Production for Graphic Designers

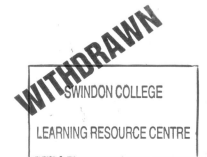

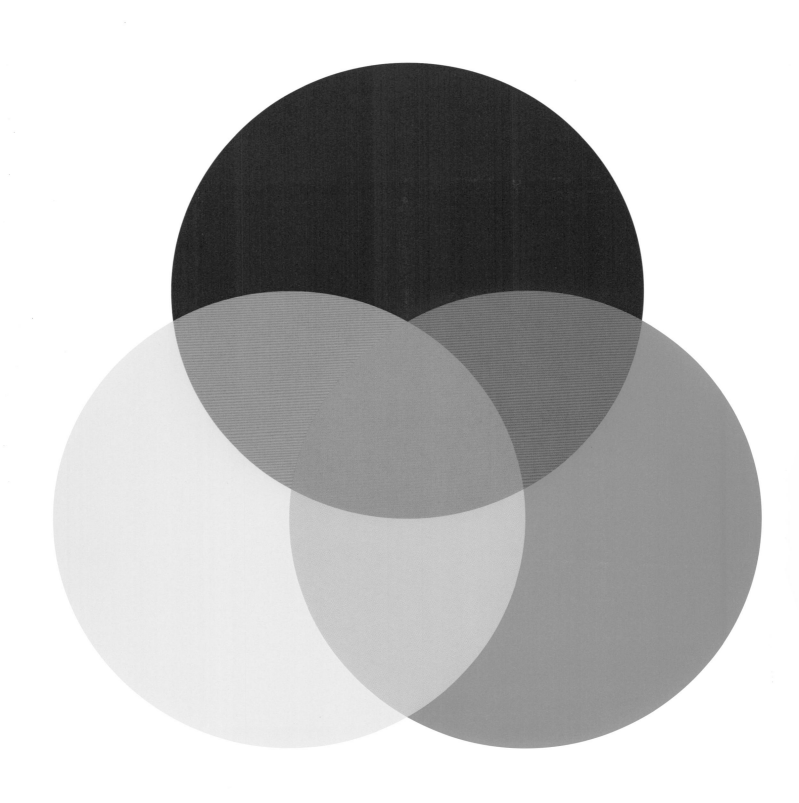

Production for Graphic Designers

Fifth Edition

Alan Pipes

Laurence King Publishing

LAURENCE KING

Published 2009, 2005, 2001, 1997, 1992
by Laurence King Publishing Ltd.
361–373 City Road
London EC1V 1LR
United Kingdom
Tel: + 44 20 7841 6900
Fax: + 44 20 7841 6910
e-mail: enquiries@laurenceking.com
www.laurenceking.com

A catalog record for this book is available from the British Library.

ISBN: 978 1 85669 601 2

Printed in China

Senior Editor: Zoe Antoniou
Designer: Ian Hunt Design
Cover Designer: Studio Ten and A Half

Frontispiece: The three process colors—cyan, magenta, and yellow—are
shown overlapping. Overprinted, they should theoretically make black,
but instead it creates a muddy brown, which is why a fourth color—black
or "key"—is added to the four-color process.

About the typefaces used in this book

Main body text: Minion Regular 10/12.5 pt
Captions: Meta Normal Roman 8/11 pt
Trailblazer life story: Meta Book Roman 9.25/12.5 pt
Trailblazer Manifesto: Meta Book Roman 8/10.75 pt
Other display text also uses Meta Plus Book

Minion is a Garalde Old style serif typeface designed by Robert Slimbach
for Adobe Systems in 1990. It supports regular and display optical sizes
in regular and italic. Different optical sizes have different stroke contrasts
and details, designed to optimize texts for specific applications.
Slimbach was born in Evanston, Illinois in 1956. He developed two
fonts—ITC Slimbach and ITC Giovanni—for the International Typeface
Corporation in New York and in 1987 joined Adobe Systems, working
on Adobe Garamond (1989) amongst others. In 1991, he received
the Charles Peignot Award from the Association Typographique
Internationale for excellence in type design.

Meta is a humanist sans-serif typeface family designed by Erik
Spiekermann (see the Trailblazer on pages 74—5) in 1984, originally
as a corporate typeface for the Deutsche Bundespost (German Federal
Post) but never adopted. It is now a whole family of typefaces, including
Meta Book and Meta Serif. In 1989 the original artwork was digitized and
the Normal face of three styles was created by Just van Rossum. Extra
weights together with the corresponding italics and small caps were later
added by Luc(as) de Groot.

Other production notes

Screen ruling: 175 lines per inch
Text paper: 157 gsm Chinese Gold East matte art
Binding: sewn in 16-page sections, cover four scored with 6-mm hinges
on either side of spine

Contents

7 Digital Design

Preface

When the first edition of this book was published, way back in 1992, computers were rarely seen in graphic design studios—there were some expensive turnkey systems around, mainly used for producing national newspapers—but the predominant means of layout was the mechanical. Now computers are not only ubiquitous in every area of the design-to-production cycle, but it is hard to imagine how books and magazines were ever produced without them.

Prepress too, that once analog world of lenses, photographic emulsions, and baths of chemicals, has also gone digital. Direct computer-to-plate, and even plateless, print are commonplace. Xerography and the newer digital print technologies are being used to produce customized short-run jobs on demand. And all the paraphernalia of prepress, currently the province of the repro service bureau, is being brought in-house.

In the past few years a completely new medium (to designers at least) has shot to prominence—the internet. There was no mention of the internet in the first edition of this book. In the second edition it was deemed important enough to deserve its own chapter, now renamed Digital Design. Through the internet, designers are able to break the bounds of traditional print and incorporate dynamic online resources that could only have been dreamed about when the first edition was put to bed. Despite the rise of the internet, print is still a large part of our lives. According to Printing Industries of America Inc, printing is still one of the largest manufacturing industries in the USA—employing over a million people in almost 39,000 establishments, and selling over $170 billion of products in 2007. The industry is dominated by small- and medium-sized businesses, most employing fewer than twenty employees—along with their computers.

This completely revised fifth edition addresses the exciting changes that have taken place since the first four editions of *Production for Graphic Designers* were published. Sustainability and standardization are the twin themes of this new edition. Print production and papermaking use large amounts of energy, water, and natural resources—but graphic designers can do their bit to save the planet for future generations by recycling, reducing toxic waste, and sourcing raw materials ethically. Some new Trailblazers and some Hot Tips address these important issues. And as the industry abandons analog to go completely digital, the process is being streamlined by adopting the PDF as a standard for print, and CSS for its perhaps greener cousin, the web.

For this fifth edition, I should like to thank Philip and Dave Clark of Brighton Print Centre for tirelessly explaining to me the finer points of practical offset printing, and the library staff of St Peter's House, at the University of Brighton. Special mention should go to: Elle Kawano of Barnbrook Design, Christine Fent of Composite Projects, Anne Brassier of airside, Richard The at Sagmeister Inc, Achim Klapp at SpiekermannPartners, Luc Schurgers at Minivegas, Oliver Hydes at Square Enough, and my other colleagues at the Brighton Illustrators Group for providing images.

I should like to thank Lee Ripley, Publishing Director at Laurence King Publishing, for commissioning me to write this fifth edition. I would also like to thank Zoe Antoniou, Senior Editor, who worked on the book in-house, Ian Hunt for his new design, and the following reviewers who offered their expertise on the subject: Jim Escalante, University of Wisconsin-Madison; Marjorie Williams-Smith, University of Arkansas at Little Rock; Priscilla Wicker, Austin Community College; and Sherri Brown, Trident Technical College.

Alan Pipes, Spring 2009

Introduction

Words and pictures. Paper and ink. And now zeroes and ones—binary digits. These are the raw materials of the graphic designer. They are about to meet, go on a journey, and undergo several transformations, before ending up in a printed and finished or electronic publication that you designed. Something that will communicate ideas and images to large numbers of people.

But how do words and pictures get on to the printed page or website? Printing has always been a mysterious craft. And until recently, graphic designers were excluded from its secrets. Now the print production process is well within the designer's realm. And designers are ever being asked to expand their expertise into newer media. The purpose of this book is to demystify and help you understand some of those arcane and cutting-edge processes.

There is a long-standing misconception that to learn the craft part of any profession can be a chore. The temptation is to jump right in there and get on with the creative stuff. Print production, in particular, with its many different stages and processes, can seem dull, the very sound of words like "mechanical" at once conjuring up visions of production lines of automatons cutting and pasting like galley slaves. On the other hand, there are some designers, and many typographers, who are so in love with the process that they forget the purpose of the job they are doing. What use is a beautiful piece of design or typography, without meaning or content? The graphic designer's role, first and foremost, is that of communicator. But if you can communicate cost-effectively with wit, economy, and elegance, then you are a very good graphic designer indeed.

In graphic design, free expression cannot exist in isolation from the process. Walter Gropius, the modernist architect and founder of the Bauhaus—a German art and design school that has become the model for most of our present schools of art, communications, and design—suggested in his manifesto of 1919 that art cannot be taught, but that craft can. "A foundation in handicraft is essential for every artist," he said. "It is there that the primary source of creativity lies."

Graphic designers are both artists and craftspeople. This book does not major on how to be an artist, but it will tell you much that you need to know about the craft of printing. And when you have learnt all about print production, the creativity will be able to come shining through. A sound understanding of all stages of the print production process will at the very least prevent your designs from failing for technical reasons.

The chapters are arranged to follow the flow of both the design process and the print process—from the choosing of type and the preparation of illustrations and photographs, through their arrangement on the page or website, to the printing and finishing of the publication. The design process may follow a linear path, but many of the design decisions up front are affected by processes downstream. Every stage of the print production process will exert some influence on your design.

The choice of paper and print technology, for example, will affect the kind of typefaces you can use and the way in which halftones are treated. In turn, the size of print run determines the print technology. You may be asked to design a range of product labels, for example—some to be printed on art-paper stock using high-quality litho presses, while others will be printed directly on to plastic yogurt pots using flexography or screenprinting. You may even be expected to "repurpose" the designs for multimedia or the internet. Your designs will have to work well across a range of substrates and media.

Some history

1.1 The *Diamond Sutra*, an Indian Buddhist text translated from Sanskrit to Chinese in about AD 400, is the world's earliest book (this copy, found in a cave near Dunhuang, is dated AD 868). It is not a book we would recognize—it is really a 16 ft scroll comprising seven panels of paper. It was printed using wooden blocks.

When you open the parcel from the printer, and you look at the finished copy of your design, it is as well to pause and appreciate that this printed product is a tribute to every advance in printing technology since the first wooden block was inked and pressed against a sheet of paper.

The history of printing began in the East: in China, Korea, and Japan. Paper was invented in China—its invention was officially announced to the Emperor by Ts'ai Lun in AD 105—and printing using wooden blocks had become a flourishing fine art by the tenth century. The oldest known printed book, the *Diamond Sutra* (Fig. **1.1**), is dated at AD 868, though books were almost certainly being printed a century before. Words and pictures were carved together on to the same wooden blocks, and a fresh set of blocks had to be cut for each new book. Printing presses with type cast from individual pieces of clay that could be used time and time again were in use in China by AD 1041, and Korean printers were casting metal type before AD 1400. But because the languages of the East use symbols for whole words—some tens of thousands of them—rather than putting together words from relatively few characters in an alphabet, the development of so-called "movable" type was not as significant there as it later was in Europe.

Textiles have been printed in Europe since at least the sixth century, and playing cards were certainly being printed, using wooden blocks similar to those of the Chinese printers, by the 14th century. But it is Johannes Gutenberg (1398–1468) who is credited with the invention of printing in the West, sometime before 1440, and who printed the first book in Europe in 1445.

Gutenberg was a goldsmith by trade, living in Mainz, in what is now Germany. All the technology necessary for the invention of printing was in place at the time—it was just waiting for the right mind to put all the pieces together. He knew how to cast objects in metal, there were presses already available (for wine-making), he had ink and paper. And he saw a market opportunity for mass-produced books, to stock the libraries of all the universities being founded at that time.

Before that, in the Middle Ages, all books were created by hand. Scribes and artists worked together to create one-off books, often copying from existing texts. They were beautiful objects, mostly "illuminated" with ornamental letters, paintings, decorative borders, and gold blocking. There was even a form of mass-production in operation. In a scriptorium, a chief scribe would dictate aloud the text to be copied by a team of under-scribes. Nevertheless, it was a slow process, and books could be possessed only by the very rich.

Gutenberg's invention was the process of letterpress: the concept of casting individual letters that could be assembled into words, printed, then cleaned and put away, and used over again. First he cut a steel punch for each character and punctuation mark. This punch was then struck into a softer metal to form the matrix in which the type was cast. Finally lead, with the addition of some antimony for hardness and tin for toughness, was poured into the mold and the type cast. The most original part of Gutenberg's process was a mold of adjustable width, used to hold the different sizes of matrix. (See Chapter 2, p. 33, for a fuller description of the process of hot-metal typesetting.)

Gutenberg's original idea was to imitate in type the handwritten books of the scribes (but without the graphic embellishments). To do that he had to create a set of over 300 characters, including all the variations of letterforms and joined letters that a scribe might use. In comparison, a 20th century printer's alphabet might contain only 50 or so characters.

The invention of printing spread across Europe. The first book in English was printed by William Caxton, who learnt his craft in Cologne, Germany, and set up a press in London in 1476, using Flemish equipment. Printing was brought to America by Joseph Glover, who imported a press and three printers from Cambridge, England, to Cambridge, Massachusetts. Sadly, Glover died on the voyage, but the press was installed by Stephen Daye and his two sons in 1638, and operated under the auspices of Harvard College (Fig. **1.2**).

Progress in the technology of printing was slow until the Industrial Revolution. Wooden wine-type presses with huge screws (Fig. **1.3**) were gradually replaced by iron presses operated by a simpler lever mechanism. The first was developed by Earl Stanhope in 1804, and this was followed by the more ornate Columbian and Albion presses. By 1812, there were presses in operation powered by steam, and huge rotary machines followed soon after.

Printing became a more industrialized process with the invention of automatic typesetting machines, first from Linotype in 1886, and from Monotype in 1887. Until the beginning of the 20th century, however, it was very difficult to combine type and pictures on the same printed page.

1.3 Benjamin Franklin (1706–90) is perhaps America's most famous printer. This wood engraving shows him at the London print shop of Cox & Sons in 1785; note the wooden screw press.

1.2 Title page from *The Whole Booke of Psalmes* (1640), the first book to be published in North America, by Stephen Daye of Cambridge, Massachusetts.

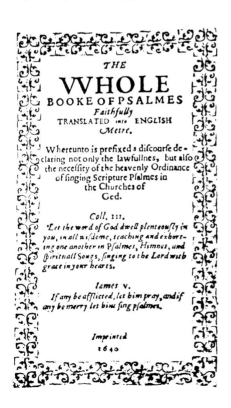

Printing pictures

Letterpress is a relief method of printing, in which a raised surface is inked and pressed against the paper. However, throughout the early history of printing almost every method of reproducing images used the **intaglio** process. The only exception was the woodcut—a relief process that predates printing—which could be used for decorative initials and simple illustrative work (Fig. **1.4**). Woodcuts are made with a knife on the long grain of the wood. The result is a rather rough image, but one that can be printed with the type.

For fine illustrative work, the only alternative was the intaglio process. Intaglio is the opposite to relief. Here it is the incised lines that print. A plate is inked, wiped almost clean, and the ink that remains in the grooves is drawn out, under pressure, to form the image on the dampened paper. Both engraving and etching are intaglio methods of printing (Fig. **1.5**).

So, before the Industrial Revolution, letterpress was used for printing text, in large print runs. Intaglio was used for refined work, where the print run was relatively small and the

1.4 Until the end of the 18th century, the only way to print type and illustrations combined on the same page was by using woodcuts. These have period charm but lacked the capacity for fine detail, as is obvious from this depiction of the 1456 visit of Halley's Comet, from Conrad Lycosthenes' *Prodigiorum ac ostentorum chronicon*, 1557.

1.5 Because etching is an intaglio process, illustrations had to be printed separately from the text and were "tipped in" when the book was bound. This baker's shop, 1635, comes from a series of 22 etchings on the arts and crafts by Jan Joris van der Vliet.

expense not so crucial. Artists had been making engravings on copper plates since the Renaissance. By the 18th century, the process was used commercially for printing invitation cards, banknotes, and stamps. The engravers used a sharp instrument called a burin to incise lines on to copper plates. And because any lettering had to be drawn by hand, it was often very elaborate. Hence the term "copperplate" is now used for a particular kind of formal handwriting. In the late 19th century, methods were developed for engraving on steel plates (Fig. **1.6**), which are more durable than copper.

A later development was etching, in which marks are made with a needle or any other sharp instrument to scratch off an acid-resistant coating on the surface of a copper plate. This is then placed in a bath of acid, and the drawing is etched chemically into the surface of the plate. The image on an etched plate was usually tidied up and detail added by hand, by engraving directly into the plate with a burin.

Another intaglio process is mezzotint, in which a burnisher is used to smooth the rough texture on the surface of the plate, created previously by the action of an abrasive "rocker" (the smooth areas would be white on the finished printed material). Aquatint is a type of etching that builds up tones using resin and stopping-out varnish. **Resist** is applied to the plate to prevent the non-printing areas from etching. Both these latter processes were used mainly to reproduce watercolor

1.6 Etchings and engravings were originally made on copper plates, which quickly wear out. In the 19th century, the problem was overcome by coating the plates with steel. This steel engraving of emigrants to America crossing the plains was first published in New York in 1869.

paintings. All of these methods are still used today by artists to produce limited edition prints, but are no longer used by commercial printers.

From Gutenberg's time until the Industrial Revolution, it was common for images in books to be printed separately from the text by using an intaglio process. The images were tipped-in (inserted among the text pages) during the binding process.

Things improved, however, when Thomas Bewick (1753–1828) developed the art of wood engraving (Fig. **1.7**). At last publishers had at their disposal the means to print fine line work and areas of rich black, in among the text.

Wood engraving is a relief process, despite the similarity of its name to copper engraving, which is an intaglio process. Wood engravings are made with tools similar to those of the engravers, most commonly on the end grain of boxwood (Fig. **1.8**). Scratchboard, or scraperboard, is a contemporary method of illustration that simulates the appearance of a wood engraving.

By the middle of the 19th century, wood engraving had become an industry, and engravers such as Joseph Swain and the Dalziel brothers were as famous as the illustrators whose work they interpreted. Magazines such as the *Illustrated London News* used a system of separating large blocks into more manageable pieces, sending them out to a team of engravers, then reassembling them—an overseer had the job of disguising the joins. Journalistic accuracy came second to visual impact, with the same blocks used over and over, whenever there was a public hanging or a shipwreck.

1.7 *The Hyena* from Thomas Bewick's *General History of Quadrupeds*, 1790. The original boxwood block is on the right. Note that the image is laterally inverted (a mirror image).

Enter lithography and photography

In fact, there was a process that could quite easily combine type and pictures on the same page, and it had been around since the end of the 18th century.

It was lithography (Fig. **1.9**), invented in Prague by Alois Senefelder around 1796–9. Neither a relief nor an intaglio process, it is better described as a planographic process. It is based on the principle that oil and water do not mix (much more in Chapter 6), and that, in effect everything happens on a flat surface.

Ironically, it was the versatility of the process that prevented it from being taken up more universally. Almost any greasy mark made on the lithographic stone, or, from the end of the 19th century, on a prepared metal plate, will print. Illustrators could at last work directly and spontaneously. By the end of the 19th century, greetings cards, postcards, decorative "scraps," maps, sheet music, and posters were all being mass-produced by lithography.

Offset lithography—in which the image is transferred from the stone or plate first to a rubber roller, and then to the **substrate**—entered the scene surreptitiously. The process was first used in about 1875 for printing ornamental decorations on to tinplate, for applications in packaging.

1.8 The tradition of Bewick is carried on today by contemporary wood engravers such as Nick Day, who are more likely to be seen cutting vinyl floor tiles than boxwood.

1.9 The process of lithography revolutionized print production, but it was a long time coming. Early lithographic illustrations, like engravings, had to be printed separately from the text, but were used extensively for color work. This express train was first published in 1870 by Currier & Ives in New York as a color lithograph. Note that here it has to be reproduced as a halftone from a photograph of the original.

Type produced by letterpress could be transferred on to the stone using special transfer paper, but this was not a totally satisfactory process. One more ingredient was necessary before lithography could take over from letterpress as the most versatile of all the printing processes: the invention of photography in the late 1830s.

Photography—analog or digital—is the basis for every print production process in use today. The first application of photography to the reproduction of illustrations was quite modest, however. It was used to sensitize the surface of the boxwood used for wood engravings. These still had to be cut by hand, but the illustrator's original drawing could be preserved and, furthermore, the method could be used to reproduce photographs.

Early photographers were eager to reproduce their work in large quantities. They were an extremely experimental group of individuals, and many of the pioneering developments in print production were made by them. **Collotype** (Fig. **1.10**) was the first method used for reproducing photographs, and this slow and expensive process was soon followed by photogravure.

1.10 It was the experimental photographers of the late 19th century who pushed forward the technology of print production, inventing better methods of reproducing continuous-tone artwork and the technique of producing color separations. This picture of Joseph Bazalgette, the architect of London's sewerage system, was first reproduced by Woodburytype—a form of collotype patented by Walter Bentley Woodbury in 1866—a process said to produce hard and brilliant prints.

1.11 The line art of such artists as Aubrey Beardsley and William Heath Robinson was as much influenced by the invention of the process block as by the importation of Japanese art at the end of the 19th century. At last an artist's spontaneity could be reproduced directly from artwork—as can be seen in this illustration by Heath Robinson from Hans Christian Andersen's *Fairy Tales* (1913).

Collotype—the name comes from the Greek word for glue—uses a plate coated with photographically sensitive gelatin which hardens in proportion to the amount of light falling on to it. A negative is exposed in contact with the plate, which is then moistened and absorbs more water where there was less light. Impressions are taken using greasy ink, as in lithography. Collotype gives an almost facsimile reproduction of pencil, pastel, and crayon. To date it is the only commercial process that can print continuous-tone originals without having them first converted, by screening, into a pattern of dots.

Photogravure, first developed in 1852, is an intaglio process characterized by rich tones and the absence of regularly patterned dots. However, the process does involve a form of screening to create the "grains" on the plate or cylinder. On etching, the grains are eaten away in proportion to the tone values on the original—the blacks become the deepest and the whites the shallowest. On printing, the darker areas are created by a greater amount of ink being deposited on the paper, and the grains are obliterated by the spread of the ink. The process relied on quick-drying spirit-based inks, and for this reason many of the early reproductions appeared in sepia or green. Photogravure is used widely to this day, and is discussed more fully as a printing process in Chapter 6.

The breakthrough that allowed images to be printed by letterpress was the development of the process block. The line block, for black and white work, was invented in Vienna by Paul Pretsch in 1853 and used a process resembling collotype—the softer portions of sensitized gelatin on the surface of the plate swell into relief. An electrotype cast is made, and the resulting plate is mounted on to a wooden block (hence the name—the block brings it up to the height of the type). This can then be assembled with the type. By the mid-1880s, zinc plates were being etched photographically from original artwork, and the profession of process engraving, or blockmaking, was born. The early process blocks could handle only relatively simple areas of black and white, and the style of illustrators such as Aubrey Beardsley and William Heath Robinson owes much to the constraints of the process (Fig. **1.11**). For the first time, an illustrator was free to draw at larger sizes than the work would be appearing in print.

Tints could be added by the blockmaker (see Fig. 3.2, p. 80), where indicated by the illustrator. Ben Day tints, the first commercially available tints, were introduced in 1901. These were sheets of celluloid stretched in wooden frames. Each sheet was embossed with a pattern and was transferred to the block, before etching, using a roller inked with lithographic ink. Areas not requiring a tint were first painted out with gum to repel the ink.

The reproduction of continuous tone by means other than collotype had to await the invention of the halftone screen. The photographer Fox Talbot first suggested in 1852 that tones could be reproduced by means of "photographic screens or veils." But it was Frederick Ives of Philadelphia who patented a method of converting a photograph into dots. This was refined in 1882 by George Meisenbach, who used a single-lined screen that was turned 90 degrees during exposure. Ives, in collaboration with Louis and Max Levy, replied in 1890 with the first cross-lined screen. Now illustrations and photographs could be freely combined with type on the same page, and printed together at the same time.

The invention of the halftone screen also paved the way for full-color printing, using three and later four "process" colors to reproduce all the colors of the rainbow (see p. 91).

The first rotary offset lithography machine for printing on paper was introduced in 1906 by Ira W. Rubel, but it was not until the 1950s that it began to take over from letterpress.

Photocomposition systems could set type, not in pieces of lead, but on rolls of photographic bromide paper or transparent film. These could be cut and pasted into designs that could then be transferred directly to a lithographic plate and printed. This technological breakthrough, and the explosion of print that followed, gave a huge boost to the young profession of graphic design. Over the years, the printing industry had become fragmented—there were separate typesetters, process engravers, and printers—and someone had to step in to plan and coordinate printing projects. That job fell to the graphic designer.

There was greater creative freedom too. No longer were graphic designers constrained to what could be done with metal type and process blocks. Type on paper could be positioned anywhere, alongside any images that could be recorded by the camera.

It was the age of camera-ready artwork—the **mechanical**. And the introduction of display faces in the form of dry-transfer rub-down lettering such as Letraset liberated the adventurous designer even further. What you saw on the mechanical was what you got in the printed product.

It was a natural next step to want to design on the computer screen, once WYSIWYG (What You See Is What You Get) displays became available in the early 1980s. Both text and graphics could be treated equally in the eyes of the computer, and could be subjected to an almost infinite variety of manipulation (Fig. **1.12**).

The introduction of **PageMaker** for the Apple Macintosh in 1984, along with the **PostScript** page-description language and the LaserWriter, are just some of the recent milestones in the history of print production for graphic designers.

Now the internet, once the domain of computer scientists, has further liberated graphic designers, setting them free to expand their horizons beyond the world of printed ink on paper and into digital screen-based multimedia.

As with the invention of lithography, it is often difficult to foresee the effect of an isolated discovery on the overall history of printing. Lithography had to wait for the development of photography before it could become a commercial proposition. In the same way xerography, invented in 1938 by Chester Carlson, has leapt forward with laser and computer technology. Who could have predicted the growth of the internet in the past few years? In just a decade, it has become as commonplace as the telephone and television, complementing print-based media with a degree of interactivity and immediacy undreamt of by Gutenberg. Broadband in every home promises huge opportunities for today's graphic designers, adding sound and time-based content to the visual media.

1.12 Old meets new. This 16th-century woodcut of printers at work is given a contemporary treatment courtesy of Photoshop, the image manipulation program from Adobe.

Milestones in the history of production technology for graphic designers

3500 BC Sumerians use cuneiform alphabet on clay tablets

2400 BC Earliest surviving papyrus scroll with writing

AD105 Paper invented in China by Ts'ai Lun

868 *Diamond Sutra*, first printed book, in China

1041 First presses with clay movable type in China

1150 First paper mill opened in Europe, in Xativa, Spain

1400 Koreans printing with metal movable type

1445 Johannes Gutenberg printed first book in Europe

1446 Earliest known copper engraving: *The Scourging of Christ*, by a German artist

1477 William Caxton issued first printed book in England

1638 First American press established by Stephen Daye at Harvard College

1690 First American paper mill established in Germantown, Pennsylvania, by William Rittenhouse

1790 Thomas Bewick perfected process of wood engraving

1796–9 Lithography invented by Alois Senefelder

1798 Papermaking machine invented by Nicolas-Louis Robert

1804 Iron press devised by Earl Stanhope

1810 First Fourdrinier papermaking machines in operation

1812 *The Times* (of London) printed on steam press

1822 J. N. Niépce first to fix images in a camera obscura on metal and glass plates

1829 Amos H. Hubbard's mill at Norwich, Connecticut, first American paper mill to install a Fourdrinier machine

1837 Invention of Daguerre photographic process

1839 Negative/positive photography invented by Fox Talbot

1841 First paperbacks produced by Tauchnitz Verlag, Germany

1852 Photogravure invented by Fox Talbot

1853 Line block invented by Paul Pretsch

1860 Photographically sensitized boxwood process developed by Thomas Bolton

1860 Principle of color separation by filters demonstrated by Clerk Maxwell

1861 First color photograph by Clerk Maxwell

1872 Process line block invented by Alfred Dawson

c.1875 Offset litho used for printing on tin

1881 Halftone process invented by Frederick Ives

1886 Linotype machine invented by Ottmar Mergenthaler

1886 First Linotype installed at *New York Herald Tribune*

1887 Monotype machine invented by Tolbert Lanston

1890 Four-color separation process invented

1890 Aniline coal-tar process (later called flexography) demonstrated at Bibby, Baron & Sons in Liverpool, England

1901 Ben Day mechanical tints introduced

1906 First rotary offset litho machine invented by Ira W. Rubel

1920s Aniline process developed for printing on non-absorbent stock such as cellophane

1938 Xerography invented by Chester Carlson

1948 Color scanner invented by Kodak

1952 Name "flexography" coined for aniline coal-tar process

1955 Linofilm photocomposing system introduced

1959 First Linofilm installation at *National Geographic*

1960 Laser invented at Hughes Laboratory

1967 Computerized Linofilm typesetter introduced

1968 Crosfield Magnascan four-color scanner introduced

1968 Ted Nelson coins the terms "hypertext" and "hypermedia"

1969 ARPAnet, the precursor to the internet, established

1971 Email invented by Ray Tomlinson of BBN

1971 Project Gutenberg began at the Illinois Benedictine College aimed at collecting as many texts as possible in electronic format

1976 Inkjet printing announced by IBM

1981 IBM PC announced

1982 Lisa, the precursor to the Macintosh, introduced by Apple

1982 Adobe Systems founded

1984 Apple Macintosh and Linotronic 300 laser imagesetter launched

1984 CD-ROM invented: Parke Lightbown builds a computer application that runs from a computer-based version of the compact disc

1984 Flash memory invented by Fujio Masuoka while working for Toshiba

1985 Adobe PostScript used to set type on LaserWriter and Linotronic imagesetter at different resolutions

1985 Aldus PageMaker launched, and term "desktop publishing" coined by Aldus founder Paul Brainerd

1987 Mac II and QuarkXPress launched

1987 Adobe Illustrator launched

1990 Windows 3 released by Microsoft

1990 Adobe Photoshop launched

1991 TrueType format and System 7 introduced by Apple

1992 Tim Berners-Lee of CERN develops software for the World Wide Web (WWW)

1993 NCSA releases Mosaic, the first WWW browser

1993 Adobe Acrobat launched

1993 First digital presses, the Indigo E-Print 1000, and Xeikon's dcp-1 launched

1994 First PowerPC Macs launched

1994 Aldus and Adobe merge

1994 Netscape Navigator launched by Mosaic Communications

1995 Windows 95 released

1996 Internet Explorer released by Microsoft

1997 Apple launches Mac OS 8

1998 Intel releases the 350 MHz and 400 MHz Pentium II processors

1998 Microsoft releases Windows 98

1999 Intel announces Pentium III processor

1999 Apple Computer releases the 400 MHz Power Mac G4 computer and 22-inch LCD flat-panel Cinema Display

1999 Adobe InDesign and PressReady launched

2001 Apple OS X launched

2001 Windows XP launched

2003 Apple releases Power Mac G5 computer

2006 Apple starts to use Intel chips

2006 Intel replace Pentium with Core 2 processors

2007 Apple drops "Computer" from its name

2007 Microsoft's Vista operating system launched

2008 PDF version 1.7 becomes an official ISO standard (ISO 32000)

Getting started: studio equipment

Some graphic designers once claimed to get by with just a pad of layout paper, a pencil, and a book of type specimens. The typographer Erik Spiekermann (see p. 74) used to boast (before he bought his first Apple Macintosh) that he could communicate clearly with his typesetter by means of a written set of instructions. This was a type specification that could be dictated down the telephone, if need be—with no graphic layout necessary. Well, you may argue that typographers have it a lot easier than graphic designers. They don't have to deal with pictures, or color.

So maybe in the past the more unprofessional graphic designers just sent rough layouts covered in keylines and instructions to the printer and hoped for the best. These days, you are expected to do more, presenting your computer-generated layouts to an imagesetting bureau or repro house on a DVD, or via the internet. And you will already have a very good idea of how the printed result is going to look.

What do you need to get started? A computer system of some sort is almost mandatory these days (see p. 111) but a sturdy tabletop or a drawing board with an adjustable angled surface and built-in parallel motion (a straight edge that moves up and down, always perfectly horizontally) will prove very useful. The drawing board has become synonymous with the cyclical nature of the design process. How many times have you heard the phrase "back to the drawing board" when contrary clients changed their minds about what they really wanted? Drawing boards are still to be seen—they are good places at which to plan and think, to scale and crop illustrations, and are ideal for spreading around the design elements during the sketch stage of design.

A surgical scalpel and a heavier-duty craft knife (such as an X-acto) are useful for cutting paper and board and making up dummy publications. Use a cutting mat with a "self-healing" surface for trimming artwork, and clean off any stickiness regularly with lighter fuel. For sticking and mounting you will need rubber cement or aerosol adhesive, such as Scotch Spray Mount, for wrinkle-free mounting. For safety's sake, adequate ventilation is essential while using spray glue. Buy a brand that uses a CFC-free propellant, to protect the environment. Low-tack masking tape and matte frosted "magic" tape are useful for mending, and for attaching tissue or **acetate** overlays to delicate artwork.

Other accessories include non-reproducing light-blue pencils, including some greasy pencils (Chinagraphs) for writing on glossy surfaces, and maybe an electric pencil sharpener. A large soft brush is indispensable for removing debris from the work in progress, and a supply of talcum powder will come in handy for degreasing and "lubricating" surfaces. However, keep it away from finished work! A bulk stock of paper towels is useful to mop up spillages. It is always good policy to keep things clean and tidy.

Paint called "process white" is used by designers for correcting mistakes and adding highlights to drawings. It is still considered good advice to buy the finest-quality sable brushes (sizes 00, 1, and 3 would be a good selection). Look after them—they should be washed and rinsed straight after use (they must never be left point down in a jar of water) and stored with the points upward. There are also some very good synthetic substitutes available.

A **loupe**, linen tester, or eyeglass (Fig. **1.13**) is a mounted magnifying glass that will prove its worth over and over. It can be used to check the dots in a halftone, examine a color transparency for suitability and any defects, and to scrutinize proofs for printing problems.

A lightbox that fits on the tabletop, and comprises a translucent surface illuminated from below by fluorescent lights conforming to the **standard lighting conditions** used by printers, is invaluable for properly examining the color temperature of transparencies. It is also a great aid to experimentation. You can try out different designs on a lightbox, tracing over those parts of an original design you wish to retain. A lightbox can also be used to check the registration of color separations. If you are to be checking and correcting color proofs, set up a corner of the studio according to **standard viewing conditions**, with the light source surrounded by neutral gray.

A proportional scale, or just a plain old calculator, will help you work out percentage reductions and enlargements. And there are all kinds of other measurement devices. A stainless-steel pica rule will become a lifelong companion, and there are plastic rules available for measuring the depth of type in different sizes, useful for casting off (calculating the length of a text) and copy fitting (making sure your typesetting will fit the space you have left for it in the layout). A transparent grid will assist you in checking that

1.13 A loupe, or linen tester, is a magnifying glass which is useful for examining transparencies and proofs, often in conjunction with a lightbox.

design elements are on a mechanical square, and well aligned, although computer layouts will always be perfectly square! A photocopier capable of enlarging and reducing is a very useful addition to any studio, as is a fax machine and a connection to the internet to keep in visual touch with the client and printer.

The computer and its peripherals (Fig. **1.14**) are now almost indispensable. And here's a word of warning, right at the start of the book. A computer can be a tireless and uncomplaining assistant, but you cannot talk to it in such subjective terms as "increase the spacing here" or "less orange there" as you would with a typesetter or the scanner operator at your repro house. Compositors and scanner operators have had years of experience in delivering the results they think you want. They can almost read your mind. They have a common understanding of what is acceptable, and what is good. The computer, on the other hand, can do either nothing or anything—depending on what instructions you give!

The computer might never question your unusual requests and never charge you for changes of mind. But it will expect you to do all the thinking, and be able to tell it exactly, to the thousandth of an inch, centimeter, or percentage point, where things should be moved. Not only does that make more work for you, but you have to know in minute detail exactly what you want—and you will have to take responsibility for the outcome.

Typesetters were in fact among the first users of computers—they could recognize a good thing when they saw it. Your computer is not going to replace printers, and they will probably always be one step ahead of you. So think of your system as complementing their computers, acting as a front end to their systems.

Use your computer responsibly, to improve the quality of design communication between your studio—the ideas house—and the printers—the production house. Their centuries of hard-won expertise are there to be used. And they will appreciate the knowledge you have of their processes, gained from reading this book.

Be a greener graphic designer

Sustainability in graphic design means looking carefully at the environmental, social, and economic impact of your print and packaging products for their whole lifecycle, from the raw materials, through production, transportation, end use, and ultimate disposal. As American physicist and Nobel Prize winner Murray Gell-Mann puts it: "Sustainability means living on nature's income rather than its capital." The idea is that things are running out so we need to use materials wisely, reduce harmful waste, and not contribute to greenhouse gases that will destroy the planet. Being greener may also save you and your client money too.

A sustainability audit for your project will consider the following:

- could the end product be replaced by a digital version, rather than being printed?
- can you make use of the whole print sheet?
- can the amount of material required for production be reduced, by using lighter paper, for example?
- can paper made with recycled, post-consumer waste be used?
- can VOC (volatile organic compound) inks be replaced by vegetable-based inks?
- can you reduce the transportation overheads by using local printers?
- do you choose vendors that use renewable energy?
- can the product fulfill more than one purpose?
- is the end product biodegradable or recyclable?
- can just-in-time production reduce the number of units produced and warehoused?
- are you using less ink by reducing solid colors and dark full-bleed photographs?
- are you using a printer that is ISO 14001 (environmental management scheme) certified or, for smaller companies, a scheme such as Green Mark?
- are you using paper certified by environmental organizations, such as FSC (Forest Stewardship Council) or EMAS (Eco-Management and Audit Scheme)?
- finally, are you printing more copies than you really need just because it won't cost much more?

1.14 The computer has transformed the landscape of the graphic designer's studio, largely replacing the traditional drawing board and drawing instruments.

The design-to-production workflow

This book follows the design process, from the prepararation of the type and images, combining them together during prepress, and finally to the actual printing and finishing of the design for publication. The print production workflow is broader than this, starting at some point earlier with a requirement from the client for something new, through the brief and the obtaining of print estimates, to the delivery of the finished product and the archiving of the files relating to the job. There is much to-ing and fro-ing between documents and interested parties (Fig. **1.15**), and designers will also be working on other jobs in parallel. There are many professionals involved, each supplying input and output, and at each stage of the process, different software programs will be used. The workflow accumulates files, proofs, and other data that needs organizing. Thankfully, the process is converging to a PDF (Portable Document Format) workflow, a standardized layout format developed by Adobe (much more in Chapter 5) while planning the progress of a job has fallen to JDF (Job Definition Format), an electronic "job ticket" administered by CIP4 (Co-operation for the Integration of Processes in Prepress, Press, and Postpress), used to specify all aspects of the job (see p. 155). It's all about inputs and outputs. For example, the input to the platesetting machine is a PDF file, the output is a printing plate; the input to the press is the plates, ink, paper, and the quantity required, the output is a pile of printed sheets, which become the input for the binder and finisher. If JDF is used right from the start of the process, asking for a print estimate on a JDF-compliant form for example, the same information can be used for the print order—the whole process will be streamlined and less prone to error. If a job is running late, a message, using JMF (Job Messaging Format) as the command and control language of JDF, can be sent downstream to the finisher and upstream to the client to inform them of the delay. This enables everyone from the designer to the printer to work more effectively with less downtime. So, onward to the first step in our production process, the type.

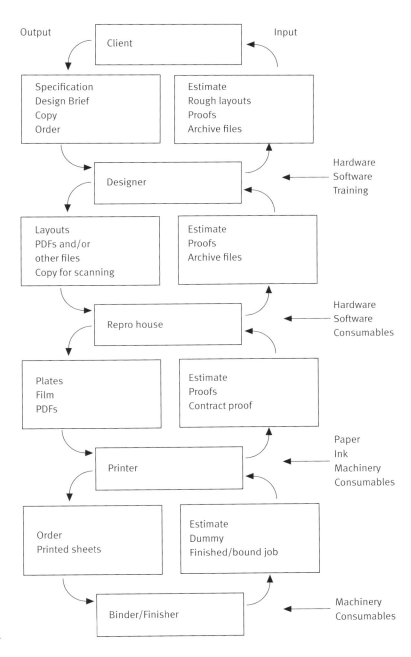

1.15 Schematic diagram of the print production workflow. Depending on the scale of the job, the relationship between the client, designer, and printer, and their involvement with one another, this will vary. There may not be a repro house in the loop—with the PDFs going direct to the printer—and the client may be responsible for buying the paper. The finisher may deal with the printer only, or be appointed by the client or designer.

Saul Bass

"His titles . . . are integral to the film . . . When his work comes up on the screen, the movie itself truly begins."

Manifesto
Symbolize and Summarize

"Bass's graphic work looked like what Matisse might have done if he'd grown up in the Bronx and had listened to jazz," says film critic Jim Supanick. Martin Scorsese once said: "His titles are not simply unimaginative identification tags, rather they are integral to the film as a whole. When his work comes up on the screen, the movie itself truly begins." A number of critics maintained his titles were in some cases better than the films that followed.

In a 1969 interview for *Communication Arts* by Richard S. Coyne, Bass said: "Years ago, if you created a modern design, it was news. You would be singled out for awards and acclaim for doing what seems now to be a janitorial job . . . removing ugliness and clutter . . . simplifying and utilizing new visual thinking.

"Magazines were full of great photography at a time when the equivalent was not happening in film. That's what distinguished my initial work in films. I was bringing to bear the visual standards that I had developed in the graphic field. That was very startling, and that's what made the work that I did then look so wild.

"Now everybody can make beautiful shots of sunsets, long-lens foreground-to-background change-focus shots . . . the nose-to-nose close-ups, fast cutting, zoomy overlaid double-image optics . . . and suddenly it's just a tool. It's understood. It's available to everyone. You can still do it poorly, but chances are, if you're reasonably proficient at what you do, you will do it well. So now the real question is: what are you trying to say?

"This process also occurred in design. Initially, the fight was to de-uglify the print environment . . . to make it more beautiful, more exciting, more visually appetizing. With that done, the issue of the day was: what does it mean? We were into content. This kicked off another swing of reaction. Ugly was beautiful—because it helped to eliminate the so-called obscuring elements. It began to undress the communication so that its essential body showed."

From the 1960s onward, Saul Bass and his Sunset Boulevard-based design company Saul Bass Associates (later Bass/Yager & Associates) fashioned the corporate face of America, with logos for AT&T, Quaker Oats, Rockwell, and Warner Communications. But he was much more than a graphic designer for print, and is perhaps better known for his film work, notably the much imitated "paper cut" title sequence for *Anatomy of a Murder* in 1959 and for collaborating with Alfred Hitchcock on the shower scene in *Psycho* in 1960. He worked as "visual consultant" on many of Hitchcock's 40-plus films, including many Hollywood classics. His more recent film credits for Martin Scorsese, which he designed with his wife and collaborator Elaine Makatura, include *Cape Fear*, *Goodfellas*, and his last film, *Casino*.

Bass was born in 1920, grew up in the Bronx, and studied at the Art Students' League in Manhattan from 1936 to 1939, then under modernist Gyorgy Kepes at Brooklyn College from 1944 to 1945. In 1948 he headed west to Los Angeles to work in advertising for motion pictures, and set up on his own in 1955. His poster for Otto Preminger's *The Man with the Golden Arm* broke new ground in 1955 with its use of bold graphic elements—before Bass, movie posters had mainly been a formulaic blend of star billing, big headlines, and photo-realistic imagery. Bass's publicity design was so dramatic that Preminger asked him to create the film's opening title sequence, which marked the beginning of a long partnership.

Bass was multi-talented, and maintained that designers should never confine themselves to a single discipline—as well as designing for print and film, he was an accomplished maker of short films (notably the Oscar-winning *Why Man Creates*), photographer, writer, and actor. He died aged 75 in 1996, but his strong, iconic, and instantly memorable approach to graphic design remains an inspiration to a new wave of web designers.

The AT&T corporate identity

One of Bass's most significant corporate-identity jobs was begun in 1968 for AT&T (then known as American Telephone and Telegraph). At the time, AT&T comprised 28 companies, 22 of which were regional telephone companies operating with a considerable amount of autonomy. The project was assigned by the parent company, AT&T. If and when they approved the designer's concept, it was still subject to the acceptance of the Bell System.

The drab look of the previous identity was designed during the depression of the 1930s. In those days the idea of a job, any kind of job, was terribly important. Institutions like the telephone company held out a solid promise of future job security. People regarded such organizations as dependable—not subject to the wild economic waves then stirring much of the business community. But with AT&T's move into the new technologies of communications and computers, it was time for a change.

The bell symbol, a trademark since 1889, was simplified, and the type within the bell deleted. New fonts were explored, but abandoned in favor of the simplicity and legibility of a modified Helvetica Medium. The corporate identity also

Neil Gower's 1994 series of posters for the British Heart Foundation were (with Bass's permission) heavily influenced by Bass's cut-up technique, in particular his design for *Anatomy of a Murder*.

HALF OF ALL DEATHS ARE FROM HEART AND CIRCULATORY DISEASE. HELP US FIGHT BRITAIN'S No 1 KILLER.

British Heart Foundation
The heart research charity

specified stripes, borrowed from the world of racing and athletics, which said: "competitive, alert, dedicated." (Stripes were also used on the AT&T globe logo designed by Bass in 1982, when the US Department of Justice decreed that AT&T divest itself of the 22 Bell operating telephone companies.)

Bass used a large sound stage in Tucson for the big presentation, which comprised eight slide and three film projectors. After the films, the screen lifted up to reveal a live set with vehicles, a simulated office, and personnel modeling proposed uniforms.

Bass's implementation manuals read more like courses in design than like the usual list of orders and prohibitions one expects. "We're still engaged in winning people over," Bass said three years after implementation had begun. "Winning them over not by charm, not by jokes, and not by fear. It's a very conscious process of patiently and logically winning them over to the program, and being so careful in our own thinking that, when we are questioned, there can be a complete openness on the reasons for what we are doing."

Resources

Website: saulbass.tv (Flash-based fan site created by Brendan Dawes and Victor Helwani, includes many interviews, images, and filmography)

Wikipedia: http://en.wikipedia.org/wiki/Saul_Bass—lists all the logos and movie posters

Pat Kirkham *Saul Bass* (with contributor Martin Scorcese), Yale University Press, 2008

Philip B. Meggs (ed.), *6 Chapters in Design: Saul Bass, Ivan Chermayeff, Milton Glaser, Paul Rand, Ikko Tanaka, Henryk Tomaszewski*, Chronicle Books, San Francisco, 1997

Gerry Rosentswieg and Saul Bass, *New American Logo*, Madison Square Press, New York, 1998

Saul Bass on the web: interview by Richard S. Coyne, *Communication Arts*

Film director Otto Preminger liked Bass's 1955 poster for *The Man with the Golden Arm* so much that he asked him to design the film's opening titles—the start of a long and creative partnership.

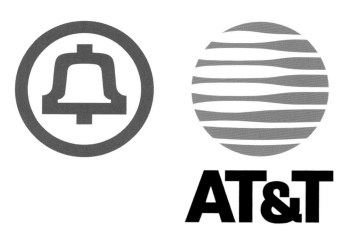

Bass simplified AT&T's Bell trademark in 1969 and, after the break-up of AT&T into "Baby Bells," in 1982 he designed a much-imitated logo for AT&T. A new 3D logo was adopted in 2005.

ABCDEF
GHIJKL
MNOPQ
RSTUVW
XYZ&123
456789C

Text & Type

The ability to use type effectively is an essential skill for successful graphic design. Just a few basic principles open the way to an infinite variety of design possibilities for all kinds of printed products. Graphic designers must endeavor to make type work hard, in harmony with other graphic elements, such as illustration, photography, and color. They are dealing with practical situations, in the real world of tight deadlines, specific briefs, and competitive pitches.

Since the introduction of digital design systems, the graphic designer has been confronted with a bewildering choice of typefaces, as well as the means to manipulate them. It has never been more important for graphic designers to become familiar with the craft and knowledge of the printers and typographers who have gone before.

People like Gutenberg designed their own type, cut the steel to make it, cast it into lead, composed it into pages, printed their own books, and bound them. They concocted their own ink, and probably made their own paper as well.

Computers give graphic designers the opportunity to take back the responsibility for almost as much of the production process as they are willing, or capable enough, to handle. But to go forward, one must first know what is possible.

This chapter aims to give the graphic designer an insight into type and how it is used. It will explain the vocabulary of print and typography, both ancient and modern. For in print production we commonly use both terminology handed down through generations of printers and typesetters, and jargon introduced from computing and digital prepress.

The chapter is divided into three sections. In the first we talk about type itself—letters and words, the basic building blocks with which graphic designers work. We see how type originated from the handwriting of medieval scribes, detail the work of pioneering printers, and learn the all-important methods of measuring type.

Then we turn to the relationship between text and house style, investigate how different typefaces are recognized, and discover how to choose the best typeface for the job.

Finally we learn how type is created. Here we discuss the systems of typesetting—from hot metal, through photosetting, to the computer systems that make the craft of typography accessible to anyone possessing a power socket.

Type

The essence of writing and lettering, according to typographer Fernand Baudin, is to make language visible and retrievable. Spoken words pass away; written words are here to stay.

Type is the basic building block of print production. The design of type is a very subtle craft, dealing with the sometimes microscopic details that distinguish one typeface from another. It is also a thankless and humbling profession. "The best typography never gets noticed," American typographer Herb Lubalin has been quoted as saying. (Typographer means here a person who designs type and designs with type. The term **compositor** is used for someone who sets type.)

Or, as another famous American typographer Beatrice Warde has pointed out, perhaps more eloquently than Lubalin: "Good typography is like a crystal wine glass, thin as a bubble and just as transparent, its purpose to reveal rather than hide the beautiful thing it is meant to contain. Good graphic design and typography should help people communicate with all the clarity an idea deserves."

When we are taught to write the alphabet at school, it probably never occurs to us that there are thousands of ways that 26 simple letters can be constructed. It is only through looking at printed matter in later life that we begin to realize that a letter g, for example, comes in two main varieties: g and g.

And while an alphabet with 26 letters and eight punctuation marks will be adequate for a message on a noticeboard, a set of over a hundred different characters and marks may still fall short of some tasks facing the graphic designer.

Some history

Our Western alphabet was invented by the Phoenicians around 1100 BC somewhere on the eastern shores of the Mediterranean Sea. Capital letters derive from Roman incised lettering, with its distinctive serifs (the little marks made by the chisel to neaten the ends of letters), slanted stress, and variations in stroke thickness. The chiseled capital letters carved on Trajan's Column in Rome (Figs **2.1** and **2.2**) in around AD 114 are still regarded as the "perfect" **roman** letters. Lower-case lettering comes from a more rounded form of handwriting, known as the uncial, developed for everyday use in the fourth century.

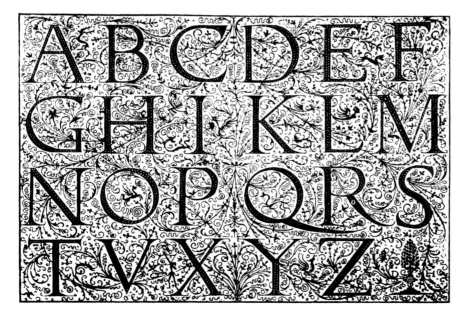

2.1 A decorative alphabet drawn as a sampler by Daniel Hopfer of Nuremburg, Germany, dated 1549. The letterforms are based on the lettering on Trajan's Column in Rome. Note the absence of J, U, and W.

ABCDEF GHIJKL MNOPQ RSTUVW XYZ&123 4567890

2.2 The lettering on Trajan's Column (opposite) is the prototype for most present-day roman typefaces, including Adobe's display typeface (above) designed in 1989 by Carol Twombly and called, appropriately enough, Trajan. Note how our serifs derive from the chiseled finishing-off marks made by the Roman stonecutter.

In the Middle Ages, scribes or scriveners created all books by hand, usually copying from existing books (Fig. **2.3**). They were beautiful objects, often "illuminated" with ornamental letters, paintings, and gold blocking (Fig. **2.4**).

The clear and manageable script established by the educational reforms of Emperor Charlemagne (742–814) in the latter part of the eighth century and early ninth—known as Carolingian minuscule—was rediscovered and refined in the Italian Renaissance by the humanists, and is the basis of the present-day roman alphabet.

In medieval Europe, there were two kinds of script: "book" hands, used in literary and liturgical manuscripts; and the more functional "charter" or "court" hands, used for business documents. In northern Europe, a narrower and heavier style of writing emerged. The use of a broad pen produced angular strokes, and the resemblance of a page written in this way to a woven pattern (*textus*) led to the name "text," "textura," or "black letter." Paper, parchment (the prepared skins of sheep or goats), and vellum (from calves, lambs, or kids) were expensive, and the scribes were encouraged to fit as many letters to a line as possible. The result is a closely packed page, with much more black than white. The humanists called this style "gothic" because of its resemblance to the pointed style of architecture in fashion at the time.

While scriveners could take their time to produce beautiful manuscripts for libraries, the clerk or secretary of a law court was more interested in speed writing and evolved a more cursive style known as "secretary," also commonly used in correspondence. By the 1450s, a more upright seriffed minuscule called "littera antiqua" was all the rage—a cursive and slightly inclined version called "italic," first used in the papal Chancery, developed from this. It did not catch on in England, however, until around 1550. It was first used alongside secretary, particularly for quoted matter and marginal asides, but came to dominate and by 1620 had become known as the "mixed" or "round" hand.

The first italic face was cut in Venice by Aldus Manutius in about 1500. It was not until two centuries later that it became partnered with roman, or plain text, and an essential part of the type family.

Other scripts included "chancery" hand, used for royal letters and patents in the Royal Chancery at Westminster, and the hand used by lawyers at the courts of the Common Pleas and King's Bench. These were banned by an act of parliament in 1733 and replaced by the round hand.

Many characters in common use in medieval England have long since disappeared. These include the thorn, which looked like a "y" and sounded like "th" (Fig. **2.5**). It lingers on in examples such as Ye Olde Shoppe, which means The Old Shop.

2.3 In medieval times all books were created individually, copied out slowly but lovingly by scribes. Only the very rich could afford books.

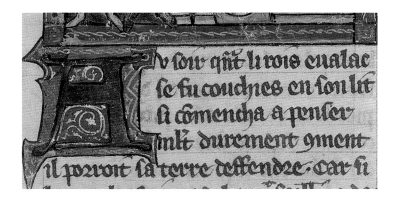

2.4 Some medieval books were illustrated or "illuminated" with watercolors and gold embellishments. The names of the artists and scribes are long forgotten, and those with recognizable styles are now known only by the names of their patrons—the Master of Mary of Burgundy, for example. To squeeze as many words as possible on to a page, most scribes used the up-and-down form of writing called textura lettering, as on this French depiction of the Montpellier riots of 1379 (left). Other manuscripts, like the 14th-century Lancelot Grail (below), used a freer, open, rounded form of script more akin to uncial, or roman lower case, writing.

2.5 Archaic English characters, including the thorn—an obsolete character that sounds like "th" but looks like a "y" (bottom row, fifth from left).

2.6 Johannes Gutenberg is credited with the invention of movable type in the Western world. No portraits of him survive from the period; this artist's impression in woodcut, made much later from the carvings on Gutenberg's tomb, shows him reading proofs while his assistant works the printing press.

2.7 To imitate the lettering of the scribes, Gutenberg's font had to contain a set of over 300 characters, whereas a later printer's alphabet might contain only 50 or so.

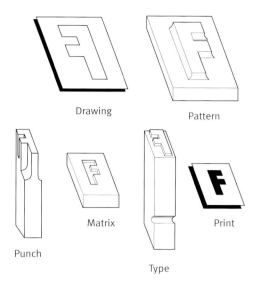

Drawing

Pattern

Punch

Matrix

Print

Type

2.8 The design for a hot-metal letterform had to go through many stages on its way to the printed page, and at each successive stage the image had to be reversed (laterally inverted).

As the skills of printing spread across Europe, craftsmen adapted their type to match the kind of lettering their customers preferred. William Caxton, the first printer in England, learnt his craft in Cologne, Germany, and bought Flemish equipment, so his books adopted the textura type.

Caxton's first book was printed in 1477. By 1509, English printers were already using roman type, mainly because of French influence. Shakespeare's plays were first printed in roman type (Fig. **2.9**), and the heavy textura type, or black letter, is now rarely seen—outside of German-speaking countries—except on newspaper mastheads, banknotes, college certificates and diplomas, on signs advertising "Ye Olde Worlde Tea Shoppe" and for the logos of heavy-metal bands.

Various historical typefaces containing extended sets of **characters** are available from type foundries such as Crazy Diamond Design and Scriptorium.

The first movable type in the Western world, invented by Johannes Gutenberg (Fig. **2.6**), closely imitated the writing of the scribes. He created a set of over 300 characters, to accommodate all the variations of letterforms and **ligatures** (joined letters, such as fi and fl) that a scribe might need to use (Fig. **2.7**).

Gutenberg's masterpiece, known as the 42-line Bible, was an impressive achievement by any standards. Each two-volume work (48 copies survive from an estimated print run of 200) comprises 1286 pages, and it was probably Gutenberg's financial undoing.

But his major legacy was the process of **hot-metal setting**. A steel punch for each character and punctuation mark is struck into a softer metal matrix, into which the lead type is cast.

Lead was used because it melts easily, flows evenly into the **matrix**, and expands slightly to make an exact replica of the punch. It hardens sufficiently to print repeatedly with acceptable levels of wear. Type for letterpress was always designed "the wrong way round" in mirror image, the production sequence being: drawing (wrong), pattern (right), punch (wrong), matrix (right), type (wrong), print (right) (Fig. **2.8**).

The fact that, in letterpress, characters have initially to be carved from steel has had a strong influence on type design ever since. It was only with the introduction of photosetting, in the 1950s, that some of the constraints were lifted.

Mr. WILLIAM
SHAKESPEARES
COMEDIES,
HISTORIES, &
TRAGEDIES.

Published according to the True Originall Copies.

LONDON
Printed by Isaac Iaggard, and Ed. Blount. 1623.

2.9 The title page of a Shakespeare edition of 1623. By the time his plays were being published, the more readable roman humanist style of type—still in common use today—had replaced the denser textura faces of the scribes.

The language of type

A **font** is a complete set *in one size* of all the letters of the alphabet, complete with associated ligatures (joined letters), numerals, punctuation marks, and any other signs and symbols (Fig. **2.10**). The word font, or fount as it is sometimes spelt in Europe, derives from "found" as in type foundry, and reminds us of the days when molten metal type was cast in molds.

Typeface, often shortened to **face**, is the name given to the *design* of the alphabet and its associated marks and symbols. Every typeface has a name. This can be the name of its designer, for example Garamond, Bodoni, or Baskerville. It can take the name of the publication it was originally designed for, for example Times New Roman or Century. Or it may just have a fanciful name intended to convey the "feel" of the face, for example Optima, Perpetua, and Futura.

The letters of the alphabet, the numerals, and all the associated marks and symbols are collectively known as the **alphanumeric character set**. Individually, they are known as **sorts**. The expression "out of sorts," meaning unwell or depressed, comes from the typesetters finding that they have run out of a particular sort when composing a job.

The two words "font" and "typeface" are often used interchangeably. This has come about because in hot metal there will be a different font for each size of type. In computer setting, as we shall see later, it is common for one design to be enlarged or reduced to make all the sizes. This confusion is compounded in a digital page-layout system or word processor, in which a computer menu item labeled "font" will display to the user a list of available typefaces.

ABCDEFGHIJKLMNOPQRSTUVWXYZ
abcdefghijklmnopqrstuvwxyzfifl.,'"-:;
()ÆæŒœ?&–$£1234567890

ABCDEFGHIJKLMNOPQRSTUVWXYZ
abcdefghijklmnopqrstuvwxyzfifl.,'"-:;
()ÆæŒœ?&–$£1234567890

ABCDEFGHIJKLMNOPQRSTUVWXYZ
abcdefghijklmnopqrstuvwxyzfifl.,'"-:;
()ÆæŒœ?&–$£1234567890

2.10 A complete font, comprising roman, italic, and bold. This font—ITC Clearface—is based on a face originally designed for American Type Founders by Morris Fuller Benton in 1907, and was redesigned in 1979 by Victor Caruso.

A complete set of sorts will also include some or all of the following:

1. alternative letters, for the ends of lines for example, and ornamented or "swash" capitals (but avoid setting whole lines of swash letters!)

2. diphthongs, such as æ and œ

3. ligatures, such as fi and fl (in books of poetry, you may even see a ligature between c and t)

4. accented letters or "floating" accents for setting foreign languages, such as à (grave), é (acute), ô (circumflex), ü (diaresis), ç (cedilla), ñ (tilde)

5. numerals or figures, which can be lining or non-lining (sometimes called "old-style" numbers). Some fonts have both (Fig. **2.11**)

1234567890
1234567890

2.11 Lining and non-lining ("old-style") numbers. The old-style ones have more charm, but lining numerals are easier to incorporate into tabular matter.

6. punctuation marks, such as , (comma) and ; (semi-colon)

7. reference marks, such as * (asterisk) and ¶ (paragraph)

8. fractions and mathematical signs, which are also known as **pi characters**, such as + (plus) and = (equals)

9. and other signs and dingbats, such as & (ampersand, see below), ☞, and © (copyright)

A font of roman type will comprise three alphabets:

1. capitals, also called majuscules or upper case, so named because of the position of the letters in the compositor's typecase (abbreviated to caps or u.c.)

2. small letters, also known as minuscules or lower case (abbreviated to l.c.)

3. and perhaps small capitals, which are the height of a lower case letter

Italic and bold fonts contain just two alphabets: capitals and lower case.

ABCDEFGHIJKLMNOPQRSTUVWXYZ
abcdefghijklmnopqrstuvwxyz
ABCDEFGHIJKLMNOPQRSTUVWXYZ

Helvetica Roman
Helvetica Italic
Helvetica Bold
Helvetica Bold Italic
Helvetica Heavy
Helvetica Heavy Italic
Helvetica Black
Helvetica Black Italic

A **family** is a set of fonts related to the basic roman type-face which may include italic and bold plus a whole spectrum of different "weights" (Fig. **2.12**). These range from ultra light to ultra bold. It will also include different widths, ranging from ultra condensed to ultra expanded.

Univers, for example, was designed by Adrian Frutiger in 1957 to have 21 fonts, in five weights and four widths (Fig. **2.13**). In the original numbering system for Univers, the tens figure indicates the weight, the units figure the width. Odd numbers are roman; even numbers italic.

A **series** is a complete range of sizes in the same typeface.

2.12 A type family contains all the fonts associated with a particular design.

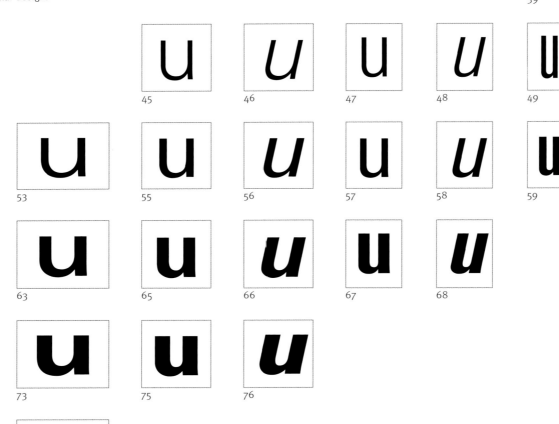

2.13 Univers is a typeface family that was especially designed to comprise a comprehensive set of variants, each of which is identified by a two-digit code number. The tens refer to the weight, the units to the width. Odd numbers are roman; even numbers italic.

How type is measured

The way type is measured dates back to the days of hot metal. Type sizes used to have quaint names such as nonpareil, long primer, minikin, minion, and brevier. Only "pica" remains in common usage.

In 1737, the Frenchman Pierre Fournier le jeune invented the **point** system of measurement, by dividing the French inch into 12 "lines" which were further subdivided into six points. Some half century later, around 1785, another Parisian, François-Ambroise Didot, settled on a standard—the **didot point**—that is used in continental Europe to this day.

In the United States, the point was standardized to be 0.013837 inch (or 0.03515 mm) by the American Type Founders' Association in 1886. Recently, the point has been further rationalized to make it exactly $\frac{1}{72}$ inch (0.01389 in or 0.3528 mm). This may seem like splitting hairs, but it means in practice that the pica rules and typescales (Fig. **2.14**) designed for traditional typesetting will give inaccurate readings when used with digital layouts.

There are 72 points to the inch. A **pica** is 12 points, and so measures $\frac{1}{6}$ inch. (The didot equivalent to the pica is the

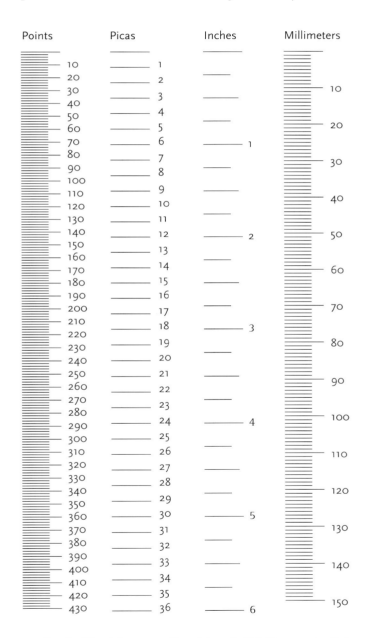

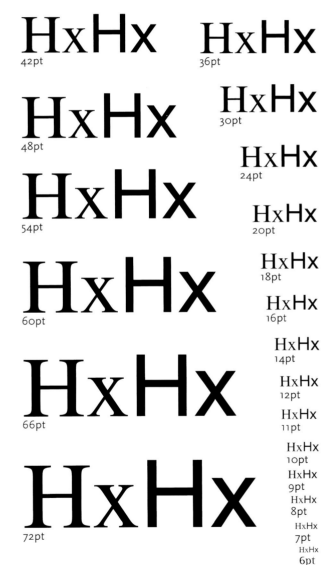

2.14 Type is still mainly measured in points and picas. There are 12 points to the pica, and 72 points to the inch. Here the two most commonplace fonts—Times New Roman and Helvetica—are shown in various point sizes.

cicero.) Although with computerized systems type can be of any height, its size is still generally measured in points, abbreviated to pt.

The use of points to specify size refers back to metal letterpress type. When a font is described as 6 pt or 18 pt, what is really being measured is the height of the body of lead that the letter sits upon (Fig. **2.15**). This is the total height from the lowest extremity of a **descender** (the long vertical stroke of a p or q) to the top of the tallest **ascender** (the long vertical stroke of a k or d), with a little extra space top and bottom. Thus in Linotype Times, for example, the distance from the top of a 10 pt letter k to the bottom of a letter p (the k–p distance, Fig. **2.16**) is not 10 pt but only 7.973 pt. The **k–p distance** of a named face can vary depending on its source, so the only sure way to identify type size is to compare your sample with suppliers' example settings.

A more exact way of defining point size is to say that it is the distance from **baseline** to baseline when type is set solid (without leading—see p. 41).

Some typefaces have longer ascenders and descenders than others, so it is quite possible for two typefaces to be exactly the same point size but to appear smaller or larger than one another. A more visually accurate method for describing size is to use the **x-height** (Fig. **2.17**). The letter x is used because all its terminals touch a line of measurement.

Type below 14 pt is called **body type**, text, or book type. Type above 14 pt is called **display type**. Some display types are so decorative as to be unsuitable for text setting and are available in capitals only.

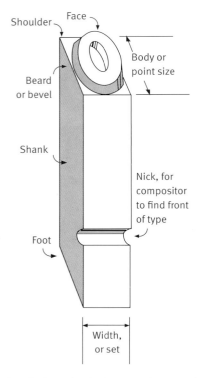

2.15 The point size of a font refers back to metal type—to the top-to-bottom size of the body that the letter sits upon, not the distance from the uppermost part of a letter to the lowermost.

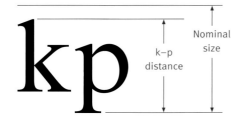

2.16 A more logical method for measuring the size of type is to measure from the top of a letter k to the bottom of a letter p: the so-called k–p distance.

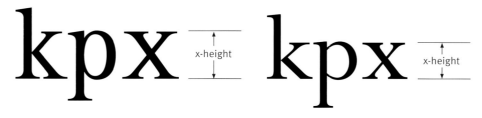

2.17 Different typefaces have different proportions of ascender to descender in relation to the bowl, say, of a letter b. So two faces of the same point size may appear to be different sizes in print. The x-height—the height of a typical lower-case letter—is a good guide to the apparent size, and thus legibility, of a particular typeface.

Width and spacing

The width of a letter is called the **set**. Every character sits on a body (real in hot metal, imaginary in computer systems) that is a number of "set points" wide; each set point being the same as the point which defines the height of the type. Typefaces with a narrow set, such as Bembo, will fit more words per page than wider typefaces, such as Baskerville.

On a regular typewriter, each letter, whether it is a thin i or a fat W, occupies the same width. The carriage moves forward the same distance each time a key is struck. The design of a typewriter font accommodates that shortcoming to some extent. Look at the length of the serifs on a typewritten i, for example, or on a t (Fig. **2.18**).

Some letters are naturally wider than others, so, in typesetting, the "body" (the letter itself plus some space either side) is divided into vertical slices or **units**. In hot metal, an 18-unit system is employed. Thus the letter i occupies five units, while an M occupies the maximum of 18. Numerals are normally all nine units wide, for ease of setting tables.

A regular typewriter uses a one-unit, or monospaced, system. An example of a monospaced computer font is Courier. A "proportionally spaced" typewriter, such as the IBM Selectric, uses a nine-unit system. In comparison, photosetting systems use as many as 96 units, the subtleties being apparent only in the very largest sizes of type.

In graphic design, the space around type is often as important as the letterform itself. When characters are allocated units, they are also given units either side to prevent consecutive sorts from touching. These are called **side bearings**, and the information about horizontal spacing built into a typeface by its designer is known as its **font metrics**.

Ems and ens

The width of a line of setting, or the column width of a publication, is called the **measure**, and is sometimes measured in picas. Other dimensions, particularly relating to page size and the positions of blocks of type, are generally measured in inches or millimeters. (In the United Kingdom, measure is also more usually in millimeters.)

Another convenient method of measurement is the **em**. This is the width of a capital M (or, strictly speaking, the width of a square space called an em **quad**). Half an em is an en, which is the width of a capital N. A complete font also provides the graphic designer with two types of dash: an en rule and an em rule—this book uses unspaced em rules.

The em is not an absolute measurement like the pica. Its size will vary depending on the set of the typeface and its point size. A one em indent in 10 pt type is 10 points; a one em indent in 18 pt type is 18 points. But it is often convenient to ask the typesetter for a paragraph indent of say an em, so that it will always be in proportion with the rest of the setting. A column width should never be specified in ems, however, for it will be different for each different font used. A 12 pt em is called a **pica em**—not to be confused with a regular pica!

Kerning and tracking

By overriding the unit allocation for pairs of certain letters, such as L and T, it is possible to bring them closer together and improve their visual appearance. This is called **kerning** (Fig. **2.19**).

2.19 To improve the visual spacing between certain pairs of letters, especially those with overhanging parts, they are kerned according to rules laid down by the type designer. It is also possible to fine-tune the kerning later, by eye, depending on the context and on the size of the type.

2.18 In a typewriter face such as Courier, all the letters are of equal width—note how the i is elongated to match the m. In more sophisticated typefaces, the width of letters varies, from the slimline l to the more expansive w. Thus different letters are allocated different numbers of units according to their set, or width.

In hot metal, kerning was only possible by physically cutting away, or mortising, the metal body of the type. Kerning characters are made with portions of the face overhanging the body (Fig. **2.20**). With computer systems, there are no restrictions on the extent of kerning possible. Most systems have routines already pre-programmed to adjust the spacing between kerning pairs automatically.

Adjusting the spacing between *all* the letters is called **tracking** (Fig. **2.21**). Tracking should not be confused with kerning, which only takes place between pairs of letters.

Tracking was never really feasible with hot-metal setting, except in special places such as the title pages of books. On the rare occasions when it was done, different materials were used to make spaces between letters: brass for 1 pt, copper for ½ pt, stainless steel for ¼ pt, and paper for the finest letterspacing of all.

In computer systems, it is common practice to use negative tracking to tighten up the spacing of text, particularly with sans-serif faces.

Jo was very busy in the garret, for the October days began to grow chilly, and the afternoons were short. For two or three hours the sun lay warmly in the high window, showing Jo seated on the old sofa, writing busily, with her papers spread out upon a trunk before her, while Scrabble, the pet rat, promenaded the beams overhead, accompanied by his oldest son, a fine young fellow, who was evidently very proud of his whiskers. Quite absorbed in her work, Jo scribbled away till the last page was filled, when she signed her name with a flourish, and threw down her pen, exclaiming:

"There, I've done my best! If this won't suit I shall have to wait till I can do better."

Utopia 10/12 pt normal tracking

Jo was very busy in the garret, for the October days began to grow chilly, and the afternoons were short. For two or three hours the sun lay warmly in the high window, showing Jo seated on the old sofa, writing busily, with her papers spread out upon a trunk before her, while Scrabble, the pet rat, promenaded the beams overhead, accompanied by his oldest son, a fine young fellow, who was evidently very proud of his whiskers. Quite absorbed in her work, Jo scribbled away till the last page was filled, when she signed her name with a flourish, and threw down her pen, exclaiming:

"There, I've done my best! If this won't suit I shall have to wait till I can do better."

Utopia 10/12 pt negative tracking

Jo was very busy in the garret, for the October days began to grow chilly, and the afternoons were short. For two or three hours the sun lay warmly in the high window, showing Jo seated on the old sofa, writing busily, with her papers spread out upon a trunk before her, while Scrabble, the pet rat, promenaded the beams overhead, accompanied by his oldest son, a fine young fellow, who was evidently very proud of his whiskers. Quite absorbed in her work, Jo scribbled away till the last page was filled, when she signed her name with a flourish, and threw down her pen, exclaiming:

"There, I've done my best! If this won't suit I shall have to wait till I can do better."

Utopia 10/12 pt positive tracking

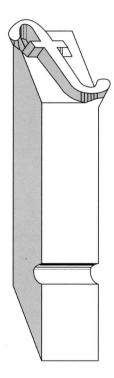

2.20 Letterpress type was kerned by cutting away parts of some metal sorts, and by placing parts of others to overhang the body of the type.

2.21 Normal tracking leaves the spaces between letters as the type designer intended them to be. Negative tracking puts the letters closer together; positive or open tracking spaces them out.

Leading

Spacing between lines of type is called **leading**, pronounced "ledding," and named after the strips of lead that were placed between lines of type in hot-metal setting (Fig. **2.22**). **Set solid** means without leading, and is written as 10/10 pt and spoken as ten on ten point. To write 10/11 pt means to ask for 10 pt type with a 1 pt space (leading) between the lines, although in hot metal it actually meant to cast 10 pt type on to an 11 pt body.

To aid legibility (see p. 58) it is now common to use 1 pt or 1½ pt leading in text setting. Computer systems often add 1½ pt leading by default. Always take into account the x-height of a typeface when deciding on a leading value. A good rule of thumb is: the larger the x-height, the more the leading; the smaller the x-height, the less the leading.

With computer systems, it is now allowable to specify all measurements in either inches or millimeters, or even mixtures of the two. However, against all odds, the point and pica persist!

Jo was very busy in the garret, for the October days began to grow chilly, and the afternoons were short. For two or three hours the sun lay warmly in the high window, showing Jo seated on the old sofa, writing busily, with her papers spread out upon a trunk before her, while Scrabble, the pet rat, promenaded the beams overhead, accompanied by his oldest son, a fine young fellow, who was evidently very proud of his whiskers. Quite absorbed in her work, Jo scribbled away till the last page was filled, when she signed her name with a flourish, and threw down her pen, exclaiming:
"There, I've done my best! If this won't suit I shall have to wait till I can do better."

Utopia 9/8 pt

Jo was very busy in the garret, for the October days began to grow chilly, and the afternoons were short. For two or three hours the sun lay warmly in the high window, showing Jo seated on the old sofa, writing busily, with her papers spread out upon a trunk before her, while Scrabble, the pet rat, promenaded the beams overhead, accompanied by his oldest son, a fine young fellow, who was evidently very proud of his whiskers. Quite absorbed in her work, Jo scribbled away till the last page was filled, when she signed her name with a flourish, and threw down her pen, exclaiming:
"There, I've done my best! If this won't suit I shall have to wait till I can do better."

Utopia 9/9 pt

Jo was very busy in the garret, for the October days began to grow chilly, and the afternoons were short. For two or three hours the sun lay warmly in the high window, showing Jo seated on the old sofa, writing busily, with her papers spread out upon a trunk before her, while Scrabble, the pet rat, promenaded the beams overhead, accompanied by his oldest son, a fine young fellow, who was evidently very proud of his whiskers. Quite absorbed in her work, Jo scribbled away till the last page was filled, when she signed her name with a flourish, and threw down her pen, exclaiming:
"There, I've done my best! If this won't suit I shall have to wait till I can do better."

Utopia 9/10 pt

Jo was very busy in the garret, for the October days began to grow chilly, and the afternoons were short. For two or three hours the sun lay warmly in the high window, showing Jo seated on the old sofa, writing busily, with her papers spread out upon a trunk before her, while Scrabble, the pet rat, promenaded the beams overhead, accompanied by his oldest son, a fine young fellow, who was evidently very proud of his whiskers. Quite absorbed in her work, Jo scribbled away till the last page was filled, when she signed her name with a flourish, and threw down her pen, exclaiming:
"There, I've done my best! If this won't suit I shall have to wait till I can do better."

Utopia 9/11 pt

2.22 The space between lines of type is called leading, after the strips of lead that were used in letterpress. Thus 9/9 pt is said to be set solid. The 9/10 pt has 1 pt leading. Type can also be set with negative leading, producing lines with ascenders and descenders touching.

Justification and hyphenation

A regular typewriter produces rows of type that line up on the left-hand side but give a ragged appearance on the right. In typesetting, this is called ragged right, **ranged left**, or flush left. Type can also be set ragged left, **ranged right**, or centered or asymmetrical (Fig. **2.23**).

In books and magazines, it is usual to see columns of type with neat edges on both sides. This is called **justified** setting, and it is achieved by introducing variable amounts of space between the words. More often than not, especially with the

For two or three hours the sun lay warmly in the high window, showing Jo seated on the old sofa, writing busily, with her papers spread out upon a trunk before her, while Scrabble, the pet rat, promenaded the beams overhead, accompanied by his oldest son, a fine young fellow, who was evidently very proud of his whiskers.

Ranged left

For two or three hours the sun lay warmly in the high window, showing Jo seated on the old sofa, writing busily, with her papers spread out upon a trunk before her, while Scrabble, the pet rat, promenaded the beams overhead, accompanied by his oldest son, a fine young fellow, who was evidently very proud of his whiskers.

Ranged right

For two or three hours the sun lay warmly in the high window, showing Jo seated on the old sofa, writing busily, with her papers spread out upon a trunk before her, while Scrabble, the pet rat, promenaded the beams overhead, accompanied by his oldest son, a fine young fellow, who was evidently very proud of his whiskers.

Centered

For two or three hours the sun lay warmly in the high window, showing Jo seated on the old sofa, writing busily, with her papers spread out upon a trunk before her, while Scrabble, the pet rat, promenaded the beams overhead, accompanied by his oldest son, a fine young fellow, who was evidently very proud of his whiskers.

Asymmetrical

For two or three hours the sun lay warmly in the high window, showing Jo seated on the old sofa, writing busily, with her papers spread out upon a trunk before her, while Scrabble, the pet rat, promenaded the beams overhead, accompanied by his oldest son, a fine young fellow, who was evidently very proud of his whiskers.

Justified

HOT TIPS & COOL TRICKS

Tabs and paragraphs

Try to use the tab and paragraph commands in your word processor to format text, rather than taps on the spacebar. Type will line up better and won't cause problems later if it has to be reflowed. Better still, learn how to use the style-sheet commands included in most word processors—it will save you time in the long run, and ensure consistency within the document. Output your text in RTF (Rich Text Format)—not everyone has Microsoft Word!

Most word processors and page-layout programs let you specify left, right, and first-line indents for paragraphs (a paragraph to a computer is all the text until you reach a carriage return, and includes headlines). So try to kick the typist's habit of hitting the tab key when you begin a new para—give the paragraph a first-line indent. And if you're setting text that's ranged left and want to move a sticking-out word over to the next line, use a forced break or soft return (shift-return) rather than a return or lots of spaces.

2.23 Type is commonly set ranged left (ragged right). It can instead be ranged right, centered, or asymmetrical. If type is to be set justified—neatly aligned on both left and right sides—variable spaces must be introduced between words to make each line the same length. Failing this, some words must be broken, or hyphenated.

narrow columns used in newspapers and magazines, it is not possible to justify a line merely by increasing the space, and so words must be divided, or **hyphenated**.

Compositors have been taught to break words according to certain rules, as found in handbooks such as *Hart's Rules for Compositors and Readers*. A word is usually hyphenated between syllables, pairs of consonants, or pairs of vowels. The part of the word left at the end of a line should also suggest the part commencing the next line. Thus starva-tion is to be preferred to star-vation. Other rules instruct to hyphenate before -ing, except in a one-syllable word such as ring, and unless preceded by d, t, or h.

Rules for hyphenation can be programmed into computer systems, along with tables of exceptions, to avoid **bad breaks**. However, it is still common to see howlers. Some careless word breaks can create unwanted meanings: the- rapist is a memorable example.

It is also generally considered good design to avoid too many consecutive hyphens. Three lines ending with hyphens or other punctuation marks is the maximum that can be tolerated. The designer should also be on the look-out for **rivers** of space running vertically in the middle of chunks of type. And for **widows** and **orphans** (Fig. **2.24**).

A widow is a single word on the last line of a paragraph carried over to the top of a column or the next page, and is best avoided by asking the copywriter or author to lose a word from earlier on in the paragraph. Orphans are single words, or small groups of words, left at the ends of paragraphs or the bottom of a page. Some experts define widows and orphans the other way round. Whichever way they are defined, they should be avoided. Try not to have fewer than two lines of type following a cross-head at the bottom of a column or page. And also be vigilant for hidden missing lines of type at the ends of

---

¶ **Type** *Tymes*

An occasional Newsletter for graphic designers, printers, and typographers that is published once a millennium, if ever at all.

Alphabet soup

Writing text that is meant to represent body type in layouts and type specimen books is probably the most difficult task a writer can ever be asked to undertake. Ideally, the text should contain examples of all the letters and sorts – in Roman, *italic* and **bold** – and include a range of words of average length so that it looks right. Above all, it shouldn't draw attention to itself. The text is not meant to be read, merely looked at – but invariably someone somewhere will grab a magnifying glass, read it and then criticize any attempted jokes therein.

Some designers take the easy route and use real or bogus Latin text, most often a famous piece of text that begins: "Lorem ipsum dolor sit amet, consectetur adipscing elit, diam nonnumy eiusmod tempor incidunt ut labore et dolo... " These are, according to the FAQ (frequently asked questions) of the newsgroup **comp.fonts**, the slightly jumbled remnants of a passage from Cicero's *de Finibus Bonorum et Malorum*, written in 45 BC, a treatise on the theory of ethics, which begins: "Neque porro quisquam est qui dolorem ipsum quia dolor sit amet, consectetur, adipisci velit..." (There is no one who loves pain itself, who seeks after it and wants to have it, simply because it is pain.)

This text has been the industry's standard dummy text ever since some printer in the 1500s took a galley of type and scrambled it to make a type specimen book; it has survived letter-by-letter essentially unchanged except for an occasional "ing" or "y" thrown in. The nonsense Latin was as incomprehensible as Greek: so the phrase "it's all Greek to me" and the term "greeking" have common semantic roots!

But this does contain some strange, to English eyes, letter combinations. Few, if any, English words contain the sequence "eiu," for example. When short pieces of text are called for, try to make a sentence containing all the letters of the alphabet with as few duplications as possible. These are called *pangrams*.

Whatever else you do, try always to avoid

The classic pangram used by typographers is: "The quick brown fox jumps over a lazy dog". Good score: all 24 letters of the alphabet in a 33-word sentence that makes sense. "Pack my box with five dozen liquor jugs" is better, with one letter less. Another common albeit longer one is: "How razorback-jumping frogs can level six piqued gymnasts!"

This one is not so good: "In the vocation of typesetting, dexterity can be gained by means of quiet, judicious and zealous work." It is more appropriate to the printing trade, but comprises 83 letters! And what about this: "Wherever civilization extends, the services of expert and judicious typographers and printers must always be quickly called upon". Is that grammatically correct? I don't think so. Or this: "The bank recognizes this claim as quite valid and just, so we expect full payment". Hmm.

Probably the shortest French pangram, at 29 letters, is: "Whisky vert: jugez cinq fox d'aplomb." Some pangrams of exactly 26 letters do exist, but rely heavily on the kind of obscure words that Scrabble players collect plus the odd Welsh and Hebrew word, such as cwm (a Welsh valley) and qoph (the nineteenth letter of the Hebrew alphabet) and, of course, proper nouns (which could in fact be made up from the left-over letters): "Vext cwm fly zing jabs Kurd qoph" is a good example. And try not to leave any

Page 1

2.24 One of the general rules of good layout is to avoid creating "orphans"—one or a few words alone on a line at the end of a paragraph—or worse still, a "widow," a single word floating at the top of a new page or column.

For two or three hours the sun lay warmly in the high window, showing Jo seated on the old sofa, writing busily, with her papers spread out upon a trunk before her, while Scrabble, the pet rat, promenaded the beams overhead, accompanied by his oldest son, a fine young fellow, who was evidently very proud of his whiskers.

For two or three hours the sun lay warmly in the high window, showing Jo seated on the old sofa, writing busily, with her papers spread out upon a trunk before her, while Scrabble, the pet rat, promenaded the beams overhead, accompanied by his oldest son, a fine young fellow, who was evidently very proud of his whiskers.

2.25 A drop cap is an embellishment found at the beginning of a chapter in a book or in the opening paragraph of a magazine article, in which the first letter is enlarged and set into the body of the text.

Its historical precedent can be found in illuminated medieval manuscripts like the ornamented title page of 1496 from the Cistercian monastery at Zinna reproduced here (above left).

columns—easy to do with computer **DTP** (desktop publishing) systems. There will be more discussion on the principles of layout in Chapter 5 (p. 138).

A revival from medieval manuscripts is the **drop cap** (Fig. **2.25**), mainly because it is easy to do on a computer system. A drop cap is an initial letter signaling the beginning of the text. It is usually enlarged to a size equivalent to three or more lines of type, with the type adjacent to the drop cap indented to make room. Drop caps work best when the first sentence begins with a single letter, such as A or I. Failing that, avoid short words, especially ones with only two letters. And take care with those words that form different words when the initial letter is removed, such as T-he, E-very, and S-elf. Another common error is to forget to remove the first letter of the body text that follows.

Text

Text is the "meaning" part of type: just plain words plus the spaces between them, devoid of any information about the typefaces, sizes, measures, or weights being used. In print production, raw text is called **copy**.

One of the designer's tasks has traditionally been **copy preparation**—adding the instructions that define how the text is going to look, which is done either by keying them directly

2.26 The style sheet for this book.

into the computer or by **marking up** the manuscript for the typesetter.

For type to remain consistent within a long document, or from issue to issue of a magazine, the graphic designer will write down and send to the compositor a **style sheet** or **type specification** (Fig. **2.26**). This will define the size, typeface, and measure of the body text, captions, headlines, and so on. In this book, for example, the text is set in 10/12.5 pt Minion Regular, with the chapter title and headings in various sizes of Meta Plus Book and Bold, and Extra Bold.

The type spec may also lay down a **grid** (see pp. 140–1) which restricts type to certain areas of the page.

Collectively, a text document is called a **manuscript**, abbreviated to Ms or ms. A single sheet is called a **folio**. (A folio is also the term given by publishers to the page numbers in books.) Each folio should be numbered and identified with a tag or catchline, usually the name of the author or job, in case the Ms is dropped or otherwise gets out of sequence. It is also customary, for short pieces of setting, to indicate on each folio whether *more follows* or that the copy *ends*.

Copy should always be clean and legible, typed or printed out on one side of the paper in double spacing with wide margins, leaving enough room for the copy editor's corrections (Fig. **2.27**). Some publishers used to provide authors with templates, sheets printed with feint blue guidelines, for the purpose. Any matter not to be printed, such as instructions to the typesetter, should be encircled.

2.27 An author's manuscript must be marked up by a copy editor before it goes to the printer for typesetting. This process brings the raw text into house style, corrects any errors, and can involve some degree of rewriting. Either the editor or the designer will also need to instruct the compositor as to which typefaces, sizes, and measures to use when converting the text into type.

Correcting text proofs

Once type has been set, it must be checked to make sure that it has been keyed correctly. The old proofreaders on newspapers were adept at reading type back to front, but for mere mortals, a proof must be taken. The first proof is traditionally referred to as the **galley proof**. Several copies are then made so that the various professionals involved in the production can each read the proof. The printer's reader is the first, and marks the printer's mistakes to be corrected, usually in green ink. One of the galley proofs is designated the **master proof**, and others go to the author or copywriter and to the copy editor, who decides which corrections should be incorporated on to the master proof (Fig. **2.28**). So-called **author's corrections** are marked in blue and have to be paid for, while any other printer's errors are marked in red.

BOOKWORM TYPESETTING
4 Harthill Street, Manchester
T: 0161-832 3034

Laurence King Publishing
Production for Graphic Designers
24.9.04 [Own Disc & Pi]
David Newton [254G]

W980BFIG.FOL

Correcting text profs

Once typp has been set, it must be checked to make sure that it has been keyed correctly. The old proofreaders on newspapers were adept at reading type back to front, but for mere morals, a proof must be taken. The first proof is traditionally referred to as the galley proof. Several copies are made so that the various proffessionals involved in the production can each read the proof. The printer's reader is the first, and marks the printer's mistakes to be corrected, usually in green ink. The printer's reader is the first, and marks the printer's mistakes to be corrected, usually in green ink.

One of the gallery proofs is designated the **master proof**, and others go the author or copywriter and to the copyeditor, who decides which corrections should be incorporated on to the master proof (Fig. 2.29). So-called **author's corrections are marked in blue and have to be paid for, while any other printer's errors are marked in red.**

Typing errors such as trasnposed letters are called *literals*, and probably constitute the bulk of the corrections. NOte that it is possible to introduce new, more serious errors into a text when attempting to correct a relatively trivial one! so that there can be no chance of misunderstanding between the copyeditor and the compositor corrections are marked neatly both in the setting and with an accompanying marginal symbol, according to an internationally agreed convention (Fig. 2.30. The marginal symbol is most important because compositors run their eyes down the edges of proofs to locate corrections. If something is wrongly corrected and needs to be reinstated, it should be marked with dotted underlining and the word **stet** written in the margin. Although there are no physical galleys in photosetting, the same procedure applies. The designer and/our copyeditor will usually recieve a set of photocopies of the bromide print which is treated in exactly the same way as the hotmetal galley proof. Once corrected, another proof may be sent, but it is more likely that the next chance to check that the corrections have been made will be on the page proof, a proof of the page layout complete with running headlines, captions, and illustrations in place.

With a digital design system, it is tempting to go straight to page layout once the text has been input. It is much safer to print out the text and to read it as if it were a proof galley. In this way there is **hardcopy**—a record of the corrections made. This also goes for website design—print out your pages and proofread them away from the computer. Better still, get a colleague to read the proof—mistakes are often invisible to those who make them. Proof reading is vital now that designers are expected to set text as they are laying out designs.

Keeping track of changes to a manuscript as it travels from computer to computer is quite difficult as word processors and layout programs always present you with a "clean' copy of the text. It is very difficult see where any changes have been made.

Programs such as Microsoft word and Adobe InCopy, which works with layout program InDesign (see p. 118) can, however, track editorial changes, including insertions, deletions, and moved text. You can display or hide each kind of revision, or display change bars in the margin of a document . To track revisoins, you can label changes by user, time and date, and navigate between them. Revisions are stored with the document until they are accepted or rejected.

And beware of computer spell checkers – they can give a false sense of security. For example, if a word is wrong but spelt "correctly," e.g. you typed "cat" but meant "cut," it won't be picked up by a spell checker. Irritatingly, spell checkers also stop at every proper noun and most numbers!

2.28 Once the marked-up copy returns from the typesetter in the form of galley proofs, it must be read, checked, and marked for correction using standard proof correction signs (fig. 2.29). Here we show the original marked-up copy (Fig. 2.27) and the typesetting after it has been marked up for correction (right).

Typing errors such as transposed letters or extra spaces are called **literals**, and probably constitute the bulk of the corrections. Note that it is possible to introduce new, more serious errors into a text when attempting to correct a relatively trivial one! So that there can be no chance of misunderstanding between the copy editor and the compositor, corrections are marked neatly both in the setting and with an accompanying marginal symbol, according to an internationally agreed convention (Fig. **2.29**). The marginal symbol is most important because compositors run their eyes down the edges of proofs to locate corrections. If something is wrongly corrected and needs to be reinstated, it should be marked with dotted underlining and the word **stet** written in the margin.

Although there are no physical galleys in photosetting, the same procedure applies. The designer and/or copy editor will usually receive a set of photocopies of the bromide print, which is treated in exactly the same way as the hot-metal galley proof. Once corrected, another proof may be sent, but it is more likely that the next chance to check that the corrections have been made will be on the **page proof**, a proof of the page layout complete with running headlines, captions, and illustrations in place.

With a digital design system, it is tempting to go straight to page layout once the text has been input. It is much safer to print out the page and to read it as if it were a galley proof. In this way there is **hardcopy**—a record of the corrections made.

STANDARD PROOF CORRECTION SIGNS

EXPLANATION	MARGINAL MARK	TEXT MARK
Delete letter(s) or word(s)	⁊	I've doner my best
Close up; delete space	⌒	I've done my best
Delete, and close up word	⌒⁊	I've done may best
Let it stand as it is	stet	I've done my best
Insert space	#	I've donemy best
Equalize spacing	eq #	I've done my best
Insert hair space	hL #	1398–1468
Letterspace	LS	I'VE DONE MY BEST
Begin new paragraph	⁋	I've done my best! If
Don't begin new paragraph; run on	no ⁋	I've done my best! If this won't suit
Move type one em	⊐	] I've done my best
Move type two ems	⊐⊐	] I've done my best
Move right	]	I've done my best]
Move left	[	[I've done my best
Center	][	] I've done my best [
Move up	⎤⎡	I've done my best
Move down	⎣⎦	I've done my best
Flush left; range left	fL	[I've done my best
Flush right; range right	fr	I've done my best
Straighten type; align horizontally	=	I've done my best
Align vertically	‖	‖ I've done
Transpose; swap the order	tr	I've done my bset
Set in *italic* type	ital	I've done my best
Set in roman type	rom	*I've done my best*
Set in bold type	bf	I've done my best
Set in lower case	Lc	I've done MY best
Set in UPPER CASE (capitals)	cap	i've done my best
Set in SMALL CAPITALS	sc	I've done my best
Remove blemish	X	I've done my best
Make superscript figure	ᵛ	1024 is 210
Make subscript figure	^	101012
Insert comma	⸲	There I've done my best
Insert apostrophe or single quotation mark	⸲	Ive done my best
Insert period	⊙	I've done my best
Insert question mark	?	Have I done my best
Insert colon	:/	She exclaimed, "I've done
Insert hyphen	/=/	Black and-white print
Insert en dash	⊥⃗N	1398 1468
Insert em dash	⊥⃗M	I've done my best
Insert parentheses	(/)	I've done my best
Insert brackets	[/]	I've done my best

2.29 To ensure that designers, proofreaders, editors, and typesetters are able to communicate with each other effectively, an internationally agreed standard for proof-correction symbols has been developed.

This also goes for website design—print out your pages and proofread them away from the computer. Better still, get a colleague to read the proof—mistakes are often invisible to those who make them. Proofreading is vital now that designers are expected to set text as they are laying out designs.

Keeping track of changes to a manuscript as it travels from computer to computer is quite difficult as word processors and layout programs always present you with a "clean" copy of the text. It is very difficult to see where any changes have been made. Programs such as Microsoft Word and Adobe InCopy, which works with layout program InDesign (see p. 148) can, however, track editorial changes, including insertions, deletions, and moved text. You can display or hide each kind of revision, or display change bars in the margin of a document.

Characters per line

2.30 Copy-fitting tables help estimate the space needed by copy in a particular typeface and point size. This old-style table (right) is for Century. In the two-part table below, each typeface is given a value. A number from the first table is used to read off characters per pica from the second.

Font size	Pica measure												
	18	19	20	21	22	23	24	25	26	27	28	29	30
8 pt	59	62	65	68	72	75	78	81	85	88	91	94	98
9 pt	52	55	58	60	63	66	69	72	75	78	81	83	86
10 pt	46	48	51	53	56	58	61	64	66	69	71	74	76
11 pt	42	44	47	49	51	54	56	58	61	63	65	68	70
12 pt	38	40	43	45	47	49	51	53	55	57	60	62	64

Alphabet lengths for different sizes
Laufweitenkennzahl für verschiedene Schriftgrößen
Longueur d'alphabet pour différents corps

alphabet length ref. no. at 10 pt
Laufweitenkennzahl in 10 pt
Référence de longueur d'alphabet en 10 pt

pt	6	7	8	9	10	11	12	14	16	18	20	24	30	36	42	48
mm	2,25	2,63	3,00	3,38	3,75	4,13	4,50	5,25	6,00	6,75	7,50	9,00	11,25	13,50	15,75	18,00
85	51	59	68	76	85	93	102	119	136	153	170	204	255	306	357	408
87	52	60	69	78	87	95	104	121	139	156	174	208	261	313	365	417
88	52	61	70	79	88	96	105	123	140	158	176	211	264	316	369	422
90	54	63	72	81	90	99	108	126	144	162	180	216	270	324	378	432
92	55	64	73	82	92	101	110	128	147	165	184	220	276	331	386	441
93	55	65	74	83	93	102	111	130	148	167	186	223	279	334	390	446
95	57	66	76	85	95	104	114	133	152	171	190	228	285	342	399	456
97	58	67	77	87	97	106	116	135	155	174	194	232	291	349	407	465
98	58	68	78	88	98	107	117	137	156	176	196	235	294	352	411	470
100	60	70	80	90	100	110	120	140	160	180	200	240	300	360	420	480
102	61	71	81	91	102	112	122	142	163	183	204	244	306	367	428	489
103	61	72	82	92	103	113	123	144	164	185	206	247	309	370	432	494
105	63	73	84	94	105	115	126	147	168	189	210	252	315	378	441	504
107	64	74	85	96	107	117	128	149	171	192	214	256	321	385	449	513
108	64	75	86	97	108	118	129	151	172	194	216	259	324	388	453	518
110	66	77	88	99	110	121	132	154	176	198	220	264	330	396	462	528
112	67	78	89	100	112	123	134	156	179	201	224	268	336	403	470	537
113	67	79	90	101	113	124	135	158	180	203	226	271	339	406	474	542
115	69	80	92	103	115	126	138	161	184	207	230	276	345	414	483	552
															491	561
															495	566
															504	576
															512	585
															516	590
															525	600
															533	609
															537	614
															546	624
															554	633
															558	638
															567	648
															575	657

Characters per line (Pica)
Zeichen pro Zeile (Pica)
Caractères par ligne (Pica)

determined alphabet length ref. no.
ermittelte Laufweitenkennzahl
référence de longueur d'alphabet déterminés

Pica	1.00	10	12	14	16	18	20	22	24	26	28	30	32	36	40	45
50	6.74	67	81	94	108	121	135	148	162	175	189	202	216	243	270	303
52	6.48	65	78	91	104	117	130	143	156	168	181	194	207	233	259	292
54	6.24	62	75	87	100	112	125	137	150	162	175	187	200	225	250	281
56	6.02	60	72	84	96	108	120	132	144	156	168	181	193	217	241	271
58	5.81	58	70	81	93	105	116	128	139	151	163	174	186	209	232	261
60	5.62	56	67	79	90	101	112	124	135	146	157	168	180	202	225	253
62	5.43	54	65	76	87	98	109	120	130	141	152	163	174	196	217	245
64	5.27	53	63	74	84	95	105	116	126	137	147	158	168	190	211	237
66	5.11	51	61	71	82	92	102	112	123	133	143	153	163	184	204	230
68	4.96	50	59	69	79	89	99	109	119	129	139	149	159	178	198	223
70	4.81	48	58	67	77	87	96	106	116	125	135	144	154	173	193	217
72	4.68	47	56	66	75	84	94	103	112	122	131	140	150	168	187	211
76	4.55	46	55	64	73	82	91	100	109	118	127	137	146	164	182	205

To track revisions, you can label changes by user, time, and date, and navigate between them. Revisions are stored with the document until they are accepted or rejected.

And beware of computer spell checkers—they can give a false sense of security. For example, if a word is wrong but spelt "correctly," i.e. you typed "cat" but meant "cut," it won't be picked up by a spell checker. Irritatingly, spell checkers also stop at every proper noun and most numbers!

Casting off and copy fitting

Casting off is estimating the number of words in a manuscript. **Copy fitting** is assessing how much space text will take up in a printed document. Both are important in ensuring that you do not end up with pages of **overmatter**.

Most computers now have built-in word counters, but these are often approximate, depending on what the program decides constitutes a word. Different programs can give different word counts for the same piece of text.

The amount of space required when the text is set into type will vary depending both on the type size and the typeface. For hot metal and photosetting, the type foundries would supply copy-fitting tables (Fig. **2.30**), which gave you the information that, for example, 11 pt Bembo averages 66 characters (11 words) in a line 24 picas long. It was thus possible to find out how many pages the copy would fill once set in type.

For smaller jobs, a plastic type gauge was used to measure the number of lines that a particular size of type would occupy. If you calculated that five lines of text would give you seven lines of type, for example, it was possible to count them off using the gauge. Many type gauges also had scales with which to count typewritten characters. On typewriters, the number of characters per inch is called the **pitch**: the normal 10 pitch is called pica (no relation to the typographic pica!), and the smaller 12 pitch is called elite.

With computer setting, there is a lot of variation in set width between the same named typeface from different suppliers. The only way to be safe is to base your calculations on a piece of sample setting from your chosen font and use exactly the same font for the eventual setting. This is particularly important when using a bureau which may claim to hold the same font: when the proof arrives you may find the words are not where you wanted them. Always overestimate the number of words, to be on the safe side. It is easier to deal with white space than to find room for unexpected text.

It is all too easy to make copy fit an awkward space by altering the tracking, the size of type, or the leading by just the tiniest amount, with a resulting inconsistency of "color" within the document. This is a temptation that you should try to resist.

House style

There are few absolutes in life, and in some cases a usage is neither right nor wrong. But **house style** is a way of standardizing spelling and codifying the way, say, that ships' names, like the USS *Enterprise*, are always italicized. There will normally also be guidelines to avoid sexist and racist usages creeping into print.

House style will regulate how the date should be written, and will also include instructions as to whether acronyms should be given periods or not (dots per inch as d.p.i. or dpi, or even dots/in), set all caps or all lower case (both WYSIWYG and wysiwyg, for example, could be used to mean "what you see is what you get").

The keyword is consistency—both within a publication, and within an organization.

Choosing and recognizing typefaces

To be able to choose the right typeface for the job, one must first know something about how typefaces are constructed and classified (Fig. **2.31**).

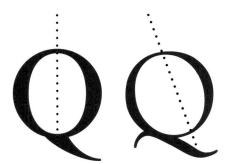

Vertical stress (Times)   Inclined stress (Goudy Old Style)

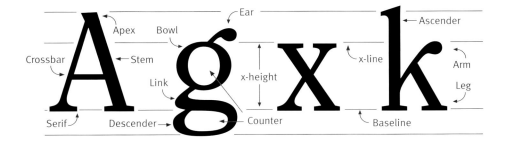

2.31 Each letter has its own anatomical details, and knowing the names for the component parts of a letterform is a great aid to identifying and specifying a particular typeface.

Zuzana Licko

"Integrating design and production, the computer has reintroduced craft as the source of inspiration."

Manifesto
Puzzles

"What is a typeface? A typeface is the ornamental manifestation of the alphabet.

"If the alphabet conveys words, a typeface conveys their tone, style, and attitude.

"Ever since I was first introduced to graphic design, I heard everybody say how bad digital type looked and how it was impossible to make it look any better. This really intrigued me. Whenever anyone makes a statement like that, I have difficulty agreeing. I was reading books on the history of graphic design and in the final chapter they would always mention something about digital type and show typefaces like OCR A and B. Some of them were interesting but never really any good for setting text.

"So I saw that here was something unexplored and interesting and I wanted to try my own hand at it. But every time I asked for advice, people kept telling me it was really a lost cause, that it couldn't be done. So I thought that anything I would do would be better than what was out there.

"I enjoy things that are like puzzles; anything that is tremendously restrictive, where there are very few choices but you have to make it work. If I get too many choices, I become overwhelmed. I just don't have the time and patience to look at every possible scenario. This is the problem I have with graphic design. I never got the feeling that I found the final solution to a problem. Although I now design more traditional and less modular typefaces, I still get most of my creative energy out of solving these problems. When nobody is able to make something work, I get inspired to find out what I might do with it.

"Integrating design and production, the computer has reintroduced craft as the source of inspiration. Because the computer is an unfamiliar medium, designers must reconsider many basic rules previously taken for granted. This has brought excitement and creativity to aspects of design that have been forgotten since the days of letterpress. With computers many alternatives can be quickly and economically reviewed. Today's designers must learn to discriminate intelligently among all of the choices, a task requiring a thorough understanding of fundamentals."

Zuzana Licko was born in 1961 in Bratislava, Czechoslovakia, and emigrated to the USA at the age of seven. She graduated with a degree in graphic communications from the University of California at Berkeley in 1984.

It was also in 1984 that Licko, together with her Dutch-born husband Rudy VanderLans, started *Emigre* magazine, a journal for experimental graphic design that ceased publication in 2005 with issue 69. The magazine garnered much critical acclaim when it began to incorporate Licko's digital typeface designs—Emperor, Emigre, and Oakland—which were created on the Macintosh computer. The 128k Macintosh was launched just as the second edition of *Emigre* was in production. The exposure and success of these typefaces in the magazine led Licko and Vanderlans to set up Emigre Inc. to manufacture and distribute the fonts to a wider audience.

When Licko designed her first fonts for the Mac (the Emperor, Emigre, Oakland, and Universal families) in 1984, bitmap fonts were the only kinds available. Her intention was to create a series of legible fonts for the 72 dpi computer screen and dot-matrix printer. After laser printers and outline fonts were introduced, she imagined that these bitmaps would be relegated to the status of novelty fonts, but with the current interest in multimedia CDs and the World Wide Web, they have been re-evaluated.

As a graphic design team, Emigre has worked for clients ranging from large multinationals such as Apple to independent art organizations such as San Francisco's Artspace. Their work has been published in *Blueprint*, *Baseline*, *Axis*, *i–D*, *Eye*, *Communication Arts*, *Print*, and numerous design magazines and books throughout the USA, UK, Holland, Germany, and Japan. Their writing has been published in the *AIGA Journal*, *I.D.*, *U&lc*, and *How*. Selections of their work are included in the permanent collections of the San Francisco Museum of Modern Art, the Design Museum in London, The National Design Museum in New York, the Italian traveling exhibit "Pacific Wave," and in the Walker Art Center design retrospective "Graphic design in America."

Emigre was the 1994 recipient of the prestigious Chrysler Award for Innovation in Design and, also in 1994, New York publisher Van Nostrand Reinhold published a ten-year retrospective book entitled *Emigre: Graphic Design into the Digital Realm*.

Licko's interest in creating more traditional typefaces for text was a result of *Emigre* magazine's publication of in-depth articles, which required fonts appropriate for lengthy text setting. Her revival of the Baskerville typeface, named Mrs Eaves, after Sarah Eaves—the woman who became John Baskerville's wife—presented her with the opportunity to design some fanciful ligatures which helped create visual interest and are reminiscent of customized lettering.

As well as designing fonts, Licko makes and sells stoneware pots with the same restraint and simplicity of design as her typefaces. She has even designed sleepwear (pajamas).

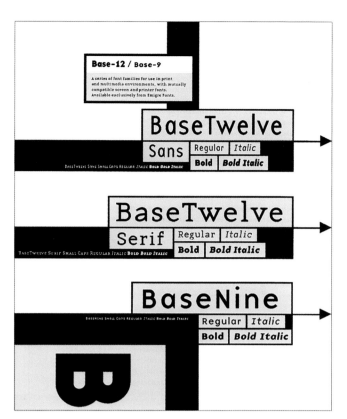

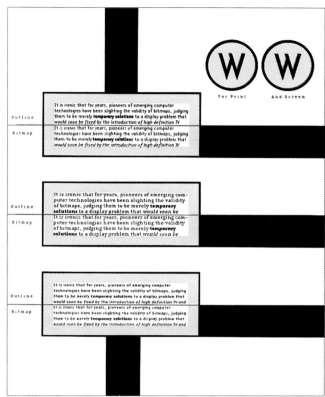

Resources

Website: www.emigre.com

Rudy VanderLans and Zuzana Licko, *Emigre* (the book): *Graphic Design into the Digital Realm*, Van Nostrand Reinhold, 1994

Emigre (the magazine): was published quarterly until 2005 by Emigre Inc., 1700 Shattuck Avenue, Berkeley, CA 94709, USA

Solex Regular

Solex Medium

Solex Italic

Solex Medium Italic

Solex Bold

Solex Black

Solex Bold Italic

Solex Black Italic

The fonts Base Nine and Base Twelve were designed by Zuzana Licko in 1995. The basic concept for the Base Twelve family started with the 24 pt and 36 pt screen fonts that Licko designed for use on the *Emigre* website. The result was one serif and one sans serif family based on 12 pt screen fonts called Base Twelve, and one family based on 9 pt screen fonts named Base Nine—a total of 24 individual faces. PostScript fonts come in two parts (see p. 68): the screen font or bitmap and the device-independent outline font or printer font. Usually, the printer-font characters dictate the look of the screen-font characters, but Licko tackled the problem from the opposite direction, designing the screen fonts first to set the exact character widths within which the outline characters were adjusted to fit. When using Base Nine and Base Twelve in situations where character display and spacing on the screen are of primary importance, such as in multimedia, they should be used at multiples of their "base." For example, Base Twelve is best used at 12 pt, 24 pt and above. Base Nine is best used at 9 pt, 18 pt and above. Carefully hand-edited screen fonts are provided at these sizes for the best possible screen display. But although Base Nine and Base Twelve were designed for a specific function, the goal was also to create a comprehensive family of typefaces suitable for traditional print.

Solex (2000) was Licko's first release in nearly two years. Inspiration came from two principal sources: Alternate Gothic and Bauer Topic (designed by Paul Renner, who also designed Futura). Solex revisits postmodern themes seen in Erik Spiekermann's Meta Sans and its cousin, Officina Sans.

Each face has its own personality (Fig. **2.32**), and typefaces are described by typographers in the same hallowed tones used by connoisseurs to talk about wine. Garamond is said to be "quiet"; Bodoni "sparkles".

Each has its place in the graphic designer's toolkit: for a bank's annual report, for example, you may wish to use a well-established "classic" face like Garamond to convey tradition and solidity; a music magazine aimed at young people will look better with a fashionable type. Some typefaces are chosen for practical reasons. Newspapers tend to use faces with large x-heights and open counters, because the ink spread on low-grade paper would fill in less robust faces.

Serif or sans serif?

The most obvious distinguishing feature of a typeface is whether it has a serif or not (Fig. **2.33**). **Serifs** are marks or flourishes around the extremities of letters, on the baseline and at the top, usually at right angles to the direction of the

Establishment
Times New Roman

Professional
Rotis serif

Fun and Friendly
Dolores Bold

Elegant
Garamond Italic

Bland but safe
Helvetica

Traditional
Baskerville

Powerful
Franklin Gothic Heavy

Fashionable
Dax

2.32 Some typefaces are so familiar as to be virtually invisible—Times and Helvetica are the main culprits—while others come regularly in and out of fashion every few years.

2.33 All typefaces can be classified according to whether they do or do not have serifs. Some serifs have brackets— smooth "fillets" between the horizontal and upright—and some do not. The size of the serif can range from slab to hairline.

Sans serif (without serifs)

Square or slab serifs

Bracketed serifs

Thin or hairline serifs

Round serifs

Novelty serifs

Cupped serifs

stroke. They help to make type more readable (see p. 58), and take several different forms: bracketed, with a smooth curved "fillet" between the serif and stem; slab, with sharper corners and almost the same thickness as the stem; hairline; or wedge. The best known serif typeface is Times.

A typeface without serifs is called **sans serif**, or just sans. The old name was grot, from grotesque, and in America they are also known as Gothic faces. The first sans typeface for text was cast in 1835 and called Seven Lines Grotesque, though sans faces have long been used for display setting and for sign-writing. They did not become popular until the beginning of this century, first with Edward Johnston's 1916 typeface—still in use—for London Transport. Later came Univers, and Max Miedinger's Helvetica (see p. 54), perhaps one of the most popular typefaces currently in use. Contemporary classics include Meta and Verdana.

Earmarks

Each typeface has its own distinctive characteristics, which are called **earmarks** (Fig. **2.34**), named after the distinctive "ear" on the lower case g. These enable us to identify one design from another. To distinguish Helvetica from Univers, for example, look for the vertical downstroke in the capital G, the curly tail of the lower case y, and the angled tail through the bowl of the Q.

Soon you will be spotting the more subtle differences. For other typefaces, a good strategy is to start with the Q (a letter so infrequently used that typographers often have fun with it, making it their trademark), then the ampersand, then the J, G, and W. Try the lower case g, then a, j, and y. For numbers, look first at 3, then 7, 5, and 2. Real italics, not the sloped oblique versions of roman type found in DTP systems, are usually distinctive and easy to identify.

Other features that help distinguish different typefaces are the overall proportions (the relation of x-height to ascenders and descenders, for example), the stress (is it oblique or vertical?), the contrast between thick and thin strokes, and the formation of the serifs. Are the characters wide and loose-fitting, or compact and tight? Some are easy: script and "black-letter" faces, for example, stand out from all the others. To the untrained eye, others look virtually indistinguishable.

Type has long been classified into groups, such as "old face," "transitional," and "modern." These sometimes vague classifications have been codified, first by French typographer Maximilien Vox, and later by national and international standards, into nine groups (Fig. **2.35 a–j**). The categories may not seem at first sight to be of great use to the graphic designer when choosing type, but they are a considerable aid to communicating with the typesetter and printer.

To this classification scheme ought to be added a group to include the digital faces created on computer systems (see pp. 65–73) mainly for the style magazines of the 1980s, e.g. Modula and Emigre, and the so-called "intelligent" faces such as Beowolf.

Despite the best efforts of the classifiers, there still remain some typefaces that defy categorization, and which can only be described as being "hybrids." These include the best-known typeface of all—Times New Roman—which has to be described as a Garalde/Didone hybrid. There are two other points to make about typefaces: first, not all versions of a named typeface are the same (Fig. **2.36**). There are many versions and interpretations of Univers and Times for example, and if you are not precise in specifying a particular vendor's Univers, you may be in for a surprise, especially when an accurate cast-off has been attempted.

Second, for copyright reasons, the same design of typeface may have a different name (often thinly disguised to give a clue to its origin) when obtained from a source other than its originator. For example, Bitstream's version of Plantin is called Aldine 721, Linotype's Futura Book is called Spartan Book and Compugraphic's Helvetica is renamed Helios.

GgyQap&4
Helvetica

GgyQap&4
Univers

GgyQap&4
Clearface

GgyQap&4
Times

GgyQap&4
Futura

GgyQap&4
Baskerville

GgyQap&4
Gill

GgyQap&4
Garamond

2.34 Earmarks are the distinguishing features of a typeface design. Easily identifiable letters include the capital Q and the lower case g, and don't forget the ampersand.

Helvetica

Helvetica:

ABCDEFGHIJKLMNOPQRSTUVWXYZ
abcdefghijklmnopqrstuvwxyz
1234567890

Akzidenz Grotesk:

ABCDEFGHIJKLMNOPQRSTUVWXYZ
abcdefghijklmnopqrstuvwxyz
1234567890

In the years following the Second World War, Swiss-style typography was the in thing. Switzerland's neutrality had allowed a continuity of development from the grid-bound modernist graphic design of the 1930s, with its integrated text and image, use of photomontage, and above all its reductive unadorned type, serving only the functional needs of communication. According to Joseph Müller-Brockman (1914–96), unornamented sans-serif typefaces expressed the age and were suitable for any job—and the typeface of choice was Berthold's Akzidenz Grotesk, aka Standard. It was favored over geometric fonts like Futura, because it could provide a closer fit of letters. It had, however, been around since 1896 and so the race was on to find a more up-to-date successor.

Max Miedinger (1910–80) was born in Zürich and trained as a typesetter, but worked most of his life as a customer service and sales representative for the Haas Type Foundry in Münchenstein, near Basle. At the age of 46, he became a freelance graphic designer in Zürich. Then in 1956, Edouard Hoffmann of Haas asked Max to redesign Akzidenz Grotesk with a higher x-height and give them something to sell. The result was Neue Haas Grotesk, renamed Helvetica (the Latin word for Switzerland) in 1957 when it was licensed to German type foundry Stempel. The commercial package was launched in 1961. Linotype took complete control of Haas in 1989 and produced a full family of variants.

Linotype's limited licensing forced a large number of unauthorized copies of Helvetica, including Helios, Geneva, Megaron, Triumvirate, and Swiss 721. Forty years after its introduction, Linotype listed 115 fonts for the family, with Helvetica Rounded being probably the least known. Max Miedinger died in 1980. Other typefaces designed by him include: Pro Arte (1954) and Horizontal (1964).

Despite the challenge of the more radical and modern Univers, designed by Adrian Frutiger in 1954 in both a photosetting and metal version and in 21 logical variants, Helvetica—a simple response to market demand—became, along with Times New Roman, one of the most popular typefaces of the 20th century.

Successors to Helvetica include Arial, designed in 1989–90 for Microsoft by Robin Nicholas and Patricia Saunders of Monotype, and, of course, "the Helvetica of the 90s," Erik Spiekermann's Meta.

Helvetica is such a famous typeface that an independent feature-length documentary movie has been made about it, produced and directed by Gary Hustwit. It looks at the proliferation of this typeface (which celebrated its 50th birthday in 2007) as part of a larger conversation about the way type affects our lives. Interviewees include such illustrious and innovative names in the design world as Erik Spiekermann, Neville Brody, Stefan Sagmeister, David Carson, and Paula Scher. *Helvetica* had its World Premiere at the South by Southwest Film Festival in March 2007. The film has subsequently played in over 300 cities in 40 countries. It received its television premiere on the UK's BBC1 in November 2007, and broadcast on PBS as part of the Emmy award-winning series Independent Lens in fall 2008. More info at www.helveticafilm.com.

Humanist: Centaur.
Mind your Ps & Qs
ABCDEFGHIJKLMNOPQRSTUVWXYZ
abcdefghijklmnopqrstuvwxyz
1234567890 (.,:;*?$["&"]'%'!)

It was after sun-up now, but we went right on and didn't tie up. The king and the duke turned out by and by looking pretty rusty; but after they'd jumped overboard and took a swim it chippered them up a good deal. After breakfast the king he took a seat on the corner of the raft, and pulled off his boots and rolled up his britches, and let his legs dangle in the water, so as to be comfortable, and lit his pipe, and went to getting his "Romeo and Juliet" by heart.

Garalde: Caslon.
Mind your Ps & Qs
ABCDEFGHIJKLMNOPQRSTUVWXYZ
abcdefghijklmnopqrstuvwxyz
1234567890 (.,:;*?$["&"]'%'!)

It was after sun-up now, but we went right on and didn't tie up. The king and the duke turned out by and by looking pretty rusty; but after they'd jumped overboard and took a swim it chippered them up a good deal. After breakfast the king he took a seat on the corner of the raft, and pulled off his boots and rolled up his britches, and let his legs dangle in the water, so as to be comfortable, and lit his pipe, and went to getting his "Romeo and Juliet" by heart.

Transitional: Baskerville.
Mind your Ps & Qs
ABCDEFGHIJKLMNOPQRSTUVWXYZ
abcdefghijklmnopqrstuvwxyz
1234567890 (.,:;*?$["&"]'%'!)

It was after sun-up now, but we went right on and didn't tie up. The king and the duke turned out by and by looking pretty rusty; but after they'd jumped overboard and took a swim it chippered them up a good deal. After breakfast the king he took a seat on the corner of the raft, and pulled off his boots and rolled up his britches, and let his legs dangle in the water, so as to be comfortable, and lit his pipe, and went to getting his "Romeo and Juliet" by heart.

2.35a Group 1: Humanist
These faces are characterized by an inclined bar on the lower case e, which points to their calligraphic origins. They are light in weight, with bracketed serifs, and an oblique stress. Also known as Venetian. An example is Centaur.

2.35b Group 2: Garalde
The faces in this group still have an oblique stress, but are less script-like, with a horizontal bar on the e. The name Garalde is a contraction of *Garamond* and *Aldus*, though where the e comes from is a mystery. Other examples include Bembo, Plantin, and Caslon. Collectively, Humanist and Garalde are called "old face" or "old style." Old style, however, does not mean old-fashioned: Galliard is a face designed with the aid of a computer by Matthew Carter in 1978–81.

2.35c Group 3: Transitional
Here the axis of the curves has become vertical, with bracketed oblique serifs. The construction of each letter is based on a mathematical formula, and the major example is Baskerville, which is wide for its x-height.

2.35d Group 4: Didone

There is an abrupt contrast between the thick and the thin strokes; the axis of the curves is completely vertical; and serifs are horizontal, unbracketed, and hairline. This grouping is also called "modern." The name is a contraction of *Didot* and *Bodoni*, and other examples include Caledonia.

2.35e Group 5: Mechanistic

Also known as slab-serif or Egyptian, these faces have heavy square-ended serifs, with or without brackets. Examples include Clarendon, Melior, and Rockwell.

2.35f Group 6: Lineal

Better known as sans serif, these faces are further subdivided into:
• Grotesque, the original 19th-century faces with a "closed" appearance, e.g. Grot and Headline;
• Neo-grot, which are rounded and open with a monoline weight, e.g. Helvetica and Univers;

Didone: Bodoni.
Mind your Ps & Qs
ABCDEFGHIJKLMNOPQRSTUVWXYZ
abcdefghijklmnopqrstuvwxyz
1234567890 (.,:;*?$["&"]'%'!)

It was after sun-up now, but we went right on and didn't tie up. The king and the duke turned out by and by looking pretty rusty; but after they'd jumped overboard and took a swim it chippered them up a good deal. After breakfast the king he took a seat on the corner of the raft, and pulled off his boots and rolled up his britches, and let his legs dangle in the water, so as to be comfortable, and lit his pipe, and went to getting his "Romeo and Juliet" by heart.

Mechanistic: Rockwell.
Mind your Ps & Qs
ABCDEFGHIJKLMNOPQRSTUVWXYZ
abcdefghijklmnopqrstuvwxyz
1234567890 (.,:;*?$["&"]'%'!)

It was after sun-up now, but we went right on and didn't tie up. The king and the duke turned out by and by looking pretty rusty; but after they'd jumped overboard and took a swim it chippered them up a good deal. After breakfast the king he took a seat on the corner of the raft, and pulled off his boots and rolled up his britches, and let his legs dangle in the water, so as to be comfortable, and lit his pipe, and went to getting his "Romeo and Juliet" by heart.

Neo-grot sans serif: Helvetica.
Mind your Ps & Qs
ABCDEFGHIJKLMNOPQRSTUVWXYZ
abcdefghijklmnopqrstuvwxyz
1234567890 (.,:;*?$["&"]'%'!)

It was after sun-up now, but we went right on and didn't tie up. The king and the duke turned out by and by looking pretty rusty; but after they'd jumped overboard and took a swim it chippered them up a good deal. After breakfast the king he took a seat on the corner of the raft, and pulled off his boots and rolled up his britches, and let his legs dangle in the water, so as to be comfortable, and lit his pipe, and went to getting his "Romeo and Juliet" by heart.

Geometric sans serif: Futura.
Mind your Ps & Qs
ABCDEFGHIJKLMNOPQRSTUVWXYZ
abcdefghijklmnopqrstuvwxyz
1234567890 (.,:;*?$["&"]'%'!)

It was after sun-up now, but we went right on and didn't tie up. The king and the duke turned out by and by looking pretty rusty; but after they'd jumped overboard and took a swim it chippered them up a good deal. After breakfast the king he took a seat on the corner of the raft, and pulled off his boots and rolled up his britches, and let his legs dangle in the water, so as to be comfortable, and lit his pipe, and went to getting his "Romeo and Juliet" by heart.

ABCDEFGHIJKLMNOPQ
RSTUVWXYZ
abcdefghijklmnopqrstuvwxyz
1234567890

ABCDEFGHIJKLMNO
PQRSTUVWXYZ
abcdefghijklmnopqrstuvwxyz
1234567890

ABCDEFGHIJKLMNOPQ
RSTUVWXYZ
1234567890

ABCDEFGHIJKLMNOPQRSTUVWXYZ
abcdefghijklmnopqrstuvwxyz
1234567890

Group 6: Lineal cont.
• Geometric, based on the geometric shapes promoted by the Bauhaus, such as circles and straight lines, e.g. Futura;
• Humanist sans serif, based on more classical proportions, e.g. Gill Sans and Optima.

2.35g Group 7: Glyphic
These faces look chiseled rather than written, with blunt elephant's-foot serifs. The example shown here is Albertus.

2.35h Group 8: Script
Script faces imitate cursive or "copperplate" writing. They can be formal, e.g. the Berthold Script shown here, or informal, e.g. Flash. They are not normally used as text faces, but are reserved for jobs such as wedding invitations or menus.

2.35i Group 9: Graphic
This group includes faces that look as if they have been drawn, rather than written. Examples are Dom Casual (shown here), MS Comic Sans, and Klang.

2.35j Group 10: Digital
Digital faces created for computer systems and style magazines, e.g. Modula (shown here), Emigre, and Beowolf.

2.36 Many classic letterpress typefaces have been redesigned over the years, first for phototypesetting and lately for digital systems. Note how recent versions often have greater x-heights, thicker serifs, and a more condensed appearance. This is to accommodate changing needs in both technology and fashion. Shown contrasted here are Monotype's Century Old Style and ITC's Century Book, and both Monotype and ITC versions of Garamond and Garamond Italic. (ITC faces are printed in red.)

ABCDEFGHIJKLMNOPQRSTUVWXYZ
abcdefghijklmnopqrstuvwxyz

ABCDEFGHIJKLMNOPQRSTUVWXYZ
abcdefghijklmnopqrstuvwxyz

ABCDEFGHIJKLMNOPQRSTUVWXYZ
abcdefghijklmnopqrstuvwxyz

ABCDEFGHIJKLMNOPQRSTUVWXYZ
abcdefghijklmnopqrstuvwxyz

ABCDEFGHIJKLMNOPQRSTUVWXYZ
abcdefghijklmnopqrstuvwxyz

ABCDEFGHIJKLMNOPQRSTUVWXYZ
abcdefghijklmnopqrstuvwxy

Legibility and readability

One of the most important concerns of the graphic designer is to ensure that any type used is legible and readable. The intention, after all, is to communicate the author's or copywriter's ideas to the reader as efficiently as possible. If the type makes an aesthetically pleasing "picture" on the page as well, then that's a bonus.

For legibility, context is everything (Fig. **2.37**). Novels, cookery books, and telephone directories are all read in different ways. The designer has to know the conditions in which the type will be read, who will be reading it, and why.

Faces with quirky letters, like the Q in ITC Bookman and the *g* in Galliard Italic, can begin to annoy when set in continuous text. And a display face for advertising or a logo has a completely different purpose to that of a face for a children's book. A logo, for example, may initially be harder to read, but in the long term is more memorable and recognizable. The instant legibility of type on freeway signs is a matter of life and death.

Legibility, however, is a cultural matter. Unless they are German-speaking, many people find "black-face" lettering difficult to understand. Graffiti on subway trains are usually unreadable by most people over 15. Designers such as David

Carson are often attacked by purist typographers for alleged illegibility, but in cases like *Ray Gun*, where the style tends to be more important than the content, a more adventurous approach to type is often expected.

There has been much research on the legibility of sans versus serifed faces. The outcome seems to be that, with some exceptions, faces with serifs are easier to read continuously over long periods than those without. Serifs serve several purposes. They help letters to keep their distance. They link letters to make words, for we read by recognizing the shapes of words. They also help to differentiate letterforms, particularly the top halves, which are apparently more critical for rapid recognition. Faces with a large x-height, favored by newspapers, do not guarantee legibility, for the relatively short ascenders and descenders may have a negative effect on the overall shape of a word.

Sans serif faces, especially geometric ones like Futura, have a (purposely) high degree of similarity between sorts. Try to distinguish for example 1, I, and l out of context! For some faces there are versions specially designed for continuous setting. Futura Book, for example, is just such a version of Futura. But the matter is highly subjective. Some assert that sans serif faces set in blocks of text look monotonous and hence intrinsically less attractive.

Italic is said to be less legible than roman, so much so that the typographer Sir Francis Meynell recommended that poetry be set in italic because it ought to be read slowly!

For print to be legible, words should be set close to each other, and certainly closer than the space between lines of type. If the gap between words is too great, the eye will skip to the next line rather than the next word. So all continuous text matter can be made easier to read by increasing the leading. Of course, there are some exceptions to this rule—for television graphics and on traffic signs, for example.

Legibility also has a part to play in deciding the width of columns. If the line is longer than about 18 words (or seven words in newspaper setting), the eye will have difficulty in returning to find the next line.

Black on white setting, too, is considered to be more legible than **reversed out** white on black (abbreviated WOB), where hairline serifs, for example, can be lost and horizontal spacing can look too cramped. Text all set in capitals, as in telexes, can be very tiring on the eye. On the internet, text that is set all in capitals means you're shouting!

Legibility is a major issue when designing typefaces for the computer screen. Verdana, designed by Matthew Carter (Fig. 2.38), and named after the verdant Seattle area, has a large x-height, yet not so big that it's hard to distinguish lower case from upper case. It is extended and has extra space between characters so they don't touch, particularly with letter combinations such as "fi," "fl," and "ff," that work well together whether ligatures or not. The bolds are very bold, so you can always tell the difference between **bold** and roman, yet the bold characters will not fill in, even at small sizes (you can still read it at 4 pt, at least in Windows).

Special care has been taken with letters like 1, I, l, i, and J, adding serifs to the capital I and J, so that they are easily recognized. The lowercase i is slightly shorter than the lowercase l, which also makes them more distinct. Curves are kept to a minimum and lower case characters are a pixel taller than their upper case counterparts at key screen sizes.

Legibility can be achieved by observing common-sense rules like these. Readability is something else. It entices readers to continue reading what you have designed, and that takes care, skill, and talent!

2.37 Maximum legibility is always required for warning signs. This poster, dated 1851, was printed by letterpress—the word "CAUTION" using wooden type, the rest in metal.

2.38 In Verdana, designed by Matthew Carter, special care has been taken with letters that look similar, such as 1, I, l, i, and J, adding serifs to the capital I and J, so that they are easily distinguished—compare with the less legible Futura (Fig. 2.35f).

Typesetting systems

There are many ways of producing type. Most graphic designers will eventually be using offset lithography for print, and this process demands input in the form of film—a photographic image of the page to be printed—although there are now also direct Computer-to-Plate (CtP) systems. This was once made from a **mechanical** (see p. 145) but now most likely comes direct from a computer system. The typesetting used as raw material in compiling a mechanical may in turn have come from metal type, in the form of a reproduction proof, or it may have been a bromide print from a phototypesetting machine, a laser print, or even a piece of hand lettering.

Other print technologies, such as flexography and silkscreen, rely on similar processes—some newspapers once even printed on letterpress machines from phototypeset mechanicals. Each method of typesetting has its role and its place, though some methods (e.g. so-called "strike-on" from the IBM Selectric typewriter) have become obsolete, and are discussed here only for the sake of completeness.

Hand lettering and calligraphy

It is an amusing exercise to try to work out the very least expensive way to produce a book, magazine, or any other publication. If you have all the time in the world, the cheapest production method of all must be to handwrite every single copy. Fernand Baudin's book *How Typography Works (and Why it is Important)* has been produced almost entirely by reproducing the author's best handwriting (Fig. **2.39**). Since the development of photolithography and, more recently, the introduction of fast, high-quality photocopying machines and inexpensive desktop scanners, the idea of handwriting a whole book is not as crazy as it may first appear. Many books have been produced this way, and curiously it is often typographers who tend to favor this quirky approach.

Calligraphy is handwriting's beautiful cousin (Fig. **2.40**), and is often used on the title pages of books. A grounding in calligraphy is essential for a proper understanding of good typography and graphic design, and its practice is to be encouraged. The famous German designer Jan Tschichold wrote in 1949, "All my knowledge of letter spacing, word spacing, and leading is due to my calligraphy, and it is for

2.39 Text does not necessarily have to be typeset. Typographers like Fernand Baudin are very fond of their own handwriting, as demonstrated in these pages from his manual *How Typography Works (and Why it is Important)*.

2.40 Calligraphy can be mixed effectively with typesetting in advertisements and on book covers, as in these examples by Carol Kemp.

this reason that I regret very much that calligraphy is so little studied in our time."

Handwriting and calligraphy have long been copied in type. Script and brush faces are "cleaned-up" versions of hand lettering. And with computers it is possible to invent your personal font based on your own hand (Fig. **2.41**).

"Strike-on" or "cold-metal" setting

Cutting and pasting of existing type, as in the punk blackmail-style designs of album covers by Jamie Reid in the late 1970s, is a form of **cold-metal setting**. Another form is the rub-down dry-transfer lettering used for display type from suppliers such as Letraset. The vinyl letters were transferred one by one on to paper or board, and then pressure applied through the backing sheet to "fix" the lettering in place. This is called **burnishing** (Fig. **2.42**).

Just Lefthand:
ABCDEFGHIJKLMNOPQRSTUVWX
YZabcdefghijklmnopqrstuvwxyz
234567890!@#£$%^&*()_+<>?

Eric Righthand:
ABCDEFGHIJKLMNOPQRSTUVWXYZabc
defghijklmnopqrstuvwxyz1234567
890!@#£$%^&*()_+<>?

2.41 Software can turn your handwriting into a usable font, as demonstrated by these commercially available typefaces from two Dutch designers: Eric van Blokland's Eric Righthand and Just van Rossum's Just Lefthand.

2.42 Rub-down lettering, symbols, and textures from suppliers such as Letraset, revolutionized graphic design in the 1970s. It had to be applied carefully to prevent break-up.

With **strike-on setting**, the marks made at the time of setting are those that will go under the camera or scanner for printing by the offset litho process. There is no intermediate processing required.

Type can be set using a regular typewriter (for menus, for example). Typeset-quality typewriters designed for the purpose were introduced during the 1960s. The IBM Selectric had fonts of 88 characters arranged around a "golfball" print head. It used a nine-unit system of proportional spacing, and had "real" fonts such as Univers and Times. For justified setting, each line had to be typed twice, as the first attempt was used to calculate the amount of space needed between words.

The VariTyper had an open carriage, to tackle greater widths of setting than the IBM, and could handle two fonts at a time, each made up of 99 characters. These machines represented a breakthrough at the time, and replaced hot metal for many low-cost jobs, but by today's standards the setting looks crude and poorly spaced.

Hot metal: hand and machine setting

The method of setting type from hot lead remained virtually unchanged from the time of Gutenberg until the invention of the punch-cutting machine by the American Linn Boyd Benton in 1884. This paved the way for the Linotype machine in 1886 and the Monotype machine a year later.

But whereas machine setting has been superseded by phototypesetting, handsetting is still used whenever beautiful typography is demanded for some high-quality publications and limited-edition poetry books.

For handsetting, the compositor takes individual metal sorts and spaces from a typecase and places them one by one into a **composing stick** (Fig. **2.43**) that has been adjusted to the correct measure. Capital letters are taken from the upper case, and small letters from the lower case. The sizes of the compartments in the typecase reflect the popularity of certain sorts. You will need more "e"s, for example, than "z"s in an average job. Less frequently used fonts are kept in drawers under the typecase.

When the composing stick is full, the setting is transferred to a galley on the **imposing table**, and the compositor returns to the typecase to set the next couple of lines. When the galley is full, a **proof** is taken on a hand-operated **proofing press**, and any mistakes are picked up and corrected by the proofreader, the designer, or copy editor.

A galley proof is a long, thin strip of paper, and gives the designer an opportunity to see the setting before it is divided up into pages. This proof, when corrected, may be good enough to be used as a **reproduction proof**, or **repro proof**, if the setting is going to be cut up using a scalpel and incorporated into a mechanical.

If the setting is going to be printed—and hot-metal setting is the only kind of setting discussed here that can be printed directly—then the type is taken from the galley and placed into a page-sized contraption called a **chase**, and "locked up" (Fig. **2.44**). The spaces and leading used to fill up the rest of the chase, often of wood, are collectively known as furniture. The locked-up chase is called a **forme**.

For small runs, the printing is made direct from the type in the chase. But for large jobs, and for newspapers and magazines, for example, where the type must be wrapped around a cylinder, a one-piece duplicate of the type, called a **stereotype** or **stereo** (Fig. **2.45**), has to be made from a papier-mâché mold called a **mat** or **flong**.

Once the stereo has been made, or the pages printed, the type is then cleaned and returned (the word used in the trade is "distributed") to the typecases. Extra care has to be taken to get this right, compositors being told to "mind their 'p's and 'q's."

The **Linotype** machine (Fig. **2.46**) was invented by Ottmar Mergenthaler of Baltimore in 1886 to automate the casting of type. Whole lines of type (hence the name, from "line o' type") called **slugs** are set in one operation. A compositor keys

2.43 Inserting sorts from the lower typecase into the composing stick, where type is set, line by line, before being transferred to the chase.

2.44 When the type, leading, and any process blocks are all flat and in place, the chase is packed with metal or wooden "furniture" and locked up. It is now called a forme and is ready to be inked and printed.

in the text and, as it is typed, molds of the letters to be cast fall into place. Wedge-shaped spacers are inserted between words, and when a line is complete, the compositor pulls a lever and these push the words apart to fill out the justified measure. Lead pours into the assembly, and out comes a slug of type. After the setting has been used, the slugs are melted down for reuse.

The **Monotype** machine, developed by Tolbert Lanston of Washington DC in 1887, sets type in individual sorts and, unlike the Linotype, uses a two-stage process. The compositor sits at the keyboard and inputs the text, which is coded on to a perforated roll of paper. When the end of a line approaches, a bell rings and it is left to the compositor's skill to calculate the spaces needed between words to justify the line. This information is keyed in at the end of each line. When the job is complete, the roll of paper is inserted into a typecasting machine *back to front*, so that the spacing information will precede the text it adjusts, and the type is cast individually.

The advantage of the Monotype machine over the Linotype one was that corrections could be made using pre-cast sorts. This was especially useful for book production.

With the Linotype method, the whole line had to be reset and replaced. As a consequence, Linotype machines were mostly used for newspaper and magazine work where speed is of the essence, and where the effect of spilling the type, a catastrophe known as "printer's pie," was minimized.

2.45 Metal type cannot be used directly on a rotary letterpress machine. It must first be made into a curved plate known as a stereotype, which is then wrapped around the press cylinder ready for printing.

2.46 The Linotype machine automated hot-metal setting. As the compositor keyed in the text, matrixes would fall into place and the type was set line by line from molten lead.

Phototypesetting

The popularity of offset litho as a printing process led to the development of new ways of setting type. With letterpress, it is not easy to mix text with illustrations and photographs, and the opportunities for creative design are limited.

Phototypesetting, or **photosetting**, was first demonstrated to the American Newspaper Publishers' Association in 1949 by Rene Higgonet and Louis Marius Moyroud, but did not become popular until the 1960s. Like a Monotype system, it comprised two separate parts. The compositor sat at a keyboard and generated paper or magnetic tape. This was then transferred to the **imagesetter**, where the bromide or film was exposed. In the earliest systems, light was projected through a matrix of tiny photographic negative images of the font's sorts on to photosensitive bromide paper or film. Later, the fonts were stored digitally, and reconstructed using CRTs (cathode ray tubes); then lasers were used (Figs **2.47** and **2.48**).

Photosetting provided the designer with many advantages over hot metal. Letters could be set closer together. They could also be set touching, or even overlapping.

It was also possible, by means of mirrors and prisms, to distort type. Oblique (slanted) letters could be created from roman type, and headlines could be condensed or expanded to fit a given width.

Type produced by photosetting was sharper than the equivalent hot-metal setting. Hot metal was always proofed to paper, and no matter how carefully the ink was applied, it was squeezed between the face of the type and the paper and there was some spread. A typeface such as Bodoni, with its extremely fine serifs, was designed to be pressed into paper—photoset versions of Bodoni had to be redesigned with thicker serifs.

With photosetting, type could be set ahead of a type specification—the text was keyed in and the size, face, and measure were added later. The same text could be used over and over, in different forms. Any metal type to be reused had to be stored as "standing matter." This was costly and took up lots of space. With photosetting, type for dictionaries and telephone directories, for example, could be stored on tape, and updated later.

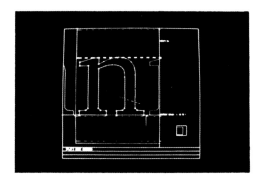

2.47 A screenshot of a letter outline being designed for phototypesetting. Note that the space between the letter n and the next letter is an integral part of the design of the "font metrics."

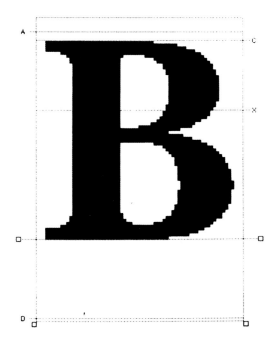

2.48 A bitmap of a Baskerville Bold capital B, showing how individual pixels are edited for optimum appearance at a laser printer resolution of 300 dpi.

Computer systems

A photosetting machine may have looked like a regular computer, but setting was all it could do. A computer system, on the other hand, makes use of a standard off-the-shelf PC or Mac to produce information that is then input to the imagesetter that generates the bromide paper, film, or plate. It does much more besides.

More choice of typefaces

Perhaps the most apparent effect of computers on graphic designers is that they have a much greater range of typefaces to choose from. With early photosetting, and even more so with strike-on technology, the user was offered any typeface . . . as long as it was Times, Univers, or Helvetica. There are currently many thousands of different typefaces available that can be used with computer systems. So-called "expert sets" add ligatures, small caps, swash caps, non-aligning numerals, fractions, and superior/inferior figures to the basic fonts.

To produce a typeface in hot metal was an enormous and costly undertaking, requiring a huge investment in both time and money. Most of the great typographers of the past are known for just one or maybe two typefaces. The same was true for photosetting. Particular typefaces were tied to particular machines. Thus if you had a Linotype machine, you could use only faces from the Linotype library. Similarly, if you had a Berthold machine, you could use only type from Berthold.

If a typographer went to Berthold with a new idea for a typeface, its production would be extremely expensive and its distribution limited to the number of Berthold machines in operation worldwide.

But with a computer system it is possible to design a brand new face, copy it on to a CD-ROM or upload it to the internet and distribute it for use by thousands of other designers within days.

Quality and flexibility of digital type

The pace of progress in computing means that the few advantages of other technologies quickly disappeared. Computers have been universally adopted by both the printing and the design industries. Yet hot metal has always held two advantages over photosetting—those of visual and tactile quality.

In hot metal, each size of a typeface has been designed individually. Thus, for the sake of legibility, the small sizes have a relatively larger x-height and a wider set width. Bigger sizes have daintier serifs and more subtle distinctions between the parts of the letterform, created by enlarging or reducing one of these **font masters**.

In computer systems, all sizes are created by **scaling** (enlarging or reducing) one font master, usually 12 pt, designed as the best compromise. There have been some concessions to creating different designs for different sizes. Times Ten Roman, for example, is a version of Times New Roman that works better at small sizes. But the problem of legibility at smaller sizes has usually been solved by tracking.

Photosetting machines could be used to expand and condense type, but this always distorted the overall proportions of the letterform. A Futura E, for example (see p. 57), when condensed, would have a vertical stroke thinner than the horizontals.

By sloping roman letterforms, a photosetting system could create an oblique—but not an italic—version of the typeface. A true italic font has entirely different designs for many of its letters. Look at the *a, f,* and *g* of an italic face (Fig. **2.49**).

Any computer system can perform these kinds of distortions. They can embolden letters, too, and produce combinations of italic, bold, outline, and shadow (Fig. **2.50**). But the results bear little aesthetic relationship to the original "plain" letterforms. The design intention of the typographer will have been lost.

With MM (Multiple Master) fonts from Adobe it was possible to create typefaces with different widths, weights, and "optical size," without losing the integrity or readability of the characters. Adobe Serif MM and Adobe Sans MM, for example, were fallback fonts that could simulate unembedded fonts used by a designer in an Acrobat PDF document that the reader didn't have installed on their computer system.

2.49 Photosetting and digital software can concoct a kind of italic by slanting the roman font. This is better termed an oblique variant, as a true italic has different designs from the roman for most letters, with more cursive serifs.

Roman & afg
Oblique & afg
Italic & afg

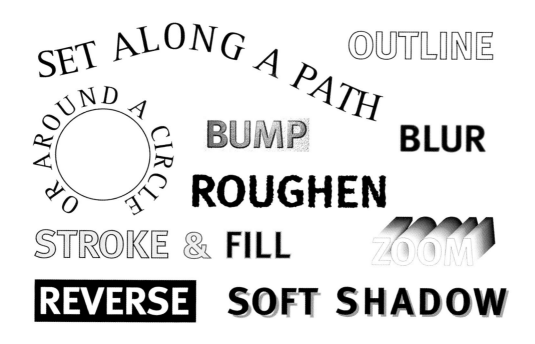

SET ALONG A PATH

OR AROUND A CIRCLE

OUTLINE

BUMP

BLUR

ROUGHEN

STROKE & FILL

ZOOM

REVERSE

SOFT SHADOW

2.50 Computer software can also take a roman font and "style" it in various ways. Most programs can create bold, outline, shadowed, and reversed-out variants. More specialized software, such as Adobe Illustrator, can be used, for example, to set type along a curve, and to apply "stroke and fill" to a letterform.

2.51 An envelope feature in programs such as Illustrator can be used to distort letters and words mathematically. Previously, the lettering would have to have been drawn laboriously by hand or distorted photographically.

These have been largely superseded by **OpenType** (see p. 73), a scalable format initially developed by Microsoft, later joined by Adobe Systems, as the successor to Apple's TrueType. Several of Adobe's OpenType fonts include four optical size variations: caption (6–8 pt), regular (9–13 pt), subhead (14–24 pt), and display (25–72 pt).

With computer setting, the graphic designer has never been restricted to the small and standard list of point sizes available from the hot-metal type foundries. In page-layout systems such as Adobe InDesign and QuarkXPress, for example, type can be set at any size in any increment, leading can be defined in increments or percentages, and letters can be kerned interactively.

Type manipulation and custom font design

With page-layout systems, such as Adobe InDesign and QuarkXPress, it is possible to adjust the size of type to fit a certain space, condensing or expanding it to the limits of legibility.

Drawing programs (more of which in Chapter 3, p. 100), such as Adobe Illustrator, allow text to be set, for example, around an ellipse or along a freeform curve—and create even more extreme distortions (Fig. **2.51**). The designer is able to create graphic "envelopes" into which the text is squeezed and contorted to fit.

With programs such as Fontographer (Fig. **2.52**), you can tweak existing faces to your own preferences or create entirely new faces from scratch. It is this power that horrifies traditional typographers. Here, a knowledge of typography, however rudimentary, is essential to prevent the novice from falling into the pitfalls learned the hard way throughout the history of type.

RAINBOW

FISHEYE

ENVELOPE

Many digital fonts are revivals of traditional fonts, adapted to the limitations of the technology. There are also several fonts designed specifically for the process, and for the changing needs of the graphic designer. Erik Spiekermann's Meta (Fig. **2.53**) has been described as an ecological face, designed to look attractive even in small sizes on problematic papers such as coarse, thin, and recycled stocks. Designers Banks and Miles developed an economical typeface for British Telecom's telephone directories and managed to achieve savings in paper of over 10 percent (Fig. **2.55**).

Some typographers are using the power of the computer to incorporate "intelligence" (or rather, chaos) into their typefaces. Beowolf, from Dutch designers Erik van Blokland and Just van Rossum, for example, is a "random" font in which the letterforms mutate subtly each time a character is produced (Fig. **2.54**). Three versions of Beowolf have differing levels of randomness built in, and they imitate the effects of wear and tear on metal and wooden type.

In a way, faces like Beowolf are a modern counterpart to Gutenberg's efforts to emulate the scribes' humanized typography. A similar point could be made about computer simulations of hand lettering in comics.

PostScript

Almost every machine or device in print production encountered today—from computer screens and scanners to high-resolution imagesetters—works on the **raster** principle. A raster (from the Latin for "rake") is the line that makes up the picture on a television screen. On digital devices like a computer screen, each line is divided into a series of dots

called **pixels**, and the **resolution** of the screen is described in terms of the number of pixels horizontally by the number of lines vertically. Thus the screen of a computer monitor may have a resolution of 1024×768 or 1280×1024.

Another way of measuring resolution is by the number of dots per inch, or **dpi**. Thus, measured in this way, a Mac's screen has a resolution of 72 dpi; a PC monitor is 96 dpi.

The higher the resolution, the better the quality. A laser printer typically has a resolution of 600 dpi. A production-quality imagesetter or platesetter will have a resolution of 2540 dpi or higher.

The same type has to look good (or at least be recognizable) on all kinds of different devices with all kinds of resolutions. A designer may work initially on the computer screen, proof the results on a laser printer, and then send off a CD containing all the type information to a bureau for high-quality bromide prints or film, or to the printers for direct digital printing.

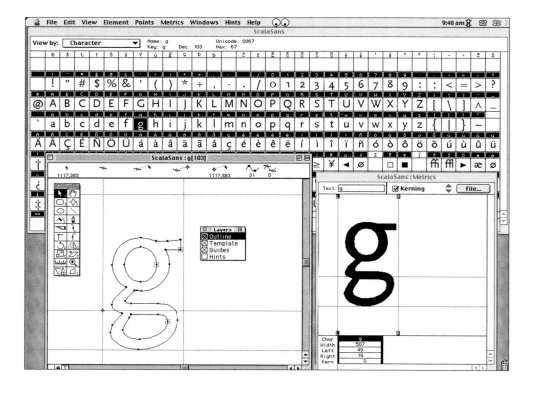

2.52 New custom fonts can be designed letter by letter using programs such as Fontographer. These programs can also import existing typefaces, which can then be adapted to your own taste—but be aware of copyright implications.

Meta Normal

ABCDEFGHIJKLMNOPQRSTUVWXYZ
abcdefghijklmnopqrstuvwxyz
1234567890!@#£$%^&*()_+‹›?

Meta Caps

ABCDEFGHIJKLMNOPQRSTUVWXYZ
ABCDEFGHIJKLMNOPQRSTUVWXYZ
1234567890!@#£$%^&*()_+Ø≠?

Meta Bold

ABCDEFGHIJKLMNOPQRSTUVWXYZ
abcdefghijklmnopqrstuvwxyz
1234567890!@#£$%^&*()_+¨Æ?

R21: ABCDEFGHIJKLMNOP
QRSTUVWXYZabcdefghijk
lmnopqrstuvwxyz1234567
890!@#£$%^&*()_+‹›?

R22: ABCDEFGHIJKLMNOP
QRSTUVWXYZabcdefghijk
lmnopqrstuvwxyz1234567
890!@#£$%^&*()_+‹›?

R23: ABCDEFGHIJKLMNOP
QRSTUVWXYZabcdefghijk
lmnopqrstuvwxyz1234567
890!@#£$%^&*()_+‹›?

ABC ABC ABC

2.53 Erik Spiekermann's "ecological" face Meta was designed as a reaction to the overuse of Helvetica, which he describes as "the Federal font" because of its widespread use by German business and government.

Design your own face

With programs such as Fontographer you can design your own typeface. First design the capital I to establish the stem thickness and overall weight of the font, then the O to establish the angles of stress and the curves, next the E to define the crossbars, and then the V to determine the thickness of the downstrokes. Test the font metrics and the overall look of the font using the word "Hamburgers." Some type foundries will turn your own handwriting into a font—for a fee.

2.54 Building randomness into a font's characteristics creates subtly mutating type. Beowolf, from Dutch designers Erik van Blokland and Just van Rossum, was the first such "anarchistic" font.

McVAY S.T,
18 Swan Copse,Mansfield Rd 25 708 0761
T, 9 Hollington Cres 33 784 7037
McVEAGH J.G.R, 211 Castle La,Solihull 743 3266
W, 69 Damson La,Solihull 705 7866
McVEICH S, 171 Jayshaw Av 43 357 5933
McVEIGH A, 63 New Coventry Rd 26 742 8955
D.F, 5 Bernard Pl,Brookfield Rd 18 554 2068
G, Warwick Rd,Solihull 705 6922
J, 16 Harvington Rd,Oldbury 422 4789
J.D, 17 Winton Gro,Sutton Coldfield 351 4406
J.M, 99 Miranda Clo 45 453 9681
J.P, 49 Round Moor Wlk 35 747 8542
M.F.P, 27 Prospect La,Solihull 744 5227
R.M, 8 Chiseldon Croft 14 474 5165
McVEIGHTY D, 82 Audley Rd 33 786 2946
D, 39 Este Rd 26 783 0454
D, 67 Hilleys Croft 37 770 1737
R, 62 Clarence Rd 13 444 4088
McVEITH T, 37 Frankley La 31 478 0534
MACVENAN M, 15 Overbrunton Clo 31 477 2547
McVERRY B.P, 4 Chalybeate Clo 45 453 8277
D, 24 Goodrest Croft 14 430 4084
D.J, 17 Duncalfe Dv,Sutton Coldfield 308 5672
McVEY C.F, 19 Brownley Rd,Shirley 745 1015
J, 31 Beeches Wy 31 477 8434
J, 158 Jayshaw Av 43 357 4988
McVICAR A.J, 158 Swan Gdns 23 373 0289
E.W, 38 Moorfield Dv,Sutton Coldfield 373 8366
McVICKER N.M, 78 Northdown Rd,Solihull 705 8822
R.P, 43 Heybarnes Rd 10 773 7558
MACVIE F.E,
Fiddlers Gn,Blackford Hl...**Henley-in-A** 2819
Mrs M.H, 72 Marsh Hl 23 373 2702
McVITTY P.J, 312 Sarehole Rd 28 777 5775
McWALTER I.M,
30 Upper St. Mary's Rd,Smethwick 429 1297
J.W, 66 Hawkstone Rd 29 475 6246
S.G, 207 Court Oak Rd 17 427 9694
McWALTERS S.B,
11 Chadwick Rd,Sutton Coldfield 378 3693
McWATTS A.C,
6 Bannersgate Rd,Sutton Coldfield 355 1647
McWEE R.M, 29 Stanmore Gro,Halesowen 422 7767
McWEENEY L, 114 Junction Rd 21 523 3828
McWHINNEY S.J, 6 Longmore Rd,Streetly 353 7526
McWHINNIE J.R.K,
282 Eachelhurst Rd,Sutton Coldfoield 351 2022
J.R.K,
282 Eachelhurst Rd,Sutton Coldfield 351 3382
W.R, 22 Widney Manor Rd,Solihull 705 8842
McWHIRTER D,
9 Spring Ho,Cooks Ct,Chester Rd 36 770 0970
D.C, 30 Greenfield Rd 17 427 9679
D.L, 24 Fugelmere Clo 17 429 4883
J, 28 St. Michaels Rd,Sutton Coldfield 354 6521
John D, 23 Maxholm Rd,Streetly 353 2850
P.J.K, 92 Devon Rd,Smethwick 429 1213
R, 17 Aldbourne Wy 38 459 4503
R.M, 127 Manor La,Halesowen 550 1718
W.H.P, 188 Northfield Rd 17 427 1736
McWILLIAM A.R, 30 Waldrons Moor 14 444 2414
I, 38 Corbridge Rd,Sutton Coldfield 354 2558
I.R, 50 Meriden Rd ...**Hampton-in-A** 2015
J.W, 55 Colesbourne Rd,Solihull 742 3228
R, 108 West Av 20 554 4261
R.C, 20 Galton Tower,Civic Clo 1 236 4901
McWILLIAMS A.G,
32 Sandhills Cres,Solihull 704 9547
B, 126 Kingswood Rd 31 477 6225
B.V, 4 Dornton Rd 30 444 3788
C, 203 Albert Rd 6 328 4676
C.P, 20 Hatherton Gro 29 427 6854
E, 20 Somerset Rd 23 384 4951
G, 306 Prince of Wales La 14 430 3917
J.B, 18 Milner Rd 29 472 7085
J.D, 3 Newells Rd 26 742 1801
K, 103 Ashbrook Rd 30 472 5807
N, 98 Manor Ho La 26 743 2498
P.W, 56 Hodge Hill Rd 34 783 7477
R, 28
R, 5 C
R, 14
S, 48
W.K,
MACWI
MACZK
MADAH
J.S, 1
T, 84
MADAN
V.P,
MADDA
MADDA
A.D,
B.M,
D.G,
G.W,
H, 41
J, 21
J.L, 2
M, 1 Chantry Dv,Halesowen 422 4339
R.G, 714 Hagley Rd Wst,Oldbury 422 7826
Sidney C, 4 Griffins Brook Clo 30 459 3814
T.A, 212 Highters Hth La 14 430 2472
MADDEN A, 54 Strathdene Rd 29 472 1469
A, 2 Wilford Gro,Sutton Coldfield 351 3998
A, 256 Witton Ldg Rd 23 350 6119
A.C, 41 Galton Tower,Civic Clo 1 233 2935
B, 113 Heather Rd 10 771 2140
C, 4 Sycamore Terr,Vicarage Rd 14 444 0919
C, 257 West Boulevard 32 427 6313
C.A, 548 Bromford La 8 786 2021
C.W, 6 St Johns Rd,Oldbury 544 7941
D, 23 Court Oak Gro 17 427 9851
D, 12 Elmwood Rd,Sutton Coldfield 353 3807
D, 40 Middle Dv 45 445 2002
D, 73 St. Agathas Rd 8 327 2379
D, 4 Sunnydale Wlk,W Bromwich 525 1518
D.M.J, 40 Sheldonfields Rd 26 743 4350
D.S, 134 Kingsdown Av 42 357 6662
E, 23 Eileen Rd 11 449 0807
E, 105 Manor Ho La 26 742 6515
E, 1/4 Ward End Pk Rd 8 327 6308
F, 34 Cecil Rd 24 373 4542
F, 19 Greswolde Ho,Cole Hall La 34 784 9304

MADDEN H.A, 85 Naseby Rd 8 327 5567
I, 11 Boldmere Clo,Sutton Coldfield 350 6027
I.M, 74 Worlds End Rd 20 554 7649
J, 44 Amberley Gro 6 356 8558
J, 266 Galton Rd,Smethwick 429 6179
J, 140 Knowle Rd 11 777 8672
J, 3 Minster Dv 10 773 3675
J, 37 Roughley Dv,Four Oaks 308 4882
James, 347 St. Benedicts Rd 10 772 0748
J, 68 Tomey Rd 11 772 0813
J, 137 Wellsgreen Rd,Solihull 743 2015
J, 5 Welwyndale Rd,Sutton Coldfield 373 6653
J, 61 Windmill La,Smethwick 565 3634
J, 21 Windsor St Nth 7 359 0115
J.A, 91 Pinewood Dv 32 422 0066
J.E, 64 Pitts Fm Rd 24 350 5780
J.T, 100 Alston Rd,Solihull 704 1390
K.W, 37 Varlins Wy 38 458 6997
L, 26 Chartley Rd 23 328 3751
L, 7 Clodeshall Rd 8 328 3186
L, 51 Ercall Clo 23 355 0845
L, 331 Yardley Wood Rd 13 449 8241
M, 12 Cecil Rd 24 373 8447
M, 323 Guardian Ct,
Francey Beeches Rd 31 477 5078
Michael, 101 Livingstone Rd 20 356 0701
M, 55 Norfolk Rd 23 373 0753
Michael, 232 Somerville Rd 10 773 9922
M, 7 Yew Tree La 26 706 6797
Michael A, 51 Courtenay Rd 44 360 4605
M.A, 75 Harrow Rd 29 472 1056
M.J, 48 Brookvale Rd,Solihull 706 3076
M.J, 29 Link Rd 16 454 7864
M.J, 50 Moorend La 24 384 4518
N, 88 Pritchett Tower,Arthur St 10 773 8947
P, 21 Ebley Rd 20 523 9924
P, 7 Rawlins Croft 35 749 3961
P.B, 101 Clodeshall Rd 8 328 7530
P.J, 48 Broadway Ave,Halesowen 550 7879
P.J, 135 Oxhill Rd 21 523 9704
R.F, 55 Hill La,Sutton Coldfield 308 4990
R.J, 3 Whitwell Clo,Solihull 744 7724
R.N, 303 Dovedale Rd 23 382 7236
S, 27 Gladstone Rd 26 706 5469
S.D, 14 St. Michaels Rd,Sutton Coldfield 355 5701
S.J, 376 Queslett Rd 43 360 1421
T, 228 Millhouse Rd 25 784 0182
T, 30 Station Rd 21 554 2344
Timothy, 16 Westbury Rd,Wednesbury 526 3558
T.A, 22 Avenue Rd 14 444 1597
T.H, 53 Allcroft Rd 11 778 1379
T.J, 68 Hazelbeach Rd 8 326 0974
T.S, 8 Daniels Rd 9 773 1741
W, 7 Hilldrop Gro 17 426 3667
W.A.L, 340 Hagley Rd Wst,Oldbury 422 8554
MADDERS G.R, 37 Quarry La,Halesowen 550 5409
G.T, 23 Rowton Dv,Streetly 353 6668
J.L, 9 Stourton Clo,Sutton Clodfield 329 3193
Max A, 6 Selly Clo 29 472 1670
41 Moundsley Ho,Baverstock Rd 14 474 5139
MADDIX C, 8/8 Broadmeadow Clo 30 459 4724
D, 33 Calder Tower,Birchfield Rd 20 356 5853
Martin, 15 Heanor Croft 6 328 3670
E.L, 16 Harbury Rd 12 440 2185
F.M, 512 Kingsbury Rd 24 350 2007
G, 31 Daimler Clo 36 747 0199
I.F, 824 Pershore Rd 29 472 2636
J, 1 Denise Dv 17 427 2395
J, 28 Tinmeadow Cres 45 453 5355
J.C, 1 Overbury Clo,Halesowen 550 4642
M, 8 Raven Hays Rd 31 477 2201
N, 29 Marsham Rd 14 430 5180
P, 38 Daisy Fm Rd 14 474 5939
P, 46 Middle Pk Rd 29 476 9146
P, 1 Pagnell Gro 13 443 3851
R.A, 178 Franklin Rd 30 458 7198
R.C, 119 Bell Holloway 31 477 3973
R.S, 178 Gregory Av 29 477 3372
S, 34 Hodgetts Clo,Smethwick 429 2362
S, 25 Pettit Clo 14 430 5011
S.C, 48 Rowheath Rd 30 459 0944
V, 8 Cherry Tree Ct,Woodfall Av 30 451 3284
W, 73 Longford Rd 44 354 5745
W.L, 129 Kineton Gn Rd,Solihull 708 2684
MADDON J, 229 Manningford Rd 14 430 6295
MADDOX A, 192 Farnborough Rd 35 747 8584
A, 12 The Hurstway 23 382 5280
A.A, 84 Hales Rd Wednesbury 556 1092

MADDOX B.T, 235 Hay Green La 30 475 6050
C.D, 347 The Ridgeway 23 331 4687
C.R, 37 Coniston Av,Solihull 743 6397
C.R, 26 Libbard Ho,Stonebow Ave,Solihull 705 8876
D, 1 Alcombe Gro 33 784 9496
D, 20 Ashton Rd 9 784 5873
D, 73 Newlands Rd 30 451 2736
D.C, 38 Duncumb Rd,Sutton Coldfield 378 3508
D.M, 71 Babbington Rd 21 523 0145
E, 139 Garretts Green La 26 742 5777
E, 149 Nuthurst Rd 31 476 6364
E, 2 Arbor Ct,Penns La,Sutton Coldfield 351 5636
E.S, 89 Monmouth Rd 32 475 1892
F.C, 49 Milstead Rd 26 784 6434
G, 54 Harleston Rd 44 360 2212
G, 57 Surrey Cres,W Bromwich 502 1184
G, 26 Elm Croft,Windmill La,Smethwick 565 1169
H, 15 Bucknall Cres 32 550 5836
H, 5 Middleton Rd,Shirley 744 4732
I, 41 Ansell Rd 24 373 1003
J, 8 May La 47 ...**Wythall** 824209
J.R, 142 Birdbrook Rd 44 360 1132
John W, 18 Elmfield Rd 36 747 5667
K, 2 Ingram Gro 27 778 2433
K.A, 28 Britwell Rd,Sutton Coldfield 355 3522
K.J, 2 Linford Gro 25 783 5073
L, 801c Warwick Rd 11 706 1305
L.L, 9 Ferndale Rd,Streetly 353 7885
M.E, 83 Stanton Rd 43 358 7530
M.I, 510 Chester Rd 36 770 5083
M.K, 42 Teesdale Ave 34 730 2350
M.P, 48 Amberley Gro 6 356 7517
N, 3 Western Rd,Sutton Coldfield 354 9278
P.W, 31 Marlborough Rd 36 747 2149
R, 78 Grestone Av 20 554 0267
R, 197 Newton Rd 43 357 1863
Roy A, 182 Northfield Rd 17 427 3322
R.L, 33 Wharf Rd 30 459 2660
S, 2 Greenway Clo 43 360 5791
S, 50 Vimy Rd 13 444 1945
S.L, 12 Boldmere Clo,Sutton Coldfield 373 3765
W, 3 Westholme Croft 30 472 8782
MADDRELL Simon, 48 Ellesmere Rd 8 326 8979
MADDY K.P, 3 Merehill Av,Solihull 745 5813
MADELEY A, 128 Dudley Rd Est,Oldbury 552 4887
A, 7 Walton Ct,High Farm Rd,Halesowen 503 0184
A.C, 98 Triumph Wlk 36 749 2685
A.E, 56 Farnhurst Rd 36 328 3619
B, 7 Dauntsey Covert 14 458 6910
B.W, 27 Leaford Rd 33 784 0412
C.E, 17 Marldon Rd 14 444 7677
D, 89 Braemar Rd,Solihull 706 0366
D, 30 Macmillan Rd,Rowley Regis 559 2793
D.H, 252 Coleshill Rd 36 747 4575
E, 5 Pryor Rd,Oldbury 544 4518
E.A, 17 Mynors Cres 47 ...**Wythall** 826651
E.G, 27 Queens Ct,Alderham Clo,Solihull 705 6750
E.S, 117 The Ridgeway 23 356 7835
J, 2/24 Taylor Rd 13 444 0057
J.M, 1 Chartwell Ct,Beardmore Rd,
Sutton Coldfield 373 1815
J.M, 40 Dower Rd Sutton Coldfield 308 1476
I, 449 Lugtrout La,Solihull 704 9849
Theo M, 38 Redthorn Gro 33 783 7684
W.E, 126 Spouthouse La 43 357 6503
MADELIN A.E,
305 Beaconview Rd,W Bromwich 588 2099
D, 152 Powis Av,Tipton 557 7026
H, 55 Glebefields Rd,Tipton 557 9450
K, 415 Sycamore Rd,Tipton 520 4748
M, 20 Kipling Clo,Tipton 557 5572
MADEN M.A, 44 Steel Rd 31 476 6493
MADER R, 107 Birmingham Rd 48 445 2366
MADEW E.A, 39 Witton Ldg Rd 23 350 0522
J.T, 226 Rectory Rd,Sutton Coldfield 378 3905
MADGE A,
60 Bampfylde Pl,Thornbridge Av 42 358 2139
C, 19 Andrew Rd,W Bromwich 588 6693
C.J, 5 Rectory Pk Av,Sutton Coldfield 378 0353
G, 1 Ravenhill Clo 34 748 7534
G.H, 78 Hathersage Rd 42 360 2845
H, 118 Finchley Rd 44 355 4840
H.E, 36 Homecroft Rd 25 783 4867
H.S, 11 Parkhall Croft 34 747 0129
J, 27 Walsham Croft 34 748 5736
J.E, 86 Preston Rd 26 708 0883
J.M, 42 Cambridge Dv 37 770 4121

MADGE M.J, 1 Station Approach,Vesey Ldge,
Sutton Coldfield 353 6347
W.H, 68 Drayton Rd 14 443 2047
MADGWICK D.J,
239 Ulverley Green Rd,Solihull 706 1349
G, 3 Beresford Cres,W Bromwich 553 3637
H.A, 78 Coopers La,Smethwick 558 8623
MADHAL C.S, 11 Raglan Rd,Smethwick 565 1487
MADHAS N, 34 Chantry Rd 21 554 7075
MADHOO G, 10 High Trees 20 523 8532
MADIGAN A, 693 Hagley Rd Wst 32 421 3971
E.G, 183 Bucklands End La 34 747 8988
E.J, 206 Gravelly La 23 350 7814
J.J, 48 Cranmore Rd,Shirley 745 4407
J.J, 48 Shakespeare Rd,Shirley 745 1712
M, 711 Kingstanding Rd 44 355 5221
M.J, 4 R.A.F Houses,Chester Rd 35 748 6327
S, 175 Balden Rd 32 429 3689
W, 18 Blakeland Rd 44 356 9967
MADILL W, 64 College Rd,Sutton Coldfield 354 8566
MADIN J, 34d Wentworthrd 17 427 7430
M.L.K, 182 Lightwoods Hl,Smethwick 429 2530
W.H, 131 Park Hl Rd 17 427 1634
MADISON J.O, 132 Raglan Rd,Smethwick 558 4789
N.A, 34 Teesdale Av 34 748 1201
MADKINS A.H,
76 Somerville Rd,Sutton Coldfield 355 3613
A.J, 39 South Gro 23 350 8551
P.E, 20 Hinton Av 48 445 2966
T.W, 433 Birmingham Rd,Walsall 358 1512
W.E, 110 Meadthorpe Rd 44 360 3535
MADLAM K, 73 Caldwell Gro,Solihull 711 1215
MADLEY Gwyn, 48 Neville Rd,Shirley 744 4881
MADOURIE C, 31 Glendower Rd 42 356 1081
MADRELL K.W, 95 Silhill Hall Rd,Solihull 705 2477
MAECHER Pictureproducts
Ltd...**Snodland** 243450
MAEER C.W, 5 Lingard Ho,Fox Hollies Rd,
Sutton Coldfield 351 7629
F.W.C, 70 Clay Pit La,W Bromwich 553 2571
G, 3 Park La 21 525 3628
J.E, 12 New St,W Bromwich 556 0285
K.M.F, 81 Riland Rd,Sutton Coldfield 378 5549
M.A, 42 New St,W Bromwich 502 1718
MAEERS G.A, 119 Kingsbury Rd 24 373 3909
MAER G.J, 14 Spiral Ct,Monkskirby Rd,
Sutton Coldfield 378 1979
MAESE R, 34 Southcote Gro 38 459 8562
MAETINEAU B.E,
Good Rest Camp Site,Good Rest La 38 459 1481
MAFFIN R.W, 64 Woodgate Gdns 32 422 1769
MAFLAHI M, 11 Birkdale Gro 29 471 4011
M.S, 22 Aubrey Rd 10 773 8415
MAGAHRAN E, 46 Doveridge Rd 28 744 5756
MAGAR K.S, 2 Greenside Rd 24 373 3709
MAGDZIARZ A, 14 Hamstead Rd 19 554 1014
MAGEE A, 20 Holte Rd 6 327 0796
7957
9226
8046
2119
0339
8640
1630
1666
5134
0260
1923
5979
9070
7482
8897
6654
R, 20 The Scotchings 36 747 9215
R.H, 153 Castle La,Solihull 743 9893
T, 11 Pavillion Av,Smethwick 429 5635
GEEAN J.J, 9 Leatherhead Clo 6 359 8471
GEED R, 27 Whetstone Clo 15 454 3927
GEN J.W, 80 Coronation Rd 43 358 6283
GENIS I, 52 Oxford St 30 459 8501
GGS B.E, 389 Warwck Rd,Solihull 704 3235
.D, 20 Greenwood Clo 14 443 4936
.I, 10 Harleston Rd 44 350 5654
, 32 Pitleasow Clo 30 451 2997
.O, 3 Garnett Av 43 360 3103
.D, 7 Meerhill Av,Shirley 745 9427
.R, 21 Whitley Ct Rd 32 422 0127
V.J.T, 17 Nevison Gn 43 325 0098
V.S, 24 Cherrywood Ct,Solihull 743 5528
GILL B, 11 Inkberrow Rd,Halesowen 550 4366
.R, 24 Morven Rd,Sutton Coldfield 354 2746
red, 172 West Hth Rd 31 475 4518
, 201 Wyndhurst Rd 33 783 2748
, 114 Clent View Rd 32 422 1576
.G, 2 Bishbury Clo 15 455 0101
GINLEY T.H, 57 St. Peters Rd 20 523 3415
GINNIS A.F, 10 Chapel St,Halesowen 501 3269
A.R, 22 Cross St,Halesowen 550 4024
J.E, 14 Grosvenor Rd,Solihull 704 2707
L.A, 43 Barcheston Rd ...**Knowle** 6840
T.W, 676 Chester Rd 36 770 7022
MAGNAY Dr A.R, 18 Crosbie Rd 17 427 3433
MAGNER P.F, 74 Fredas Gro 17 427 9846
R.D, 10 Lottie Rd 29 472 7916
MAGNESS C.R,
50 Slater Rd,Bentley Hth...**Knowle** 3189
MAGONS F, 61 Burney La 8 783 6389
MAGOR D.C,
6 Linden Ct,Hampton La,Solihull 704 9722
M, 7 The Avenue,Rowley Regis 559 1674
MAGOWAN S.C, 21 Tansy Badgers Bank Rd,
Sutton Coldfield 308 3265
MAGRATH G.F, 90 Wentworth Rd 17 426 2485
MAGRAW W.L,
42a Maney Hl Rd,Sutton Coldfield 354 5063
MAGRI S, 69 Tedstone Rd 32 427 5127
MAGRIS G.L,
5 Far Highfield,Sutton Coldfield 378 2470
MAGSON A.G, 109 Stoney La 25 783 0170
A.M, 243 The Avenue 27 707 3712
D.C, 26 Scott Rd Olton 706 9854

2.55 The condensed typeface designed by Colin Banks of London-based designers Banks and Miles addresses green issues. It allows four columns per page of the telephone directory, and this, along with the decision not to repeat surnames, has resulted in huge savings in both paper and ink. As only one size (5.75 pt) was required, Banks was able to design the bitmaps pixel by pixel. Note the traps in some letters to prevent ink spread from filling in the junctions.

Type descriptions have to be stored in a device-independent format, and converted to a form readable by the particular device as and when necessary. **PostScript**, developed by Adobe, is such a format (Fig. **2.56**).

PostScript describes the outline of the letterform in terms of vectors (lines and curves) rather than dots, and this outline is converted by software into a pattern of dots specific to each output device. PostScript is, strictly speaking, a page-description language (more in Chapter 5; see p. 148) that describes not only letterforms, but also drawings created on the computer, and the layouts of type and drawings on pages.

As PostScript is a proprietary piece of software; anyone wanting to make PostScript-compatible typefaces or printing devices has to pay Adobe a license fee. To try to break Adobe's monopoly, Microsoft, the developers of Windows for the PC, and Apple developed a rival format called **TrueType** (Fig. **2.57**), which has now been replaced by OpenType (see p. 73).

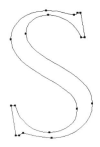
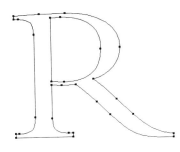

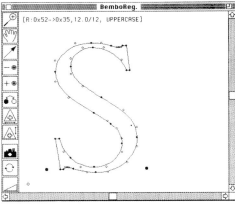
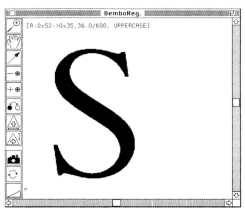

2.56 PostScript is an outline description format, developed by Adobe and adopted worldwide as a de facto standard. Letterforms are described in terms of outlines using the math of Bézier cubic spline curves. These outlines are later converted to bitmaps appropriate to the resolution of the output device being used.

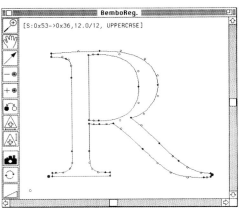
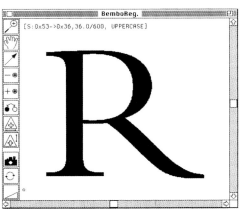

2.57 TrueType is a rival format to PostScript, developed jointly by Apple and Microsoft. It is similar in principle to PostScript, but its mathematical basis is different—it uses quadratic curves. It is linked to Apple's operating system, but also runs under Windows on a PC. These samples were produced using TypeMan from Type Solutions, Inc.

Adobe's licensed fonts are called Type 1 PostScript fonts. Other PostScript fonts are called Type 3. There is no Type 2! Type 1 fonts have **hinting** (Fig. **2.58**), which subtly changes the shape of a character so that it better fills the pixel grid of the target device. It is not the same as non-linear scaling.

Before PostScript and TrueType, fonts were stored as arrays of dots called **bitmaps** (Fig. **2.59**). These can, when printed, be every bit as good as the equivalent PostScript version, but you need a separate bitmap for every font and every resolution of the target device. With PostScript you need just two: a screen font to give an idea of the look of the typeface on the relatively low resolution of the computer screen; and a printer font, to cover all the different kinds of output device. TrueType and OpenType use just one: the printer font is used to generate the screen font.

2.58 Hinting is the name given to the process of slightly adjusting the pixels in a scaled bitmap to give a consistent weight and to make the letterform more legible at smaller sizes.

Inconsistent weights

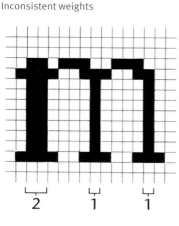

2 1 1

Consistent weights

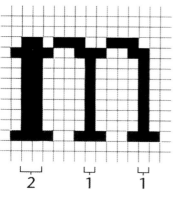

2 2 2

Without hints

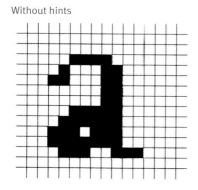

With hints

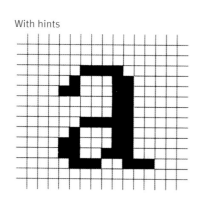

2.59 A bitmap is a pattern of dots that approximates the outlines of a letterform. On a low-resolution device, such as a computer screen or dot-matrix printer, a bitmap looks crude and jagged. But on a high-resolution device, such as an imagesetter, the dots would be too small to see.

72 dpi

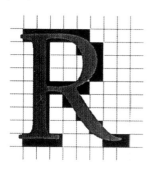

144 dpi

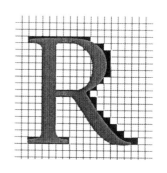

300 dpi

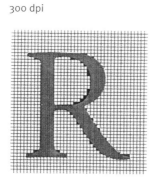

OpenType

With PostScript and TrueType fonts you will need different versions for use on Macs and PCs. OpenType is a format developed jointly by Adobe and Microsoft that is compatible with both platforms and also supports expanded character sets.

An OpenType font uses a single font file for all of its outline, metric, and bitmap data. Based on **Unicode**, an international standard for character encoding covering most languages, OpenType can make multilingual typesetting easier by including several accented character sets, for example Turkish and Polish, within one font.

Unicode, adopted by Apple, HP, IBM, Microsoft, and many more vendors, allocates a unique number for every character, no matter what the platform or language. Each character defined in Unicode has a code point—a hexadecimal number used to represent that character. The Unicode for a lower-case Latin "a" for example is 0061; a capital "Z" is 005A.

In the past, a typical Western PostScript font was limited to 256 **glyphs**, forcing you to install and manage two or more fonts to access "expert set" characters. A glyph is the specific form that a Unicode character can take. Lower case "a" and an alternate swash lower case "a" are the same character, but they are separate glyphs. OpenType fonts can contain more than 65,000 glyphs, including old-style figures, small capitals, fractions, swashes, and ligatures.

Some OpenType fonts include four size variations: caption, regular, subhead, and display. Called **opticals**, these variations are optimized for use at specific point sizes: caption (6–8 pt), regular (9–13 pt), subhead (14–24 pt), and display (25–72 pt).

The OpenType format is an extension of TrueType SFNT (SFNT stands for "spline font") that can also support PostScript data. Fonts containing PostScript data have an .otf suffix; TrueType-based OpenType fonts have a .ttf/file name suffix.

Adobe InDesign (see p. 148) and Photoshop can also automatically substitute alternate glyphs, such as ligatures, small capitals, swashes, and old-style figures, via a pop-up menu on the character palette.

Summary

What, then, are the pros and cons of the various typesetting technologies?

Hot metal or letterpress

Advantages Quality: each font is designed specifically for its particular size; printed result gives an impressed look and feel which conveys care and expense. Uses original type designs. Can be quick to set up for small jobs such as business cards. Nowadays reserved mainly for short-run prestigious invitations, overprinting diplomas, and for private press editions of poetry books.
Disadvantages Handsetting is labor-intensive, and thus costly. Must hold a large inventory of metal type, which takes up space. Can run out of sorts in the middle of a job. Machine setting is noisy and highly skilled. Metal type is inflexible, does not enlarge well, and cannot be set close. Limited availability.

Cold-metal or strike-on

Advantages Quick and direct setting by relatively unskilled operators. Inexpensive.
Disadvantages Poor selection of typefaces, crude intercharacter spacing. Justified setting difficult. Low quality.

Photosetting

Advantages Fast and relatively inexpensive. Large range of typefaces. Letters can be set closer than in hot metal. Set by skilled compositors, ensuring a good-quality result.
Disadvantages All sizes produced by one font master. More "sterile" look than hot metal. Mechanicals usually needed to produce pages. Becoming obsolete.

Computer setting

Advantages Wide range of typefaces available. Type can be adjusted and manipulated in different ways. Type can be imported directly to page make-up systems, so no intermediate mechanical stage required. Possibility of "do-it-yourself" setting, so no typesetting costs.
Disadvantages Designs of traditional typefaces vary between suppliers. Unless set by skilled compositor, possibility of errors going unchecked. Choice of sizes, leading, and tracking can result in unimaginative use of defaults. More responsibility for the designer.

Erik Spiekermann

"A typographic designer starts from the word up; a
graphic designer starts from the picture down."

Manifesto
You Cannot *Not* Communicate

Spiekermann's philosophy is: think before you
act, do a little more than is required, and keep it
simple. "Each single solution has to function in
every small detail," says Spiekermann, "while at
the same time being seen as part of a larger total.
Nothing is irrelevant: a picture chosen arbitrarily,
sloppy printing, inappropriate choice of paper,
or messy typography can destroy even the most
profound design concept. The aim is always to
achieve a distinct, coherent visual style, which can
be identified and attributed even without showing
the logo."

Spiekermann's specialty is to create order
out of chaos: information design. This is
achieved through care in type selection, or
sometimes type creation, and especially
through typographic clarity.

"We're constantly bombarded by messages,"
says Spiekermann, "all trying to make us look, to
make us listen, to make us react. Some of these
messages, however, are more important than
others. How you interpret some information could
even be a matter of life or death. The difference
between being a survivor and a casualty may be as
simple as finding the 'Way Out' sign.

"When the design of information is left to
chance, the result is information anxiety. And
when things become too complex, when an
environment defies common sense, when technical
requirements are allowed to prevail over human
considerations, then someone has to intervene.

"Many designers regard the design of
information as something that is somehow
beneath them; they'd rather be left alone to
design posters, logos, and glossy brochures,
which probably pay better anyway.

"But more and more businesses are
now discovering the advantages of clear
communications. Good information design
must communicate by convincing us, not just
browbeating us. And information designers need
to know, as clever advertising people have long
known, that nothing convinces people more than
being entertained. Show me a form that's fun to
fill out, a sign that makes me smile, or a set of
instructions I'll want to take to bed to read, and
maybe all this information won't seem so painful
after all."

Erik Spiekermann was born in 1947, in Stadthagen,
Germany. He funded his own studies, in art history at the
Free University in Berlin, by setting metal type and oper-
ating a printing press in the basement of his home.

He spent seven years working freelance in London in
the 1970s, principally for Wolff Olins and Pentagram. He
also lectured at the London College of Printing, consoli-
dating his involvement with all aspects of typography, including type design.
Spiekermann calls himself a typographic designer: "A typographic designer
starts from the word up; a graphic designer starts from the picture down." His
trademark signature is a "tectonic" narrow rectangle or bar bleeding off the
confines of the page, usually in just one of two colors: black or red, with type
dropped out in white.

Never long away from Berlin, Spiekermann also developed a success-
ful relationship with Berthold AG, which led in the late 1970s to commissions
to redraw and digitize some of their classic typefaces. He returned to work in
Berlin, founding the first incarnation of MetaDesign with Dieter Heil (based in
London) and Florian Fischer in 1979. In 1984, the company was bought by Sedley
Place Design, while Spiekermann worked nearby as MetaDesign Mk 2. The first
Mac computer (in Germany) arrived in 1985. MetaDesign Mk 3 was set up on
January 1, 1990 with Uli Mayer and Hans Christian Krüger.

In 1992 Spiekermann co-founded MetaDesign West in San Francisco, with
Terry Irwin and Bill Hill, ostensibly because he needed "a work excuse to spend
more time in California." In 1995, to close his typographic circle, Spiekermann
formed a partnership with Tim Fendley and Robin Richmond in London, completing what has become an international network. In July 2000, he withdrew from
the management of MetaDesign Berlin. In 2001, he set up UDN United Designers
Network with offices in Berlin, San Francisco, and London and in 2007 this was
renamed SpiekermannPartners. The partners are Fabian Rottke, Ralf Weißmantel,
Oliver Schmidthals, Susanna Dulkinys, and Marianne Schuler. Clients include
Bosch, Lufthansa, and Nokia for corporate design, magazine layouts, and exclusive fonts. The DB Type type family developed for Deutsche Bahn was awarded
the design prize of the Federal Republic of Germany in 2007. Recently, he even
designed a cup for the Ukrainian soccer championship.

As a type designer, Spiekermann is best known, so far, for ITC Officina, FF
Info and FF Meta (see p. 69), which is now approaching a Helvetica-like ubiquity.
Meta began life as a corporate typeface for the German Post Office to try to end
the "chaos" created through the use in the organization of dozens of versions of
Helvetica, but ended with the client's decision to stick with Helvetica because to
change would "cause unrest."

No conference about type and typography is complete without an appearance by Erik Spiekermann. If not in person, then on tape or by satellite link. The
newcomer in the audience is struck first by his bilingual articulation and then by
his humor, at once acerbic and self-deprecating. His ability to communicate ("not
called speaker-man for nothing") has speeded his international recognition.

Erik Spiekermann is honorary professor at the HfK in Bremen, honorary doctor at the Art Center College of Design in Pasadena, USA, as well as committee member of international design institutes. In 2004 he was honored with the Gerrit Noordzij Award of the Royal Academy of The Hague and in 2007 was made an Honorary Royal Designer for Industry by the Royal Society for the encouragement of Arts, Manufactures and Commerce.

The German railway company Deutsche Bahn is now a worldwide logistics service provider. When it comes to visual communication, Deutsche Bahn aims to deliver as clear an image as possible to the outside world. SpiekermannPartners developed a design system that strengthens the visual identity of DB as a brand and integrates its acquisitions worldwide. The corporate design program was divided into individual projects: an exclusive DB Type font, literature concepts, passenger information materials, and style guides. All images © SpiekermannPartners.

Resources

Website: www.spiekermannpartners.com
blog: www.spiekermann.com/mten/
Erik Spiekermann, *Rhyme and Reason: A Typographic Novel*, H. Berthold AG, Berlin, 1987
Erik Spiekermann and E. M. Ginger, *Stop Stealing Sheep and Find Out How Type Works*, Adobe Press, CA, 2002 (2nd edition)
Fay Sweet, *MetaDesign: Design From the Word Up*, Thames and Hudson, 1999
Emigre, 11, 1989 Ambition/Fear issue
Mike Daines, "Erik Spiekermann: Serious But Not Solemn," *Baseline*, 19, 1995, pp. 22–7
William Owen, "Meta's Tectonic Man," *Eye*, 18, 1995, pp. 34–45
i–D magazine Jan/Feb 1996, p. 78

Illustration

As the ancient Chinese proverb says, "a picture is worth more than a thousand words." Well, that may be a gross undervaluation in our image-rich and visually literate society. And while beautifully set typography can have "shape," "form," and "color," there is nothing to compare with the real thing.

Words and pictures are the raw materials used by the graphic designer. We have looked at the production of words, and now it is the turn of images in all their diversity.

Until the middle of the 19th century, there were very few ways that images could be combined with type. Today, any image is immediately accessible to the resourceful graphic designer. How individual designers choose to communicate the message of their particular publication is no longer limited by printing technology. But an under-

standing of the process is essential if designers are to realize their dreams.

We explore the differences between line and tone, find out the finer points of flat color and the four- and six-color processes, learn the secrets of successful screening, and discover how the digital scanner "sees" the copy we put before it. We look at practical methods of sizing and cropping images, and investigate the best ways of preparing artwork and photographs for the service bureau, repro house, or printer.

We look at the psychology and symbolism of color and how to take into account the needs of disabled people. Finally, we investigate the important issue of copyright and develop some winning ways to get the best from our professional colleagues, the illustrators and photographers.

Line and tone

Line, to the printer, is any copy that will print in a single color requiring no other intermediate treatment. When the printer mixes ink, the machinery is not capable of diluting it to produce grays, or tints of a color. Black cannot become gray; dark green cannot become pale green. The ink is either there on the paper or it's not. Line means solid areas, dots, or lines of a single color, with no gradation of tone.

There are ways of fooling the eye into perceiving tints and tones. Illustrators use techniques such as stippling or cross-hatching to simulate tones. Victorian engravings can look almost photographic, but look closely and you will see only lines and dots of one color (Fig. **3.1**).

The line process is both the cheapest and the most satisfactory for printing on inferior papers. As mentioned in Chapter 1, the line block for letterpress was invented by Paul Pretsch in 1853, and, by the mid 1880s, zinc plates mounted on wooden blocks were being used to reproduce black-and-white illustrations in newspapers and books.

For the first time, an illustrator was able to work at larger sizes than the image would appear in print; any imperfections of the line would thus be proportionally reduced. It became common, therefore, to work "half-up"—at 45×30 to become 30×20—or "twice-up," at 60×40 to become 30×20. Too great a reduction in size, however, can lose much of the original quality and spontaneity of the work, and over-reduced lines may break up or disappear under the pressure of printing.

3.1 Line art includes much more than just black lines on paper, as can be seen in this Victorian engraving of Prince Albert by D. J. Pound, from an original photograph by Mayall. Look closely at the full picture and at the detail opposite and you will not be able to see anything that cannot be reproduced directly.

From 1901 onward, the blockmaker could add Ben Day mechanical tints to a line drawing as indicated (usually with a blue wash on the original) by the illustrator (Fig. **3.2**). Later, self-adhesive film such as Letratone, printed with various tints and patterns, could be added to line work to achieve the same effect.

For offset litho, line illustrations were reproduced photographically on high-contrast **bromide** paper, usually reduced down in size from the original. This print was then pasted on to a board along with the typesetting. Bromide prints were also produced as **PMT**s (photomechanical transfers), or **diffusion transfers**, by a proprietary method developed by Kodak (Fig. **3.3**). It was a much drier process than the original method, in which the bromide paper was processed in trays of photographic chemicals in a darkroom.

To produce a PMT, original artwork was exposed on special negative paper through a process camera. This negative was then fed into a processor which activated the in-built developer and then laminated it to a receiving sheet of paper or film.

If more than one copy was required, or there was a need for the image to be retouched, a negative film was first made from the original. (It is easier, for example, to clean marks on the white areas of an image by opaquing out the black areas on a negative.) This was then used to produce contact prints on bromide paper, by means of the conventional and messy method of processing.

For low-cost work, it is also possible (and much cheaper) to reduce artwork on a laser photocopier using smooth, good-quality paper.

3.2 "Overcoming the difficulties of serenading in New York City," a cartoon with a mechanical tint, from William Heath Robinson's 1934 collection *Absurdities*. Note the Ben Day tint in the sky.

3.3 Before computers, graphic-design studios used a combination of process camera, like this WLTC 184, and PMT machine to produce enlarged or reduced copies of line art good enough to use on the mechanical.

Screens and halftones

A photograph or piece of artwork that contains tonal values other than just plain black and white must be converted into a **halftone** before it can be printed (Fig. **3.4**). Before an original containing continuous or intermediate tones can be printed, it must first be converted to "line"—into a form in which there can be either ink on the paper or not. The most common method is to use a halftone **screen** which converts the continuous tone original into a pattern of single-colored dots (Fig. **3.5**).

Screening is done digitally these days, but used to be achieved by placing a glass or plastic screen between the lens of the process camera and the bromide paper or film being exposed. As mentioned in Chapter 1, the method devised by George Meisenbach in 1882 used a single-lined screen that was turned 90 degrees during exposure. The first cross-lined screen was introduced in 1890 by Frederick Ives, in collaboration with Louis and Max Levy.

Halftone screens came in two varieties: glass screens and the cheaper plastic contact screens. Glass screens had a finely ruled grid pattern and were situated between the lens and the film. Contact screens contained a pattern of vignetted holes and were placed in direct proximity with the film. The term halftone is perhaps a misnomer: they are thus named because it was thought that half of the tone is eliminated during the process. Half the image maybe—but all of the tone. Just black and white remain.

The optics of how this happens is not really important to know. Suffice to say that different tones are converted into

3.4 Tone art, such as this print of Bill Gates, below, has to be converted into a pattern of dots before it can be printed, by a process called screening.

3.5 A conventional halftone contains dots of different sizes, but in a regular array conforming to the screen being used. Light areas are represented by small black dots. At 50 percent, you will see a checkerboard of black-and-white squares, while the darker tones appear as white dots on black. It is rare to find either pure white (no dots at all) or pure black (a solid area of black) on a halftone.

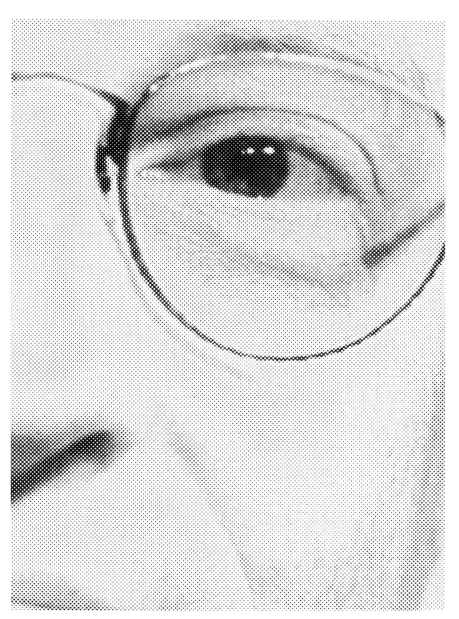

ILLUSTRATION   81

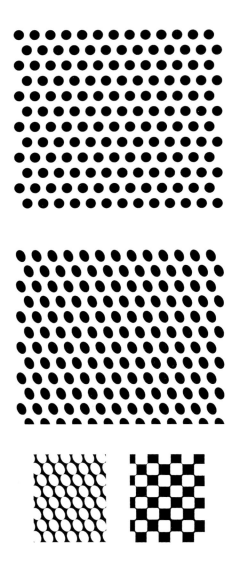

3.6 Imagesetters can make various shapes of dot electronically. Elliptical dots score over conventional ones, as they are less prone to dot gain—the abrupt darkening of areas where the dots are beginning to join up.

dots varying in size, shape, and number which, when viewed from a distance, seem to melt back into continuous tone.

The traditional crossed-line screen of 1890 gives a round dot, which becomes a square in the midtones—a checkerboard pattern at 50 percent density. More recently, various shapes of dot have been tried. An improvement on the conventional screen is one with elliptical holes which produce kite-shaped dots that join first in one direction, then the other, giving a much smoother gradation in the middle tones.

On modern electronic imagesetters, the dots are "written" on to the bromide paper or film directly by a laser beam—no screen is involved. These machines are capable of producing any shape of dot you like: square, round, or elliptical (Fig. **3.6**). The operator at the repro house will choose the best type of dot for the printing process and paper stock being used, and the tonal quality of the original.

Halftone screens are measured in lines per inch (lines per cm in continental Europe), usually abbreviated to lines or lpi (Fig. **3.8**). The higher the number of lines, the finer the dot pattern, and the better the quality of the reproduction. But there is a trade-off. Newspapers, for example, use cheap, rough paper and thin ink that is prone to spread. Too fine a screen, and the dots in the darker areas of the image will merge and **fill in**. Thus, for newsprint, a coarse dot pattern of 100 or 120 lines for offset is standard. Magazines are printed on smoother papers, and so a finer screen of, say, 150 lines can be used. The very finest screens are reserved for glossy art papers (see Chapter 6, pp. 167–80, for an in-depth discussion about paper).

The lines of the screen are usually aligned at 45 degrees to the horizontal, as this seems to produce the pattern that is easiest on the eye. There are dangers, however, when screening photographs containing regular patterns—on a person's clothing, for example. The screen dots and the pattern in the picture can interfere with each other to produce **moiré** (wavy or basketweave) **patterns** (Fig. **3.7**). This can be avoided or lessened by adjusting the angle of the screen. The moiré effect is put to good use in devices that can tell you what screen is being used in a printed publication.

3.7 When the two screens are superimposed and are not quite in alignment, there is a chance that moiré patterns will result. This happens most commonly when a previously screened halftone, cut from a magazine for example, is put through another screening process.

3.8 Detail of Rajarani Temple at Bhuvanesvar, India (opposite), at screen rulings of 65 (coarse), 120 (general purpose), and 175 (the ruling used throughout this book).

ILLUSTRATION 83

3.9 Publicity shot of Tina Turner. It does not have to be dots! But use special effect screens with discretion!

3.10 Publicity shot of Tina Turner. FM or stochastic screening uses a random scattering of spots to reproduce tone, rather than the regular pattern of dots used in AM screening.

3.11 A halftone is not always "squared-up." It can also be cut out around a profile, have the highlights dropped out, or it can be made into a vignette with the usually elliptical edges fading away to white. (Bartholdi's Statue of Liberty at the entrance to New York Harbor.)

There are also special-effect screens available that convert continuous tone into straight lines of varying weight, wavy lines, concentric circles, and textures that simulate canvas, linen, and random grain (Fig. **3.9**).

Conventional screening is now referred to as **AM** (amplitude-modulated) **screening**: the dots are arranged in regular columns and rows, but vary in size. In **FM** (frequency-modulated) screening, all the dots are same size, but they are randomly scattered (Fig. **3.10**). This eliminates the possibility of moiré patterns, and produces much smoother vignettes. And because the final image is built from single pixels, rather than composite halftone dots, the imagesetter can be run at lower resolutions. However, subsequent platemaking is so sensitive it must be carried out in almost "clean-room" conditions. The familiar rosettes (see p. 92) you see when you magnify areas of constant color in four-color work will be absent. FM screening is also sometimes referred to as **stochastic screening**, from the Greek for "random."

Halftones were traditionally squared up, i.e. rectangular in shape. Sometimes you might want to specify a thin black border or **keyline** around them to define the edge. There are other effects that can be used by the discerning graphic designer (Fig. **3.11**). These include **cut-outs**, in which extraneous matter is removed (once by hand, now using an image-manipulation program such as Photoshop); **drop-outs**, in which the dots in the very whitest areas are eliminated to accentuate the highlights; and **vignettes**, usually oval, in which the image fades gradually to nothing at the edges.

In work destined for offset lithography, halftones were once made into negative film and "stripped in" later, occupying the clear holes on the negative page left by black squares placed on the artwork. For some jobs, however, it was cheaper and more convenient to put correctly sized halftones, called

ILLUSTRATION   85

Scanning line artwork

Most black-and-white artwork is routinely scanned as **grayscale** at 300 dpi. This is fine if the artwork contains a range of tones, but if it is meant to be a solid black (or solid color) logo with crisp edges, or a cartoon drawn in Indian ink, for example, it should be scanned at a higher resolution, say 1200 dpi, in bitmap. Otherwise, when printed, the image will be converted to halftone and solid areas may appear blotchy and edges fuzzy.

If your scanner does not have such high resolution, scan in grayscale at the highest resolution you can. Then, in Photoshop, resample the image to 1200 dpi—the software will interpolate and add pixels to the image—you may have to apply the "blur" filter to the image then sharpen it with "unsharp mask" to remove any jagged or irregular edges. If you feel confident, you can attempt some retouching with the brush and eraser tools. Then go to "threshold" and adjust the slider until all the pixels— now either solid black or white—are showing. Finally, convert from grayscale to bitmap and save as a TIFF.

veloxes, into place along with the type and line, and shoot the whole page in one operation.

Sometimes it may be necessary to produce a halftone from copy that has already been screened. It may not be possible to locate the original of an old illustration from a book, for example. To put a screened picture directly under the camera or on the scanner will more often than not result in unwanted moiré patterns, but there are ways of avoiding this.

Use your loupe (eyeglass) to see if the dots on the original are sharp and black. If the screen does not exceed 120 lines, it can be shot as line copy. This is called **dot-for-dot** reproduction, and will often result in an increase of contrast. In Photoshop, you can use a despeckle filter, or blur the image to remove the screen followed by "unsharp mask" to put it back into focus— minus the screen.

Where lines and tones appear on the same piece of artwork, for example in a pencil drawing or an ink and wash illustration, a compromise has to be made. Either the whole illustration is treated as tone, in which case the white of the paper will appear light gray and the black lines will lose their crispness. Or the artwork is shot twice, as line and as tone, and combined at the film or platemaking stage as a line and tone combination.

Color

The use of color in printing is almost as old as printing itself, but the process has always been labor-intensive and has required painstaking amounts of skill. The chromolithographs of the mid-19th century sometimes used as many as 12 separate hand-drawn plates. This created correspondingly enormous problems of positioning the successive printings into correct alignment, one on top of the other—what printers call **registration**.

Flat color

Printers can mix up any color of ink you like—you will just be charged for the cost of special ink and for cleaning up the machine afterward.

An additional color used as a design element in a layout is called **flat color**, or sometimes **match** or **spot color**. In theory, you could use any number of different colors in a design. In practice, most printing presses are designed to handle two, four, or six colors printing, and the more printings you ask for, the higher the cost of the job. Printers can match almost any color—from a color chart, a piece of printed work, or even the color of your eyes. But if it is consistency you're after, between jobs and other related printed items, you're going to have to be a little more scientific.

The **Pantone Matching System** (PMS) is an industry-standard collection of over 1000 colors that printers recognize

3.12 The Pantone Goe System for specifying flat color.

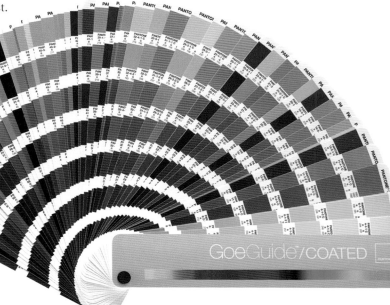

and are comfortable using. It is worth purchasing a color guide, in the form of a fan chart or **swatch book**. It will show you all the shades, along with the formulas for mixing the ink, and the effect of colors printed on both coated and uncoated paper (Fig. **3.12**). The easiest way of specifying flat color is to give the printer the Pantone number and perhaps one of the tear-off samples that come with the swatch book.

The Pantone Goe system, launched in 2007, has 2058 colors based on a smaller set of 10 base colors—medium yellow, bright orange, bright red, strong red, pink, medium purple, dark blue, medium blue, bright green, and natural black—plus Pantone Clear. No color uses more than two base colors plus clear and/or black in its formulation. More colors have been added mainly in the greens and blues and are orga-nized in a more logical chromatic way. PMS consists of 1114 colors (not counting metallic, Hexachrome, and other spe-cialty products), produced by mixing 13 base colors plus black and transparent white. There are also complementary sets of colors incorporating metallic inks, and specialist selections, such as pastel colors for packaging designers.

Flat color can be printed solid or as a percentage **tint** (Fig. **3.13**). Charts are also available that show Pantone colors in a range of percentage tints. Type can be combined with a tint of flat color in three ways: **surprinted**, with the tint and in the same color; reversed out of a tint block; or **overprinted** in another color (Fig. **3.14**). Legibility is an issue, so check with printed samples to see what will work with different percent-ages of tint.

Printers do not like to have flat colors overlapping, because it slows down the rate of drying of the inks and introduces the possibility of smudging. A color will change shade, too, when printed over another one. But adjacent areas of flat color will need to overlap to a small extent to allow for misregistra-tion (misalignment of successive printings). This allowance is called **trapping** (Fig. **3.15**) and is particularly important where, say, lettering is reversed out of a block of one color and printed in another. Without trapping, the slightest amount the printing slips **out of register** will cause a thin white line to appear around part of the boundary, resulting in an unwanted bas-relief effect. Generally, it is the lighter color that is extended into the area of the darker color.

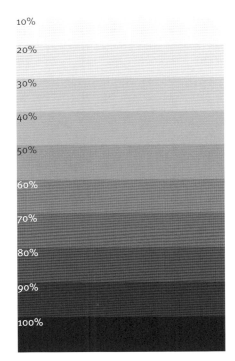

3.13 Color tints are effective when used under typesetting to draw attention to a particular passage, quotation, or checklist, as in our Hot Tips boxes.

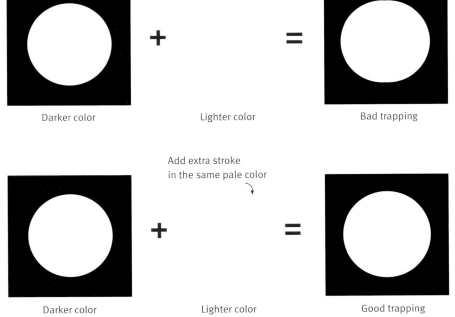

Darker color + Lighter color = Bad trapping

Add extra stroke in the same pale color

Darker color + Lighter color = Good trapping

surprint

reverse out

overprint

3.14 Text that has been surprinted, dropped out of a tint of the same color, and overprinted in a different color.

3.15 If a graphic or type in one flat color has to fit with a background of another color, there is always the possibility that misregistration might cause a sliver of white where they should abut—this is called bad trapping. The prevention and cure is to add a "stroke" width all round the lighter component, which will be hidden when the darker ink is overprinted.

ILLUSTRATION   87

Duotones

A halftone cannot always reproduce the full tonal range of a photograph. A **duotone** is a superimposition of a contrasty black halftone over a one-color halftone, which is shot for highlights and middle tones (Fig. **3.16**), using the same image. The most commonly used colors are yellows (Fig. **3.17**), browns, and reds. The intention is to create a rich range of tones, and at the same time add a colored tint to the result. For high-quality work, where cost is not a constraint, a duotone may even comprise two printings in black, or in black with a shade of gray. A basic shot with the screen at 45 degrees is used

for the black plate, and a second shot at 15 degrees is used for the second color.

For very high-quality publications, three passes of black or gray ink may be used to reproduce the full tonal range of a halftone. A less impressive duotone effect can be achieved by printing a black halftone over a color tint of the same size. This is called a **flat-tint halftone** (Fig. **3.18**). The tint must be kept quite light, as the highlights in the halftone can only ever be as light as the underlying tint.

3.16 A duotone is a halftone reproduction comprising two (or sometimes more) printings—one for contrast and the other for the highlights and middle tones. Here the underprinting is Pantone PMS 1205 yellow, to demonstrate how they can be created in Photoshop. The lower window shows how the contrast is adjusted by manipulating the "curves." As no spot colors are used in this book, these examples are simulations. The image is Dorothea Lange's 1936 photograph of migrant agricultural workers during the Depression in the United States.

3.17 More often than not, the underprinting for a duotone is in a spot color other than black, in this case a Pantone yellow. On the left is the black, the center is yellow, and right shows both combined.

3.18 A flat-tint halftone is a simple way to achieve a duotone effect. A contrasty black-and-white photograph is printed above as a flat tint of a spot color. Highlights will be a problem as nothing can be lighter than the underlying tint.

3.19 Pure white light contains all the colors of the rainbow. Add together the three primaries—red, green, and blue-violet—and you get white. Where the primaries overlap, the secondaries appear: yellow, magenta, and cyan. No light, as in the shadow of the pushpin, equals black.

RGB and CYMK

If you are working in full color, always convert imported Pantone colors to CMYK in drawing programs such as Illustrator. Remember that the bright colors you see in RGB on screen may not print that way—especially the blues. In paint programs, such as Photoshop, work in RGB until you've nearly finished, then—unless your printer prefers an RGB workflow (see p. 154)—convert to CMYK. This makes each operation faster and keeps file sizes down.

Full-color reproduction

It is neither economic nor practical to mix up ink and print every individual color to be found in a piece of artwork or color photograph, so another method has to be used. It should be possible to create any color from a mixture of the three primary pigments: red, yellow, and blue. Mix any two primary colors and you have the secondaries. Thus blue and yellow produce green, red and yellow produce orange, and blue and red produce purple. Theoretically, if you mix all three, you get black. Experience tells us, however, that what we really end up with is an unpleasant muddy brown. A similar result occurs with combinations of **reflected light**.

With **transmitted light** (Fig. **3.19**), things are a little better. Here, the three primaries are red, green, and blue-violet; the secondaries are yellow, **magenta** (reddish purple), and **cyan** (turquoise). Mix three such primary beams of light, and the result is pure white. Grass is green because it absorbs

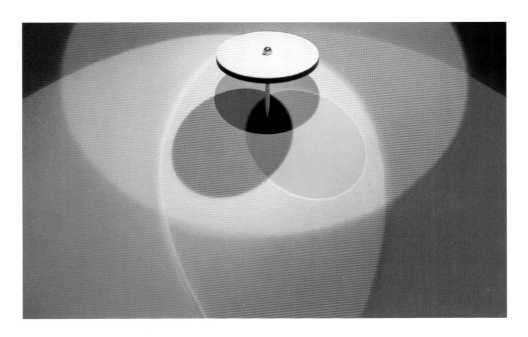

ILLUSTRATION   89

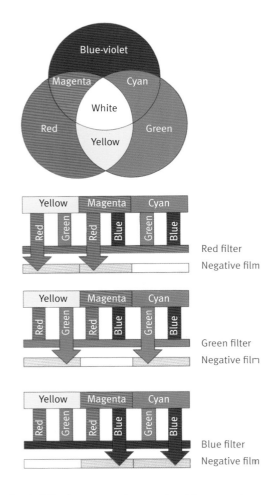

the red and blue-violet components of white light and then retransmits the green.

The secondary colors of transmitted light—yellow, magenta (process red), and cyan (process blue)—are the ones used by printers to reproduce full-color work. In 1860, Clerk Maxwell demonstrated how colored filters could be used to record the blue-violet, green, and red constituents of any full-color subject. Filters of red, green, and blue-violet—the primaries of transmitted light, also known as **additive colors**—are used to produce **separation** negatives (Fig. **3.20**). Using the red filter results in a negative of the red light transmitted by the subject. When a positive is made, the dark areas correspond to the blue and green components of the color, i.e. cyan. The green filter allows through only red and blue, creating magenta, and the blue filter lets through only the red and green, creating the yellow. The negatives taken through these filters, known as **color separations**, are screened and the positives are then used to make plates to be printed in sequence and in register (correct alignment) in the **process colors** of yellow, magenta, and cyan.

The colors of pigments or printing inks are subtractive—in theory all the colors added together should produce black, but in practice printing ink, like school paint, never does produce a pure enough black. So a fourth color—black—is added to deepen the dark areas and increase contrast. This makes the scheme a **four-color process**. In print jargon, black is referred to as **key**, so the system is known as **CMYK**. Other systems of defining color include **RGB** (**red green blue**), used for computer displays, and the more theoretical **HLS** (**hue, luminance, saturation**). Hue is the part of the rainbow the color occupies—whether it is red or blue. **Luminance**, lightness, or **value**, is the amount of black or white that has been added, to make yellow into brown, or red into pink. **Saturation**, or

3.20 All the colors in full-color copy can be reproduced from a mixture of the secondaries—yellow, magenta, and cyan—and these components of any color can be extracted using filters of the primaries—red, green, and blue-violet.

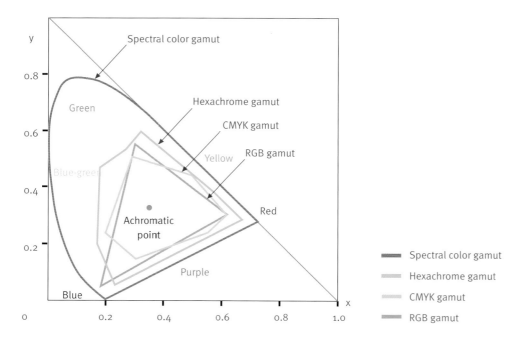

3.21 The gamut of colors that an RGB monitor can display differs from the gamut of colors capable of being reproduced by CMYK four-color printing. Hexachrome adds orange and green to increase the gamut. Here, the various gamuts are plotted in a CIE (Commission Internationale de l'Eclairage) standard color space diagram. RGB can only display approximately 70 percent of the colors that can be perceived by the human eye. The CMYK color gamut is much smaller, reproducing about 20 percent of perceivable colors.

intensity, is a measure of the color's position in the range from neutral gray to fully saturated, or bright, color.

L*a*b color is a device-independent model proposed by the CIE (Commission Internationale de l'Eclairage) in 1931 and refined in 1976. L is for luminance; a and b are chromatic components—a for green to red and b for blue to yellow. Photoshop uses the L*a*b model internally when converting from RGB to CMYK.

Pantone's **Hexachrome** system uses six colors: brighter (fluorescent) versions of CMYK plus vivid orange and green. This expands the color **gamut** (the limited spectrum of colors that a particular device can reproduce; see Fig. **3.21**) and is also referred to as HiFi color. When the image is separated, green and magenta are prevented from appearing in the same area, as are orange and cyan, so can share the same screen angles (see Fig. **3.22**) and avoid any moiré patterns. When printing, black goes down first, followed by green, cyan, magenta, yellow, and finally orange.

Color separations

A color tone original, once separated by the **process camera**, is now commonly separated using an electronic **scanner**. Separations by camera were made on to continuous-tone film using three-color filters, and these were then converted into halftones by exposure through screens.

Scanners work by reading the artwork as a series of horizontal lines, or rasters. The **transparency** or artwork is wrapped around the scanner's transparent drum, which revolves at around 90 miles per hour (150 km/h). A beam of light is used to pick up the three color components. These split beams are digitized, and pass into a computer where color correction and some manipulation of the image can take place.

Finally, a laser is employed to "write" the dots of the screened separations directly on to film.

The screens are laid out at different angles to keep the dots separate—the apparent "mixing" of the colors is done by the brain and the eye—and in a pattern designed to eliminate moiré effects (Fig. **3.22**). The screens of the main colors are oriented at 30 degrees to each other, with the stronger colors at 45, 75, and 105 degrees, and the less intrusive yellow at the "difficult" angle of 90 degrees.

Some combinations of the three process colors cancel each other out to produce neutral grays, and since black is being used anyway, this can be seen as overkill. **Gray component replacement** (Fig. **3.23** and **3.24**), also known as **achromatic stabilization**, is a technique used at the scanning stage for cleaning up the color and reducing the amount of ink that gets to the paper. Not all the "chromatic" gray is removed and replaced by a tint of black, however. **Undercolor addition** (**UCA**) is a method of returning some of the process color, usually cyan, beneath the black to add depth and density to areas of deep shadow. **Undercolor removal** (**UCR**) reduces the amount of color in areas of shadows, to save ink and

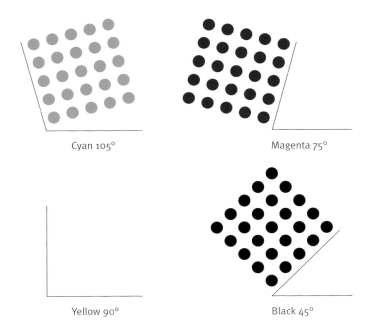

Cyan 105°

Magenta 75°

Yellow 90°

Black 45°

3.22 To prevent moiré patterns, the screens for the different color printings are set at specific angles: 45 degrees is easiest on the eye, so that is reserved for black; 90 degrees is the least satisfactory angle, so it is used for the relatively pale yellow. When printed together they produce the rosette pattern as seen in Fig. 3.24.

ILLUSTRATION   91

3.23 In theory, any color can be reproduced from a combination of yellow, cyan, and magenta. In practice, though, black is added for extra punch. Gray component replacement trades off some of the neutral gray created by combinations of the process colors for tints of black—it saves ink and quickens drying (see bottom row). Detail of *Scene in Harlem (Simply Heavenly)* by Edward Burra (1905–76).

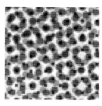

3.24 The screen angles of the four process colors produce a "rosette" pattern when printed, here shown magnified.

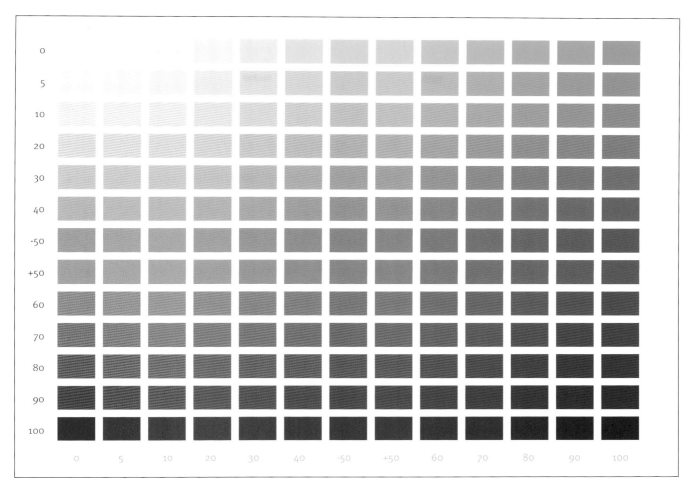

3.25 Charts showing combinations of various percentage tints help you make the most effective use of process color in layouts. This chart shows the effect of changing the percentages of magenta and cyan while keeping yellow constant at 60 percent. Along the axes, −50 refers to dots that are not touching and +50 refers to ones that are.

prevent problems that may occur if a new layer of ink is printed on to ink that is not quite dry.

If a solid area is to be printed in a Pantone shade along with four-color illustrations, it will be cheaper to match the color by using a combination of tints in two or more of the process colors. Pantone publishes charts illustrating various combinations of process tints printed one over the other (Fig. **3.25**). But if you plan to substitute in this way, check first with your clients. They may have strict rules about the use of specific colors for corporate-identity work—the color of a company logo, for example—and may be willing to stand the cost of an extra printing in a specially mixed Pantone shade.

To prevent potential muddiness when too many colors are mixed together, a rule of thumb has evolved that the sum of percentage components of the process colors should never exceed 240. A color comprising 30 percent yellow, 10 percent cyan, and 60 percent magenta (= 100 percent) is fine, but one containing 70 percent yellow, 100 percent cyan, and 80 percent magenta (= 250 percent would not be allowed on the press. The color bar on a color proof has checks for this (see p. 161).

Cultural implications of color

You're wearing white for a special occasion. Where are you going? In a Western country, you'd be the bride at a wedding; in Korea, you'd be at a funeral. In China, brides wear red. The bride in Jan van Eyck's Renaissance painting *Giovanni Arnolfini and His Bride* wears green—a symbol of her fertility. Color provides both visual and psychological information. But in different cultures, colors can have different meanings.

ILLUSTRATION   93

Chris Ware

"I'm only trying to present as honest a portrayal of the grimness of human ambition as I can. I'd hope it's rather uplifting."

Manifesto
File under Self-help

The advice to booksellers on the cover of *Jimmy Corrigan* is "File under: Literature/Self-help." The story of Corrigan, a crushed, middle-aged man who fortifies his existence through fantasy can be seen as autobiographical. The *New York Times* called it "arguably the greatest achievement of the form ever." Three-quarters of the way through the book, Ware's father made contact. "It was spooky," he says. They met for a few hours, but before they had a chance to meet again, Ware's father died of a heart attack. Now he regrets having hated him all those years.

"I'm only trying to present as honest a portrayal of the grimness of human ambition as I can. I'd hope it's rather uplifting, actually, since I find the sort of blind optimism and empty laughter of a great deal of 'contemporary culture' to be more depressing than something that admits to a potential for disappointment and a gnawing sense of existential mockery. I don't trust art that promises a 24-hour joyride. In fact, there seems to be a modern sense of entitlement for such constant 'ups,' which is a repugnant attitude any way one chooses to look at it. I definitely believe in the possibility of happiness, though; it's just something that I think, rightfully, is rare in its genuine form, and that it can't be counterfeited."

Ware, with characteristic modesty, says that the only graphic arts "training" he had was a "commercial art" vocational class in high school in 1984, where he learned how to use a photostat camera. "I owe the rest of what I know to the pressmen and particularly the extremely helpful and tolerant prepress guys at *The Daily Texan*—not to mention the subsequent printers of my comic books. I should mention here that I don't consider what I do to be classified as graphic design or illustration, and while I have done illustration in the past to pay the bills, I consider what I've done in that regard pretty much to be hackery."

Fans of the *The Acme Novelty Library* will instantly recognize Ware's oddly formatted comic books (either infuriatingly large—"taller than most bookshelves, good luck archiving this with the rest of your collection"—or "adorably tiny," but never "standard"), which star the existential adventures of Quimby the Mouse, Rocket Sam, Big Tex, et al, all drawn like 1930s trademark characters. Many will have been intrigued by Ware's mix of hand-rendered Victorian lettering (taken from sheet music and cigar labels), flowery language, and over-ornamentation with precise, minimal art deco drawings, somber colors, and cutting-edge computer production, all informed by the visual language of cartoons. Others might be perplexed by the seemingly impenetrable text and painfully complicated three-dimensional cut-out-and-assemble paper projects (will they really work?), but nevertheless delight in the sheer visual joy of the understated compositions.

Franklin Christenson Ware was born in 1967 in Omaha, Nebraska, the cultural and geographical middle of America. His father left home shortly after Ware was born. He moved to San Antonio, Texas, at 16 and later went to the University of Texas in Austin where he discovered the dream-worlds of Winsor McCay's "Little Nemo," the lyrical abstraction of George Herriman's "Krazy Kat," and European "clear line" artists, such as Joost Swarte.

As a sophomore, Ware's work caught the eye of Art Spiegelman and he was promptly invited (by phone call) to contribute to *Raw* magazine. Many of the *Novelty Library* publications were collections of strips published in *The Daily Texan* and *New City*. When collecting the strips, Ware restructures, redraws, and rewrites much of the work.

Ware controls the total production of his books; his publisher Fantagraphics doesn't usually see anything until they are printed. He has been lucky enough to pick and choose his "outside" projects.

He is the designer of the ongoing Fantagraphics reprints of George Herriman's classic "Krazy Kat" strips. In addition, he designed a vast public mural for San Francisco's 826 Valencia center depicting the development of the human race, along with its efforts at, and motivations for, communication.

Resources
Daniel Raeburn, *Chris Ware*, Laurence King Publishing, London, 2004

Chris Ware Bibliography: http://quimby.gnus.org/warehouse/

Chris Ware, *Jimmy Corrigan: The Smartest Kid on Earth*, Pantheon Books, New York, 2000.

Chris Ware (ed.), *McSweeney's Quarterly Concern: Issue Number 13*, McSweeney's Ltd, San Francisco and Brooklyn, 2004. A large fold-out comic strip broadside, with "free" 264-page hardcover book featuring new or little-seen contributions from Daniel Clowes, Robert Crumb, George Herriman, Charles Schulz, Seth, Art Spiegelman, and many others

George Herriman, Bill Blackbeard (ed.), Chris Ware (designer), *Krazy & Ignatz 1925–1926: "There is a Heppy Land Furfur A-waay"* (Krazy Kat), Fantagraphics Books, Seattle, 2002. At the time of writing, eight further volumes had been published, with more in the pipeline.

One of Ware's rare excursions into commercial graphic design, a 7-in record cover for *Waiting on the Eclipse* by 5ive Style, a Chicago-based trio, on the Seattle label Sub Pop Records. Their first release in 1994 has become a collectors' item thanks to the brilliant, witty design of Chris Ware.

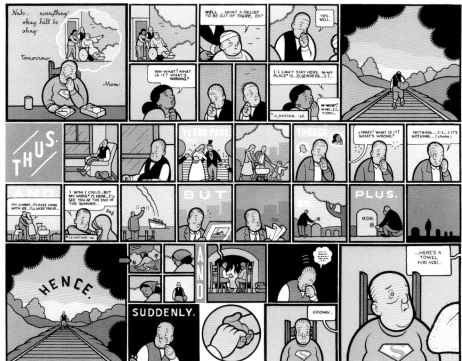

Front cover of *The Acme Novelty Library* number 7 (Fantagraphics Books, Seattle, 1996), one of Ware's large-format comic books (17⅞ × 10¼ in/455 × 273 mm)—"taller than most bookshelves, good luck archiving this with the rest of your collection"—starring Rocket Sam and Big Tex, with a brief appearance by Jimmy Corrigan. The topsy-turvy design was based on a board game. The retro futuristic illustration in the central porthole anticipates "Tales of Tomorrow" in number 15; the robot is a self-portrait.

This left-hand page toward the end of *Jimmy Corrigan: The Smartest Kid on Earth* (Pantheon Books, 2000) has a cross-shaped design, starting and ending with Jimmy's reality, with the other two corner squares housing Hollywood "happy" sunsets. The other squares are what Jimmy is thinking, indicated by the thought bubble in square one. One of the delights of Ware's comic strips is that no spread can be singled out as typical.

Designers can control what the viewer perceives, but must always be aware that they could sometimes be sending the wrong messages.

Some colors seem to convey universal truths, and have been codified by organizations such as the Occupational Safety and Health Administration (OSHA) of the US Department of Labor. Yellow, for example is a very visible color; that's why it is used on school buses. OSHA regulations designate yellow for caution and for marking (usually with a yellow and black chevron) physical hazards you might trip over. Red, for danger, is the color used for identifying fire-protection equipment and emergency stop buttons on dangerous machinery.

Colors can change their meanings over time with fashion and changing social awareness. Green used to be an unpopular color for automobiles—it was an unlucky color. This probably dates back to the 19th century when "Paris green" became a fashionable emerald shade—until it was discovered that this arsenic-based pigment had caused several deaths and was aptly renamed "poison green." Now green is back in fashion, along with greater environmental awareness. The names of colors, too, can have an influence on the perception of the color. In 1962, Binney & Smith renamed the Crayola color "flesh" to a less culturally charged "peach," and in 1992 introduced so-called "multicultural" crayons in many subtle shades of brown.

We often use colors to describe our emotions and feelings: "I was so angry, I saw red," we say, or "I'm feeling blue," or "I was green with envy." "Paint it black" sang the unhappy Rolling Stones. But do these descriptions translate easily into other languages? Probably not that successfully, because the color may lose its associated symbolic meaning.

One link between color and emotion is the perception that red, orange, yellow, and brown hues are "warm"—inducing excitement, cheerfulness, stimulation, and aggression—while the blues, greens, and grays are "cold"—implying security, calm, and peace, or sadness, depression, and melancholy. A cross-cultural study has shown, however, that in Japan blue and green hues are perceived to be "good" and the red–purple range "bad." In the United States, the red–yellow–green range is considered to be "good," with oranges and red–purples "bad."

Colors are not the same for everyone. Some languages do not contain separate words for green and blue, or for yellow and orange, and the Inuit, for example, are supposed to have 17 different words for white, as modified by different snow conditions. All languages have words for black and white. If a third hue is distinguished, it is red. Next comes yellow or green, and then both yellow and green. Blue is the sixth color named, and brown is the seventh. Finally, in no particular sequence, the colours gray, orange, pink, and purple are given names.

Architects and designers use color psychology to modify our behavior. Fast-food restaurants and coffee shops are painted orange and pink in conjunction to induce excitement. They excite you to come in, eat quickly, then vacate the table for the next set of excited customers. Better restaurants do this more subtly using colors like burgundy. Blue is rarely used in restaurants, because it is a relaxing color. Once in the restaurant, the customers will be so relaxed that they won't want to leave. Hospitals used to be painted green to soothe patients. Pink can be energizing or calming. Prisons are painted pink to cheer up those who work there and subdue the prisoners.

Color has a significant effect on both our minds and bodies. Young children are attracted more by color than shape. As we mature, we will often become more form-dominant; however, creative people often remain color-dominant all of their lives. Eye-tracking studies of infants indicate that, regardless of sex, red and blue are the most preferred colors. Color has been shown to affect human moods, physiological responses, and perceptions of temperature, size, and ambiance. Colored light is used to treat some illnesses, and to soothe patients in hospitals and institutions. Warm colors (particularly red) increase human attraction to external stimuli, induce states of excitement, produce higher arousal levels, quicken muscular responses, and increase grip strength. In contrast, cool colors (particularly green) reduce anxiety states, and are associated with calm and tranquilizing moods.

Designing for disability access

Color-blindness is the inability to distinguish one or more of the three colors red, green, and blue. Blindness to red is called protanopia; to green, deuteranopia; and to blue, tritanopia. Red-blind people are unable to distinguish between red and green, while blue-blind people cannot distinguish between blue and yellow. Green-blind people are unable to see the green part of the spectrum. Color blindness, which affects about 20 times as many males as females, is a sex-linked recessive characteristic. A woman must inherit the trait from both parents to be color-blind.

In the United States alone, approximately 19 million people possess some form of color-blindness. While they are not technically blind, there may be some colors which are inaccessible to them, appearing as a confusing blend of grays. Designers must be ever aware of the problems of those who are color-blind, have age- or illness-related degenerative vision, or who have limited sight.

Elderly people see colors differently, but are not color-blind in the usual sense of the term. Vision declines with age, with yellowing and darkening of the lens and cornea, and a shrinking pupil size. Yellowing selectively blocks short wavelength light, so blues look darker. Moreover, the elderly have difficulty discriminating colors which differ in their blue content: blue-whites, blue-grays, green-blue greens, and red-purples. Ageing also reduces the amount of light reaching the photoreceptors. All colors will be dimmer and visual resolution lower—a moderately bright yellow may appear brownish, and dimmer blues will appear black. When designing for elderly people, use bright colors and make sure that brightness contrast is especially high.

Choosing and preparing illustrations

Briefing an illustrator or photographer

Graphic designers and illustrators have much in common. The most famous illustrator-turned-graphic designer, Milton Glaser, has always encouraged illustrators to do as he has done. Not only will you earn more money as a graphic designer, but you can then commission yourself to do the illustrations! Be that as it may, not every graphic designer can draw as well as he, nor is every illustrator as passionately interested in type.

A graphic designer may commission artwork and photography, or may be presented with a package of words and pictures to put together according to a design brief. If the graphic designer is involved at an early stage with the commissioning of illustration and photography, a careful eye can be kept on the quality and content of the finished job.

Perhaps the two most important pieces of information an illustrator needs to know are the deadline date, and the size of the artwork required. The content and style will be different for each job, and the choice of a particular illustrator or photographer will be made on their ability to deliver what you want, on time, and to a professional standard. There are, however, some further general principles that can be outlined.

There are two kinds of original copy. Flat artwork from the hand of the illustrator and photographic prints is termed **reflection copy**: it is viewed by reflected light. Color transparencies and film positives are referred to as **transmission copy**.

Unless artwork has been produced digitally, copy is scanned in and separated on a drum scanner, so try to encourage illustrators to produce their artwork on flexible media that will wrap around the drum. Check with the repro house the maximum size of artwork that the scanner can take. Black-and-white line artwork is often scanned as grayscale, so if you want black line, make a point of telling the repro house that black line is what you want! An illustrator may use different densities of black ink for the outline and solid color. Under the process camera, all would come out as solid black; but scanned as grayscale, you might end up with an illustration in two distinct unintended shades of gray.

Many illustrators like to work on rigid board. There is a kind of board available with a surface that can be peeled off from a rigid base and then wrapped around the drum of a scanner, but this is not to be recommended. Originals sometimes get damaged and some kinds of paint crack, so it is wise to have a scan or transparency made first. Bear in mind, however, that there will be a loss of quality whenever an original is copied.

Where you do have commissioning power, and when selecting images that already exist—from picture libraries, for example—insist on the following:

- Line reflection copy, such as cartoons, should be in black Indian ink on good quality artboard, with any corrections made in process white paint. The original should be drawn no larger than twice-up, unless the lines are simple and thick enough to withstand reduction below 50 percent. Scratchboard illustrations, with their sharp lines, generally reduce successfully. If a line-and-tone effect is required, for example in comic book illustration, the line work and lettering should be drawn on an acetate **overlay**, in register, over the tonal element.

- Halftone reflection copy, such as photographic prints or airbrush drawings, should have a wide tonal range with not too much contrast. Check for the correct exposure, the graininess, and whether the part of the image you require is correctly in focus. The original should ideally be same size and, at any rate, not more than half-up. Photographs should be printed on glossy paper.

If you have access to a slide scanner, or attachment to a flatbed scanner, it is possible to scan a negative directly into the computer, where it can then be turned positive using a program such as Photoshop.

Never risk scratch marks by attaching anything to a photograph with a paperclip or staple. If color copy is to be reproduced in black and white, be prepared for a loss in clarity and contrast.

Artwork intended for flat color should be supplied in black on a baseboard, with each color drawn, in register, on a separate overlay. Artwork in which the separate flat colors do not touch or overlap can be drawn on the same board, provided that the portions to be printed in different colors are clearly indicated on an overlay. Photoshop is not very flat-color friendly—you have to save the flat-color element in black line or grayscale and color it within the page-layout program. Some designers have been known to use the duotone function to produce flat-color separations. You can also allocate a process color to a flat color and tell the printer to substitute a Pantone color on the press, but it will be impossible then to produce meaningful color proofs. Adobe Illustrator is much better at handling two- and three-color work.

Artwork in full color should not contain any fluorescent paints or inks as they do not reproduce well when separated into process colors. Nor do very pure secondary colors, such as purples and lime greens.

ILLUSTRATION   97

- Halftone transmission copy, such as photographic transparencies, should be chosen on a lightbox equipped with standard lighting conditions. Transparencies come in various formats: 35 mm, 5 × 4 inches, and 10 × 8 inches, for example. Because they will undergo considerable enlargement when reproduced, choose as large a format as you can afford. Check for graininess—it will increase as the transparency is enlarged. And because a transparency's tonal range will be compressed by the printing process, look for detail in both shadow areas and highlights. Check for correct exposure (ask the photographer to "bracket" the exposures, by shooting at apertures above and below the optimum f-stop, and choose the best result). Look, too, for the **color cast** found on a subject photographed against a strongly colored background. Also, scrutinize the transparencies for fingerprints, scratches, and other blemishes. Colors can be corrected to some degree at the repro house, and some retouching can be done using Photoshop, but beware—you will be charged for the service.

  Ensure that each transparency is right reading—the repro house will assume that the image is correct when the transparency is viewed with the **emulsion side** facing away from you. This is not always the case, especially if the "original" is a duplicate. Double check by supplying them with a sketch of the subject on a traced overlay.

- Halftone digital copy, direct from digital cameras, for example, should be at a resolution of at least 300 dpi at the size you require or bigger. Images can be successfully resampled in Photoshop to a smaller size, but increasing the size of a low-resolution image can produce disappointing results. For print, the image should be CMYK (unless your printer prefers an RGB workflow) and in **TIFF** (**Tagged Image File Format**) format. A high-quality **JPEG** (**Joint Photographic Experts Group**) can also be acceptable, and files at 72 dpi straight from a digital camera or grabbed as screenshots are not necessarily too small for use—in Photoshop, uncheck the "Resample image" button in "Image size" and if the resulting width or height is what you want (or higher) then all is well.

Scaling and cropping

Copy to be reproduced at exactly the same size as the original is called same size and marked S/S. More often than not, artwork will have to be reduced in size to fit your layout, and transparencies enlarged. This is called scaling, or reproportioning.

The simplest and clearest way to indicate the required size of artwork or photographs is to mark the limits of the image with a double-headed arrow and write "Reduce to 4 inches" or whatever you want the width (or height) to be. To avoid damaging the artwork, this is best done on an overlay, or flap, of layout paper or tissue. If you are using only a portion of the photograph or artwork, the area you need can also be outlined on the overlay. This is called **cropping**, or recomposing.

It must be said, however, that few photographers and probably no illustrators like to have their work cropped by a graphic designer. Some sensitivity and diplomacy is required if it just has to be done. It is much better to have the size and shape of the illustration or photograph worked out in advance so that the illustrator or photographer can be briefed thoroughly. Obviously, photographs come in standard formats, and some cropping is inevitable. But give the photographers the opportunity to crop their images and you will be rewarded with better results.

If you are ever tempted, for the sake of a composition, to **flop** or invert a photograph laterally, i.e. turn it into a mirror image of itself (and it can be done quite simply at the stripping-in stage), get out your loupe and watch out for the giveaways. These include obvious ones such as lettering and signs, but also more subtle telltales such as clocks and maps in the background, or the position of a man's suit breast pocket, or specialized equipment with controls and buttons that the reader will recognize as inverted. Some of these can be retouched, but it is often better to prevent potential embarrassment by leaving well alone, or paying out to have the photograph reshot.

It is difficult to draw **crop marks** accurately on such a small area as a portion of a 35 mm transparency, and it is better to make an enlarged photocopy, and to mark that with your instructions. These copies can be placed in position and at the correct size on the artwork (there is more information on this in Chapter 5, p. 145).

It is often useful to know the size an image will appear once it has been reduced or enlarged, so that you can plan your layout with confidence that the scanned image or dropped-in color separations will fit. There are two methods for making this calculation. The first is to use a **reproduction calculator** or **proportional scale**. This is a kind of circular slide rule, comprising two disks that rotate relative to each other. Find the width of the original on the inner wheel, line up the width of the space into which is has to fit on the outer wheel, and you will be able to read off the corresponding reduction or enlargement in height. It will also give you another useful figure—the percentage reduction or enlargement.

An ordinary pocket calculator is most likely to be used to determine the size of an illustration after reduction or enlargement—just substitute your figures into the following formula:

$$\frac{\text{height after reduction (or enlargement)}}{\text{height of original}} = \frac{\text{width after reduction}}{\text{width of original}}$$

Suppose you have a photograph 10 inches high by 8 inches wide that you have to reduce so that it will fit a column 3 inches wide. What will be the resulting height after reduction? How much room should you allocate in the layout?

Using the above formula:

$$\frac{x}{10} = \frac{3}{8}$$

Now, cross-multiply and divide to find x, thus:

8x = 30
x = 30 ÷ 8 = 3·75 in

The main thing to remember when using a regular pocket calculator is to ensure that your units of measurement are consistent. All units must be in either inches, millimeters, or picas—but never a mixture!

To calculate the percentage reduction or enlargement, divide the intended width (or height) by the width (or height) of the original and multiply the result by 100. In this example:

$$\text{percentage reduction} = \frac{h}{8} \times 100$$

$$= 37·5\%$$

Percentages can seem confusing at first: 100 percent, for example, is same size; 50 percent is half the width or height,

but a quarter the area; 200 percent is twice the width or height, but four times the area. If you increase or reduce the width, do not forget that the height will also be increased or reduced, in direct proportion. When in doubt, always mark the copy with the width (or height) at which you want the image to appear. Writing exact measurements on the copy will also make it easier to check that the correct reduction or enlargement has been made when you receive your picture proofs.

The diagonal method (Fig. **3.26**) uses geometry to help you to work out the final size of your scaled artwork. Draw a rectangle around the cropped area on the overlay, using a triangle (set-square) or transparent grid to make sure that the corners are square. Protect the original, and draw a diagonal

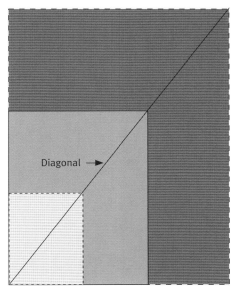

3.26 Diagonal scaling is a quick and easy way of estimating the space an enlarged or reduced illustration will occupy. Note that this photograph has been intentionally flopped.

ILLUSTRATION 99

from the bottom left corner to the top right. If the artwork is to be reduced, measure the width you want it to appear along the bottom edge of the rectangle using the bottom left corner as your starting point, and draw a vertical from the other end, up to meet the diagonal. Where these two lines intersect, draw a horizontal line to meet the left vertical edge of your original box. This is the height that your scaled artwork will appear when reproduced.

If the artwork or transparency is to be enlarged, trace the crop outline to the bottom left corner of a piece of paper, draw the diagonal as before, but extending it beyond the crop rectangle. Also extend the bottom edge of the box and the left vertical. Now measure off the intended width of the enlargement, draw a line vertically to meet the extended diagonal, and read off the enlarged height. A lightbox will make the process a lot easier.

Most pictures have to fit a specified width—a column width, for example. This method can, however, be used to calculate the width of an image that has to fit a specific height.

Always label illustrations, and do so in soft pencil, preferably a non-reproducing light-blue one, or in fibertip pen (checking first that it will not bleed through the overlay). Do not stack photographs while the marks on the back are still wet without first protecting the front, and never write on the back of a photograph with a ballpoint pen. A greasy pencil such as a Chinagraph, or a CD-ROM pen, are best for writing on glossy surfaces. If you will be handling a lot of transparencies, invest in some lint-free cotton gloves to avoid introducing fingerprints on to the images. And always remove transparencies from glass mounts before sending them to the printers—they will break, damaging the transparency, and showering the recipient with thin shards of glass.

Desktop scanning

Artwork can be scanned in the studio using a desktop scanner. The quality of the scanned images produced will be lower than that of illustrations originated on the scanners found in repro houses, but they are improving, and coming down in price all the time.

Desktop color scanners and special slide scanners are not always up to repro quality, but they do have a place in giving the graphic designer an idea of how the layout is going to work. And they are being used as a creative tool by a new breed of computer graphics illustrators. With digital cameras, it is possible to bypass even the scanning process, and input digitized images direct to the computer (see p. 119).

Drawing and painting by computer

On a computer such as the Macintosh, there are two different ways of producing illustrations, referred to as "draw" and "paint" (Fig. **3.27**). A "paint" document is stored in the computer's memory as a bitmap, a one-to-one array corresponding to the pixels (dots) appearing on the screen—although the image can be much larger than the size of the screen. In a **paint program**, a circle intersected by a line, say, is just a pattern of dots and can only be moved en bloc. It is not possible to edit "globally"—modify every circle in a picture, for example—by using just one command.

A "draw" or **vector** document has more in-built "intelligence." It is stored in the computer's memory as a display list of the points and lines that make up the illustration, plus the formulas for any circles, ellipses, and curves. This is also known as object-oriented graphics, because every object—a circle, line, or curve—can be accounted for separately. In draw programs, it is possible to move the line without affecting the circle. And because the lines are not stored in terms of bitmaps, the output resolution to, say, a PostScript printer is independent of the image's resolution. The output of a paint system is a TIFF or JPEG; the output of a draw program is generally an EPS.

MacPaint was the first program for the Macintosh to use bitmapped graphics. MacDraw was the original object-oriented draw program.

The original **paint system** was the Quantel Paintbox (Fig. **3.28**), best known for producing special effects for broadcast television. With ever more powerful computers and cheaper memory, much of the functionality of the Paintbox can be reproduced by programs such as Adobe Photoshop. There are also paint systems around that do their best to emulate real paint. Corel's Painter, for example, can simulate so-called "natural media"—the wet appearance of oil paint and watercolor—and produce convincing chalk and pastel effects through the use of a pressure-sensitive stylus.

It is as a medium of photomontage, however, that paint systems such as Adobe Photoshop are being put to work in most design studios (Fig. **3.29**). Originally developed for **retouching** photographic images, Photoshop is now the de facto image-manipulation program. Here, so-called source or "reference material" (beware of copyright infringement!) can be scanned into the system, or "framegrabbed" by a video card, to be combined, manipulated, and recolored. This is analogous to sampling and remixing musical quotations to produce today's electronic dance music.

Some graphic designers also use paint systems as a concept design tool. If you are designing packaging for a new range of TV dinners, for example, a convincing illustration can be montaged from illustrations "grabbed" from cookery books or other sources. When the concept has been approved for go-ahead by the client, these roughs can be used as a brief for the commissioning of original illustration or photography.

The power of the computer as a conceptual tool is grossly underestimated. Some designers use it for nothing else, preferring to produce finished artwork traditionally, by hand. The computer allows you to play around with ideas—trying out different type, alternative positioning of elements, another color, and so on—for as long as your schedule will allow. As

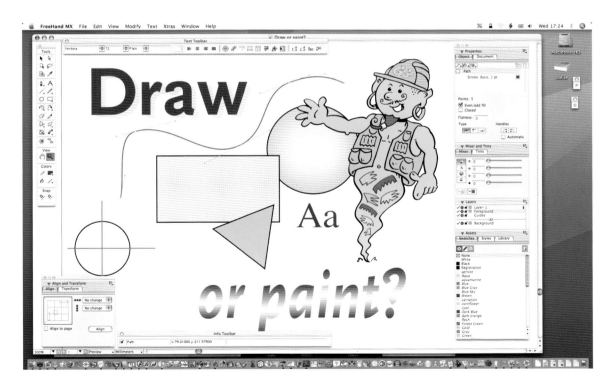

3.27 The main difference between "paint" and "draw" software lies in how the image seen on the screen is stored in the memory. A paint document is a bitmap—just a representation of the screen—whereas a draw document is stored in terms of the points, lines, and formulas used to create it. Thus a draw document is not restricted to the resolution of the screen, and the image can be "deconstructed" for editing and amendment.

ILLUSTRATION   101

3.28 The Quantel Paintbox was originally designed for television graphics. The Q Paintbox Pro has a much higher resolution, more suitable for print applications.

3.29 This "paint" illustration by Gary Thompson was created using Photoshop to combine multiple paint layers with typographic, EPS, and 3D elements.

West Coast designer April Greiman says: "The paint never dries." And so long as you have the different versions, there is no chance of ever spoiling the original.

Retouching covers a multitude of sins: it can be as innocent as adding a few crocuses to a countryside scene, or it can be used to subvert reality completely, placing well-known characters in compromising positions, for example. Thankfully, it is mainly used to clean up images or as a purely creative

3.30 Paint systems are used for making "paintings" from scratch or, more usually, for retouching or montaging photographs and "found" artwork. "Karona's Conflagration" by illustrator John Avon was drawn and painted entirely in Photoshop for "Magic: The Gathering," a trading card game. He used an A4 Wacom tablet and a G4 Power Mac. © 2004 Wizards of the Coast.

medium—in fact, just as graphic designers use any other form of illustration (Fig. **3.30**). What is certain, however, is that photographs are retouched routinely because it is so easy to do. And the adage that "the camera never lies" has little credibility these days.

Draw programs such as Adobe Illustrator are now closely linked to page-layout packages. They can be used not only for color or black-and-white illustration, but to manipulate type too (Figs. **3.31** and **3.32**).

Both use controllable freeform curves (called Bézier curves) which can be manipulated to produce complex drawings. Scanned images or bitmapped drawings from a paint program can be "imported" and traced over.

Other tools are used to create boxes, lines, ellipses, and corners at any angle. Layers (overlays) are available, so that the drawing can be split up into separate elements which can be displayed and edited individually. Line attributes, pattern fills, and colors can be saved on a computer style sheet and applied to other elements later to maintain a consistency throughout

HOT TIPS & COOL TRICKS

Photoshop PDFs

Native Photoshop files (.psd) can store layers of vector data (crisp PostScript text and shapes) as well as raster data (pixels from paint layers). The same is true for Photoshop PDFs, even after being imported into a page layout program and printed/exported. But be sure to turn on "Include Vector Data" in the PDF Options dialog box. If you place/import these images into a new, blank InDesign or QuarkXPress file and output to a PostScript printer, you'll see that the type is crisp and clear. A .tif or .psd file would be rasterized, with blurred anti-aliased edges.

ILLUSTRATION   103

Simplify your illustrations

A lean and efficient illustration from Adobe Illustrator will output faster at the repro service bureau and save you time and money (they'll put complex jobs to the back of the queue so they don't hold up other jobs). Use straight lines in preference to curves whenever you can. Or use paths with as few points as possible. The number of segments the output device uses to simulate curves depends on the "flatness" value. The flatness is a number between 0 and 100 and is the difference between the polygon the output device draws and the mathematical curve. The higher the number, the rougher the curve but the faster it will print. A value of 3 should be your default, but you can probably get away with a much bigger number before detecting a loss of quality. And delete any object you can't see in preview mode—it might be hidden behind another object, but it will still have to be processed!

3.31 Illustrator Peter Greenwood created "Scooter girl" using Illustrator 9 on a Mac G4: note the exhaust smoke—it is possible to render almost airbrush effects in a vector program.

3.32 A completely different use of a "draw" program is shown in this image by Henry Lyndsey—a dodo containing the names of 2000 endangered animals (below left). It is a virtuoso demonstration of FreeHand's ability to set text along freeform lines.

a series of illustrations. There are commands for rotating, scaling, mirroring, skewing, and stretching elements. Text can be wrapped around a line or shape. Drawings thus created can be exported directly, as **EPS** (**Encapsulated PostScript**) files to page-layout packages such as QuarkXPress or Adobe InDesign. There they can be combined with text originated on a word-processing system.

Clip art (Fig. **3.33**) is royalty-free artwork that can be bought ready-made and en masse on a CD-ROM or from the internet and incorporated into your layouts. It has always been around in book form, to be copied at will, but lately has proliferated. Some is good, most is awful, and none of it is either original or unique. It should be used with discretion, and never in work where clients are under the impression that they are paying for original artwork. Clip-art maps can usually be copied with confidence, especially when they are to be customized in a program such as Adobe Illustrator.

Three-dimensional design programs are also increasingly being used by illustrators, especially in comic books, where cartoon characters need to be viewed from different angles and against different backgrounds (Fig. **3.34**). Programs such as DAZ's Bryce can be used to create fantastic fractal landscapes for use as backgrounds.

Increasingly so, illustrators are creating work on computers—images that can be shipped directly to page make-up programs with no intermediate artwork needed. There will always be a place for original illustration and photography, however, produced using traditional materials. Today's graphic designer needs to know how to make the best use of both.

Copyright

What is **copyright**? Put simply, it is the right to prevent copying of your work. It protects the form your work takes, but not the underlying idea. Copyright for designers cuts both ways—it protects your intellectual property, but also protects the creator of the piece of work you may be tempted to copy.

Copyright is a property right—that of intellectual property—in that it can be bought, sold, inherited, willed, and leased. You can assign it, license it, or you can sell it. In some countries, such as Germany, however, copyright is an inalienable right, which cannot be bought or sold.

How do you acquire and protect your copyright? Well, you don't really have to, as the only criterion to qualify in the case of an artistic work is that it must be original. Work that you copy (your own, of course) has a new copyright in each version you do. The main exception is in "work made for hire," when you are in full-time employment and in which case the employer, and not the employee, is considered to be the creator. It is advisable, however, to append a copyright notice to your work thus: © 2009 John Doe.

3.33 Samples of digital clip art from the Clipper Creative Art Service.

ILLUSTRATION   105

3.34 Pepe Moreno used 3D graphics combined with paint software to produce the artwork for the DC Comics graphic novel *Batman: Digital Justice*.

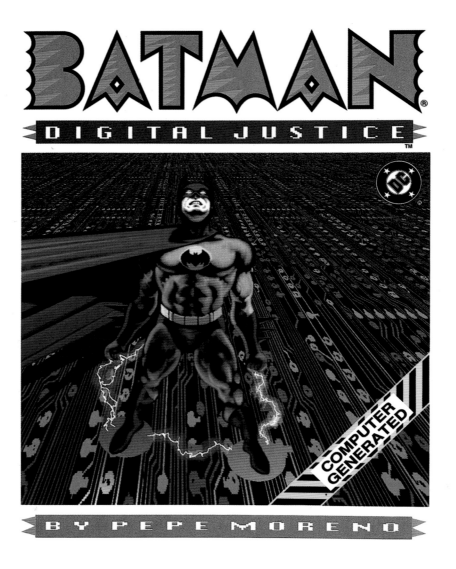

In the United States, copyright protection is provided under Title 17 of the US Code and the 1976 Copyright Act. In addition, certain authors of works of visual art have the rights of attribution and integrity. While federal copyright law is fairly specific, state variations make nationwide advice difficult to provide. The law was written before computers became commonplace, but computer-generated work is covered.

Failure to protect copyrights can lead to fines of up to $10,000 per infringement. Some state laws provide even greater fines. However, copyright law does provide some protection to intermediaries such as designers and printers. But the burden falls on you to prove that you were misled, a sometimes difficult and expensive proposition.

Measures such as requiring clients to affirm that the materials you are about to incorporate into a design are in the public domain, that the copyright is owned by the customer, or that the customer has received the copyright owner's permission to print the work can all help establish proof of innocence.

Include a release in your contracts (the US Copyright Office website, www.copyright.gov, provides an example), and be certain that the customer understands the significance and the consequences for you and them if a copyright violation charge is brought.

In the United Kingdom, the 1988 Copyright, Designs and Patents Act gave works of art new moral rights, aimed at protecting their paternity (the right of the creator of the work to be credited as such) and integrity (the right not to have the work subjected to derogatory treatment or to be falsely attributed). The right to be identified as the author of the work can be asserted but cannot be assigned to anyone else. It can however be waived in writing.

How long does copyright last? Until 70 years after your death in most cases. Your children and grandchildren will probably be able to earn a fortune out of your work even if you don't!

Summary

Illustrations can be line or tone. If tone, they must be screened to convert the image into a pattern of dots for reproduction. Artwork can be drawn or painted conventionally, or created on a computer. Photographs can come in one of three forms: as reflection copy prints, as transmission copy transparencies, or as digital images. Before origination, they will need to be scaled, and maybe cropped, so as to fit the size and shape of their position on the page layout. And they can be manipulated by computer, either on the level of merely correcting or changing colors, or in terms of undergoing more drastic treatment, using the image as a basis for a photomontage.

Whether you choose the mechanical or the digital method for the production of your illustrations will depend quite a lot on the processes being employed, and on the type of project. Conventionally drawn line work, such as cartoon illustrations, will have a sparkle and a fluidity that a computer program is unable to replicate. On the other hand, the consistent line weights and perfect geometry of a computer "draw" program are ideal for technical diagrams. But as desktop scanners come down in price, a hybrid approach may rule: scanning in line art drawn conventionally, to be manipulated further on the computer and output as a file ready to be placed in a page-layout program.

The constraints on black-and-white and color illustrations are different. If you are using a computer, it is easy enough to scan in black-and-white artwork and place it straight on to your page layout. Where photographs are concerned, the desired quality will be the decisive factor as you choose between scanning in a coarsely screened picture or leaving its origination to the repro house. With a computer-generated or stored illustration, there is the distinct advantage that the all-important artwork cannot get lost or damaged in the mail. It can even be sent to its destination via the internet. And once the image is inside the system, it can be used over and over in different shapes and forms.

For color work, illustrations sometimes arrive in the form of transparencies, though original artwork can produce much better results. Whichever form they take, they must be flexible enough to be wrapped around the drum of the scanner at the repro house or printer. Desktop scanners can be used to input images intended for photomontage and other forms of creative retouching. Alternatively, the scanner can produce low-resolution scans to indicate positions and crops for illustrations that will later be processed at the repro house, on better-quality equipment, as we shall discover in Chapter 5.

You must be aware that colors can mean different things to different cultures, and the psychology and symbolism of color can affect our behavior. We must also take into account the needs of disabled people, especially the elderly and people with color blindness.

Computers have made it easy for anyone with the right skills and software to copy and modify text, artwork, and photographic images. As a result, knowing all there is to know about copyright has never been more important.

ILLUSTRATION   107

Stefan Sagmeister

"Witty and provocative, mixing sexuality with the sinister,
his technique is often simple to the point of banality."

Manifesto
How Good is Good?

Good Design + Good Cause = Good
"Most current graphic design done by professional design companies is used to promote or sell, which is fine, but design can also do so much more."

Design can unify
"Francis Hopkinson, a writer, artist, and a signatory of the Declaration of Independence designed the American Flag (never got paid for it though)."

Design can help us remember
"The Towers of Light by Julian LaVerdiere and Paul Myoda, at this moment proposed as a temporary memorial down at Ground Zero, are a beautiful emotional response. They are ghost limbs; we can feel them even though they are not there anymore."

Design can make someone feel better
"After we designed the CD cover for the Rolling Stones there was quite some press interest in Europe and a number of Austrian and German TV stations came to New York for an interview. This was just around the time my Mom was celebrating her 70th birthday. I made a T-shirt saying 'Dear Mom! Have a great birthday,' and wore it during the interview. The Austrian station agreed to air the interviews exactly on her birthday. Mom felt better."

Design can help people rally behind a cause
"There is this entire subsection in design, the peace or environmental poster, where hundreds are actually printed, but only dozens go up in the street and the rest are distributed to design competitions. This of course does NOT help people rally behind a cause, it only helps the ego of the designer."

Design can make us more tolerant
"Winter Sorbeck, design teacher and fictional main character in Chip Kidd's new novel *The Cheese Monkeys*, says at one point: 'Uncle Sam is commercial art, the American flag is graphic design. Commercial art makes you BUY things, graphic design GIVES you ideas.'"

"If I'm able to do that, to give ideas, that WOULD be a good reason to get out of bed in the morning."

Edited from a lecture to the AIGA National Conference in Washington, 23 March 2002.

New York-based Stefan Sagmeister was born in 1962 in Bregenz, in the Austrian Alps. He is best known for designing album covers for Lou Reed, the Rolling Stones, and David Byrne.

Sagmeister studied at Vienna's University of Applied Arts and in 1987 received a Fulbright scholarship to study at the Pratt Institute in New York. After returning to Austria for compulsory military service, he moved to Hong Kong in 1991 to work with Leo Burnett. In 1993, he returned to New York to work at Tibor Kalman's M&Co design firm, but when Kalman retired to Rome to edit *Colors* magazine for the Benetton Group, he founded his own studio, Sagmeister Inc. He followed Kalman's advice to keep his company small with a team of three: himself, a designer (since 1996, Icelander Hjalti Karlsson), and an intern. His first CD cover was for a friend's album, H.P. Zinker's *Mountains of Madness*, which won Sagmeister the first of his four Grammy nominations. Lou Reed invited him to design his 1996 album *Set the Twilight Reeling*, and the following year, Sagmeister depicted David Byrne as a plastic GI Joe-style doll on the cover of *Feelings*.

When asked to design the poster for an AIGA lecture he was giving at Cranbrook near Detroit in 1999, he had the details carved onto his torso with an X-acto knife and the result photographed. That poster sums up Sagmeister's style: witty and provocative, mixing sexuality with the sinister. His technique is often simple to the point of banality, for example spelling out words from roughly cut strips of cloth for a 1999 brochure for the fashion designer, Anni Kuan. He has also designed branding, graphics, and packaging for clients such as AIGA, the Guggenheim Museum, Zumtobel, and Time Warner.

In 2000, Sagmeister treated himself to a long-promised year off to concentrate on experimental projects and his book *Sagmeister: Made You Look*, sub-titled "Another self-indulgent design monograph (practically everything we have ever designed including the bad stuff.)"

Solo shows have been mounted in Zurich, Vienna, New York, Berlin, Tokyo, Osaka, Prague, Cologne, and Seoul. He teaches in the graduate department of the School of Visual Art in New York and has been appointed as the Frank Stanton Chair at the Cooper Union School of Art, New York.

He received a Grammy Award in 2005 in the Best Boxed or Special Limited Edition Package category for art directing *Once in a Lifetime* by Talking Heads.

Resources

www.sagmeister.com
Stefan Sagmeister, *Things I have learned in my life so far*, Abrams, New York, 2008
Peter Hall, Stefan Sagmeister and Chee Pearlman, *Sagmeister: Made You Look*, Booth-Clibborn Editions, London, 2004
Stefan Sagmeister, *Visible Music: CD Jacket Graphics*, Gingko Press, CA, 2000
Stefan Sagmeister, *Postcard Graphics: The Best Advertising and Promotion Design*, Rockport, MA, 1997
Adrian Shaughnessy, *How To Be a Graphic Designer Without Losing Your Soul*, Princeton Architectural Press, New York, 2005 (Foreword by Stefan Sagmeister)

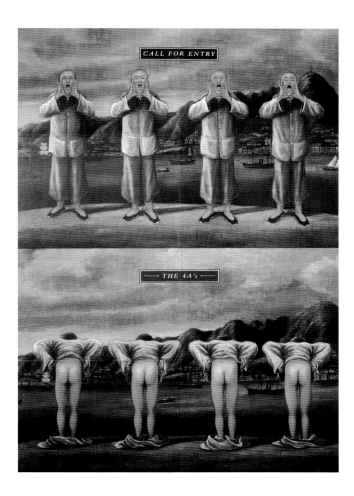

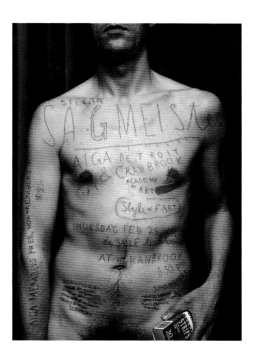

Poster for AIGA lecture in Cranbrook, 1999, 27½ x 39 in (690 x 990 mm). Sagmeister tried to visualize the pain that seems to accompany most of their design projects. Studio intern Martin cut all the type into Sagmeister's skin. Yes, he said, "it did hurt real bad." Art Direction: Stefan Sagmeister. Photography: Tom Schierlitz. Client: Aiga Detroit.

Call for Entries poster for 4As (Association of Accredited Advertising Agencies) awards, Hong Kong, 1992. The four naked As created quite a scandal in Hong Kong. It was discussed for a month in the trade press and was shown on the cover of the South China Morning Post, Hong Kong's largest newspaper. Young and Rubicam attemped to organize a boycott of the show. At the end participation was up 25 percent and it won a gold award. Art Direction & Concept: Stefan Sagmeister. Design: Peter Rae.

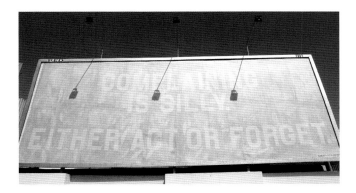

Complaining is silly. Either act or forget. 2005, photogram on newsprint, 26 x 10 ft (8 x 3 m). After "exposing" the newsprint on their studio roof in New York, the poster was shipped to Lisbon where under further exposure to the sun, it slowly faded away. Design: Stefan Sagmeister. Typography: Matthias Ernstberger, Richard The.

Once in a Lifetime by Talking Heads, 2003, 16 ¾ x 5 ½ in (425 x 135 mm). Containing three CDs and a DVD, this panoramic collection features cover paintings by the Russian contemporary artists Vladimir Dubossarsky and Alexander Vinogradov. They contain all of Sagmeister's favorite visual icons: babies, bears, severed limbs, and naked people (except a guy in boxers on the inside front cover). The format allows for easy storage in standard record store bins and will also obstruct access to all CDs behind it. It contains over 100 rare photographs and extensive essays. Art direction: Stefan Sagmeister. Design: Matthias Ernstberger.

Computers & their Peripherals

Not so long ago, a graphic designer's studio would contain a drawing board, a Grant enlarger, and maybe a wax-coater, along with a toolkit comprising scalpels, technical pens, and sheets of Letraset rub-down lettering. Today the landscape has changed completely, with everything the designer needs—and more—all contained within a computer system.

The computer brings control and flexibility to the designer's desktop. It won't do the designing for you, of course. A computer is merely a tireless tool, to be put to work as and when necessary, alongside the pencil and layout pad. It is an extremely powerful tool, nevertheless, and it is waiting to be used.

In the past few years much of the equipment described in this chapter has become commonplace in designers' studios. It is important, therefore, to know how it works, what it is capable of, what its limitations are, and what trade-offs you will be expected to make. Thus forearmed, you will be able to take on the suppliers' salespeople, and make sound buying decisions that will ensure a successful implementation.

Simply having a computer does not make you into a better designer. If you need any evidence, take a look at the advertisements at the back of any computer magazine, especially for dealers and bureaux. Those people have offices bristling with computers, use all the software daily, and possess just about every font you could imagine. And still their ads look terrible.

But a good designer, armed with a computer, can do wondrous things. The main advantage is almost total control of your design, from initial concept to finished product. There is a down side to this, though. If it is control you want, you'll have to take responsibility for all your design decisions—you won't be able to blame the typesetter, for instance, if you don't get the setting you thought you'd specified. And you'll have to learn something about the way computers work. This chapter will take you some of the way.

Finally, the health and safety aspects of a computer installation are discussed, so as to safeguard the well-being of the most valuable component of the production system—the graphic designer.

Hardware and software

First, some basic definitions. The stuff you can see and touch—the computer and all the ancillary equipment, the peripherals—is the **hardware**. **Software** is the unseen factor of a system which supplements the brainpower and experience of the designer and makes the hardware come alive. It arrives on a **CD-ROM** in an over-large box, or as a download via the internet, and is copied on to the computer's own **hard disk**. (The originals are kept in a safe place, in case anything should go wrong with your hard disk.)

The word **system** is used a lot in computer parlance. It is a catch-all term, and usually means "everything"—the hardware and software together, as in a digital prepress system. The software that looks after the internal workings of the computer is called the **operating system**. And an item of software can be referred to as a program, a package, or, again, a system.

Most people recognize a computer from the name it has on the front: it may be an IBM PC, a Dell (Fig. **4.1**), or an Apple Macintosh (Fig. **4.2**). These are all **personal computers**. A personal computer is a self-contained system that sits on the desktop, that you do not have to share, and that is powerful enough to do the job you have in mind.

Although the abbreviation PC stands for personal computer, it refers to a specific class of personal computer, namely the original IBM PC and compatible computers from suppliers such as HP Compaq and Dell.

The Apple Macintosh is a personal computer, but not a PC. It operates in a fundamentally different way to the IBM PC and compatibles. Programs designed for the PC will not work on a Macintosh, and vice versa, although versions of a program such as QuarkXpress and InDesign are available for both kinds of computer and will operate in similar ways. It is possible to emulate PC software on a Mac, and generally a Mac will find it easier to read PC files than vice versa.

Software

There are many levels of software inside the computer which are mainly invisible to the user. At the lowest level, you need a program built into the machine that loads (or boots, as in "pull yourself up by the bootstraps") all the other programs.

At the next level is the operating system. This looks after the computer's internal workings, particularly the operation of the hard-disk memory. It is often specific to the make of computer: PCs use Microsoft Windows. The Macintosh's operating system is just a number, such as OS X (ten). Other PCs use Linux, a public-domain operating system for PCs based on AT&T's Unix. The operating system comes with the computer when you buy it, and upgrades can be bought on CD-ROMs and installed on the hard disk. You usually see evidence of the operating system at work only when you switch

4.1 This Dell Precision 490 is a PC running Windows XP Professional, built around a 2GHz dual-core Intel Xeon processor. The UltraSharp 2407WFP-HC 24 in widescreen flat-panel LCD monitor has a maximum resolution of 1920 × 1200 dpi.

4.2 An Apple Mac Pro combines two of Intel's 45nm Quad-Core Xeon processors running up to 3.2GHz with up to 4Tbytes of internal storage. It is shown here with a 30 in (762 mm) Cinema HD screen capable of 2560 × 1600 dpi resolution.

the computer on. It checks that everything is in working order, then awaits your instructions. If anything is wrong, it will put an error message on the screen and you will have to refer to the manual and take remedial action.

The most visible level of software is the **application**, which you buy on CD-ROM, along with an operating manual, or download from the internet. Applications software converts the general-purpose computer, which cannot do anything, into the kind of system the user wants. It can be one of a number of things: a spreadsheet, a page-layout package, paint software, or a computer game. Software suppliers each have their own methods of numbering versions. It is important to know which version you have, to ensure compatibility, for example, between your program and the one at the **service bureau**. New versions of software packages are being released all the time—some are really significant improvements on the previous release, some are merely "fixes" that correct bugs.

A **bug** is an error in the program, hidden away in the depths of the computer code—a mistake made by the programmer. The term was coined in the late 1950s by computer pioneer Grace Hopper, who found a real insect interfering with the workings of her computer.

All programs have bugs, just as all computers crash and do inexplicable things from time to time. Thus there is all the more reason to save your current job to the hard disk as frequently as possible, rather than leave it in the short-term

RAM (**random access memory**; see p. 114) memory. A few but by no means all programs do this automatically. It is a good idea also to back up (copy) anything important on to an external hard disk or a CD-ROM at the end of every session. Then put them in a safe place.

A **virus** is worse than a bug—it is a self-replicating piece of mischief, introduced surreptitiously into your computer by malicious computer addicts called "hackers."

Software is written in a programming language. The computer's own language is called **machine code**, which is expressed in hexadecimal numbers (numbers in base 16). It is gibberish to all but the most hardened hacker. Computers "think" in binary code (using the numbers in base 2: 0 or 1; on or off), but this is too cumbersome for humans to get to grips with. Binary, however, is conveniently convertible to hexadecimal. So-called high-level languages such as Basic (beginners' all-purpose symbolic instruction code) and C use English words, arranged using simple grammar, which is later "compiled" or "interpreted" into machine code. Even higher-level languages are sometimes available—so-called scripting languages—so that users can customize (adapt) the applications software to their own preferred ways of working.

But today it is completely unnecessary to learn a programming language. Today's operating systems contain an "intuitive" **GUI** (**graphical user interface**; Fig. **4.3**) which simplifies communication between the human and the computer. Commands are chosen from lists called **menus**, and most things can be done using **tools**. A pen tool, for example, allows you to draw lines on the screen. The user selects tools by pointing at small pictures called **icons**, using a device such as a **mouse** (more of which on pp. 117–9).

4.3 This screenshot shows a WIMP (windows, icons, mouse, and pull-down menus) GUI (graphical user interface): Apple's Mac OS X version 10.5, codenamed Leopard.

The processor

The "brain" of a computer is usually housed in a featureless box, perhaps with a CD/DVD slot in the front, and with the odd light flashing to show that the hard disk is working. The display screen rests on the box. The processor may also come in a "tower" that stands on the floor or on the desk, next to the display.

At the heart of the computer is the **CPU** (**central processing unit**), comprising a microprocessor silicon chip or set of chips (chipset). The main manufacturer is Intel, who have always supplied the chips for the PC and who now supply the chips for the Apple Macintosh.

Raw speed in computer terms is measured by the internal **clock speed**. Clock speed is measured in Hz (cycles per second). For example, a Macintosh Classic built around a 68000 CPU chip ran at 8 MHz (megahertz), a PowerMac 9500 ran at 200 MHz, and a G5 runs at 3.2 GHz (gigahertz).

At every tick of the clock, the CPU processes an instruction, or part of one. These are not the instructions you key into the computer, though. The computer breaks down your complicated instructions into millions of simple ones, which it calculates very quickly.

Computers for graphics applications have special requirements. Compared with text, pictures take up enormous amounts of memory and to move them around, the CPUs on these systems require some help. They are therefore augmented with various speed-increasing subsystems—such as printed circuit-boards (PCBs), or cards, to control the color graphics on the screen.

All this, however, is pure speed, and, like the top figure on an automobile's speedometer, is an abstract quantity. Some computers may be able to redraw the screen after a tricky manipulation more quickly than others. But how quickly a designer actually completes a given job ultimately depends both on the efficacy of the software and on the proficiency of the operator.

ROM, RAM, and flash memory

Computers have different types of chip-based memory. **ROM** (**read-only memory**) chips have instructions manufactured into them, and they cannot be altered. These instructions remain on the chip even when the computer is switched off. ROM chips contain some of the computer's operating system, and give a computer its "personality."

Local memory, containing the immediate job in hand, is in the form of RAM (random access memory) chips which are wiped clean each time the computer is switched off (Fig. **4.4**). This, of course, includes any form of power failure, however fleeting. The amount of ram a computer has available is measured in **bytes**, each equal to eight **bits** (bit is short for binary digit). A Kbyte, k, or kilobyte is not a thousand bytes as you may have expected, but 1024 bytes, which is equal to 2^{10}, (2 to the power of 10, or $2 \times 2 \times 2 \times 2 \times 2 \times 2 \times 2 \times 2 \times 2 \times 2$). A megabyte, written 1 Mbyte, is more than a million bytes. A gigabyte, or Gbyte, is more than 1000 Mbytes.

The reason for the strange number 1024 is as follows. Computers count in binary numbers, 0s and 1s. (Hexadecimal, referred to earlier, is easily converted to binary and is more convenient for computer scientists to deal with.) Thus, to a computer, "round numbers" are always powers of 2 (such as 4, 8, 16, 32, 64, 128, 256, 512, and 1024), and that is why you will often see these particular numbers associated with computers.

ASCII (**American Standard Code for Information Interchange**), the worldwide format for encoding alphanumeric text, allocates a single byte per character. This chapter contains over 64.5 kbytes of information. The hard disk on my G5 iMac is capable of containing 250 Gbytes, and that is quite modest by graphic design standards.

Saved data is stored in a hard-disk drive. It is advisable to backup important data to CDs, DVDs, or external drives.

External hard disks can be added to your system. They are useful for overflow, archiving, and backing up your data. CD-ROM drives, now commonly built into Macs and PCs, are compact-disc players for computers which can hold up to 700 Mbytes of information over several sessions. DVD-ROM drives burn DVDs (digital versatile disks) capable of storing over 5 Gbytes of data.

Data travels round the computer on "buses," which are like clumps of wires. There are two main buses: the memory bus and the data bus. A 32-bit computer has a data bus 32 bits wide, i.e. 32 bits of data can travel around the computer and be processed at the same time. The "width" of the bus determines how much data can be processed at each tick of the clock, and how much RAM can be managed.

A typical home PC from the early 1980s had an 8-bit processor and a 16-bit memory bus. It could thus address only 2^{16} permutations of 0s and 1s, which equals 64k possible memory locations in RAM. Modern processors can handle several Tbytes (terabytes). Computers also commonly have "cache memory." This is a portion of ram that holds the most recently used data from the hard disk ready for further action, thus increasing the apparent speed of access to the user.

A third kind of chip-based memory is **flash memory**, a technology that is primarily used in digital camera memory cards and portable USB (Universal Serial Bus) devices used for general back-up and transfer of data between computers. It was invented by Dr Fujio Masuoka in 1984, while working for Toshiba and so-called because the erasure process reminded a colleague of his of a camera flash. Intel produced the first commercial chips in 1988. Unlike ROM, it can be electrically erased and reprogrammed and, unlike RAM, the slower flash memory needs no power to maintain the information stored in the chip. Flash memory devices have no mechanical parts so are much more durable than hard disk drives, but at present they are more expensive per gigabyte.

VRAM (**video random-access memory**) contains the current image in the form of a bitmap of pixels (picture elements;). It comprises several layers or planes, with one bit (a 1 or a 0) stored for each pixel on each plane. The number of planes, and hence the number of bits allocated to each pixel, determines how many colors or "grayscale" shades the displayed pixel can be.

A mono screen, without grayscales, had one bit per pixel. An 8-plane system can handle 2^8 (256) different colors or grayscales. A 24-plane system can display 16.8 million, a number considered sufficient to produce realistic-looking images. A 32-bit system has 24 bits allocated to color, the rest for other things—on a Mac, for example, the extra eight bits are called the "alpha channel" and are available for animation and masking effects.

Displays

The computer's display is the window through which we view whatever is being designed, and through which we interact with the software. The output quality is dependent on the output device—whether it be a low-resolution laser printer or a high-resolution imagesetter—not on the quality of the screen.

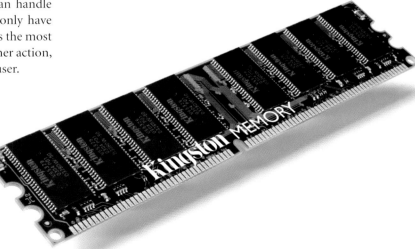

4.4 RAM comes in the form of tiny silicon chips which are encased in plastic. In a Mac, they are mounted in lines on long, thin, printed circuit-boards and are called SIMMs (single inline memory modules) or DIMMs (dual inline memory modules). This is Kingston DDR (Double Data Rate) SDRAM (Synchronous Dynamic Random-Access Memory).

4.5 The LaCie 526 is a professional prepress flat LCD screen with built-in hood. It has a wide color gamut, representing 98.5 percent of ISO coated stock and 95 percent of Adobe's RGB range. With a 25.5 in diagonal screen in 16:10 format, it has a resolution of 1920 × 1200 dpi. The included LaCie Blue Eye pro software for color management includes automatic hardware calibration and ICC profile creation, and ambient light analysis.

Conventional computer displays were based on the CRT (cathode ray tube), the tube that takes up most of the space in a television set. Computer and television screens are called raster displays, from the Latin *rastrum*, or rake. The electron gun at the back of the CRT scans the whole screen in horizontal lines, top to bottom, usually 60 times a second (60 Hz). Each scan line is chopped into chunks called pixels (picture elements). Pixels are the screen equivalent of dots (see p. 85), and, as discussed earlier, each pixel on the screen is described by one or more bits in the graphics card or VRAM. The resolution (fineness) of a raster display is measured by the number of pixels horizontally by the number of scan lines vertically. The resolution of a 17-inch display is typically 1280 × 1024. A multiscan screen can display different resolutions: from 640 × 480 to 2560 × 1600, for example.

Flat-panel **LCD** (**liquid crystal display**) screens, originally found in laptop computers, are now widely available for the desktop. These take up less space on the desk, are flicker-free, and use up less power than CRTs.

Meanwhile, software optical illusions such as **anti-aliasing** are used to improve the perceived resolution of screens. Anti-aliasing smooths out the staircase effect seen on sloping lines.

It does so by coloring the pixels around the diagonals that actually define the line or edge in subtle shades of the current foreground and background colors.

If you are doing lots of design work you will need a large-format display: 17-inch (432 mm), 21-inch (533 mm), or even larger. Prepress operators and designers doing lots of color work will need the highest-possible quality of screen to make sure the transmitted RGB color of the screen faithfully predicts the CMYK color of the scan and finished printed page. The LaCie 526 monitor (Fig. **4.5**) is a professional prepress screen with an integral hood to prevent reflections and glare. Blue Eye is its matching display calibrator that adjusts the monitor and for color management creates a ColorSync profile.

The color coming from a color monitor, being transmitted light, will never be the same as the color reflected from a printed page (see pp. 92–3), and the color output will change as the phosphors age. To make the colors on the screen as faithful as possible, you must **color calibrate** your screen regularly, recalibrating for color "temperature" appropriate to the application and local lighting conditions. Color management is the controlled matching and mapping of color representations from devices with different color gamuts, such as scanners, digital cameras, monitors, and printers. The ICC (International Color Consortium) was established in 1993 by eight industry vendors (including Adobe and Apple) to create and promote an open, vendor-neutral, cross-platform color management system. The ICC specification has since been approved as an International Standard—ISO 15076. When a device is calibrated, a profile is created. This profile is then embedded into the image file, so the device's color space information can then be read and interpreted by any ICC-aware application. Some colors, which otherwise wouldn't be represented on the output device will need to be rearranged inside of the target gamut. For example, a saturated blue seen on an RGB monitor cannot be reproduced on a typical CMYK printer. Conversely, the bright cyan of an inkjet printer cannot be represented on the average computer screen. Color management in Windows Vista is handled at the OS level through an ICC-compatible standard known as WCS (Windows Color System). Apple's Mac OS has long been capable of color management through ColorSync.

LCD technologies make it possible to have much thinner monitors, commonly known as flat-panel displays. LCDs work by blocking light rather than creating it, while light-emitting diode (LED) and gas plasma work by lighting up display screen positions based on the voltages at different grid intersections. They have a crisper image, and produce less heat and radiation.

So-called active-matrix LCDs depend on thin film transistors (TFT). Basically, TFTs are tiny switching transistors and capacitors. They are arranged in a matrix on a glass substrate. Liquid crystal materials emit no light of their own and most computer displays are lit with built-in fluorescent tubes above, beside, and sometimes behind the LCD. A white diffusion panel behind the LCD redirects and scatters the light evenly to ensure a uniform display.

To address a particular pixel, the proper row is switched on, and then a charge is sent down the correct column. Since all of the other rows that the column intersects are turned off, only the capacitor at the designated pixel receives a charge. The capacitor is able to hold the charge until the next refresh cycle. If the amount of voltage supplied to a crystal is carefully controlled, we can make it untwist enough to allow some light through. By doing this in very exact and very small increments, LCDs can create 256 levels of brightness per pixel.

A colour LCD has three subpixels with red, green, and blue color filters to create each color pixel. By control and variation of the voltage applied, the intensity of each subpixel can range over 256 shades. Combining the subpixels produces a possible palette of 16.8 million colors (256 shades of red × 256 shades of green × 256 shades of blue). Color displays use an enormous number of transistors. For example, a computer with a resolution of 1024 × 768 needs 2,359,296 transistors etched onto the glass! If there is a problem with any of these, it creates a "bad pixel" on the display, showing as a tiny dot.

Input devices

The input device is the means by which the designer tells the machine and the software what to do. The particular method used for human/computer interaction is called the computer's graphical user interface (GUI). Originally, you would have had to type commands using the computer's keyboard. Apple Macintosh then introduced the "point and click" approach,

4.6 Digitizing tablets are essential for precision drawing and tracing. Wacom's Intuos3 A5 Wide is available in 16:10 format and comes with the Intuos3 Grip Pen, with stroke and felt pen nibs pressure-sensitive to 1024 levels.

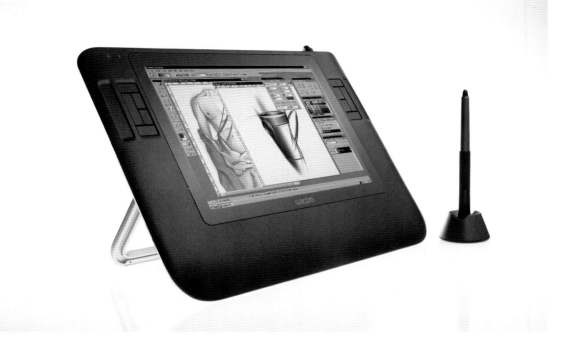

4.7 Wacom's Cintiq 12WX is described as a digital sketchbook: lightweight with an ergonomic pen with 1024 levels of pressure sensitivity and a built-in smooth, flat 21 in (310 mm) screen, with 1280 × 800 resolution and 24-bit color depth.

and almost all applications now make use of a mouse to "pull down" menus (lists of options), select icons (pictures that represent tools and documents), and open and close windows (active areas of the screen). Microsoft's Vista for PCs and X-Windows for workstations are other examples.

Computer graphics users have long abandoned exclusive use of the keyboard that always comes with the computer, in favor of other methods for manipulating on-screen cursors and entering shape descriptions. However, keyboard-entered shortcut commands remain popular with experienced so-called "power" users, who find mouse operations slow compared with typing "command-P" to print, for example.

There are many alternatives to the mouse, however. There are rolling balls, joysticks, thumbwheels, and digitizing tablets—which come with a pen-like stylus or a mouse-like puck with buttons, depending on the user's preference.

Digitizing tablets like the Wacom Intuos or Graphire (Figs. **4.6** and **4.7**) perform a dual role: they can be used to point and pick software commands from a menu, or to make pictures. Most are electromagnetic devices containing a grid of fine wires embedded into the work surface; others make use of sonic techniques to detect the position of the stylus or puck.

A digitizer with a cordless pressure-sensitive stylus, from a supplier such as Wacom, can be used with some draw-and-paint programs to create images more intuitively than with a mouse and keyboard. **Bluetooth** is a wireless protocol that is used to communicate between devices such as mobile phones and computers over a short range, usually less than 30 ft (9 m).

The conventional mechanical mouse (Fig. **4.8**) suffers from friction, or the lack of it (use a special mouse pad rather than the slippery surface of the desk, or an optical mouse). And, as it works in relative coordinates rather than absolute

4.8 Most computers come with a standard mouse, but you don't have to stay with it. The Logitech MX Air mouse works both on the desk and in the air using a combination of MEMS (microelectromechanical systems) sensors and RF (radio frequency) wireless technology.

4.9 A rolling ball is more touch-senstive than a mouse, has a smaller "footprint," and is more robust. The Logitech cordless Trackman Optical is a finger-operated trackball with "cruise control" scrolling buttons, scroll wheel, drag-lock button, and forward and back buttons.

4.10 Logitech's NuLOOQ navigator is used in conjunction with a mouse and a keyboard to manipulate images and documents. It is designed for use with the Mac versions of Adobe Illustrator, InDesign, and Photoshop. The size and shape of half a tennis ball, it sits under the non-mousing hand and a moveable rubber-like "navring" at the base allows designers to navigate images and documents, while embedded buttons (trigger-point buttons) call up frequently used tools or adjust text leading or brush size.

ones, it can get lost in space. It is fine for menu picking, but little use for drawing. Turn a mechanical mouse upside down, however, and you have the **rolling ball** (Fig. **4.9**)—a device that has been used in air-traffic control for decades. These are much more touch-sensitive than joysticks. Furthermore, they are less prone to breakage, don't trap dirt, and have a small "footprint." Other devices can augment the work of the mouse or rolling ball (Fig. **4.10**).

Digital cameras

A **digital camera** looks and feels just like a conventional analog camera, but it has one big difference. Instead of capturing an image on light-sensitive **film** that has to be sent away to be developed and printed, a digital camera (Fig. **4.11**) uses an array of CCD (charge-coupled device) sensors in order to convert the image into a form that can be stored in the camera's memory and then downloaded onto your computer.

The advantages of digital cameras are that you don't need to buy film, you don't have to wait for the film to be developed, and there is no need to scan the photograph or transparency into your computer. The original disadvantages—that digital cameras are relatively expensive, the images are generally at a lower resolution than the silver crystals of photographic film, and can only

4.11 Canon's titanium-bodied Digital IXUS 960 IS has a resolution of 12.1 Mpixels, a 3.7x zoom wide-angle lens, red-eye correction, and "face detection technology" to prevent blur and overexposure in portraits automatically.

store a limited number of images—are rapidly diminishing. If you are working away from the studio, and need to take many pictures, you will need a portable memory device to use as mass storage.

The nominal quality of a digital image is determined by its "pixel count"—the number of pixels captured by the sensor chip. For example, a 10 Mpixel camera is capable of capturing a 3872 × 2592 image, i.e. 10,036,224 pixels. This is at 72 dpi, so would convert in Photoshop to a 300 dpi file for print that is 328 × 220 mm in size. However, the camera's lens and the size of the sensor also play a part, and a compact camera may have a sensor so small that its theoretical resolution will be greater than the lens could deliver.

There are currently many different types of memory: **CompactFlash**; the largely defunct **SmartMedia**; the smaller SD (Secure Digital) card, which is almost identical to the MMC (MultiMedia Card); the Sony Memory Stick; and the xD (extreme digital) Picture Card developed by Olympus and FujiFilm. Flash memory is a solid-state non-volatile memory that can be electrically erased and reprogrammed, and it retains its data after power is removed.

Although CompactFlash cards are available up to 64 Gbytes at the time of writing, it may be preferable to buy several smaller cards in case one fails. A 1 Gbyte card will store around 100 images at 5 Mpixels, depending on the amount of JPEG compression and the selected resolution of the picture. **PictBridge** is an open standard for connecting a digital camera directly to a dye-sublimation or inkjet printer (see p. 127). Another consideration is battery life—how many photographs you can take before the camera needs recharging.

If you already have an investment in camera lenses, you can buy a digital SLR (single lens reflex) camera such as the Canon EOS (Fig. **4.12**) with all the advantages of a digital camera but with the design of a conventional film SLR and accessories.

Many digital cameras now store images as **RAW** files, rather than compressed as a JPEG or TIFF. They are termed RAW because they are not yet processed and are "digital negatives," in that like film negatives in traditional chemical photography, they are not directly usable as images, but comprise the information needed to create the image within image-processing software, such as Photoshop. RAW files are larger than compressed files, but can be tweaked later for white balance, color saturation, contrast, and sharpness. A digital camera has become one of the essential parts of the designer's toolkit.

4.12 The Canon 21-Mpixel SLR EOS-1Ds Mark III uses a 35 mm full-frame sensor to produce files that convert to 16-bit TIFFs over 100 Mbytes in size uncompressed. Dual processors enable you to take five frames per second in continuous shooting, producing up to 56 JPEGs (or 12 RAW files).

Scanners

A scanner converts flat artwork, photographs, or transparencies into a form that can be "seen" by your computer software. You will have a desktop scanner in your studio and you may also make use of the drum scanner at your repro service bureau.

Desktop scanners (Fig. **4.13**) allow the designer to input already existing images into the system—commissioned photographs, drawings, or images plagiarized from magazines. Scanned data, whether it comes from a digital camera or a scanner, is in its raw form a bitmapped image (see p. 72). A bitmap is good enough for a paint system such as Photoshop to get to work on. However, a drawing package will need some conversion, and the scanned image is best used as a background layer, to be traced over.

The most popular scanners for the studio are the single-pass flatbed desktops, which look similar to photocopiers. The early models worked like photocopiers, with a moving scan head containing a fluorescent tube slowly moving from end to end of the original. More recent models use CCDs (charge-coupled devices) to recognize and store images.

A rule of thumb says you should scan at a resolution that is twice the screen you plan to use for printing, if the image is to be reproduced at same size. So scanning with a resolution of 300 dpi will be able to produce a halftone at same size with a screen of 150 lines. Although this will be good enough for newspaper or newsletter reproduction, for other jobs a scanned image should be used for position only and replaced with a professionally screened image at the film stage.

Flatbed scanners work by scanning the image using red, green, and blue lamps and arrays of CCD sensors. Even the cheapest scanners now can scan at true (rather than interpolated) optical resolution of 600 dpi. Scanners of 1200 dpi are within the reach of most designers. Color depth of 24 bits used to be common, but this has evolved to 36 and even 42 bits. The greater the resolution and color depth, the greater the information at your disposal when you begin to manipulate the image. Some scanners offer a larger flatbed area; others may have a lamp in the lid and adaptors for scanning different sizes of transparencies.

Scanners use **USB** (universal serial bus) or **FireWire** (IEEE 1394 or I-Link) to connect to the computer; a serial bus interface standard offering high-speed communications between computers, scanners, video cameras, and hard disk drives.

FireWire can link together peripherals in a tree-like structure. It allows peer-to-peer device communication, such as communication between a scanner and a printer, to take place without using system memory or the CPU. It is also designed to support plug-and-play and hot swapping. The cable can supply up to 60 watts of power, allowing low-consumption devices to operate without a separate power cord.

The standard means of connecting a scanner to application software such as Photoshop is something called **TWAIN**, from Kipling's "The Ballad of East and West"—" . . . and never the twain shall meet . . . ," reflecting the difficulty, at the time, of connecting scanners and personal computers. The standard was first released in 1992. Because it is often seen in caps, people believed it to be an acronym, and a contest was held to come up with an expansion. None were selected, but the entry "Technology Without An Interesting Name" continues to haunt the standard!

4.13 A desktop scanner such as this A4-size ($8\frac{1}{2} \times 11\frac{11}{16}$ in) Epson Perfection V700 Photo has a resolution of 6400×9600 dpi for film scanning and 4800×9600 dpi for reflective copy and contact-sheet scanning, up to a document size of 216×297 mm (A4, US letter) and film from 35 mm to 203×254 mm. It uses a white cold-cathode fluorescent lamp to produce 48-bit output equivalent to 281.5 trillion colors. Kodak's Digital ICE (Image Correction and Enhancement) is used to remove dust and surface defects.

Paul Rand

"Visual communication of any kind . . . should be seen as the embodiment of form and function."

Manifesto
A Language of Clarity

Laszlo Moholy-Nagy, the Bauhaus typographer, photographer, and designer, described Rand as "an idealist and a realist using the language of the poet and the businessman. He thinks in terms of need and function. He is able to analyze his problems, but his fantasy is boundless."

Paul Rand advanced the cause of modernism in graphics and introduced the so-called New Typography to the US, insisting that type should carry a message rather than be used solely as decoration: "Artistic tricks divert from the effect that an artist endeavors to produce, and even excellent elements such as bullets, arrows, brackets, ornate initials, are at best superficial ornamentation unless logically employed."

His guiding principle was that "the designer experiences, perceives, analyzes, organizes, symbolizes, and synthesizes."

"Visual communication of any kind . . . should be seen as the embodiment of form and function: the integration of the beautiful and the useful."

In advertising, he encouraged art departments to raise their aesthetic standards: "Even if it is true that commonplace advertising and exhibitions of bad taste are indicative of the mental capacity of the man in the street, the opposing argument is equally valid. Bromidic advertising catering to that bad taste merely perpetuates that mediocrity and denies him one of the most easily accessible means of aesthetic development."

He was not at all happy with the new breed of deconstructivist typographers and in 1992 wrote: "Today the emphasis of style over content in what is alleged to be graphic design and communication is, at best, puzzling. Order out of chaos is not the order of the day."

Born in Brooklyn, New York, in 1914, Paul Rand took night classes at the Pratt Institute (1929–32) while a high school student in Manhattan. He later studied at Parsons School of Design (1932–3) and the Art Students' League (1933–4).

Rand's first job was for the George Switzer Agency in New York, designing lettering and packages for Squibb and other clients. In 1935, he opened his own studio on East 38th Street and a year later he began designing pages for *Apparel Arts* magazine. He became art director of *Esquire* magazine at the age of 23 and to developed an expressive 'visual dynamics" style of page layout, which broke away from narrative and symmetry. He also designed covers for *Direction*, an arts and culture magazine with an anti-Fascist focus. He moved back into advertising, working from 1941 to 1954 for an agency started by William Weintraub, a partner at *Esquire-Coronet*. Here, he pioneered a "creative team" approach, collaborating with Bernbach and clients such as Dubonnet, Lee Hats, and Auto Car Corporation.

Rand was influenced by the European modernist design of De Stijl and Bauhaus and merged their visual vocabulary with American culture to form his recognizable bright and witty style. He combined elements from modern art—color, texture, and collage—with contemporary typography in his advertisements for Orbach's department store, Playtex, and El Producto Cigars, as well as on book jackets and covers for Alfred A. Knopf and other publishers.

In the 1950s, Rand concentrated on logos and trademark design and he is perhaps best remembered for his corporate identity for IBM. He was hired as graphic design consultant and produced typography and icons for stationery, packaging, signage, and publications, plus the design guides on how they should be used. Other clients included Westinghouse (1960), United Parcel Service (1961), and American Broadcasting Company (1962).

Rand was a prolific communicator and writer, publishing his *Thoughts on Design* in 1947 (re-issued and revised as *Paul Rand: A Designer's Art* in 1985). His career as educator started at Cooper Union in 1942. He taught at the Pratt Institute in 1946 and from 1956 he was Professor of Graphic Design at Yale School of Art and Architecture until his retirement in 1985, when he wrote two other memoirs: *Design, Form and Chaos* (1993) and *From Lascaux to Brooklyn* (1996). He died aged 82 in 1996 in Norwalk, Connecticut. His work is in the public collections of the Museum of Modern Art in New York, the Library of Congress, Zurich's Kunstgewerbeschule Museum and the Cooper-Hewitt Museum of the Smithsonian Institution in New York.

Resources

American Icons: www.areaofdesign.com/americanicons/rand.htm
Paul Rand, *Paul Rand: A Designer's Art*, Yale University Press, New Haven, CT, 2001 (paperback edition)
Paul Rand, *Design, Form and Chaos*, Yale University Press, New Haven, CT, 1993
Paul Rand, *From Lascaux to Brooklyn*, Yale University Press, New Haven, CT, 1996
Anne and Paul Rand, *Sparkle and Spin: A book about words*, Chronicle Books, San Francisco, 2006
Steven Heller, *Paul Rand*, Phaidon Press, London and New York, 2000

IBM's simple typographic logo, in a typeface called Beton Bold, replaced the globe of the International Business Machines Corporation in 1947, as the company began to move into computers. In 1956, Paul Rand changed the font to City Medium, and the letters took on a more solid, grounded, and balanced appearance. In 1972, Rand added the horizontal "scan" stripes to lighten and unify the heavy slab letters, and suggest speed and dynamism. With some variations in color, the logo is still in use today.

In 1961, after the success of the IBM branding, Rand was invited to update the UPS logo. He kept the shield shape from past logos, but added a "package" with string and bow, instantly identified by his eight-year-old daughter, Catherine, as a "present" (above left). In 2003, Rand's design was replaced by a 3D emblem by FutureBrand in New York (above right).

The almost Bauhaus rebranding of the American Broadcasting Company logo (1962) comprises a simple rhythmic combination of four circles. It is still in use today.

For the book cover of H. L. Mencken's *Prejudices* in 1958, Rand was supplied with an uninspiring portrait, which he incorporated into a playful modernist collage using paper cut-outs with informal hand-lettering. Note that Rand always signed his book covers prominently.

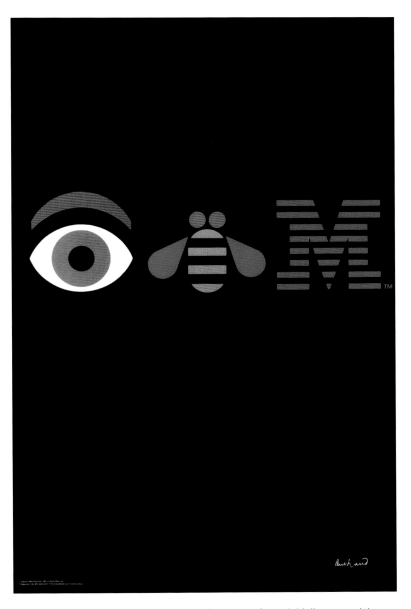

The rebus (visual pun) of Eye Bee M for Rand's poster of 1981 initially annoyed the managers at IBM for its irreverence, but it has since become a design icon.

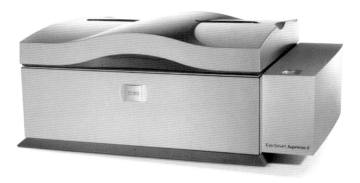

4.14 A professional flatbed scanner such as this Kodak EverSmart Supreme II can perform 120 scans an hour at an optical resolution of 5600 dpi everywhere on the scanner glass. An 8 × 10 in (203 × 254 mm) image can be scanned in several strips at a resolution of 14000 dpi. Oil mounting can be used when images are to be enlarged by more than 800 percent, or if the original is scratched.

High-end scanners (Fig. **4.14**)—the kind found at your repro service bureau—come in two distinct types: flatbed (like studio desktop scanners) and the more traditional drum scanners (Fig. **4.15**). It is important to mount the artwork very precisely. With a flatbed scanner, you just lay the artwork on the glass plate or place transparencies into a carrier with pre-cut frames and you're ready to scan. Mounting film or flexible artwork on a drum scanner is more complicated;

the drum spins very quickly, so you must secure the film well. Oil mounting (which reduces problems created by dust and scratches on the film) can be used on drum scanners: bending the film around the drum creates tension which holds it evenly against the glass. Oil mounting is also possible on some of the top-end flatbed scanners.

Flatbed scanners use a line of CCDs (charge-coupled devices), just like studio desktop scanners. Drum scanners use photomultiplier tubes. Separations are made by a beam splitter, which divides the light transmitted through the transparency or off the artwork into its three color components. Each beam goes through a filter corresponding to one of the additive primaries (see p. 90) and is detected by a photocell. These signals are then converted into CMYK by color-correction software.

When changing levels of magnification, both types of scanner maintain a 1:1 aspect ratio. To do this, drum scanners change the rate at which the optics scan across the drum. At the same time, they change the frequency with which the photomultiplier samples the image. Scanning at a lower rate captures finer lines horizontally; higher-frequency sampling keeps the vertical density the same. Flatbed scanners use lenses to map a smaller or larger area of the film on to the CCDs: when a smaller area is captured, a shorter movement by the stepper motor keeps the density of pixels the same vertically and horizontally.

Until all photographers use digital cameras, there will still be a need to scan in slides or negatives. High-end flatbed and drum scanners are happiest with large-format transparencies: 35 mm slides are small and often come in mounts that lift the emulsion away from the glass and the optimum focusing distance. Dedicated slide scanners are optimized for this kind of work and can deliver high-quality scans quickly (Fig. **4.16**).

4.15 The ICG 380 drum scanner has 12000 dpi optical resolution with a 2000 rpm drum speed. Its enlargement range is continuously variable between 20 and 6000 percent. A one Gbyte file can be scanned in 12 minutes. The A3 external drum is designed for scanning all traditional media, including transparencies, reflection artwork, line artwork, and color negatives. Maximum scan area is 18¾ × 12⅝ in (476 × 320 mm).

4.16 Film scanners, such as this Nikon Super Coolscan 9000 ED, produce scanned images of 35 mm slides and film strips, positive or negative, black and white, or color at an optical resolution of 4000 dpi. Kodak's Digital ICE (Image Correction and Enhancement) technology is built in and works by reading the surface defects of color film, such as dust and scratches, and recording them in a separate channel.

Output devices: laser printers and imagesetters

A graphic designer will be most likely to output to a nearby laser or inkjet printer for proofing, and send a PostScript file to a repro service bureau for imagesetting on film or direct to an offset litho plate. In addition, many of the output devices on the following pages can be used for undemanding short printing runs.

Laser printers work on a similar principle to laser photocopiers (Fig. **4.17**). In a photocopier, the light reflected from the white areas of an image causes a rotating drum charged with static electricity to lose its charge, so the toner doesn't stick. In a laser printer, however, there is no "original," so a laser draws a negative image on to the drum, removing charge from the white areas.

Black-and-white laser printers are great for proofing, producing artwork for publications such as newsletters, and printing short runs of simple documents. Color laser copiers have fallen in price and are increasingly being used for proofing. Most are 600 dpi; some are 1200 dpi or even 2400 dpi.

The original phototypesetters could only set type. With the introduction of PostScript came the imagesetter, which could output graphics and pictures as well as type (Fig. **4.18**). The ability to output all page elements in position streamlined the traditional camera and stripping operations, paving the way for totally digital prepress.

The resolution of an imagesetter is measured in dpi (dots per inch), and these should not be confused with halftone dots, which are measured in lpi (lines per inch). A halftone dot is a cluster of many imagesetter dots (which, to avoid confusion, we'll call spots). An imagesetter might deliver a resolution of up to 4876 dpi—in other words, 847 distinct spots can be laid along a line one inch long with their edges just touching. Most, however, will output at 1200 (actually 1219) or 2400 (actually 2438) dpi.

The size of a laser's spot cannot easily be altered, and so halftone dots are built up by overlapping the spots (Fig. **4.19**). The **addressability** of an imagesetter is the accuracy with which the centers of the spots can be placed in proximity with each other. Thus an addressability of 2540 dpi means that the centers of two spots can be positioned $\frac{1}{2540}$th of an inch apart. So, when we talk about resolution, we are more correctly talking about addressability. Other important parameters are the dot (spot) size, measured in **mils** (thousandths of an inch) or **micrometers** (aka μm or microns—millionths of a meter) and the repeatability, also measured in mils or microns, which is a measure of how well separations will register together.

We are told that the higher the resolution (but read: addressability), the better the print quality. But this is not always the case: there comes a point where there is so much overlapping

4.17 This Xerox Phaser 7760 color laser printer has a resolution of 1200 dpi and can print 35 pages of A3 (11¹¹⁄₁₆ × 16½ in) per minute.

4.18 A large-format imagesetter such as this Agfa Avanxis VIII is a high-speed external drum recorder for 810 × 1120 mm (31⅞ × 44 in) format and eight-page-up output. At a resolution of 2400 dpi, it can expose 20 flats per hour.

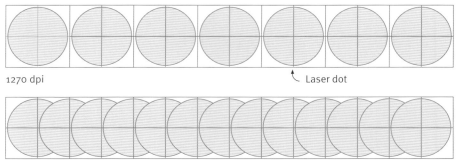

4.19 Resolution and addressability are two different, but related, parameters of an imagesetter. Resolution is the number of dots edge to edge in a line measuring an inch; addressability is a measure of how close, center to center, those dots can be placed next to one another.

1270 dpi

Laser dot

2540 dpi

of spots that any difference in quality is marginal. Similar results could probably be obtained using a lower setting.

There are two main types of imagesetter: capstan and drum (Fig. **4.20**). In an internal drum imagesetter, film enters and exits through a gap at the base of a large, stationary drum. Tension rollers on either side of the gap hold the film flush against the inside of the drum. In a capstan or roll-fed imagesetter, film enters and exits the imagesetter between tension rollers, which hold the film taut and flat. Photo material—

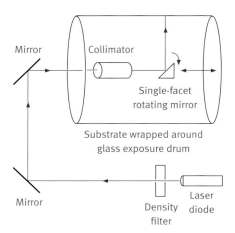

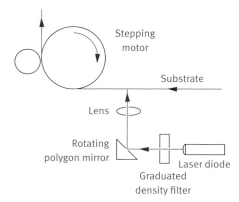

4.20 Drum imagesetter (above) and capstan (below) configurations. Each has its particular pros and cons, but the drum-based ones seem to offer the better and more consistent quality of output.

film or bromide paper—is stored in a light-tight cassette or box and then pulled across the imaging area into a receiving cassette or direct to an inline chemical processor.

Drum-based imagesetters are either internal-drum, where the film is positioned inside the drum and the imaging system moves, or external-drum systems, where the film is positioned on the outside of the drum and the drum rotates while the imaging system remains stationary. Internal drum image setters have an imaging laser attached to a screw which runs down the middle of the drum. As the laser spins, it slowly moves across the drum, writing the image, line by line. The film is always at the same distance from the laser. Capstan imagesetters have a stationary laser: a spinning mirror located directly above the film reflects the beam from side to side across the film.

A drum imagesetter's imaging area is limited in both width and length by the diameter and length of the drum. These imagesetters typically accept wider film sizes than do capstan devices, which are limited by the tolerance to distortion at the edges of the imaging area where the laser beam is being reflected at a steeper angle. Capstan imagesetters have to use complex optical systems to ensure that the beam reaching the film or paper is uniform in strength. Imperfections in all the extra optics can lead to slurring, and loss of brightness and contrast. This results in weaker (less sharp) dots. Typically these devices use narrower film than drum imagesetters do, but can run longer lengths of film.

Drum-based imagesetters produce more accuracy and repeatability of images for each of the four films. They use sheets of film capable of four-up standard pages. Each of the four color separations can be output on one sheet of film, or four sheets can be output on four-up pages, one for each CMYK color.

Imagesetters which, along with imposition software, produce film negatives with pages in position ready for plate-making are sometimes referred to as **imposetters**.

There must also be some means of processing the film or bromide paper, and imagesetters will have either an inline film processor attached, or cassettes of exposed film will have to be taken to a separate unit. Dry imagesetters output film without the need for wet chemicals and all the problems of recycling and disposal.

4.21 Heidelberg A52 and A74 Suprasetters are modular thermal external-drum CtP (computer-to-plate) platesetters directly producing plates for sheetfed and web offset. They have a resolution of 2400 dpi.

In a **platesetter** (Fig. **4.21**), the film is replaced by plate material. Although some imagesetters have always been able to output polyester plates for black-and-white work, color CtP (computer-to-plate) technology is becoming more commonplace (see p. 189 in Chapter 6).

To print documents containing PostScript files (see p. 71)—such as type, a page layout from QuarkXPress or InDesign, or an image from a program such as Adobe Illustrator—an imagesetter has to operate with a device called a **RIP** (**raster image processor**). These are sometimes built into the imagesetter, but can be housed in a separate box. A RIP is a computer in its own right, and often is just that—a standard Mac or PC with lots of RAM—and all it ever does is convert PostScript into the raster bitmap an imagesetter can read and output. The RIP also takes care of the screening of halftones. A 3600 dpi imagesetter with a spot size of 7.5 µm will have a maximum screen of 500 lpi.

To do all the "ripping" on the designer's computer would be very time-consuming. A way to get around this is to send only the text, rules, and non-scanned graphics to the RIP, along with instructions describing the size, cropping, and position on the page of the scanned pictures (the high-resolution files). This is a process known as **APR** (**automatic picture replacement**).

The picture commands, tagged on to the PostScript file, are part of a standard known as the **OPI** (**open prepress interface**), originally proposed by Aldus. A page description can thus be transferred from a Mac or PC to a faster, more powerful **workstation** at the repro service bureau and then to the RIP. A designer's computer is thus liberated to do what it does best—page design and layout.

Hardcopy: other technologies

There are many other forms of output, especially for color, and one or more of the machines described here will be found in the designer's studio. **Dot-matrix printers**, once commonplace, are now virtually obsolete.

Inkjet printers (Fig. **4.22**) spray jets of microscopic electrically charged droplets of ink on to a moving roll of paper. These jets of ink are deflected by electromagnets—just like

4.22 An inkjet printer, like this Canon Pixma iP4500 prints borderless A4 (8.5 × 11 in) photos at resolutions up to 9600 × 2400 dpi. The five-ink system includes a pigment black for better text prints, and dye-based black, yellow, cyan, and magenta for color printing.

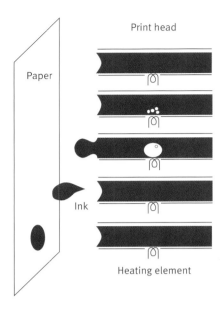

Print head

Paper

Ink

Heating element

4.23 In bubblejet printers, a heating element causes bubbles to form in the print head, thus forcing drops of ink to fly on to the paper.

the electron beam in a television tube—to build up the image. **Bubblejet printers** have an array of thin nozzles in the print head, each of which is full of ink, held there by surface tension. A small heating element causes a bubble to form which forces the ink out of the nozzle and on to the page (Fig. **4.23**). Another variation is the **thermojet printer**, which sprays melted plastic on to the paper (Fig. **4.24**). These are gradually being ousted by cheaper color laser printers, except for

some display purposes where their bright, light-fast colors are an advantage.

Wide-format inkjet printers such as the Epson Stylus Pro 11880 (Fig. **4.25**) are used for color proofing and artists' prints. **Giclée** printers (from the French for "spraying" or "spreading") are medium- to large-format inkjet devices for printing on to substrates such as watercolor paper using archival ink. Output is specifically targeted to creating fine-art prints. Large-scale inkjets can be used to print posters up to A0 in size, and some can print the huge banners that hang outside buildings.

Thermal-transfer printers use an inked-roll cartridge sandwiched between the mechanism and the drawing. This acts like carbon paper, "ironing" the image on to clay-coated paper. The three process colors (and sometimes black) are applied, one at a time, by melting dots of wax on to the paper or acetate at a resolution of 300 dpi (Fig. **4.26**). The machines are cleaner and dryer than inkjets, but consumables are more expensive. Thermal-transfer machines produce solid, bright colors, but tend to print blues and greens darker than inkjets. **Direct thermal printers** "burn" a monochrome image into specially coated paper using thermal heads.

Lower resolution thermal-transfer and inkjet printers produce their colors by a process called **dithering** (Fig. **4.27**), which is analogous to halftone screening. Pixels of cyan, magenta, and yellow (and sometimes black) are interspersed in regular patterns. Some printers use a fixed pattern of dithering, which results in a distinct step between colors. Others can make use of different patterns, leading to much smoother gradations.

4.24 The Xerox Phaser 8860 is a solid-ink printer with a maximum paper size of 8½ × 14 in (216 × 356 mm). It can print 30 pages per minute at a resolution of 600 dpi, tweaked by Xerox's FinePoint image, enhancement to an optical equivalent of 2400 dpi.

4.25 Large format inkjet printers such as this A0 Epson Stylus Pro 11880 can print 64-in (1626-mm) wide media in nine colors of pigmented ink: light cyan, cyan, vivid light magenta, vivid magenta, yellow, light black, light light black, photo black, and matte black. Photo or matte black is chosen automatically by the medium selected. Resolution is 2880 × 1440 dpi. Lightfastness is up to 75 years for color prints; 100 years for black-and-white prints.

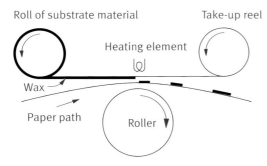

4.26 In the thermal-transfer process, rolls of transfer paper containing colored wax are "ironed" on to smooth paper by hundreds of individually controlled heating elements.

Laser, thermal-transfer, and inkjet printers are available with or without a PostScript driver, the PostScript versions being more expensive. For most graphic designers committed to PostScript, and who need fast and consistent output, a PostScript-compatible printer will be essential.

Dye-sublimation printers (Fig. **4.28**) have found themselves a niche in producing postcard-sized, photo-realistic prints from digital images, often connecting direct to the camera without the need for a computer. Machines from Sony, Canon, and Olympus mix the ink on the treated paper, without dots or dithering. So 16.7 million possible colors and 256 grayscales are smoothly blended together into a photographic-quality image that is almost good enough to go as artwork straight to the printer.

Sublimation is the phenomenon whereby certain substances change directly from a solid to a gaseous form, without the usual intermediate liquid stage. The thermal head on a dye-sublimation printer varies the temperature so that the amount of dye emitted is continuously controlled.

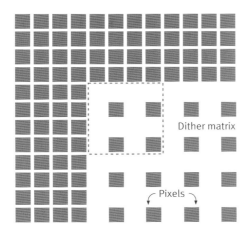

4.27 Most output technologies can produce only one size of dot in just one intensity. This is fine for line work and flat color, but for smooth blends between colors, thermal transfer and inkjet printers have to resort to a trick called dithering, which introduces deliberate randomness into a dot pattern.

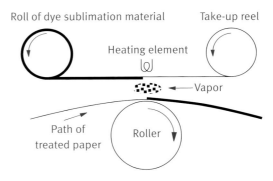

4.28 Dye-sublimation printers can produce an almost photographic quality of output, without dots or dithering, by melting and merging the inks right on the surface of the paper.

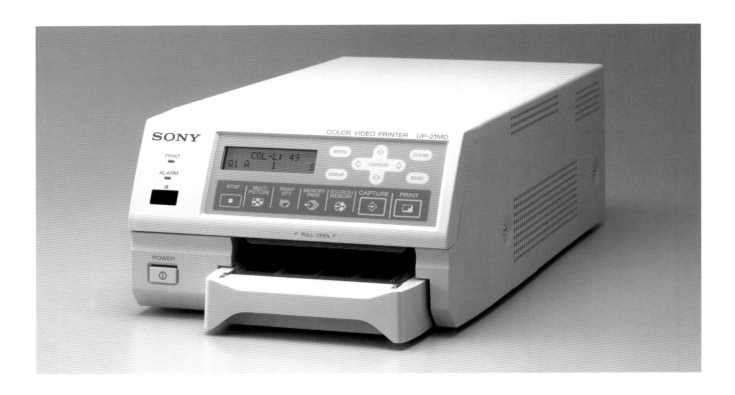

4.29 The Sony UP-21MD uses dye sublimation to produce A6-format prints at 400 dpi, each taking 17 seconds to print.

At present, both the machines and the media for dye sublimation are expensive. Dye-sublimation printers such as the Sony UP-21MD (Fig. **4.29**) can produce prints of near-photographic quality.

Designers may sometimes want to take a 35 mm or larger-format transparency off the system. A **film recorder** (Fig. **4.30**), from companies such as Lasergraphics, captures the image on a small, flat CRT built into the device, making three consecutive exposures through red, green, and blue filters.

A **pen plotter** will have limited use in most graphic design studios, but with a cutting knife replacing the pen or pencil, can be used to prepare flat-color masks for silkscreen printing (see p. 200), and for cutting out vinyl letters for large-scale displays and signs (Fig. **4.31**). Roland's CAMM-1 is a plotter modified for cutting vinyl and Rubylith film in which the pen moves in one direction and the paper in the other.

Plotters and cutters are vector devices, moving from point to point as on a graph, and the code that drives them conforms to a standard called HP-GL (Hewlett-Packard graphics language). PostScript is a vector format too, even though most computer devices encountered by the graphic designer work on the raster principle. PostScript to HP-GL conversion is necessary to drive a plotter directly from a PostScript package.

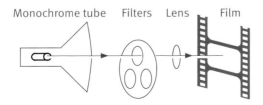

4.30 Film recorders are used to produce photographic transparencies direct from computer disk. They work by exposing the film three times—once for each of the primary colors—using small, flat cathode-ray tubes.

4.31 Pen plotters are rarely used by graphic designers. An exception is when they are equipped with a cutting knife in place of the pen, like this Roland CAMM-1, and are used to produce masks for screenprinting or to cut vinyl letters for large signs.

Choosing a system

Turnkey systems

A **turnkey system** is a complete package of hardware and software dedicated to a particular task. You turn the (imaginary) key, and off you drive. The system may be assembled from standard pieces of equipment, bought in from well-known manufacturers and "badge engineered" (i.e. the turnkey vendor's logo is stuck on the front). Or perhaps the vendor will have modified it somewhat. The software that does the job is usually only available from the turnkey vendor. (If it is subsequently sold separately from the turnkey system, it is said to be unbundled.)

The attraction to the user is that everything needed for a working system is purchased from one source, with a single maintenance contract and one technical support person to call if things go wrong. The disadvantages are that the system cannot usually be used for other tasks—to run the studio administration, for example. And you are "locked in" to one supplier for any future updates of the hardware and software. The trend today is toward "open systems" with standardized GUIs, and the ability for programs to be able to pass information between each other. This may not be possible with a turnkey. It may have a quirky interface, and once you have learnt to use it, that knowledge will apply to that system only.

Nevertheless, there are still several turnkey systems around, aimed at highly specialized applications. There are systems targeted at packaging designers, with their need to design in three dimensions and then produce flat-pattern developments of cartons, for example. Another group of turnkeys is aimed at screenprinters and signwriters, who need to cut letters and masks out of vinyl and Rubylith.

Turnkey systems are usually much more expensive than an equivalent system assembled from component parts selected by you. The vendors have been guilty of trading on people's fear of computers by stressing that their menus, for example, make use of the terms and language peculiar to that trade. But these days, much more flexible systems can be assembled quite painlessly from standard PCs or Macs, plus any make of plotter or cutter and inexpensive, off-the-shelf software.

4.32 Networking means that you can link computers together to send files or to share resources, such as a laser printer. You can also work with others on large projects communicating wirelessly or via the internet.

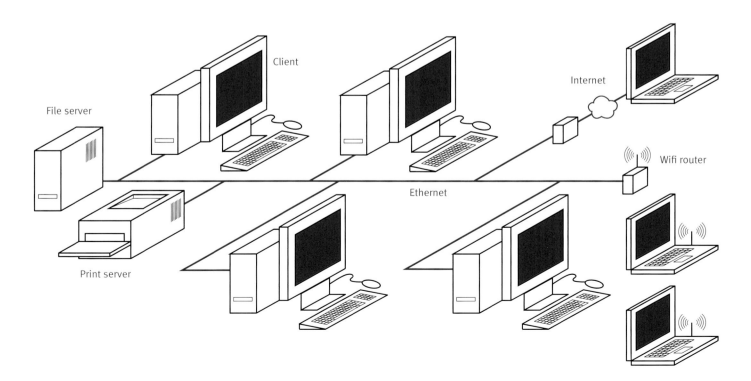

Selecting, upgrading, and networking the system

Selecting and cost-justifying a system is a very personal business. Read the computer magazines, visit trade shows, and talk to other users doing similar work to that of your studio. Methodologies exist that use spreadsheet programs to enable you to quantify the benefits of introducing a particular computer system into your studio. These may be understandable to an accountant or bank manager and be instrumental in securing you a loan to make the purchase. But of course they cannot predict the future.

Ultimately, the success of an installation is down to you. You will have to understand what the system is capable of doing, and how it can save you time and materials, while producing a quality product.

Once a successful installation has been established, however, expansion happens rapidly. This can take two forms: expansion of hardware—adding more systems, more memory, more output devices—and expansion into new application areas. On the Macintosh, particularly, programs have a common look and feel, which reduces the culture shock when you encounter new software.

As soon as you have more than one system, they can be networked together (Fig. **4.32**). There are three main reasons for **networking**: to exchange files and messages with nearby members of your team; to share expensive resources such as laser printers and disk drives; and to co-operate jointly with others in your studio on a large-scale project—in a workgroup.

Networking has a language all of its own, but all you need to know is that the most famous LAN (local-area network) is called **Ethernet**. It operates via a single length of cable, and was developed by Xerox, DEC, and Intel and introduced in 1980. With Ethernet it is possible to mix PCs and Macs on the same network.

On the Macintosh, networking is fairly straightforward—Ethernet is built-in. Two systems can be linked using just one cable—a cross-over cable. When more than two systems are linked, one system is designated the server—the place where files are stored—and the others are called clients. Any computer in the network can act as a server. (In larger networks the file server is a dedicated computer with a large disk drive, but with no screen.) This provides shared storage for programs (though it is faster to keep your own local copy), files, or fonts that everyone on the network can access. It is the responsibility of the applications software to say who has read-only access and who has the authority to make changes to the master files.

Networking, though complicated, is not really difficult. It does, however, ultimately take you into a new league of computer management. While your studio may not want or be able to afford a systems manager, someone will have to take responsibility for the smooth operation of the system: developing filing systems, watching out for viruses, maintaining the shared resources, and so on.

Health and safety

As computers become commonplace, so must health and safety issues be taken seriously. It is not yet normal, for example, to find ergonomically adjustable desks and chairs in large organizations, so what chance does the smaller design studio have? But they cost little compared with the total investment in hardware and software, and can prevent lower-back damage to the most valuable component of the system—the designer. If that is not an incentive, then it should be noted that many of the recommendations are or will become legal requirements (Fig. **4.33**).

Desks should be as thin as possible and adjustable for height; chairs should be grounded sturdily and give good lumbar (lower-back) support. When you sit on your chair, upper and lower legs should be at right angles and feet comfortably on the floor. A footrest may have to be provided,

4·33 If you are to be working at the computer for long periods, it is vitally important to have the correct ergonomic conditions to reduce the possibility of computer-related health problems such as repetitive strain injury, backache, and eyestrain.

subject to sufficient leg clearance, if desk height is not adjustable. The angle between your upper and lower arm, when typing, should be no less than 90 degrees.

There is a body of knowledge existing on such hazards as WRULD (work-related upper-limb disorders) and RSI (repetitive strain injury)—a disorder of the hands and wrists causing numbness, swelling, tingling, and ultimately complete seizure. Keyboard operators have already suffered severe damage, and employers have already been sued for large sums, so do not wait until it is too late. Educate everyone to take frequent "thinking" breaks away from the system. To rest the eyes, a break of 15 minutes in every 75 minutes of continuous computer use is recommended.

Lighting should be diffuse and indirect. Fluorescent lights should have diffuser shades and should run parallel to the user's line of vision. Avoid glare and reflections, and excessively bright or dark color schemes. No user should have to face a window directly, and vertical blinds should be fitted, to be closed on sunny days. Regular eye tests are recommended. Because of the possibility of radiation, pregnant women should have the right to keep away from computers during pregnancy, without loss of pay or career prospects.

The health risk from static build-up and electromagnetic radiation from computers is an issue still hotly debated. The computer screen should be at arm's length from your body—anyone sitting closer than 28 inches (711 mm) from the front is at some risk. Nobody should sit closer than 36 inches (914 mm) from the sides or back of a computer screen. LCD screens are flicker-free and emit less radiation, but the color reproduction and brightness may not be acceptable for some applications.

Photocopiers and laser printers should be placed where the air is changed at least once an hour, at least 3¼ yd (3 m) away from the nearest person, and preferably in a separate, well-ventilated room to disperse the fumes produced by the toner. Noisy printers should also be fitted with hoods and be kept well away from the workers.

Finally, stress and anxiety can be reduced through appropriate and thorough training. This can be as simple as sitting down with the software manual for an hour or two each week to practice shortcuts, or spending time looking over the shoulder of the "resident guru" at work. Or it can involve taking time off from your paying projects regularly, to attend more formal training courses.

Summary

Computers are here to stay. However, there is no such thing as a free lunch. There is a price to be paid for working on computers. The machinery will never be a panacea. It will never do the design work for you—in fact, it will probably make you work harder! You have to do things that maybe designers before you left for the typesetter or printer to sort out. The entire print-production process has become your concern … and your responsibility. The benefits are enormous, however, not only in cost savings, increased creativity, and improved quality, but also in job satisfaction and personal fulfillment.

Neville Brody

"I think intelligent, questioning design that can somehow help extend and open up people's awareness is valid."

Manifesto
There is No Such Thing as Bad Design—Only Inappropriate Design

Brody on website design: he quotes with approval designer David Berlow's complaint that web design is "DTP all over again." After desktop publishing first appeared, it took a long time for designers to learn how to use it in a way that wasn't led by technological novelty. Online design has been going through the same process.

Web designers still have to get over what he calls "feature fascination": "Netscape announces a new feature and everyone immediately redesigns to take advantage, whether it works for their site or not. Start with what you want to say, not with how many ways you can say it."

The biggest problem for online design, Brody argues, is not technical. The right tools and software packages won't help if designers don't develop a new mindset. They need to stop porting print methods over to the net and start working with its distinctive features. He talks about recognizing the fluid, unfinished nature of digital design and text, about the way you can "play with time" online.

Brody suggests building websites so that no individual user ever experiences quite the same site as anyone else. "What you need is a smart site that recognizes where you've been, learns from it, and responds, so it's more of a dialogue, more user-affected. Digital data has a fluid form to it. As April Grieman once said, digital design is like painting where the paint never dries. It's always shiftable. It can always respond."

"It also means incorporating design evolution, making sure that the site feels alive to people visiting more than once. You can change information on a site all you want, but if it looks just the same after the tenth visit, those changes are no longer perceived. It feels like the same old site, like there's no more reason to visit. So design evolution becomes part of the design solution. Often people just don't get it. They think you are trying to pad your bill."

Brody is also an ethical designer: "I think intelligent, questioning design that can somehow help extend and open up people's awareness is valid. I wouldn't work for cigarette or oil companies, or even alcohol. I would find it immoral to have my persuasive skills used to encourage people to start smoking."

Neville Brody was born in 1957 and grew up in Southgate, a suburb of North London. He studied fine art at Hornsey College of Art and graphic design at the London College of Printing (1977–80), where some of his tutors said he had no commercial potential. He joined the post-Punk music scene of the early 1980s, designing sleeves for Rocking Russian, Stiff, and Fetish Records, where he experimented with a graphic language that combined painting with constructivist typography. Between 1981 and 1986 he was art director for style magazine *The Face*, where his typographic experimentation influenced the look of magazines, advertising, and retail worldwide. In 1986 he set up a design studio with Fwa Richards. Jon Wozencroft's book, *The Graphic Language of Neville Brody* (see Resources below), was the best-selling art book of 1988. Brody was also honored with a retrospective exhibition of the same name at London's Victoria & Albert Museum. He was just 31 years old.

For *Arena* magazine from 1987 to 1990, Brody tried to cool down the frenzy then surrounding design by developing a minimal typography, which, as the Apple Macintosh came into widespread use, he then developed into a more expressive approach. He started his own London studio The Studio in 1987 using the Mac to provide companies with templates that would enable them to carry out their own design needs in-house. He also began designing his own typefaces, such as Blur, Industria, and Insignia.

Commissions from Germany and Japan, and postage stamps for the Dutch PTT, were followed by two major television graphics projects: the German cable channel Premiere and the Austrian state broadcasting company ORF.

In 1990, Brody founded FontWorks with Stuart Jensen and became a director of Erik Spiekermann's FontShop International, with whom he launched (with Jon Wozencroft) the experimental type magazine *FUSE*. In 1994, he changed his studio's name to Research Studios, with a subsidiary Research Publishing, a web production company. In 2001, Lionel Massias opened Research Studios Paris. Sandra Steinebrunner, who was at that time working as production manager in London, joined the Paris studio soon after. During 2002, Jason Bailey and Daniel Borck, formerly senior designers at the London studio, moved to Germany and opened Research Studios Berlin. After helping to establish the studio in Paris, Sandra Steinebrunner moved to Berlin and now manages the studio there. Research Studios Barcelona was opened in 2007 by Pablo Rovalo.

Clients include Deutsche Bank, Nike, Macromedia (if you use Macromedia products you will have seen Brody's designs on the boxes and intro screens), the *Guardian* newspaper and its website, and Channel 4. Brody now sees his role as nurturing the international team of designers at Research Studios rather than working on his own projects.

Brody is best known for his work as Art Director on post-punk "style bible" *The Face* magazine (1981–6). He used radical Russian Constructivism-inspired typography and bold cropped images to define the design.

Poster for Fuseday—lectures and an exhibition—at Manchester Metropolitan University in 1999.

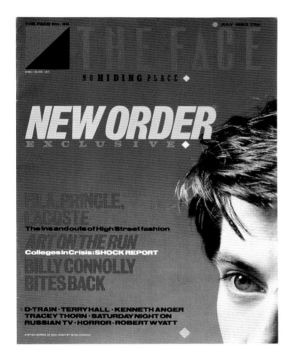

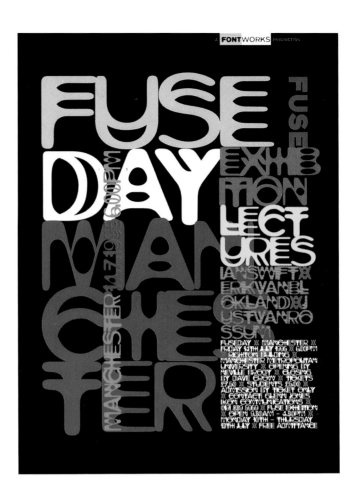

Research Studios designed a new visual language for the *Times*, which included the creation of a new font called Times Modern, a major restyling of the navigation of the newspaper, a new masthead, and a new crest. The changes took effect from Monday, November 20, 2006. The Times Modern typeface encapsulates the paper's heritage while adapting to the demands of the new compact format. The *Times* is the only newspaper to create and use bespoke fonts—all other UK newspapers purchase ready-to-use fonts. The project was led by Ben Preston, Deputy Editor of the *Times*, in partnership with Research Studios' founder Neville Brody who acted as Art Director. Neville also worked on the redesign of the *Times 2* supplement in 2005. Collaborating with Neville was lead designer Jon Hill, supported by Research Studios' Luke Prowse, who created the Times Modern headline font for the newspaper.

Resources

Website: www.researchstudios.com

Jon Wozencroft, *The Graphic Language of Neville Brody*, Thames and Hudson, London, 1988

Jon Wozencroft, *The Graphic Language of Neville Brody 2*, Thames and Hudson, London, 1994

Lewis Blackwell and Neville Brody, *G1*, Laurence King Publishing, London, 1996

Graham Vickers, "Brody," *Creative Review*, May 2000, pp. 113–15

Prepress

Prepress is the part of the print process in which all the design elements—the words and the pictures—are assembled into a unified whole. It is the stage in print production that ends with the making of lithographic plates, silkscreens, or gravure cylinders. This marks the point of no return, after which the presses begin to roll.

But in recent years that decisive moment has shifted. The involvement of the graphic designer has been extended, and is now much more closely tied to the outcome. A publication used to be "put to bed" with the dispatch of the mechanicals to the printer or repro house. Now, as all the data that makes up a page is digitized and stored electronically, it is feasible (though not always desirable) to make essential changes much later in the process—right up until press time, in certain cases.

This chapter begins by covering the principles and terminology of layout, with tips for avoiding common design pitfalls. We take a look at grids and their usefulness in providing structure to a page; they save time too. Then imposition schemes are explained—a good grounding in how and where pages are arranged on printing plates or cylinders is important for effective prepress planning. We move on to repro and discuss the various methods of checking picture proofs, and outline what you can discover from a detailed examination of a proof's color bar.

Until only a few years ago, graphic designers could send corrected galleys, a rough layout, and marked-up illustrations along to the repro shop and expect the rest of the job to be completed by others. Now it is difficult to believe that books and magazines could possibly be produced without the use of computers!

Digital prepress can roughly be divided into what you, the designer, can do in your studio with a computer, desktop scanner, and color printer, and what still has to be done at the repro service bureau or printers with their high-end drum scanners, RIPs, imagesetters, and digital proofers. But this divide is blurring all the time, and many large design practices are effectively bringing repro in-house.

Layout

In design, all rules are there to be broken. But first you have to know what they are. Most graphic designers are, so to speak, in the fashion business, and if asymmetrical or off-center designs are in vogue this year, then maybe a symmetrical or centered design will get noticed (Fig. **5.1**). Whenever someone writes down the rules, you can bet that someone else will come along before the ink is dry to rewrite them.

Having said that, however, there are some rules that endure and, for the majority of jobs, the desire will not be to shock, but to communicate ideas clearly, in a visual language accessible and understandable to all.

Very few designers are given a completely free hand—an open brief—to design what they will. There are always constraints, and therein lies the challenge: how to be different and eye-catching, while getting the message across, to time and to a budget. The client will expect the design to relate to the job it has to do—an annual report for a prestigious company will look very different, for example, from a newspaper advertisement for a cut-price corner store.

Designers must develop skills in communicating their concepts to the client clearly and unambiguously, through presentations, which may include rough sketches and more polished visualizations. Designers are also sometimes asked to help "sell" an idea to a client's clients by producing highly finished mock-ups or dummies that will convey a flavor of how the printed product will look.

There are technical constraints in planning your layout. Paper comes in stock sizes, and so do printing plates. Insisting on so-called **bastard sizes** and non-standard shapes can be wasteful of resources. Folding machines have their limitations, too. Packaging designers, in particular, may be restricted by the print technology—for example, only two, non-overlapping colors may be allowable when printing a plastic container by flexography (see p. 199).

Thankfully, the offset litho process has given designers almost complete freedom over where the design elements—the type, line illustrations, and photographs—can be positioned on the page. And computer layout systems offer the chance to try out many more potential design solutions. So where do we start?

For magazine and book work, there are certain conventions to be observed. Here we are dealing with pages. Most pages are the shape of an upright rectangle, and this orientation is sometimes called **portrait**. A page with a width greater than its height is denoted **landscape**.

Page sizes are written thus: US Letter is 8½ inches wide and 11 inches tall, and is written 8½ × 11 in. The European equivalent is called A4 (see p. 139), and its dimensions are written 210 × 297 mm. In inches, that is 8¼ × 11¹¹⁄₁₆ in. In the United States and most of Europe, it is sometimes usual to write the width before the height; in the United Kingdom and the Far East the opposite is the case—the height precedes the width.

5.1 Layouts can be symmetrical—with almost everything centered—or asymmetrical, or can combine elements of both approaches. The look you decide upon is very much dependent on the sort of job in hand, the message you wish to get across, and the fashion at the time.

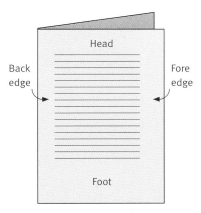

5.2 The page has a vocabulary of its own to describe the various parts of its anatomy. The blank spaces—the margins—are as important as the image and type areas: at the top is the head; at the bottom, the foot; nearest the inside, the back edge; and nearest the extremities, the fore edge.

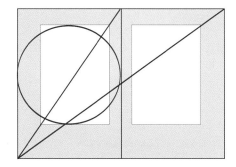

5.3 The standard proportions of medieval book pages, as discovered by the German designer Jan Tschichold. The text area and page size are in the ratio 2:3, the depth of text is equal to the width of the page, and the margins are in the proportions 2 (back edge):3 (head):4 (fore edge):6 (foot).

The white areas that frame the printed portion of the page are called the **margins** (Fig. **5.2**). The one at the top is the **head**; the one at the bottom is the **foot**. On the outer edge of the page is the **fore edge**; and the space between the printed material and the spine or fold is the **back edge**. The combined back edges of a double-page spread are called the **gutter**. This is also a term used for any vertical space—between two columns, for example. Traditionally, the foot is greater in depth than the head, and the fore edge approximately twice the width of the back edge. This means that two facing pages will be united visually as a spread.

Much has been written about what constitutes "good" and "elegant" design. The German designer Jan Tschichold discovered that the margins of medieval manuscripts followed certain rules of proportion, which are still thought pleasing (Fig. **5.3**). The ratio of text area to page size was 2:3; the depth of the printed area was the same as the width of the page; and the back edge:head:fore edge:foot margins were of the ratio 2:3:4:6. The famous **golden section** format of the Renaissance has proportions of 34:21 or 8.1:5. Superimposed on to a sheet of US Letter stock, the golden section is just over 1¾ inches narrower (Fig. **5.4**).

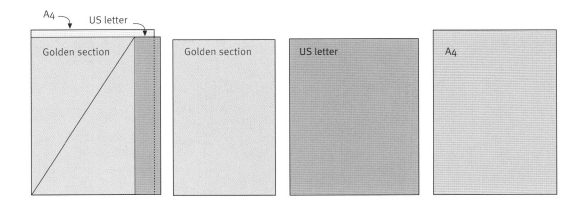

5.4 The golden section is a proportion (34:21) that people through the ages and in different cultures have found pleasing. It has many parallels in nature—the way a snail's shell grows, for instance. Here, a sheet of paper to golden-section proportions is compared with US Letter and A4 sizes.

Grids

The layout of columns, margins, and area for text and images is usually marked out as a grid (Fig. **5.5**). It also shows the positions of any repeating headlines, or **running heads**, plus the page numbers, or folios. Before computers, a grid was drawn out on to a board or sheet of heavy paper in non-reproducing blue pencil for a one-off publication. On regular publications or books, the grid would be preprinted on layout sheets. A page-layout system will have an invisible (or visible—you choose) grid set to whatever increments of whatever units you specify. Items can be made to snap to these grids. In addition, it is possible to set up non-printing guidelines on master pages (more of which later).

Type is set in columns. As discussed on p. 59, too wide a measure (column width) affects the readability of text.

Try not to specify more than 18 words per line for books, or seven words for newspapers and magazines. Novels and most small-format books are usually set in one column (Fig. **5.6**). If the single column goes right across the page, you are severely restricted as to where you can place any illustrations. Two or three columns give more flexibility to illustrated books. But there again, an art book may have just one relatively wide column, situated asymmetrically, with lots of white space around it.

In newspapers and most popular magazines, white space means wasted space, and space is at a premium. So there will typically be many narrow columns to the page, with the possibility of photographs straddling two, three, or more of them (Figs **5.7** and **5.8**).

5.5 The grid used for this book has been underprinted on this spread. A grid is the backbone of a good layout, and a great aid to consistency. It should not be a straitjacket, however. A grid that is too detailed and tight will result in a cold and static design.

5.6 While magazines and newspapers are meant to be browsed, books are generally intended for reading calmly and sequentially, hence the simple and comforting one-column format found in most fiction.

5.7 The front page of UK newspaper The *Guardian* has a five-column grid and nothing in this example breaks out of it—even the lively "advertsement" above the masthead conforms to the grid. The sober symmetrical layout identifies this as a serious broadsheet: there is one main story, with "turns" along the bottom of the page that refer to stories within.

Horizontal lines built into the grid can be used to impose further discipline on the layout, allowing you to align the edges of photographs, say, with blocks of text. Six to eight horizontal divisions should be sufficient. Too many, and the layout will seem fussy, with no apparent thought-out design. Too few will not allow enough variety in the layout—it will appear static if the illustrations always fall in the same positions. Some grids may show a numbered horizontal line marked out for each line of type.

A grid can seem confusing at first sight, but not all the lines and divisions have to be used on every page. Seen as an underlying structure, the grid can become an indispensable time-saving aid to producing clear and consistent layout, quickly and painlessly.

Design elements such as **cross-headings** (subheadings within a block of text), boxed copy, captions, rules, borders, and tint blocks are all devices for adding "color" to an otherwise "gray" layout. They will assist the readers' eyes, helping them follow the flow of the text, especially if it has been split to accommodate the placement of illustrations. And, if the copy does not fit exactly, they are useful and unobtrusive space fillers.

Keep your initial rough layout on paper and a complete copy of the galley proofs (see p. 47) for reference, to check that paragraphs have not been moved out of sequence or missed out altogether, and make any adjustments to the layout to avoid widows and orphans (see p. 43). The rest is up to you!

HOT TIPS & COOL TRICKS

Bleeds

Having an image, text, or block of color go right up to the edge of the page requires a bleed. The object to bleed must overlap the print area of the page by at least ⅛ inch (or 5 mm—check with your printer), so that when the page is trimmed the ink will truly reach the edge. Avoid fiddly bleeds that need precise trimming. Adjust the design so that any accidental cropping looks intentional.

5.8 This double-page spread from *Time* magazine has a basic four-column grid, with a three-column variation at the bottom of the left-hand page. The way that the photographs break out of the grid slightly in places gives a more contemporary and relaxed feel to the layout—news magazines in the United States once exhibited a much more serious style to convey depth.

NoteBook

cred of embattled Pakistani President Pervez Musharraf. Although outwardly supportive of Musharraf's government, U.S. military officials have quietly been questioning just how intensely it is battling the Taliban and al-Qaeda fighters who cross routinely between Pakistan and Afghanistan. U.S. casualties in Afghanistan have increased in recent months. And some Pentagon officials have been privately critical of Pakistan for harboring al-Qaeda members in unpoliced areas along the border—the region where, according to Islamabad, the unidentified al-Qaeda mastermind believed to be behind the British plot is said to be hiding.

But Pakistan may have won points with the U.S. for its steadfastness in the Rauf case. British authorities had wanted to wait for the alleged plotters to do a dry run of their mission before striking. Washington vigorously disagreed, and while Pakistan was officially neutral in the spat, an Islamabad official points out, "The last thing we want is for something to happen and everyone says it's linked to Pakistan." According to one source, the U.S. threatened to take Rauf with Pakistan's help even if London didn't move. Washington won, the British swooped on their suspects, and Pakistan delivered Rauf.

Rauf's networks haven't yet been fully mapped. For instance, investigators say his phone records show a number of calls to contacts in Germany. Who were they? He made numerous phone calls to South Africa. What were they about? Several of his 23 suspected co-conspirators being held in Britain are said to have attended Koranic study sessions run by a hard-line Islamic group known as Tablighi Jamaat (the name roughly means "missionary group"). Did they know Mohammed Sidique Khan and Shehzad Tanweer—who took part in July 2005's London subway bombings and are believed to have been regulars at a Tablighi Jamaat mosque? Were they acquainted with Richard Reid, the jailed, failed shoe bomber, who frequented a Tablighi Jamaat mosque too? Pakistani intelligence officials aren't done with Rauf but expect eventually to hand him over to Britain. "He can be extradited," says an official, "once we get the maximum out of him." One can imagine that will not be a pleasant process. —*By Bill Powell. Reported by Aryn Baker, Jessica Carsen, Ghulam Hasnain and Talat Hussain*

The U.S. may now have more trust in Musharraf's government

North Korea's Rising Waters

In a country as secretive as North Korea, even natural disasters are shrouded in mystery. With international aid groups struggling to determine the extent of damage caused by July's torrential rains and floods, Seoul-based NGO Good Friends last week reported that the disaster left more than 54,700 dead or missing and 2.5 million homeless—a startling contradiction of Pyongyang's claim that "hundreds" were dead. Good Friends also warned that large areas of farmland were washed out, raising the specter of another famine, reminiscent of the one that cost the lives of as many as 2 million North Koreans in the mid-1990s. "It is a very horrific and devastating situation," says Good Friends' manager Erica Kang.

Other North Korea-watchers are skeptical of the estimates, but with accurate data hard to come by in the Hermit Kingdom, "we simply don't know and can't know" the extent of the fatalities, says Gerald Bourke, spokesman for the World Food Program in Beijing. Bourke has no doubt, though, that "there are a lot of hungry people" in North Korea right now.

Whatever its scope, international attention on the catastrophe could benefit dictator Kim Jong Il, whose neighbors have toughened their stance toward the Stalinist state since it test-fired seven ballistic missiles in July. Seoul, which suspended food shipments after the tests, quickly reversed course, promising $10 million in aid earlier this month. And while Washington has favored isolating the North to pressure Pyongyang into dismantling its nuclear weapons and missile programs, cutting off aid in the face of a humanitarian crisis could be difficult. "There will be more pressure on the U.S." to change course if the reports prove true, says David Steinberg, director of Asian studies at Georgetown University.

So far Washington hasn't resumed the food aid it suspended last year. Pyongyang remains equally defiant and shows no signs of returning to talks aimed at ending its nuclear program. Unknown millions of North Koreans might be struggling to survive, but Kim Jong Il is still sitting pretty. —*By Michael Schuman. With reporting by Jennifer Veale and Douglas Waller*

Famine could strike again in North Korea

STAR RECRUITS

Army sergeants usually inspire fear. Not Sergeant Star. He's soft-spoken, approachable and, well, kinda cute. Oh, and he's not human. Star is the U.S. Army's newest recruiter—a camouflage-wearing avatar at GoArmy.com who answers the questions of visitors to the site. He's straightforward: ask "Will I go to Iraq?" and he'll say it's "likely." If he's stumped, Star will direct you to a live recruiter, who is waiting to chat.

Star's debut on Aug. 2 was the Army's first step toward the planned October unveiling of its new interactive Web portal. Thousands have chatted with Star, typically staying on-site for 15 minutes—three times longer than the average visit before he went live. Major Brad Van Poppel, who works on the Web-outreach program, credits Star's "cool factor" and says he's fulfilling his mission: "When 85% of teenagers are online every day, the Army wants to be there." —*By Sally B. Donnelly*

The World Cup gave a boost to German retailers

The Summer Just Got Hotter

After several false starts and much delay, Europe has finally managed to crank up its economic growth engine. But how long before it once again sputters? Preliminary second-quarter figures published by the E.U.'s statistics office last week showed that the 12 euro-zone countries, led by a resurgent Germany and France, enjoyed their strongest growth in six years, catching up with Britain, which continues to perform more robustly than even the prudent government anticipated.

The 0.9% quarterly rise in the euro zone was fueled by a sequence straight out of the textbook: firms enjoying robust exports have been increasing their investment at home, which is creating jobs. Jobs, in turn, are giving a vital boost to consumption. The World Cup may have helped a bit too, especially in Germany, where some retailers and restaurants did extra business. Governments have been quick to take credit. "We've finally cut the knot," enthused Michael Glos, the German Economics Minister. "Solid growth has returned," crowed Thierry Breton, his French counterpart, predicting that 2007 will be "a good to very good year."

Many economists are more skeptical, pointing out a slew of significant risks that could nip the Euro-recovery in the bud, including the prospect of interest-rate hikes and the introduction of a higher VAT rate—up to 19%—in Germany next year. One of the biggest risks is what happens in the U.S., whose economy is just starting to cool as the Europeans heat up. "Much will depend on how abruptly the U.S. slows," says Barbara Böttcher at Deutsche Bank in Frankfurt, who nonetheless expects that the Continent will be able to sustain faster growth for some time. Her peers at Credit Suisse in London are less optimistic, pointing to surveys that suggest business confidence is already starting to decline. And some countries, especially Italy, remain stuck in a rut. Still, for much of the Continent, it all amounts to the first piece of good economic news for a long time. Pity everyone was on vacation. —*By Peter Gumbel*

Euro-zone states are enjoying their best growth rates in six years

Much Ado About Abe

With outgoing Prime Minister Junichiro Koizumi due to step down next month, Japan's neighbors are breathing a sigh of relief and focusing their attention on his likely successor, Chief Cabinet Secretary Shinzo Abe. Koizumi's visits to the controversial Yasukuni shrine—the latest on Aug. 15—have long outraged China and South Korea, who view them as deliberate celebrations of Japanese militarism. But Beijing and Seoul have signaled their willingness to give Abe a chance to repair ties—if he forgoes Yasukuni.

Don't bet on it. A lifelong right-winger from conservative stock (his grandfather was arrested as a war criminal after World War II, though never charged), Abe has visited Yasukuni repeatedly in the past. So far he has refused to say whether he would go as PM, but even if Abe defuses tensions over Yasukuni, he has other ways to rile Japan's neighbors. For a start, local media reported last week that he has plans to revise the country's pacifist constitution to allow Japan's self-defense forces greater participation in allied military operations—a signal that he's eager for Japan to become a more assertive player on the world stage. If so, Beijing and Seoul may have second thoughts about celebrating Koizumi's departure. —*By Bryan Walsh. With reporting by Toko Sekiguchi*

Abe wants Japan to be a bigger global player

French hunters have bullfrogs in their sights

OPERATION: KILL KERMIT

Most nights, armed men stomp through the Perigord-Limousin Regional Park in southwestern France with orders to shoot ... frogs. But not just any amphibians. They're after *Rana catesbeiana*—the North American bullfrog—introduced to France in 1968 by a French aviator who liked the idea of the critters croaking in his garden. They're now an ecological menace. Weighing up to a kilo, these voracious predators gorge on crustaceans, fish, other frogs, salamanders and even the occasional bird. "It's capable of attacking anything it can swallow," says Tony Dejean, the naturalist at Perigord-Limousin leading the operation. Worse, it was recently discovered that bullfrogs carry chytrid fungus, which kills other amphibians. Prior attempts to eradicate invasive species have failed in France. But the park service has already killed thousands of the frogs, their tadpoles and eggs, and residents nearby are praying this eradication mission succeeds: "Thousands of bullfrogs croaking all night is unbearable," Dejean says. —*By Jeffrey T. Iverson*

Imposition

Unless you are designing a solitary jar label, or a single-sided folder, it will help the printer considerably if you know about imposition. **Imposition** is the term used for the planning of **pagination** in folders, magazines, or books in a pattern such that when the printed sheet of paper is folded and trimmed, the resulting pages **back up** correctly and run consecutively. Page layout programs allow you to view the pages as spreads, but bear in mind that these may be broken apart when imposed. Some printers like to receive layouts and film in "printer's pairs"—like double-page spreads—if they are to do simple imposition themselves.

A sheet of paper has two sides: front and back (Fig. **5.9**). Fold it once and—to the printer, at least—it becomes a four-page folder. Fold it again and, when one of the short sides has been cut, it becomes an eight-page folder, comprising two folded sheets, one nesting inside another. Fold a third time, and the result after trimming is a 16-page folder. It is a curious fact that it is impossible to fold paper more than seven times, regardless of the size of the original sheet, or the thickness of the paper stock.

Most printers work in 16-page sections, with plates that print eight pages on each side. If your 16-page folder is numbered consecutively, with the first right-hand page as page 1, the first left as page 2, the numbers will fall as follows:

front: 1   4,5   8,9   12,13   16
back: 2,3   6,7   10,11   14,15

It is important to know which page numbers are on which side of the sheet, because you may wish to introduce flat color, or full color, into an otherwise black-and-white publication. It will save you money if you can restrict it to one side of the sheet (Fig. **5.10**).

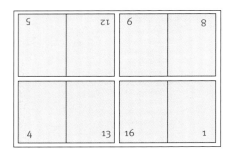
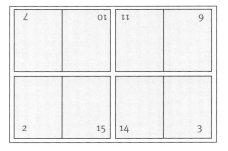

5.1c Sheetwork—the simplest form of imposition. Several pages are printed on one side of a sheet of paper, which is then turned over and printed again on the other side.

Work-and-turn

If you are designing a greetings card, your first thought might be to put the front side of it two-up on a plate, and the reverse two-up on a second plate. You can, however, print both sides of the card using just one plate! How's it done? Using work-and-turn. Say you need 1000 cards: you print 500, wait until they're dry, flip the cards over and print the other side, making sure that the half of the plate with the verso is on the back of the half of the card's recto. Guillotine the result, and you have two stacks of cards, both printed both sides (see also p. 144).

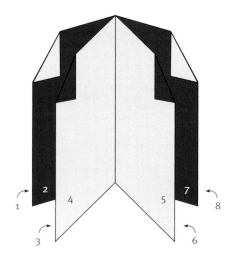

5.9 Imposition schemes can look complicated in diagram form, but all should become clear if you make a folded dummy in miniature—for your own benefit and to show the printer.

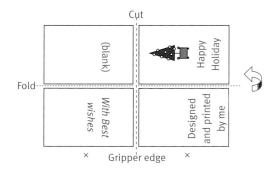

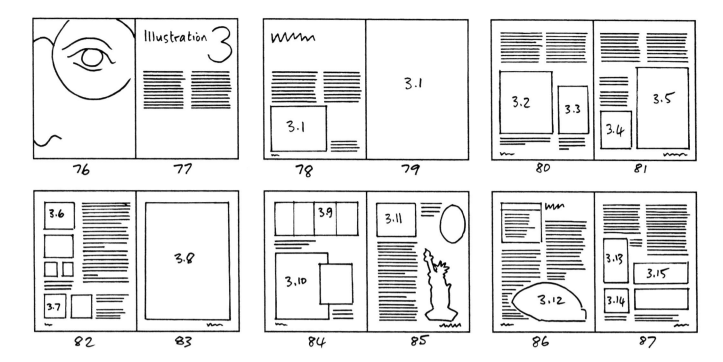

5.11 Part of the flatplan for this book. It shows, at a glance, not only picture sizes and text position, but gives an overview of where black-and-white and color sections fall.

The odd numbers are always, by convention, on the right-hand side; the even numbers on the left. In bookwork, right or front is called **recto**; left or back is called **verso**. A 16-page section of a book is called a **signature**, and each signature will usually be marked with a **backstep mark**—a letter, number, or black strip to help the binder **collate**, or assemble, the signatures in the correct order.

If the cover of a 16-page folder is to be printed in the same stock as the rest of the publication, as a **self cover**, the first page will be the outside front cover (or OFC), page 2 will be the inside front cover (or IFC), page 15 will be the inside back cover (or IBC), and page 16 will be the outside back cover (or OBC). If, however, the cover is to be printed in heavier stock, or if it alone is to be printed in color, then it will be treated as a four-page section, printed separately. This leaves you with 16 pages for the inside, making a 20-page publication.

Generally speaking, printers like to handle only 4-, 8-, or 16-page sections (though novels are often printed in 32s and 64s). A 64-page magazine with a separate 4-page cover comprises four 16-page sections, which is convenient and economical. If you increase the pagination to 68, a 4-page section would have to be added somewhere. It is possible to add a two-page section, but not recommended. If the publication is to be saddle-stitched, this would leave an unsightly strip of paper at the other side of the wire staples. It would probably be just as economic to create another two pages.

To help you find your way around an imposition scheme, it is common to draw out a **flatplan** (Fig. **5.11**). This shows diagrammatically what goes where in a publication. It also makes clear which sections or signatures can accommodate flat or full color to best effect. It is a good medium of communication on a magazine, for example, between the editorial, advertising, and design staff.

There are many ways of drawing up a flatplan, and it is best to consult your printers first, so as to take into account the way they are used to working, and any peculiarities of their folding machines. If in any doubt about imposition, do not be afraid of making up a folded **dummy** out of scrap paper. This would be a miniature version of your publication marked with page numbers and the position of any color.

There are two distinct ways of feeding paper through printing presses. It can be done either with pre-cut single sheets (**sheetwise**) or with a roll of paper (for **web** printing). The sheetwise method uses one plate to print the front of a sheet, and another for the back. Both sides share a common **gripper edge** (Fig. **5.12**). The gripper edge is the leading end of the sheet, and is held in place on the press by finger-like grippers. An allowance of ½ inch (15 mm) must be made on this

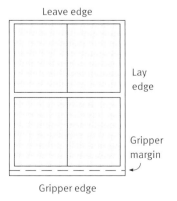

5.12 The way a sheet of paper goes into the printing press has a bearing on the layout. The gripper edge, for example, must contain an area that is free of all text or graphic material.

edge when estimating the printed area of a sheet. Opposite the gripper edge is the **leave edge**, and the left side of the sheet as it passes through the press is called the **lay edge**.

An alternative, and a method used when printing booklets or sections of publications with fewer than 16 pages, is to put both sides of the sheet on the same plate. This may sound crazy, but when it is cut and folded correctly you end up with twice as many half-size sheets.

Work-and-turn (Fig. **5.13**) is a technique in which the sheet goes through the machine first one way, then the paper is turned over sideways and printed once more, such that page two prints on the back of page one. The gripper edge remains the same. The sheet is cut in two, and the result is two piles of paper printed on both sides that can be folded and trimmed as in sheetwise imposition. **Work-and-tumble** (Fig. **5.14**) is similarly ingenious, but the paper is flipped head over heels, and the gripper edge changes ends.

Using work-and-turn or work-and-tumble is economical. This is not only because just one plate is made and there is less **spoilage**, but also because for smaller jobs the printer can **step-and-repeat** (duplicate), a set of pages and print **two-up**—twice as many again in one printing.

If you are designing a whole range of stationery, to be printed in the same Pantone colors and on the same paper stock, you can make similar savings by **ganging up** the individual items on to one plate and printing, say, three compliments slips on one sheet of A4 paper.

Web printing is usually reserved for large print runs. The possible imposition schemes are quite different from those for sheetwork. If you are going to use this method, it is best to consult the printers at the outset.

There are other design considerations relating to the imposition scheme. A **double-page spread** (DPS) will be a problem if text or an image runs across two facing pages. They will only align correctly on a center spread, and even here you must take care to keep anything important—the eyes in a portrait, for example—well away from the position of a magazine's wire staples. For consistency of print density, it is best to have DPSs printed on the same side of the same section,

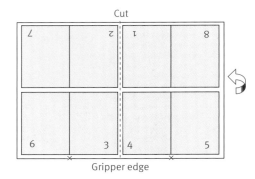

Cut · Gripper edge

5.13 Work-and-turn is an ingenious imposition scheme that gives twice as many products as you would expect, using just one plate. It is often more economical to use large plates, so one side of the sheet is put on one half of the plate, the other side on the other half. The sheet is printed, and the pile is turned over and printed again on the other side. Later the pile of sheets is cut down the middle to give you two identical half-size piles of printed sheets. Both sides share the same gripper edge.

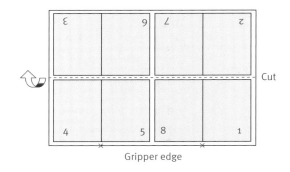

Cut · Gripper edge

5.14 Work-and-tumble is similar to work-and-turn, except the pile is flipped head over heels and the gripper edge changes ends.

if at all possible. **Starvation ghosting** is an unwelcome effect that results in uneven printing and is due, to some extent, to the placement of dense black elements in certain positions on the plate. If you think you may have problems, check with the printer about an alternative imposition.

There are all kinds of other imposition schemes that relate to non-standard folders and booklets—those with fan or **accordion folds**, for example, and those having unusual shapes and sizes. Computerized imposition systems arrange page files on to large sheets of film inside an imagesetter, which are then used to produce plate-ready flats.

Factors that influence the choice of a particular imposition scheme include: the total number of pages, the print run, the untrimmed page size, and the type of folding and binding. Discuss all these with the printer before you start, and together you will be able to plan for the most economical sheet size, as well as the most cost-effective press, the lowest spoilage, the highest quality, and the fastest turnaround.

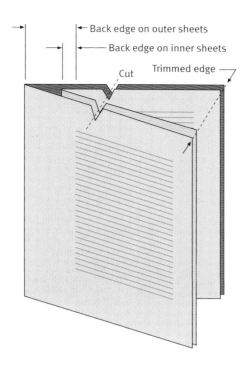

5.15 Paper creep allowance—made to counter the effect caused by the thickness of the paper in the fold of saddle-stitched publications with lots of pages. Otherwise, after the pages have been trimmed the text area will creep nearer the fore edge as the center of the publication is approached.

Back edge on outer sheets
Back edge on inner sheets
Cut
Trimmed edge

Paper creep allowance

A book will be bound, stitched, or glued in 16-page sections. A saddle-stitched publication, however, may have quite a number of sections nested one within the other. When these sections are collated, the thickness of the paper at the fold will add up to make pages toward the center stick out more than those near the covers. More paper will be trimmed from the fore edges of these pages, making them significantly narrower than those near the covers. To allow for this paper creep, it is important that you vary the position of the margins, especially those at the outer edges.

A simple method of **paper creep allowance**, or **shingling**, is as follows (Fig. **5.15**). Make a folded dummy, using the same paper stock as the proposed publication. Looking down at the top edge of the dummy, measure off the inner margin of the center pages and make a scalpel cut through the rest at the same point. Disassemble the dummy and use the position of the scalpel cuts as an inner margin reference on the layout. It will appear to move toward the fold as you approach the center pages. It is not necessary to make an allowance on every page—a cumulative allowance can be made every few pages. Trim and center marks must remain to the same measure on all the pages, and remember to mark your design "paper creep allowance made" in case a "helpful" printer decides to straighten up your seemingly wandering margins.

Page layout

The layout of the page is the graphic designer's very own domain. It is what the canvas is to the fine artist. It is the key stage in which all the copy—both text and line illustration—comes together as a unified whole ready to go to film or plate.

Crossovers

A **crossover** is an image, text, or tint that extends from one page to a facing page. Unless you are designing a center spread or the center pages of a signature, the two halves of a crossover will be printed on separate sheets of paper. After trimming and binding, your crossover may well misalign—so avoid thin rules, small text sizes, and objects that are not placed horizontally. And consult your printer about imposing the two sides of a crossover, so that ink and color coverage are consistent.

Once, designers merely provided a rough cut and paste of photocopies to indicate their ideas to another professional, known as a **finish artist**, who did the neat job of preparing the layout for the later stages of prepress.

Before computers, designers had to prepare a mechanical (Fig. **5.16**), also known as **camera-ready copy** (**CRC**) or just plain artwork (A/W). This skill is still relevant, though almost obsolete. A mechanical is sometimes necessary for old jobs that need simple updating or when you're in a hurry and the computer is down! The difference is that the mechanical is now more likely to go on to the glass of a scanner than under the lights of a process camera.

At the printer, a negative film is made from the mechanical. After retouching work to opaque-out scalpel marks and any other imperfections, it is contact printed direct to a **negative-working plate**. Alternatively, it may first be contact printed to film to produce a positive, which is then used to produce a **positive-working plate** (see Chapter 6 for a fuller explanation of platemaking).

5.16 A mechanical layout can contain all kinds of design elements: text on bromide paper, PMTs, or photocopies of line art, rules, and boxes, and maybe even headlines created using rub-down lettering.

Bruce Mau

"If process drives outcome, we may not know where we're going, but we will know we want to be there." from *An Incomplete Manifesto for Growth*

Manifesto
A Studio Built for Special Projects

Bruce Mau's nine-point work philosophy is outlined on his website, an edited extract of which is printed here:

1. It takes two (or three or four). Collaboration is our wellspring—both within the studio and without. We enter into projects looking for the work that lies between our clients' ventures and our studio practice, finding that area where we can make the greatest contribution.

2. We see projects, not accounts. Our clients come to us with ambitions that we can build on. They are ongoing projects that are never "closed."

3. We see readers, not viewers. We privilege the receivers of our work as readers—as people who are intelligent and appreciative of subtlety.

4. The root of studio. We look at the studio as a place of study in service to its projects. Our projects, and the intensive research we favor, provoke us to learn about the world, and we are enriched and changed by that level of engagement. But this rigorous process has also proven to be the way to produce the best people with the highest capacity for tackling the most difficult projects.

5. Re-Iteration moves design upstream. Solving a design problem is not a linear practice; it's an iterative one. Rather than focusing at the outset on producing that "perfect" thing, our method is loose and consequently very productive. We visualize a range of ideas to the point that we can say to our clients, "this is actually what you are asking us to do." This affords our clients the ability to see business decisions and their attendant implications early in the process.

6. Upstream the water's deeper. Rather than flowing downriver, we prefer to labor against the current, to resist the simple solution, because that's where we find the real opportunity within a project.

7. We love things. And we love making them. We aspire to a level of quality you could call perfection . . . our creative input does not cease until the receiver sets their eyes or hands upon it.

8. The studio is not a tree. The studio's trajectory could best be described as rolling. Our capacity is constantly evolving in response to projects undertaken and as a defense against unhappiness.

9. We're claustrophobic. If we feel we are contributing something of value, our ambition has no boundaries.

Bruce Mau was born in Sudbury in Ontario, Canada, in 1959, and grew up on a farm outside the city. As a teenager, he gave no thought to a career in design: "There were two or three jobs that you could get: a bus driver, a miner, or you could work in the smelter—graphic designer is simply not even on the list."

At high school, Mau studied electronics, but then decided—almost too late—that he wanted to study art. He joined the Special Art Program, designed for people like him who had decided late in their education to pursue art.

Mau was accepted into the Ontario College of Art & Design in 1978 but, frustrated by what he considered low standards, he quit before graduation. In 1980, he began two years with the Toronto design firm Fifty Fingers, and then went on to spend a couple more at Pentagram in London, before becoming part of the founding triumvirate of Public Good Design and Communications.

In 1985, the opportunity to design *Zone 1/2* (a collection of essays about the contemporary city) presented itself and he set up Bruce Mau Design (BMD). He designed everything from the books themselves to Zone's overall visual identity, its advertising and catalogs, business cards, CDs, and exhibitions, as well as sharing in editorial and planning responsibilities. He has remained as design director of Zone Books, and from 1991 to 1993 he was also creative director of *i–D* magazine. In 1995, the studio gained global attention with *S,M,L,XL*, a 1300-page compendium of projects and texts designed and conceived by Bruce Mau with architect Rem Koolhaas.

Life Style, Bruce's monograph on design culture and the work of the studio, was published in 2000. He was awarded the Chrysler Award for Design Innovation in 1998, and the Toronto Arts Award for Architecture and Design in 1999. In 2001, he received an Honorary Doctor of Letters from the Emily Carr Institute of Art and Design in Vancouver. In 2007, Bruce Mau was the recipient of the AIGA (American Institute of Graphic Arts) Gold Medal in the field of communication design.

Mau has always been a vocal critic of the way design is taught and practiced, so in 2003, he introduced his own postgraduate course at George Brown–Toronto City College. Institute without Boundaries bills itself as "the first Canadian college postgraduate design program to offer a public-private model of education that addresses the market need for multi-disciplinary designers."

BMD has gained international recognition for its expertise and innovation in identity articulation, research and conceptual thinking, print design and production, environmental signage and way-finding systems, and exhibition and product design.

Resources

Website: www.brucemaudesign.com

Bruce Mau, *Massive Change: A Manifesto for the Future Global Design Culture*, Phaidon Press, London and New York, 2004

Massive change: The Future of Global Design. www.massivechange.com

Institute without Boundaries: www.institutewithoutboundaries.com

"The Aura of Power," a critique of Bruce Mau by Rick Poynor and others: www.designobserver.com/archives/000106.html

"An Annotated Manifesto for Growth": www.textism.com/maunifesto/

Rendering of interior typographic and graphic design scheme for the Bloor Street ROOTS store in Toronto (2002). Mau developed the identity for Canadian lifestyle brand ROOTS, designing logos, graphic standards, packaging, marketing campaigns, and the interiors of their flagship stores.

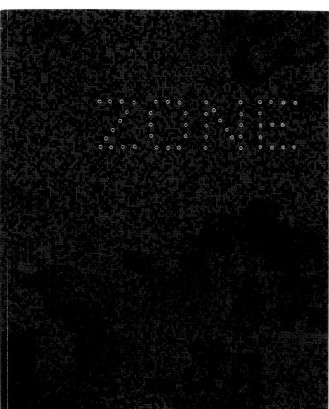

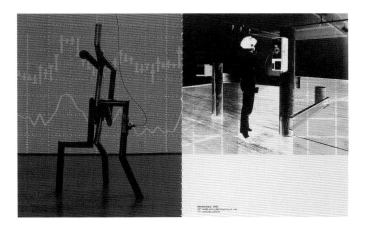

Life Style, written by Bruce Mau in 2000, documents the BMD process and clients, starting with Zone Books in 1985.

In collaboration with its editors, Mau encouraged *Zone 1/2* (1986) to behave like the city that is its subject, with all the city's attendant abrasions and multiphonic aspects—readers are pulled out of their passive reception of the text into an active involvement in the unfolding of ideas.

Digital make-up

With a computer system, it is possible to design "on the fly," though this methodology is not always recommended! What is certain, though, is that you will be able to try out lots of "what-if?" layouts, and always end up with clean, seamless artwork, with no changes in density where paragraphs have been corrected, no scalpel cuts to be retouched, and no chance of last-minute corrections dropping off the mechanical on to the printer's floor.

Digital make-up is an immensely powerful tool, but it brings with it a great deal of responsibility for the finished product. There is no one to blame for a less than perfect layout except yourself, or perhaps a bug in the program. And there is much to learn: about operating the system, making use of the flexibility it offers, and about computers in general.

As with the totally manual method, it will always pay to sit down with a pencil and paper to plan your layout. A layout pad has been designed for that purpose, with leaves thin enough for you to trace the best parts of a previously attempted design before it is consigned to the trash. Make a sketch layout of the page. It does not have to be completely accurate, but it should be good enough for you to see what a spread is going to look like at full size. This should include the margins, columns, and the position of page numbers and running heads.

Next, select your typeface. This will depend on the type of job, and what's available—both on your system, and at the service bureau. Don't forget practical considerations, such as the number of words per line and the relative x-heights (see p. 38) of the different faces. Try running off some sample lines of type in the face and at the point size and measure that you have chosen, and place it on the layout. That way you will be able to judge whether you require more or less leading and tracking. Try out different sub-headings, and decide now whether the text is to be set justified or ranged left. Remember: type on the screen only approximates the output from the laser printer or imagesetter, so it is important to have a reasonable idea of what to expect.

Next, calculate how much space the type will occupy. If the text has been input using a word processor with a word counter, then that figure will be a good guide. Otherwise use one of the methods outlined in Chapter 2 (see p. 48). If it is going to be too long, or fall short, adjust the layout.

Now draw up a grid. Although the digital make-up system will have built-in rulers and construction lines, the page on the screen—even on a large format display—will look deceptively different from a piece of board on your desk. So double-check with a ruler and a same-size reference grid. Then you can key the specifications into the computer.

If the publication is mostly words, with only a few or no illustrations, then you can start to place the text on to the page. If, however, there is a large number of illustrations, it is best to draw up a rough plan showing where you expect them to fall. It is much easier to manage the layout (and make sure that nothing is left out) if you know exactly which elements have to be included, and roughly where.

Finally, make a written record of your specification and keep it nearby. Although it is in the computer somewhere, it can be time-consuming and disruptive to have to stop what you are doing to find a reminder of what measure, margin, or horizontal division you have been using.

Page layout programs

It is possible to make up complete pages and even multi-page documents in some of the so-called drawing programs, such as Adobe Illustrator, especially where their versatile type controls are required. Most off-the-shelf word-processing programs can now handle several columns of text integrated with graphics. And there are some packages on the market developed for specific design tasks: producing display advertisements for newspapers and magazines, for example. At the other extreme, there are programs such as FrameMaker (discontinued for Macs in 2004), aimed at the market for very large but relatively unsophisticated publications, such as technical manuals.

Most designers come across all kinds of jobs, however, and need a more general-purpose program. The best-known and most versatile are Adobe InDesign—a successor to PageMaker—(Fig. **5.17**) and QuarkXPress (Fig. **5.18**). Aldus released the first version of PageMaker for the Apple

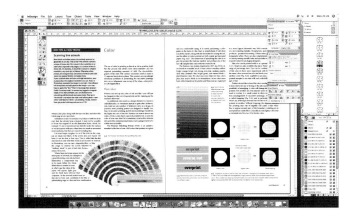

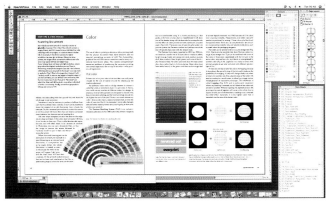

5.17 In a digital make-up system such as Adobe InDesign the mechanical is replaced by an "electronic pasteboard." Text is imported from a word-processing system and placed on to a grid. Text can also be wrapped around illustrations.

5.18 QuarkXPress is similar to InDesign in many ways, but uses a different approach to placing text and graphics—QuarkXPress has linked text and graphic frames.

Macintosh in July 1985, and for the IBM PC in January 1987. QuarkXPress was not introduced until later in 1987. It was Aldus founder Paul Brainerd who coined the phrase "desktop publishing." PageMaker can thus rightly claim to be the original desktop-publishing package. Aldus was taken over by Adobe in 1994.

Both QuarkXPress and InDesign are based on the PostScript page-description language. Both boast a WYSIWYG (what you see is what you get) display, but the term is not strictly accurate. The printed result is far superior to the page you see on the screen, even at full zoom (magnification), because screen fonts are fundamentally different from printer fonts (see p. 71) and the illustrations may only be visible in "preview" quality. Nevertheless, what you see is far superior to

what compositors have seen on screen at the typesetter in the past. Both QuarkXPress and InDesign make extensive use of the **WIMP** (windows, icons, mouse, and pull-down menus) methodology, with "palettes" of tools (for drawing boxes, for example) and such things as style-sheet information that can be available on the screen all of the time (Fig. **5.19**).

Both systems are functionally similar; QuarkXPress gained a reputation as "industry standard," but today most practising designers are expected to be able to use InDesign also. But

5.19 Both InDesign and QuarkXPress allow you to compile and edit a style sheet outlining highly specific instructions for components such as the font, leading, and tracking of body text, headlines, and captions. Thus you can maintain consistency between publications.

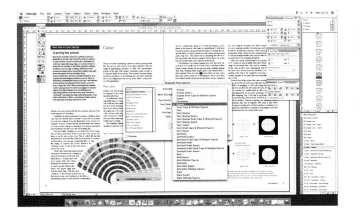

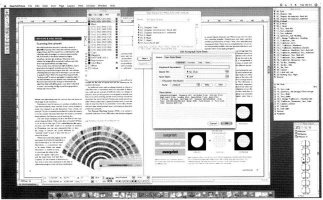

still there is no clear division, and designers will argue into the night about the relative merits of *their* program and its suitability to do a particular job. PageMaker will be remembered as being intuitive and simple to use. InDesign made great play about being able to output directly to PDF format (more of which later) and its ability to open QuarkXPress files. Quark has always claimed to be more accurate and with more "bells and whistles" appropriate to professional print production.

In PageMaker, and now in InDesign, the user is presented with a picture on the screen of a "pasteboard" for electronically pasting on text or graphics. Any elements not being used can be placed outside the page area on a virtual desktop until they are needed. When you open a new **document**, you are asked to enter the page size and margins in a "dialog box." (In computer language, any job you are working on is called a document, whether it is a drawing, a piece of text, or a page layout.) You will also be asked how many pages the publication will have. It is then possible to specify the number of columns, their width, and the spacing between them. All of these parameters can be changed later, if need be.

In QuarkXPress, you open a new **project** and then a layout by creating text and graphics boxes for the design elements. It has sophisticated drawing tools based on Bézier curves

Scanning and overscanning

Scan at your target output resolution—if you are going to print at 600 dpi then scan at 600 dpi. The rule of thumb for scanning halftones is to use the following formula:

scanning resolution in dpi =
[(target width (or height)/original width (or height)]
× screen ruling in lpi × 2

So if the image to be scanned is the same size as it will finish up in the final layout, then just double the screen ruling your printer recommends. Many photographs can be scanned at lower resolutions without affecting the print quality (down to 1.5 times the screen ruling), as long as they do not include geometric patterns, repeating textures, or straight lines. Adding the reproduction percentage (the part in square brackets) is unnecessary if your scanner allows you to set the enlargement or reduction.

Scanners use a row of CCDs (charge-coupled devices) to capture the image. If there are 600 of them per inch, then try to scan at a multiple of that. For the web, for example, instead of scanning at 72 dpi, scan at 100 dpi. This will use every sixth CCD—using regularly spaced CCDs will produce better results. You can then resample the scan to 72 dpi in Photoshop.

Rotate images before you import them

You can save time by cropping and rotating images in Photoshop before importing them to a page-layout program such as InDesign or QuarkXPress; it will also save time at the imagesetting stage. To straighten a crooked scan in Photoshop, select the crop tool and draw a box around the image to be straightened, leaving plenty of room between the image and the edge of the scan. Now rotate the crop box. Once the edge of the box is parallel with the image, press Return in order for Photoshop to straighten and crop the image at the same time.

and freeform paths. Complex shapes can be created by using Boolean operations (intersection, union, difference) to carve away or merge together simpler shapes—and a picture box can be created from the shape of a selection of text, to be filled, say, with an imported graphic. Text can be set on a path, can flow around all sides of an object, and clipping paths can be built around, say, the non-white areas of an imported TIFF image file. It can deal with text styles at the character level, rather than just at paragraph level: the styles palette shows the two current styles simultaneously.

Text can be imported from a word-processor document, and a symbol is placed in the position you wish the text to start. In "auto-flow" mode it will flow down the columns until all the text is in position. In regular mode, text will flow down the first column, and then stop.

In PageMaker, the text block took the appearance of a window-shade (roller blind). A red + in the "handle" indicated that there was more text in there to be placed. A blank handle indicated that all the text was accounted for. Once placed, the text could be moved around en masse. InDesign retains this ability to place text (and pictures) directly on to the page without first creating boxes (as you must in XPress), but now the text frames are created automatically.

There are several aids to consistency. Anything placed on "master pages" will appear on every page selected. This is useful for positioning construction lines, effectively creating a grid, and for inserting running heads and folios. You can compare alternative designs by creating a master for each idea and applying them in turn to a page of content.

Style sheets allow you to specify body text, captions, headlines, and different grades of subheadings, as well as instructions about indents for paragraphs, kerning, and hyphenation. Entire "skeleton" documents can be saved as templates, which can be used over and over to produce documents that are going to look similar—future issues of a newsletter, for example.

e-books

An **e-book** is a book in digital form. It can be a document scanned into **PDF** (**portable document format**), retaining all the formatting, typography, and illustrations of the original paper document; it can be output into PDF directly from a layout program such as QuarkXPress or InDesign, or it can be just pure text. An e-book can be read from a computer screen, or—to counter the argument that you can't curl up with an e-book on holiday—from a dedicated reader, such as Amazon's Kindle. Since the content is digital, text can be browsed, searched, annotated, or bookmarked in ways impossible with a traditional book. Usually, you pay the e-book vendor and then receive either an encrypted document or a password to a download site.

The ideas behind e-books are older than the internet itself. Back in 1945, Futurist Vannavar Bush imagined a "Memex"—a supplement to memory—in which people could store all their books, records, and communications to be consulted with speed and flexibility. In 1968, Ted Nelson coined the terms "hypertext" and "hypermedia" to include non-sequential text that could branch off in any direction. Project Gutenberg—an attempt to collect as many texts as possible in electronic format—began in 1971 at the Illinois Benedictine College.

The resolution of the average laptop, handheld, or desktop screen is only 72 or 96 dpi. This means type can appear jagged on-screen. Adobe has developed CoolType to improve on-screen text resolution using color anti-aliasing to individually manipulate the red, green, and blue subpixels on an LCD (liquid crystal display) screen. Microsoft's version is called ClearType, used in its Reader for notebook and desktop computers, pocket PCs, and tablet PCs.

Traditional computer font rendering assumes that each pixel is either "on" or "off," appearing as tiny black squares. Letters appear jagged on the computer screen because they are formed from many of these tiny squares. Grayscale anti-aliasing smooths the jagged edges but sacrifices edge sharpness. ClearType uses a human visual model to choose the brightness values of the color subpixels so that letters appear smooth and sharp.

What's next? Xerox PARC has developed a technology called **Gyricon**, described as "digital paper." It has many of the properties of paper, but is electronically writeable and erasable. A Gyricon sheet is a thin layer of transparent plastic in which millions of tiny beads—black on one side, white on the other—are randomly dispersed. The beads, each contained in an oil-filled cavity, are free to rotate within those cavities and are charged so that when voltage is applied they rotate to present one colored side to the viewer. The image will persist until new voltage patterns are applied.

A similar technology, called e-ink, was developed at MIT's Media Lab. An electrophoretic display is a liquid containing microcapsules, each containing white particles suspended in oil containing a dark dye. When an electric charge is applied,

5.20 Amazon's Kindle is a portable reader that wirelessly downloads books, magazines, and newspapers, without the need for a computer, to a crisp, high-resolution electronic paper display that looks and reads like real paper, even in bright sunlight.

the particles either show on the surface or remain hidden in the dye. The first commercial applications were signs in J. C. Penney stores, all of which could be updated simultaneously from a central computer. An e-book made from e-ink could look just like a regular book, but could be rewritten many times—"radio newspapers" could be updated wirelessly. Unlike LCD displays, e-ink requires no back lighting and draws current only when the text is changed. The first consumer application of electronic paper was Sony's Librié.

In 2007, Amazon launched the Kindle in the USA (Fig. **5.20**), an electronic paper display that downloads content from Amazon Whispernet, over Sprint's EVDO network. This means that the Kindle can be used without the need for a computer or a broadband account. The battery lasts roughly two days with wireless on, and one week wit wireless off. It has a 6 in (150 mm) four-level grayscale electrophoretic display with a resolution of 600 × 800 and weighs 10.3 oz (292 g). It also has built-in access to an online dictionary, and the online encyclopedia Wikipedia.

The advantages of electronic paper include low power usage, flexibility, and better readability than most displays, but color is still a problem. Other applications of e-paper include school books, price labels in shops, timetables at bus and railroad stations, electronic billboards, and on T-shirts.

I-Paper is an "intelligent" paper developed for security applications by Arjo Wiggins Carbonless Paper and PaperGate. It is a magnetic data storage medium that looks, feels, and prints like paper. An A4 (8¼ × 11¹¹⁄₁₆ in) sheet is capable of storing up to 1 Mbyte of data, which can be changed, erased, or rewritten using a standard magnetic printer with modified writing heads. It consists of two layers of conventional paper with a layer of magnetic data storage material in the middle and can be made from 100 gsm to around 300 gsm in plain, matte, silk, or gloss finishes.

Find out more

Adobe's e-paper website: www.adobe.com/epaper/ebooks/
Project Gutenberg website: promo.net/pg/
E-ink: www.eink.com
Gyricon: www2.parc.com/dhl/projects/gyricon

Make a preflight check

Your printer isn't telepathic, so before handing over the completed job on a CD or removable hard disk along with proofs and/or thumbnails, take time to produce a list of all the settings, files, fonts, colors, bleeds etc. in a **preflight** check, so called because just as an airplane pilot runs through a standard checklist before take-off, so should anyone signing off electronic files. QuarkXPress 7 can preflight a document. It works within the layout application itself and allows the user to jump directly to any problem or conflicting objects.

Account for every page in the publication, even blank ones. Indicate the number of color separations expected for each page, and note any details requiring special attention, such as instructions to position the saddle wires to avoid spoiling an illustration on the center spread. Keep notes brief—and include your name and telephone number just in case there are any unforeseen problems.

The "eyeball method" of evaluation is fine for simple jobs; for more complex workflows there are third-party programs such as Enfocus's Pitstop Professional and Markzware Flightcheck which can be helpful.

FlightCheck scans various file types including QuarkXPress, PageMaker, Multi-Ad Creator, Illustrator, Photoshop, FreeHand, CorelDraw, and PDF, and warns you of over 150 potential problems, such as incompatible graphic elements or font types. FlightCheck can investigate native document files without needing the application that created it. After verification, it reports a menu of possible problems like missing images or fonts, including fonts in EPS files.

Preflighting has grown from merely correcting PostScript errors to becoming a front end to a fully automated workflow and quality control system based on PDFs. Unlike most production lines, printers need to be more flexible with short runs and more complex jobs using miscellaneous machinery and systems that don't necessarily talk to each other, and so are turning to workflows standardized on PDFs.

JDF (job definition format) takes this one step further, integrating production planning, scheduling, project management, and management information systems. It is a proposed industry standard monitored by a consortium called CIP4 (Cooperation for the Integration of Processes in Prepress, Press, and Postpress) and based on their PPF (Print Production Format) and Adobe's PJTF (Portable Job Ticket Format) partial solutions for streamlining information exchange between different applications and systems.

In theory, and if adopted, it will allow different computer systems, equipment, and presses to be integrated seamlessly, bridging the communications gap between designers and production teams, and eliminating the need to re-key project information. By establishing end-to-end job-processing instructions upfront, JDF helps reduce the errors and costs associated with manual or redundant tasks. Once a job reaches prepress and production, JDF helps automate the workflow through each process step, increasing productivity and speeding job turnaround.

It is an open, extensible, job-ticket standard based on **XML (extensible markup language)**, see p. 237, containing details about the job—both the item itself (the intent) and the steps to completion (the process), with the ability to carry a print job from estimating and design, through prepress, onpress, postpress, and to delivery. Schedules can be re-adjusted based on feedback from the production machinery.

Trueflownet is Dainippon Screen's JDF-compliant implementation and is based on its web-based PDF/PostScript workflow system Trueflow. It features file checking, OPI, trapping, and imposition, and is designed to drive optimized CtP (computer-to-plate) production and digital printing presses (see Chapter 6).

Find out more

Flightcheck: www.markzware.com
CIP4: www.cip4.org

PageMaker incorporated a story editor which was virtually a word-processing package in itself—with a spelling checker, a search-and-replace command, and a word counter—and could be used for fast text entry and last-minute editing while you were working on the layout of a publication. InDesign didn't have this feature originally, but it was reinstated in version 3 (InDesign CS). Adobe InCopy is a separate text-editor that you can use to write and edit text while designers prepare the layout. With InCopy, you can track changes, add editorial notes, and fit copy.

InDesign can handle process and flat (spot) color, which can be specified by Pantone number (the color libraries also include Trumatch, Focoltone, Toyo Color Finder 1050, and DIC Color; further libraries can be imported from Illustrator), percentage tints and gradients, and also the 216 websafe RGB colors.

Objects can be grouped, resized, rotated, or cropped—and text can still be edited while remaining in the group. Any part of the layout can be masked using objects created with the drawing tools: ovals, rectangles, and polygons. Kerning and

Parkitecture

are our new public buildings too much fun?

a talk by Stephen F. Hutchinson
at Evesham Library

7pm, thursday 29 March, admission free

5.21 Jo McLaren of UK design group Square Enough created this poster entirely in InDesign, using different-shaped text frames like a child's set of colored wooden blocks.

Adding text to PDFs

You can edit text in a PDF using the TouchUp Text tool. But you can also add text to an area of a PDF where none exists by option-alt-/clicking (PC) or alt-cmd-clicking (Mac) the tool. A dialog box will appear asking which font and mode you'd like to use, then you can start typing. For more control over text formatting, a contextual pop-up menu can be opened by right-clicking (PC) or ctrl-clicking (Mac) the text block. Choosing "Properties" will take you to the TouchUp Properties panel where you can change the typeface, size, character, and word spacing, fill and stroke color, and even choose whether or not you want to embed and/or subset the selected font. Note that your ability to add text is limited by the degree of security added to the PDF in question.

feathered edges and soft drop shadows, and more versatile controls for creating tables. With the "separations preview" palette, you can visually check single or multiple plates, preview what is overprinting, and view ink-limit warnings.

With each new upgrade, InDesign and Quark continue to leapfrog each other—if a feature in one of them proves popular, then the rival will adopt its own interpretation. InDesign has introduced frames (Fig. **5.21**) and a control palette like in Quark; and QuarkXPress has changed over to the pasteboard metaphor. (It is a truism in computing that you only realize what something cannot do when they bring out a new version.) InDesign has plug-ins to add functionality to the basic program; Quark has its equivalent Xtensions. Both are also expanding

tracking can be in 0.0001 em increments. There are four kerning options in InDesign: manual, optical, metrics using kern pairs (the default), and range (what we call tracking).

Output will generally be to a laser printer or desktop color printer for proofing and low-grade output (for a newsletter, for example), to an imagesetter for bromide or film, or direct to a digital printing press. InDesign has built-in automatic trapping, and non-printing objects, such as production notes, can be defined. A "print fit" preview shows where the document will fit on the output page, complete with register and trim marks. Limited imposition schemes can be set up, to produce booklets, for example.

At the time of writing, QuarkXpress was on version 7, which added support for OpenType, Unicode, JDF, and PDF/X (a subset of PDF with printing and graphics related requirements) and built-in support for the Photoshop format (.psd). It also supports shadows and transparency. InDesign CS3 (an integral part of Adobe's Creative Suite) has built-in support for OpenType, Photoshop-like layers, pixel transparency,

Reducing PDF file size

There two ways to make a PDF file smaller in size: the Reduce File Size command under the File menu or, for more options, the PDF Optimizer under the Advanced menu. Using the Optimizer's "Audit space usage" function lets you see exactly what is affecting to the size of the file. The "Clean up" tab in the Optimizer will then let you eliminate it. Like Reduce File Size, PDF Optimizer lets you specify the level of Reader compatibility for the optimized PDF. But Optimizer also has Distiller-like controls over image and font compression. You can set exactly what pixels per inch resolution you downsample the images to, what method it should use for compressing the images, and whether it should unembed fonts, allowing you to choose which commonplace fonts you can safely remove.

Color management

One of the biggest headaches is making sure that the colors you see on your computer screen and in the images you have scanned stay faithful to the originals in the finished printed publication. Of course, it is just not physically possible to reproduce on a printed page the colors we see in nature, nor is it possible to print the colors we see on a computer monitor. This is because they all inhabit different color spaces, or gamuts. RGB can only display around 70 percent of the colors that can be perceived by the human eye. The CMYK color gamut is smaller, reproducing about 20 percent of perceivable colors. These gamuts are shown diagrammatically in Fig. 3.21 (p. 90) against a CIE (Commission Internationale de l'Eclairage) standard color space diagram.

Scanners, computer programs like Photoshop and QuarkXPress, monitors, printers, proofers, imagesetters, and printing presses all work within their own color spaces. It is unlikely at the outset of a project that you will know the type of printing press that will ultimately be used. Nor is it likely that the printing-press operator will be able to see the photographs and artwork you have been scanning.

If all of these device-specific color spaces could be mapped into a device-independent color space, such as the CIE color space, aka L*a*b color, and if all of the computer and applications vendors could agree on the interpretation of that color space, then it would become much easier for you to mix and match equipment from different vendors into one workflow and maintain color consistency throughout the production process.

Usually, scanners have a wider gamut than printers, but optimum reproduction cannot always be attained simply by making the color space smaller. So success can either be measured subjectively, by seeing if the grays appear gray and colors such as flesh, grass, and sky look acceptable, or objectively—using a colorimeter to measure how many colors from the input device have been faithfully reproduced.

In 1993 several companies, including Apple, Microsoft, Adobe, and Kodak, formed the International Color Consortium (ICC) to tackle this problem. One of their first decisions was that color space transformations are the responsibility of the operating system. Device profiles, containing information on the color behavior of a particular peripheral, would provide the data necessary to perform these transformations.

To build a scanner profile, for example, you would scan in a reference image and compare it with what the scanned values should be. Building a profile for a printer inverts the process. Here, a set of patches evenly distributed in the output ink color space are generated and printed. These patches are then measured to provide colorimetric data. Thankfully you don't have to do all this calibration and characterization yourself, although there are instruments available to calibrate monitors. Meanwhile, Apple's **ColorSync** had been gaining industry acceptance. It uses device profiles, usually stored as part of an image file (in the file's header or "table of contents"): these provide a description of how this image was captured, what its color space is, and more besides.

CMMs (**color-matching modules**) convert images from one color space to another and simultaneously apply the information in the profile to correctly render the image.

In each step of the workflow, ColorSync compensates for any deviations in the image-capturing systems of scanners, the display anomalies of monitors, and the color-imaging components of printers and output devices. The CMMs from vendors such as Heidelberg, Kodak, and Agfa are packaged in each version of ColorSync along with a CMM from Apple.

The device-independent color space used by ColorSync (and also by Photoshop to convert from RGB to CMYK, for example) is CIE L*a*b—a three-dimensional color space based on the theory that a color cannot be both green and red at the same time, nor blue and yellow at the same time. L is the lightness component, ranging from 0 to 100; a is the green–red axis; and b is the blue–yellow axis. Both can range from +128 to −128. The white reference point is usually based on the whitest light that can be generated by a given device.

RGB workflows

Although a CMYK workflow is logical and more commonplace, an RGB workflow can capture and retain a far broader gamut of colors—Pantone's Hexachrome system can, for example, print a gamut 30 percent larger than the four-color process. With image capture from desktop scanners and digital cameras, there are obvious advantages to the designer, since their images start in the same color space as their monitors. Printers can scan multiple images on a flatbed scanner rather than one at a time on a drum scanner. You can position low-resolution files in QuarkXPress or InDesign documents and then have the repro house or printer replace the color-adjusted file. You must, however, work with all RGB images or all CMYK images, and not mix the two. Furthermore, because many clients repurpose work for the web, which is also RGB, this allows designers to use the same source files for cross-media projects, streamlining workflow and helping to maintain better color consistency across media. Always check with your printer to see if a CMYK or an RGB workflow is preferred.

Find out more

International Color Consortium: www.color.org/
ColorSync: www.apple.com/colorsync/

from print into newer media such as CD-ROM production and the internet, with features that help convert page layouts into HTML (hypertext markup language—see Chapter 7, p. 228) and Adobe Acrobat's PDF (Portable Document Format).

The essence of digital make-up is that you can be as rigid or as flexible as you choose. InDesign is said to be more intuitive than QuarkXPress, but some designers are convinced that Quark has more functionality, with just about every typographic control you could wish for. It is beyond the scope of this book to describe every feature of each program. The above can only give you a flavor of what both Adobe InDesign and Quark have to offer. Check with a dealer for the specification of the latest update. Both will continue to change and improve, and ultimately the choice between them continues.

Full-color digital prepress

In some workflows, layouts are designed on a system using only low-resolution images, in the same way that photocopies of halftones on a mechanical were once used "FPO (for position only)," with transparencies sent to the repro house to be "stripped-in" later.

Printers and repro houses have been using digital scanners coupled with computers for many years. Organizations with digital prepress systems from suppliers such as Scitex and Dainippon Screen have been able to scan in and retouch color transparencies since the early 1970s. Of course, these systems have been capable of much more, but were so expensive to buy and run that printers, afraid that designers might develop the "bad habit" of asking for alterations to their images, adopted an almost conspiratorial silence.

With OPI (open prepress interface), you, the designer, use low-resolution images, called proxies, as position-only visuals to produce the "electronic mechanicals" on your desktop make-up system. High-resolution scans, straight from the original transparencies, are reunited with the layouts in the imagesetter at the repro house.

The low-resolution scans used in the computer until the proofing stage can be straight from your desktop scanner, or they can be "compressed" versions of scans from the repro house's system. As you lay out the images, the system remembers all the scaling, rotating, and cropping alterations made to the image, and conveys them to the operator at the repro house. This makes considerable savings on set-up time compared with conventional repro techniques, in which the operator has to check and measure position mark-ups on overlays.

5.22 A regular desktop design system can be used as a front-end to the system at the repro house, mixing and matching the abilities of both to the best and most economical advantage. Transparencies are sent to the repro house, where both high- and low-resolution scans are made. The low-res scans are used in your layouts and the high-res ones are substituted later, when the final pages are made up.

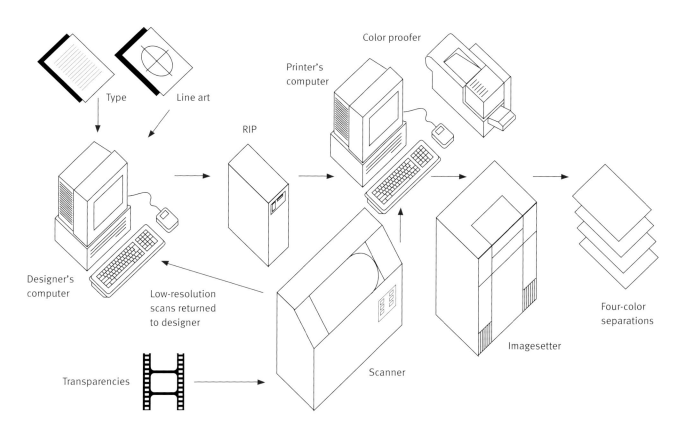

Spot the difference

Have you ever played spot the difference between two similar documents? Export them both to PDF, using the same settings, and choose Document > Compare Documents. Select the two PDFs you want to compare and choose either "Page-by-page visual differences," which will highlight differences in image, color, and text; or "Textual differences" which focuses on the copy alone and indicates which words were inserted/deleted or changed format. For best results you may need to run the compare twice, once for each method. It won't tell you exactly what's different, but by helping you to zoom in on problem areas it can considerably improve troubleshooting, or give you the reassurance to discard a redundant identical document.

An EPS (encapsulated PostScript) file can be a resolution-independent graphic from a vector program such as Illustrator, or a complete page containing bitmap images from Quark (called DCS—Desktop Color Separations—in Quark). They can also include OPI comments, which can link to other documents, such as high-resolution versions of an image.

Complex cut-outs and **masks** can be made and these are automatically translated into smooth high-resolution masks at the repro house, using a technique called mask-density substitution. In the same way, graduated tints (called dégradés in Scitex talk) are recreated automatically in high-resolution versions.

Most page layouts are output to an imagesetter via a RIP (raster image processor), which changes the PostScript outlines of the letters and drawings into a bitmap (an array of dots) that the imagesetter can print out. Once all color and mono elements are in place, the page can be proofed on a digital proofing system.

After corrections have been made, the PostScript file can be sent via CD, removable hard disk, or via the internet to the repro house. This assumes, of course, that the repro house already holds the original transparencies! At the repro house, all type, tints, and images are plotted directly on to final output film, with no need for intermediate typesetting, imagesetting, or stripping-in.

The system at the repro house (Fig. **5.22**) is built around a top-quality drum scanner, a RIP, and a high-resolution imagesetter, and one difference between it and the kind of system you may find in a designer's studio is that at the repro house all operations are carried out in CMYK. Desktop systems generally use RGB for image capture and manipulation and only convert to CMYK right at the end of the process. Color-management systems, such as ColorSync and constant calibration, are critical for the color you see on your screen to end up on the printed page.

Late binding is a term used to mean last-minute changes within PostScript files while they are in the RIP, such as adding trapping and imposition information, particularly for digital presses. The advantage of supplying the repro house or printer with the job in PDF format is that late changes—including rearranging pages—can be made and viewed regardless of whether they have a Mac, Windows, or Unix system, or whether they have access to the application that originally created it.

Quick PDFs

When using Acrobat's "Print to PDF," the engine that creates your PDF is called Distiller, which comes with preconfigured profiles, also called settings or joboptions files. In Windows, you can change the profile by clicking the Print dialog's Properties button. On Macs, select PDF Options from the Copies & Pages dropdown menu. When creating a PDF for print, ask the printer for a joboptions file to use. You can then select your printer's or service bureau's particular profile when creating a PDF for them. You can "Save As PDF" or PDF/X straight from the Macintosh OS X print dialog box. Apple's proprietary PDF graphics system is called Quartz. You can reduce the file size of a PDF (for emailing, for example) by choosing a Quartz filter from the ColorSynch dropdown menu in the Print dialog box. In Leopard (10.5), hit the "Preview" button instead to open the PDF in the Preview application where Quartz filters are available in the "Save As" dialog box.

Repro

Film make-up

For most high-quality work, and multicolor printing, the design elements may still be assembled together on film (Fig. **5.23**). It is unlikely that the average graphic designer will ever be asked to do film make-up—the **assembly** will be done by a professional called a "stripper." But graphic designers effectively have to brief the strippers with their roughs, and check the results, so it is important to know what is going on.

Film used by printers has a high-speed, high-contrast emulsion on a polyester base. The emulsion side of the film is slightly duller than the other side, and it may be possible to see the image on the film if it is held up to the light and viewed at a shallow angle. If in doubt, scratch the film—well away from the image area, naturally—to discover which side the emulsion is on.

Film can be right reading, or wrong (reverse) reading. As you can view film from either side, it is important to specify "emulsion up" or "emulsion down" as well.

When the printing plates are made, the film is always put in contact with the plate for maximum sharpness. The emulsion touches the plate, i.e. the film is emulsion-side down.

The type of film most commonly used is **right-reading emulsion down** (**RRED**), also known as **wrong-reading emulsion up** (**WREU**). The image appears the correct way round (is right-reading) when the film is viewed from the shiny side, and wrong-reading from the dull emulsion side. RRED film is used for litho printing—and for all offset processes. When the film is contacted with the plate, the image is transferred so that it is right-reading. During printing, the ink on the plate transfers as wrong-reading to the rubber blanket, and then as right-reading to the paper (Fig. **5.24**; there is more about the offset litho process on p. 187).

Wrong-reading emulsion down (**WRED**) film, also known as **right-reading emulsion up** (**RREU**), has a wrong-reading image when viewed from the shiny side and is right-reading when viewed from the dull emulsion side. WRED film is used for direct printing processes, such as gravure. When the cylinder is made, the image is wrong-reading. It transfers ink to the paper directly, and becomes right-reading (see p. 193 for further information on gravure).

Pages can be assembled using positive or negative film. Negative film, with all the white space turned to black, is often too dense to use accurately. So most color **stripping-in** is done using positive film. The stripper uses a white board, on to which the grid (or layout) plus all the trim and center marks have been drawn or preprinted. A clear carrier sheet of polyester or acetate is laid on to this guide, and for each page the design elements (type, line illustrations, and halftones) on film are assembled into place with the emulsion side

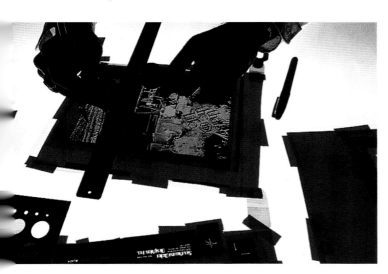

5.23 At the printer's, halftones and tints are "stripped-in" to the spaces left in the text films. Opaque material such as Rubylith is used to blank out black or solid flat-color areas on positive film or white areas on negative film.

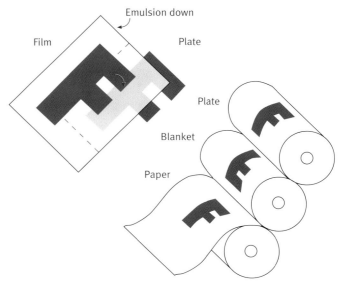

5.24 For offset litho work, strippers most often use positive right-reading emulsion down film. Thus the emulsion comes into contact with the surface of the plate; the blanket is wrong-reading; and the final printed image is right-reading.

uppermost. The film elements are cut to size with a scalpel and attached to the base sheet with pressure-sensitive tape, in order to leave a uniformly flat surface, with none of the elements overlapping.

If the layout is quite complex, with lots of design elements stuck down with tape, a copy is made on to positive-working daylight film. This is called the **final**. Every time a duplicate is made, however, there is a slight degradation in quality. The best results are obtained when film is copied emulsion to emulsion. Using normal negative-working film, the image would be reversed and another copy would have to be made to right it. Special **auto-reversing film** is used instead to keep the number of steps to a minimum.

For multicolor work, a separate clear carrier sheet is used for each of the process colors. The registration (alignment) between the separate finals has to be observed meticulously, using a **pin-register** system to line up the trim marks and multicolor elements (see below).

As discussed earlier, it is generally most economical to print several pages together, in one pass of the printing press. Putting together the **flat** (Fig. **5.25**), or forme, to make a 16- or 32-page plate is the stripper's job, and here's how it is done.

A single-color flat with no registration problems to worry about is usually made up from film negatives, assembled together on an opaque, orange-colored paper called **Goldenrod**. Goldenrod contains a dye that prevents ultraviolet (UV) light from passing through it, and acts as a mask to protect the non-printing areas of the flat. The negative film is placed in position emulsion side up, and the whole assembly is turned over. Windows are then cut into the Goldenrod to allow UV light to pass through the image areas. The assembled flat is placed on the press plate and exposed in a **printing-down frame**.

Goldenrod can stretch, so, for work requiring close registration, the negatives are assembled first on to clear acetate or polyester sheets, emulsion side up. The assembly is turned over

HOT TIPS & COOL TRICKS

Getting film made

Until everyone uses direct computer-to-plate technology, you will still need film. It can save a lot of hassle to get film made at a service bureau, rather than letting the printer do it—you can even use the film as a final last proof. But talk to your printer first. Positive film may be easier for you to read, but many printers prefer negative film, which is easier to touch up and cheaper to make plates from. If you're doing a job that doesn't require a black separation—in two spot colors, for example—make sure that the registration and trim marks have been included on the separations.

and non-printing areas are masked using either Goldenrod or a red/amber masking film.

For multicolor printing, a positive flat is made for each of the process colors. To ensure close registration, these are pin-registered (Fig. **5.26**) with pins and a special punch used to make holes in the flats. They can be correctly located with pins on the press plate, and again the plates can be located on the press cylinder with further pins and clamps.

An alternative method is called **blue and red keys**. The first flat is assembled using either the cyan or the magenta elements. This is exposed in contact with a sheet of blue or red **dyeline** film, which produces a key image of the original image in blue or red. With blue keys, each color flat is registered in position using the blue to give accurate sightings. When complete, the flat is used for platemaking in the normal way, as the blue does not record on the plate. Red does record, however, so when red keys are used, the flat is assembled on to a clear acetate sheet with the red keys underneath, acting as a guide.

5.25 The stripper assembles all the pages for one printing into a flat ready for platemaking, opaquing out any blemishes or marks not to be printed.

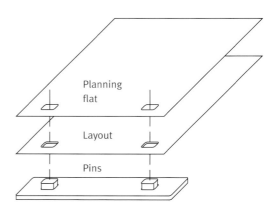

5.26 For color work, each printing must be in close register. Pin registration is a system of precisely placed holes and corresponding pins which ensure that all the films, flats, and plates are correctly aligned.

Picture proofing

Film for a single color is commonly proofed as a positive dyeline or **diazo** print (contact ammonia print), called an **ozalid**, **brownline**, **blueprint**, or **blue**. Blues (which may also be gray, brown, or other colors) often give the only opportunity to check the **alignment** of halftones and other elements. This is absolutely the last chance to make any changes before the job is "put to bed."

It may be necessary to see the printed quality of halftones, either all together in random order, as **scatter proofs**, or—probably more expensively—in their correct position on the page, as page proofs.

Color separations of illustrations and photographs can be proofed photographically or digitally, as inkjet, **dye-sublimation**, or **thermal-transfer prints**, or on plastic laminate systems. These are called **prepress proofs**, or **dry proofs**, and are all approximations to the finished printed result, but will give you an idea of what to expect.

Photographic systems work by exposing each process color separation in turn on to a three-layer photographic paper, using filters. The material is then processed to produce the color proof.

One-off transfer or integral proofs, such as DuPont's **Cromalin** and Kodak's **Matchprint**, take colored powders or pre-coated sheets representing the process colors. They are laminated in register on to white paper. With some systems it is possible to use the same stock as you will be using for the final printing, which is useful for checking color and inking accurately.

Plastic laminate proofs, such as Kodak's **Color-Key** and DuPont's **Cromacheck**, build up an image layer by layer on to a plastic substrate using mylar or acetate overlay film; one for each process color.

Digital proofing systems produce proofs direct from the computer's memory, using inkjet, thermal-transfer, dye-sublimation, or electrostatic technologies (Fig. **5.27**).

Wet proofs require four plates to be made from the separations and printed on a flatbed proofing press. This should produce the most realistic representation of the finished job, and allows several sets of proofs to be made. Ensure that a complete set of color bars (see Fig. **5.28**) is run with the proof—these can later be compared with the values being recorded on the press. And ask for standard inks to be used.

A full set of **progressives** can be obtained in this way. Progressives are color proofs printed in the same order in which the process colors will be applied at press time. Each color printing is shown separately and also surprinted with the other colors. A typical set comprises the individual process colors of yellow, magenta, cyan, and black, accompanied by the cumulative combinations: magenta on yellow; cyan on yellow and magenta; and finally black on yellow, magenta, and cyan. Some printers vary the sequence by running the cyan printing before the magenta. Make sure to ask for progressives in the **laydown sequence**—the order in which the finished job will be printed.

For flat color, the printer may offer a **drawdown**—a smear of ink from a smooth blade on a particular paper stock. This should not be relied upon, however, to give an accurate impression of how a particular color will print on the press.

5.27 Most proofing is now done on inkjet printers such as these HP Designjet Z2100 series printers available in 24-in and 44-in wide versions. They output to high-gloss, semi-gloss, or matte proofing paper at up to 2400 × 1200 dpi using eight HP Vivera pigment inks: cyan, light cyan, magenta, light magenta, yellow, light gray, photo black, and matte black. ColorByte's Imageprint RIP supports five standard viewing conditions and the ability to produce neutral black and white prints.

Checking proofs

Remember that contract color proofs will not reproduce exactly the way that ink will appear on your chosen paper stock: this is especially true for any varnishes, spot colors, and metallic inks. Check that colors are even and consistent, and check tints to make sure they are not mottled. Use printed swatches to check spot colors. Examine the color bar for lost detail. Make sure bleeds and crossovers extend beyond the trim marks. Check for weak or breaking-up type. Use a loupe to look closely at highlights and shadows. Pay attention to flesh tones and hair. Bright reflected light in the eyes should have no dot, only paper white. On fluffy clouds, magenta and yellow dots should be as small as possible, with cyan dots only slightly larger.

It is important, when viewing color samples, to ask for the same paper stock as will be used for the final printing. Always make allowance for the fact that **press proofs** pulled from a proofing press will be sharper and show less dot gain (see p. 208) than a high-speed production press.

Check the proofs to see that the images are the right way around—it's amazing how often they are upside-down or reversed (flopped) left-to-right, or both—and at the correct resolution. Low-res images sometimes slip through! Check also for the correct crop, size, position, and sharpness, and mark any obvious imperfections such as spots and scratches. Black-and-white proofs need to be checked for contrast—they should have the entire tonal range from shadow to highlights.

When it comes to marking proofs for color correction, tell the printer or repro house as plainly as possible what you think is wrong. Color judgment is subjective, and there may be many routes to a better end result. Just because something has a blue cast, it does not necessarily mean that there is too much cyan—the cyan may be all right but the other colors may need taking up. It is better to say "too blue" than to instruct the printer with technical certainty to "take down the cyan."

Soft proofing is a way of simulating the look of a paper proof on your computer screen, mainly to preview proper color assignments, overprints, separations, transparency, and other issues that might cause problems later at the printers. The screen should first be properly calibrated (make sure it has been switched on for at least an hour), and ICC profiles obtained for the paper stock and ink to be used. Control the ambient light to create a neutral environment with no direct sunlight.

To preview a PDF as it will look printed offset, for example, use an ICC profile such as US Web Coated (SWOP) v2.

You can simulate the whiteness of the paper and blackness of the ink. To preview the PDF document as it theoretically is printed on paper, choose from either an ICC profile you created or from the preset profiles such as Euroscale, SWOP, and so on. For printing on offset press on coated stock use US Web Coated (SWOP) v2. The "proof" image on screen will look washed out compared with the original image because the whites will no longer be as bright as the monitor can display. The trick is to eliminate all user interface elements from the screen so that your eye sees nothing whiter than those whites in the proofed image.

ICS's Remote Director and Kodak's Matchprint Virtual are soft proofing systems that are SWOP (Specifications for Web Offset Publications) certified and allow real-time collaboration throughout the workflow—upstream to content creation and production approval and downstream to press-side proofing.

Some workflows use email to pass around PDFs to be proofread. **Web proofing** stores the PDF centrally so everyone always has access to an up-to-date proof, with a full history of changes. You can track the changes made to the text and you can make comments and annotations about the layout. This is also called web-to-print or web2print. A **contract proof** is the final proof before going to press. Currently the de facto standard for a contract proof is a Matchprint or laminate proof but some digital proofs are now considered good enough to accurately predict color on press.

Color bars

Color bars (Fig. **5.28**) yield vital information about the performance of both the press and the inks being used. To be able to interpret them arms you with the knowledge to improve the quality of the job without being "blinded by science" at the printer. They contain a whole range of tests: some are visual checks; others require special instruments such as a **densitometer**. And they are totally independent of the job, thus representing a consistent guide to the standard of printing you can expect.

Color bars comprise most or all of the following components:

1. Printing-down controls. There will be a series of micro-lines and highlight dots to assess how accurately the job has been printed down from film to plate.

2. Solid density patches for each color. These monitor ink-film thickness, and should be read using a densitometer.

3. Trapping patches. These show solid process colors printed on top of others in different combinations, and they test how ink is being accepted in wet-on-wet printing. There will also be a dense black made up from 100 percent black, 55 percent cyan, 42.5 percent yellow, and 42.5 percent magenta (= 240 percent the maximum recommended percentage of tints; see also p. 93).

4. Screen patches. Patches for each process color at different screens are used to monitor dot gain. Dot gain happens as the ink spreads around just-joined-up dots in the middle tones, tending to make these areas look darker than they should be. At one tone lighter, where the dots are not yet touching, density does not gain to the same extent. This effect can cause a visible jump in an otherwise smooth gradation of tone. Elliptical dots can help alleviate the problem.

5. Coarse and fine halftone scale. This quick visual check comprises ten steps in the form of the numerals 0 to 9 set using a screen of 200 lines, which are dropped out of a background tint screened at 65 lines. Dot gain shows as the numbers fill in and become visible—the theory is that fine tints are more sensitive to dot gain than coarser ones.

6. Slur gauge. These patches reveal any directional dot gain caused by slurring or doubling, and take the form of star targets and/or oblongs containing both horizontal and vertical lines.

7. Gray balance. If all is well, a 50 percent cyan, 40 percent magenta, and 40 percent yellow, printed on top of each other, should produce a neutral gray.

5.28 A color bar is used by printers to assess the performance of their presses—giving information, for example, about dot gain and slurring. It appears away from the image area and is trimmed off the sheets later.

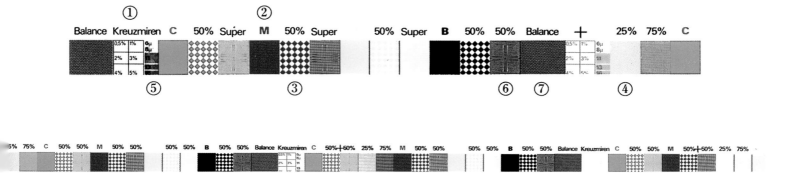

Summary

Prepress is where the text set in type, the illustrations and photographs, and any other graphic elements, such as rules, boxes, and areas of flat color, all come together in a form that can be printed. The prepress process starts with the page layout on to which graphic elements—typesetting, line art, and photographs—are assembled. For simple black-and-white work, the job is completed.

For close-registration color work, however, halftones may be processed on to film, and stripped in at the printers on to flats.

For medium- and large-scale jobs, it is important to give some thought to imposition schemes. Early planning in this area can have a substantial effect on the cost-effectiveness and smooth running of a project.

The preparation of type and graphic elements at the prepress stage can also be carried out on a computer, using the electronic cut-and-paste of desktop programs such as QuarkXPress and Adobe InDesign. Layouts can then be output by laser or inkjet printers on to plain paper, or by higher-resolution imagesetters as bromide prints or film.

Whichever method or system is used, it is essential to see and to be able to understand the prepress process of proofs and color bars, so that you can be sure of quality . . . and know that your design is going to be printed as you envisaged it!

Jonathan Barnbrook

"It is far more important to do the work that you are excited by,
not work that you feel you should do."

Manifesto

"I would like to say this very simply—graphic design is not just about marketing, it is not just an industry; it is an area of mass communication which means you have the potential to communicate what you believe in to an amazing amount of people. Unfortunately there are plenty of designers who believe that everything has to be framed within the market economy, that things are 'indulgent' if they do anything else. This is utter utter rubbish—design does not just serve the market economy; this is an imposed political ideal based on abstract idea called profit, not human need. If people want to show their own human responses in their work they should do so, if they feel that their work should connect with others in different areas over and above the client's message they should do so. To treat design as a marketing tool is a political decision amongst many and not the only one.

"When I teach at colleges the first thing I usually say is forget about the idea of producing a portfolio to get a 'job.' The work you want to do will attract more of the work you want to do.

"I don't believe your work is separate from your life, it's part of it, so I regard what I do in design as an extension of my philosophy in the way I live my life rather than the other way around. So in short, although I am not perfect I do try to practice what I preach as a good citizen in everything that I do.

"We don't work with companies we don't agree with, which has cost us a lot of money. I live in a modest house and get to work on a bicycle I have had for ten years, or the subway. We do charity work, but not as often as we would like and I think you have to start out with these kind of values otherwise you become like every other 'suit'. Finally after all this ranting I would say that it is important to laugh, if you can't see your own self as funny then that is a problem. On a wider scale I would like to quote a favorite writer of mine called Hermann Hesse who said 'Eternity is just long enough for a joke.'"

British graphic designer and typographer Jonathan Barnbrook was born in Luton in 1966 and trained at Barnfield College in Luton, Croydon College of Art, Central St Martins School of Art, and the Royal College of Art in London. He is most recognized for his work on the cover artwork of David Bowie's 2002 album *Heathen* which featured the debut for his Priori typeface. Other well-known fonts designed by Barnbrook (first released through Emigre, and now Virus Fonts) include Bastard, Exocet, False Idol, Infidel, Moron, Newspeak, Sarcastic, Shock & Awe, and Tourette. The emotive and controversial titles reflect the style and themes of Barnbrook's work.

From 1997 to 2003 Barnbrook collaborated with British artist Damien Hirst, most notably on the design, layout, and typography of his book *I Want To Spend the Rest of My Life Everywhere, with Everyone, One to One, Always, Forever, Now* and on artwork associated with his restaurant *Pharmacy*.

A recurring theme of Barnbrook's graphic design is political work and work with a social conscience. He describes as a major influence to his work "an inner anger which is a response to all the unfairness that is in this world" and has stated his ambition to use "design as a weapon for social change."

As such he was a signatory to the *First Things First 2000* manifesto, in which graphic designers, including Erik Spiekermann and Zuzana Licko, pledged to put their skills to worthwhile use and address the environmental, social, and cultural crises that they see in the world. This former sentiment is expressed in part by his 2001 artwork "Designers, stay away from corporations that want you to lie for them," a quote from Tibor Kalman, which took the form of a large-format advertising billboard displayed in Las Vegas during an AIGA convention.

Barnbrook has also contributed work to, and art-directed, two editions of *Adbusters*, the anti-advertising magazine edited by Kalle Lasn in Canada that seeks to expose the harm that advertising and large corporations do to us all.

Barnbrook is big in Japan, designing the logo and corporate identity for Roppongi Hills, the largest post-war development in Tokyo, and which includes the Mori Art Museum. They used Priori for all the signage, although Barnbrook was annoyed to find they decided to use Jan Tschichold's Sabon in the main building where the staff work.

An exhibition of his work entitled "Friendly Fire" took place at the Design Museum in London in 2007: work in response to the first and second Iraq conflicts, the *First Things First Manifesto*, and examples of Barnbrook's typography and film work. A 320-page hardback collection of his work—*The Barnbrook Bible*—was also published in 2007.

Resources

www.barnbrook.net

Jonathan Barnbrook and Kalle Lasn, *Barnbrook Bible: The Graphic Design of Jonathan Barnbrook*, Booth-Clibborn Editions, London, 2007

Paul Felton, *The Ten Commandments of Typography/Type Heresy: Breaking the Ten Commandments of Typography*, Merrell, London, 2006 (Foreword by Jonathan Barnbrook)

Damien Hirst, *I Want to Spend the Rest of My Life Everywhere, with Everyone, One to One, Always, Forever, Now*, Booth-Clibborn Editions (Compact edition), London, 2006

Designers, stay away from corporations that want you to lie for them—Adbusters billboard, Las Vegas, 2001.

Cover of *Heathen* by David Bowie, 2002, which featured the debut for his Priori typeface.

I Want To Spend The Rest Of My Life Everywhere, With Everyone, One To One, Always, Forever, Now—cover of Damian Hirst monograph, 1997.

On Press

The secret of a successful print job is a well-designed layout, some good scans for color repro, and the correct choice of paper and ink. If all these aspects are right, a good printing company can be relied upon to produce a pleasing result.

On press is the one part of the process that the graphic designer scarcely influences. It's now time to say goodbye to the layouts, leaving the printing work in the experienced hands of the printer.

Paper is one of the basic foundations of a good print job, but so often its choice is an afterthought. The first task in specifying paper is to think hard about what the finished item has to achieve. Then, after carefully considering the budget and availability of the stock, the designer can decide which particular characteristics of a paper are required.

Ink, too, plays a crucial role in the printing process, and the right formulation must be used for the right technology. Knowing about how inks perform will allow you to predict accurately how a job will come out. We discuss the effect of varnishing and laminating on an ink's performance, and explain the difference between die-stamping and thermography.

The printing process itself has a profound effect on print quality. The majority of designers will probably use offset litho or direct digital for most applications, but in some circumstances, gravure can become a cost-effective possibility. And when should you use flexography, or even screenprinting? What are the pros and cons? This chapter gives an insight into the process of choosing the right supplier, and suggests how to go about ensuring the best-quality job.

Finally, we come to finishing—all those operations of folding, gathering, stitching, and trimming that happen to a printed sheet after it leaves the press. What are the options? Is perfect binding better than saddle-stitching? This chapter explains.

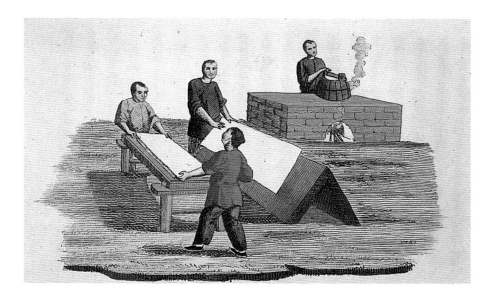

6.1 Papermaking in China, from a sequence of miniatures dating from 1811. Note that two people are required to make large sheets, a feat of coordination usually avoided by Western papermakers.

Paper

Papermaking is older than any of the other printing crafts. Paper is largely a natural product—organic fibers held together by their own molecular forces. It is easy to make, but hard to make well. You can make it at home, with the help of a blender, some torn-up paper and other fibrous material (flowers, straw, cotton), and some kind of mesh to let the water drip through. Whether it will have the right degree of absorbency, strength, and surface finish required for fine printing is another matter.

The word "paper" comes from the Greek word "papyrus," the name of a plant that grows on the banks of the River Nile in Egypt. The writing material made from papyrus was not the kind of paper we are familiar with today. It was produced from strips peeled from the stem of the plant and pounded together into sheets.

The invention of paper made entirely from vegetable fibers—in this case tree bark, hemp, rags, and fishing nets—was announced to the Emperor of China in AD 105. However, a quasi-paper, made from pulped silk, was being made at least 200 years before that date.

Papermaking flourished in China (Fig. **6.1**), but the techniques took a thousand years to reach Europe. The first documented paper mill was established in Spain, at Xativa, around 1150. Mills were later set up in Italy, at Fabriano (a name still famous for the manufacture of beautiful paper) around 1260, and in Hertfordshire, England, around 1490. Papermaking was brought to America by a German, William Rittenhouse. The first American paper mill was established in Germantown, Pennsylvania, in 1690. Paper mills couldn't be built just anywhere. The process depends on huge amounts of pure running water—150,000 US gallons (120,000 UK gallons or about 500,000 liters) of water, for example, are required to manufacture just one ton (or metric tonne) of handmade paper.

Until the 19th century, all paper was made by hand. The first papermaking machine was invented by Nicolas-Louis Robert in 1798 and built in France. His patents were taken up by Henry and Sealy Fourdrinier, and further developed in England. The Fourdrinier process, as it is known, allowed paper to be made in a continuous operation, producing a web (Fig. **6.2**), or roll, at the end of what are still some of the largest machines in existence.

6.2 Papermaking is a continuous process, producing huge webs, or rolls, of paper. These are cut into sheets or made into smaller webs to feed the huge web litho, gravure, or flexo presses. Here, recycled paper is shown drying, at a mill in Minnesota.

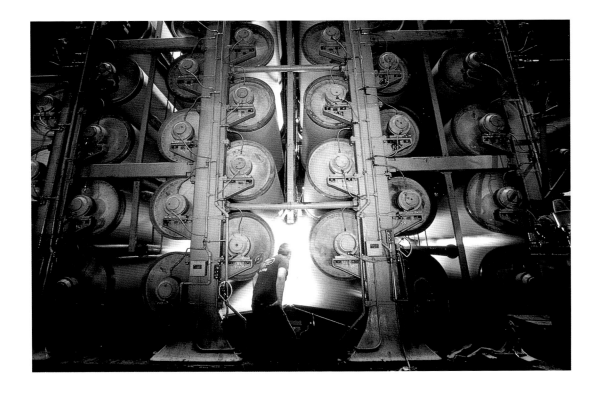

The raw materials

Paper is made from cellulose fibers, and these come from plants or trees. Cellulose is a chemical compound of the elements carbon, hydrogen, and oxygen, and constitutes the cell walls of plants. Cellulose fibers are tubular, and swell when immersed in water. Allowed to dry in close contact with one another, they create their own gelatin "adhesive." Along with the bonding from the fibrillation (splitting and fraying) of the fibers, this produces an extremely strong material. The resulting paper is naturally porous and will absorb the inks and dyes used in printing. And it can be made less porous by adding a substance called **size**. It is also inert enough not to be affected by inks or photographic chemicals. The fibers are colorless and transparent, yet produce paper that is white and opaque.

Early paper mills made paper from rags. Textile production requires strong, long fibers for spinning and weaving. Papermaking is not as exacting, so papermills could recycle the shorter fibers from de-buttoned cast-off clothing and offcuts from shirt manufacturers, turning them into paper. Synthetic fibers such as nylon and rayon have put a stop to that. Artificial fibers (and animal fibers such as wool) are much more inert than cellulose. They do not bond as it does, and if they find their way into paper, they weaken it and produce clear specks among the opaque white of the natural fibers.

One remaining source of pure cotton "rags," however, is the T-shirt industry, and its waste clippings are used to produce some of the finest papers. Another source of cotton for papermaking is from **linters**. These are the fibers left on the seed once the longer fibers for yarnmaking have been removed. The best linters come from the southern states of the United States, and from Egypt.

Clippings and linters are sorted, shredded, and placed in a large boiler. Under pressure and steam, any contaminants are removed. The fibers are washed and pulped. The dirty water is then drained off, clarified, and reused. The pulp is bleached, and any chemicals left over are recycled into the next batch.

Designers have always demanded whiter and brighter papers. Pulpmills used to use chlorine gas in the bleaching process, but the combination of chlorine and organic molecules in the wood fibers creates cancer-causing dioxins. Virtually all mills have now converted to at least **ECF** (**elemental chlorine-free**) bleaches, such as chlorine dioxide. **TCF** (**totally chlorine-free**) means that the virgin fiber is either unbleached or bleached using non-chlorine compounds, such as hydrogen peroxide. **PCF** (**processed chlorine-free**) means that the recycled fiber in the sheet is unbleached or bleached with non-chlorine compounds. Any virgin fibers in a PCF sheet must be TCF. To promote their environmental credentials, some mills say that their papers are PCF and ECF. However, a paper can only be one or the other. If there is any ECF pulp involved in the making of this paper, it cannot be called PCF. The best you can do is a sheet that is completely PCF, made from recycled pulp that is PCF, with the virgin portion of the pulp TCF. In 2005, ECF pulping using chlorine dioxide accounted for 75 percent of bleached kraft pulp globally, with only 5 percent of paper bleached using TCF sequences, mainly in Finland and Sweden—the pulp and paper going to the German market, where regulations and consumer demand makes it viable.

Most paper for general-purpose use is produced from wood. There are two kinds of **woodpulp**: mechanical and chemical. Mechanical, or groundwood, woodpulp is made by grinding logs under a stream of water, after first removing the bark (Fig. **6.3**). This results in the cheap but not very strong pulp used in **newsprint** and rougher grades of wrapping paper. It is the lignin left in mechanical pulp that makes the resulting paper turn brown and brittle in sunlight.

Chemical pulp relies on chemical agents such as calcium or sodium bisulfite to separate the wood fibers (Fig. **6.4**). This way they are damaged less than in mechanical pulping, and thus paper from chemical pulp is of a higher quality. Oddly, chemical pulp is sometimes known as **woodfree**.

There are two sources of woodpulp: from softwood (coniferous) and hardwood trees. When softwood is beaten, it loses opacity. Well-beaten softwood is thus used for hard, translucent papers, such as glassine (in the windows of envelopes,

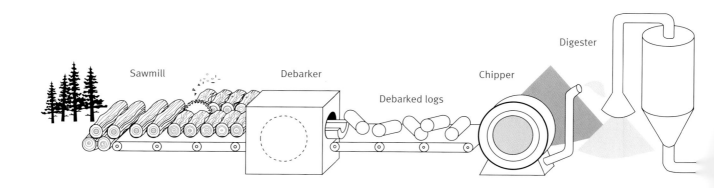

Sawmill   Debarker   Debarked logs   Chipper   Digester

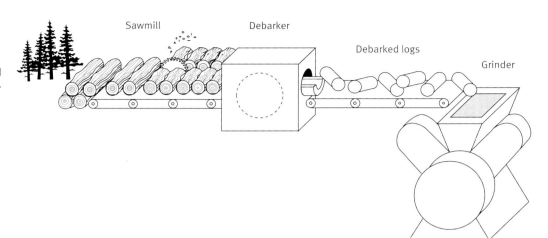

6.3 Mechanical woodpulp is made directly from logs. They are first debarked, then cut into smaller logs, and finally ground into fibers to be mixed with water and made into low-grade newsprint.

Sawmill

Debarker

Debarked logs

Grinder

and also used to wrap after-dinner mints), greaseproof, and tracing papers. Hardwoods, such as eucalyptus, produce more opaque and bulky pulp than softwoods, and can be used to produce a wide range of different papers.

Cotton products and woodpulp are the most common raw materials for papermaking. **Kenaf**, a plant from Asia and parts of Africa, and now grown in the USA, has many environmental advantages over trees. A hardy crop, it requires less fertilizers, pesticides, and water than conventional row crops. In 1960, the United States Department of Agriculture surveyed more than 500 plants and selected kenaf as the most promising source of "tree-free" newsprint. In 1970, kenaf newsprint produced in International Paper Company's mill in Pine Bluff, Arkansas, was successfully used by six US newspapers. As kenaf fibers are naturally whiter than pine pulp, less bleaching is required. The energy requirements for producing pulp from kenaf are about 20 percent less than those for wood pulp, because of its lower lignin content, and one acre of farmland can produce 10 to 20 times more fiber than Southern pine.

Other plants are used for producing specialized papers. Esparto grass from North Africa and Spain is used in Europe for the body of the coated papers used in color work, and for good-quality writing papers. The fibers are small and flexible, and combine to form a paper with a closeness of texture and smoothness of surface. It also watermarks well. Straw is used for the rough board found in book jackets, and in cigarette papers. Hemp has short fibers that bond well, and is used for papers that must be thin but strong—for Bibles and airmail paper.

Manila fiber comes from the leaves of a plant that grows in the Philippines. It produces tough, almost untearable paper mostly used for envelopes and wrapping papers.

Other trees and plants that yield fibers for papermaking include corn (maize) stalks, bamboo, bagasse (from sugar cane), seaweed, citrus peel (a by-product of the food industry), and nettles.

Japanese papers are made from a wide range of plants, from the short-fibered *gampi*, which gives a thin, transparent paper with a fine, smooth finish, to the longer-fibered and thus stronger *mitsumata*.

6.4 Chemical woodpulp is also debarked, but then the chips are cooked in chemicals to remove the lignin that makes newsprint brittle and liable to turn brown. The pulp is reduced to fibers, washed, screened to remove knots and splinters, bleached, beaten, and mixed with various additives.

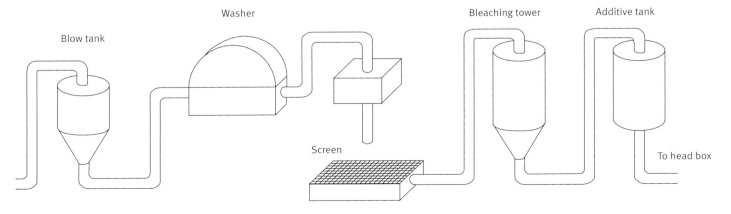

Blow tank

Washer

Screen

Bleaching tower

Additive tank

To head box

Composite Projects

"Don't let going green affect your creativity—it is the essence of design to embrace working within set boundaries."

Manifesto
Christine's tips

"Becoming a more environmentally conscious business is a gradual process. Don't try to aim too high and get frustrated if you can't keep your promises."

"Put it in writing. State your environmental commitments as bullet points in a brief environmental policy. Let everyone who is working with you know about it."

"Help with writing an environmental policy can be found at Envirowise (www.envirowise.gov.uk/page. aspx?o=119327)."

"Be specific and meaningful with your environmental claims. 'We do as much as we can' doesn't say anything! You should be accountable for what you promise. For advice on writing environmental claims, see the Defra (Department for Environment, Food and Rural Affairs) website (www.defra.gov.uk/environment/consumerprod/ pdf/genericguide.pdf)."

"Don't let the restrictions in choice affect your creativity."

"After all it is the essence of design to embrace working within set boundaries."

Christine Fent is a graphic designer who believes in memorable design that communicates successfully, but is produced with a minimal impact on the environment. She studied typography and book design with Hans Peter Willberg in Mainz, Germany, and after completing her diploma she headed straight to London, where she worked for Roundel Design among other design companies. After a spell as freelance designer with contracts at Landor in Hamburg and SalterBaxter in London, she set up her own practice, Christine Fent Design. In 2005 Christine co-founded the graphic design consultancy Composite Projects (with Marek Gwiazda, who has since left) with the focus on print communication, branding, and online projects. In 2006 they took the conscious decision to make the business more sustainable by implementing an EMS (environmental management system) that was accredited in 2008.

They chose an EMS specifically designed for smaller businesses, the IEMA (Institute of Environmental Management and Assessment) Acorn Scheme, based on British Standard BS8555 "Guide to the phased implementation of an environmental management system including the use of environmental performance evaluation," as it offers a phased implementation process.

The accreditation process is a one-day workshop where the accreditor assesses if all requirements of the scheme have been fulfilled. Specific goals for future improvement must be defined and will be reviewed annually.

One specific goal they set was to prepare a "certificate" for each project, presented to the clients after project completion. This certificate states all data relating to the environmental aspects of the job and shows the measurements that had been taken to reduce the impact on the environment.

To make the decision to be more environmentally friendly is one thing—to actually stick to it is another. Particularly during busy periods, high-flying aims can easily fall by the wayside as more expedient options are used.

Writing an environmental policy (or as they prefer to call it, an environmental commitment) has helped them to define promises and commitments and, as it is published on the website and made known to clients, they are forced to do what they said they would.

To save resources, they use electronic rather than paper-based communications, reuse and recycle paper and stationery items in the studio environment, and encourage clients to have digital proofs rather than wet proofs.

They only specify paper that is either recycled or from sustainable forestry (FSC-certified), use only recycled paper during the design process, and specify materials from sources that have the least impact on the environment.

They work with printers that are ISO140001- or FSC- (Forest Stewardship Council) certified and offer volatile organic compound (VOC) emission-free printing. To reduce fuel consumption they avoid unneccessary journeys, using public transportation, cycling, or walking.

Resources
www.composite-projects.com
www.iema.net/acorn

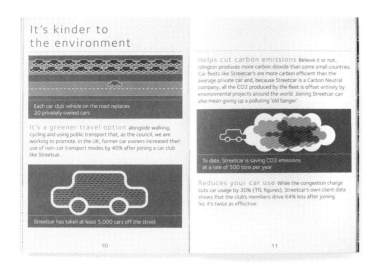

Cycle Islington promotional brochure. The brief was to design a guide to encourage young professional males to take up cycling for their daily commute. The solution was a pocket-sized guide featuring cycling routes through various areas of Islington, in north London. The illustrator was Peter Grundy. Six inspirational interviews show the diversity of cyclists in Islington. To create a tactile experience, the 100 percent recycled paper used changes from rough to smooth surfaces. It was winner of "Best Use of Art Direction" at the Green Awards.

This promotional report on green consumer behaviour and green branding, called "Green. Who cares?," was an economic design that integrated the packaging into the cover and used only recycled materials and eco-friendly printing, avoiding design clichés such as scribbled type and the color green. Naturally they used recycled paper—Colorset, manufactured from 100 percent recycled pre-consumer fibers. This carries the "Blue Angel" certification, which specifically indicates that a paper has the highest environmental credentials on a "cradle-to-grave" basis.

Giant Green poster. The illustrator was Mick Marston.

Identity for Sustainserv management consultancy. The brief was to create an identity to reflect how Sustainserv brings expert environmental knowledge and business competence together. The outcome was a marque using two colored shapes that overlap to create a third color—applied throughout the identity.

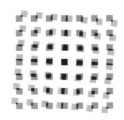

sustainserv

Recycled paper

More than a third of the raw material fiber US papermakers use now comes from recycled paper. The US paper industry recovers for recycling 48 percent of all paper Americans use—well on the way to meeting the American Forest and Paper Association's goal of recovering 55 percent of all paper used in the United States by 2012. In 2005, 51.5 percent of the paper consumed in the USA—51.3 million tons—was recovered for recycling. Recovered paper is the most important raw material for the UK paper and board industry. It represented 4.6 million tonnes, or 74 percent, of the fiber used in 2004. The paper industry is the UK's most successful recycler and recycling is crucial because only 11 percent of the UK is forested.

All paper contains some recycled material, in the form of "broke," the waste from the papermaking process created within the paper mill. This is returned to the refiner, beaten, and turned into more paper. So-called "post-consumer" waste has always been used to manufacture board—the gray kind with specks of ink and sometimes whole letters visible.

Paper mills specializing in recycled paper prefer good clean clippings from printers—all the trimmings, with no ink or other "pernicious contraries," such as glue or metal staples, present. That apart, the next best source is office or domestic paper. There is not very much demand for newsprint, which is low-grade stock to begin with. And what mills definitely do not want are fax paper, self-adhesive envelopes, and plastic-coated papers such as milk and fruit-juice cartons. Problems are also caused by foil-stamped papers, varnishes, and anything containing ultraviolet inks.

Material for recycling is first put through vibrating sieves and centrifuges, where metal objects such as staples and paper-clips are removed. Next it is liquefied in a hydro-pulper, and washed to remove the fillers. The sludge then goes for de-inking (Fig. **6.5**). Steam and detergents are used to loosen the ink from the fibers. Air is blown through the sludge and the ink flocculates (attaches to the bubbles) and floats to the surface, where it is scraped away. The ink removed from recycled pulp, along with clay, short fibers, and other substances removed during the de-inking process, can either be burned to generate energy to run the mill, or sold to make compost or road-making material.

The resulting pulp is mixed with a percentage of virgin stock and printers' waste and made into paper. Virgin pulp is sometimes added for strength, for the more times that fibers go through the process, the shorter they become. Recycled paper is rarely pure white. If the ink from previous usages has not been completely removed but merely redistributed, then the paper will have a grayish tinge. This is something that has to be allowed for in color printing. Good results can be achieved by reducing the black component in four-color work, but do not expect miracles. Recycled paper tends to have greater absorbency than conventional papers. This results in dot gain (see p. 208) and reduced sharpness, and it dries more quickly after printing. It is important that you discuss the use of recycled paper with your printer. Cylinder pressure may have to be adjusted, presses run slower, and different inks used.

Off-whites and colored recycled paper can, however, have a subtlety of appearance and finish not found in conventional papers. Recycled papers are getting better all the time, and ironically, it is not always obvious to the purchaser that you are using them. Clients who want to demonstrate

6.5 More and more paper is being produced from recycled material, but it is ironic that removing and disposing of the ink can produce an ecological cost of its own.

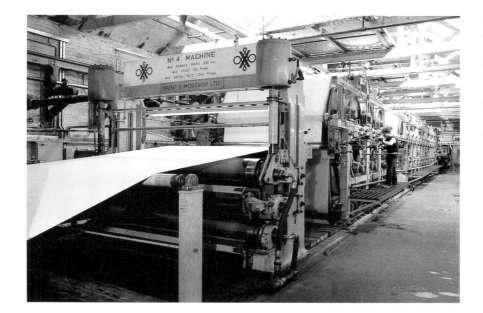

6.8 Papermaking machines are among the biggest production machinery in existence—some are over a mile long. This No. 4 machine at James River Fine Papers at St. Andrews in Scotland has since been modernized and largely enclosed to conserve heat.

After forming on the wire, the paper is still around 70 percent water. Water drains through the mesh, and the screen is vibrated from side to side. The fibers thus tend to align in one direction, along the length of the roll, and this gives machine-made paper its characteristic **grain**. The pattern of the wire mesh gives the paper its texture. **Laid** papers have a pattern of mainly horizontal or vertical stripes; **wove** papers are created with a woven mesh.

Paper is formed as it lies horizontally on top of the wire. To create texture on the top of the sheet, a hollow dandy roll is located above the wire. This device presses a pattern on to the top surface of the paper corresponding to the pattern on the wire.

A **watermark** is created by placing a raised symbol, fashioned in wire, on the dandy roll (Fig. **6.9**). In handmade paper production, it forms part of the mold. The watermark is thinner and thus more transparent than the rest of the sheet. For large print runs, it may be possible to have your own watermark incorporated into specially ordered paper stock. It can be an attractive design element in its own right (Fig. **6.10**), especially if it falls in the margins of a printed publication. But it can interfere with the printing, for example, by weakening a solid area of ink.

From the Fourdrinier wire onward, most of the immense length of a papermaking machine is concerned with drying the damp paper. First, it passes through a series of presses

6.9 The dandy roll of a paper machine in the mill of James River Fine Papers at St. Andrews, Scotland.

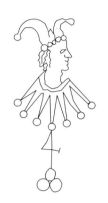

that squeeze out most of the water. These presses can also be used to impart surface texture, and the amount of smoothing affects the final bulk (though not the weight) of the stock.

The paper can then be surface coated or sized with starch, and carried on a felt belt between staggered rows of huge, steam-heated cylinders. It must not get too dry, however. After leaving this section, it will still contain two to eight percent water, necessary to ensure a paper stock with good printing and folding characteristics, and the ability to **cure** in balance with the relative humidity at the printers.

Once dry, the paper is pressed in a vertical row of polished steel calender rolls, or nips. This operation, called **calendering**, increases the smoothness and degree of gloss. The more calenders, the higher the gloss.

The distance from headbox to calenders can be a mile or more. But the elapsed time of a fiber traveling that distance could be as little as two minutes. From the calender stack, the paper is wound into large rolls called webs. These are slit and rewound into more manageable smaller rolls for shipping. If the paper mill has the capacity, they may be cut into sheets. Some papers may also require off-machine finishing such as **super-calendering** (polishing), **coating**, or **embossing**.

Cover paper, or board, is made in much the same way as book paper. The furnish contains more recycled material, and is beaten less, to ensure efficient drainage on the wire. Board can be single-ply, or multi-ply. Multi-ply board comprises a top liner, under liner, middle liner, and back liner. Generally, the liners are given conventional amounts of beating to develop strength. The middle stock, which is there as padding, is given very little. The plies may be combined on the machine or off it.

The characteristics of paper and board

By altering the furnish, and making adjustments to the paper-making machinery, mills are able to produce papers exhibiting very different characteristics. Which kind of paper you choose for a particular job will be determined mostly by the printing process. Offset litho presses require papers that are hard sized, whereas gravure presses need fast ink penetration, and hence "slack" sized paper. If you are dealing with high-quality halftones, you will need a smooth coated paper to do them justice. Economics, too, play a part. Newspapers are cheap and ephemeral, so mechanical woodpulp is a cost-effective choice. Legal documents have to last, so a good-quality rag paper is appropriate.

Paper is specified by its characteristics, and the main ones are weight, bulk, opacity, color, and finish. In the United States, the **basis weight** (also called poundage or substance) is measured in pounds per ream of paper cut to its basic size. A **ream** is 500 sheets. The basic size is 25×38 in for book papers, 24×36 in for newsprint, and 20×26 in for cover boards. To avoid misunderstandings, a 60 lb book paper is written $25 \times 38 - 60$ (500). In the rest of the world, the weight is measured in grams per square meter (g/m^2, gsm, or grammage). To convert lbs to g/m^2, multiply by 1.5 (the exact factor is 1.48), and to convert g/m^2 to lbs, multiply by two-thirds (or, more exactly, by 0.6757).

Another common measurement is the **M weight**, which is the weight of 1000 sheets. To convert poundage to M weight is simple: simply double the poundage figure.

The **bulk**, or **caliper**, of the paper is its thickness. Rough papers tend to be thicker than smooth papers of the same weight. Thickness is measured by a bulking number—the number of sheets to the inch, under test conditions. The ppi (pages per inch) is twice the bulking number (because there are two pages to the sheet). Another way to describe bulk is to measure four sheets of paper with an instrument called a micrometer. This "four-sheet caliper" is expressed in thousandths of an inch, which are commonly referred to as mils or points. In both continental Europe and the United Kingdom, thickness is measured in micrometers and bulk in cm^3/g.

Opacity is one characteristic not complicated by the metric system. It is the property of a paper affecting the **show-through** of printing from the other side of the sheet. Opacity is obviously influenced by both weight and bulk—the heavier and thicker a paper is, the more fibers there are blocking the passage of light. But it is also a function of the fillers added to the paper.

Visual opacity—the opacity of the unprinted sheet—is measured using an instrument called an **opacimeter**, and is expressed as a percentage. A sheet with 100 percent opacity is completely lightproof. A general idea of visual opacity can be gained by placing a printed opacity gauge under the sheet (Fig. **6.11**).

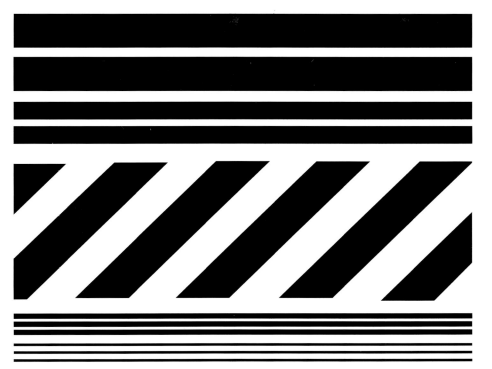

6.11 The opacity of paper is now measured using electronic instruments, but until recently the only measure was a subjective one, obtained by placing a printed opacity gauge like this below the sheet and assessing the amount showing through.

Printed opacity depends partly on how absorbent the paper is (the more absorbent, the more **strike-through** of ink), and on the paper's ink **holdout** (its capacity to keep ink on the surface). This is a difficult parameter to measure, and the subjective terms high, medium, or low strike-through are used.

The color of a paper is determined by dyes added during the papermaking process, or by coatings added afterward. Color can be affected by the raw materials used. Recycled papers are sometimes grayer than those made from virgin pulp, but this and the speckled appearance can be used as design elements in their own right. Paper also comes in several grades of whiteness, produced by adding **optical brighteners** and other chemicals. The color of paper stock always affects the color of the ink printed on it, determining the lightest highlight in any halftone. You cannot have a highlight that is whiter than the paper, nor a shadow deeper than the color of the ink.

The finish of a paper is a description of its surface. Its texture first takes shape on the wire and under the dandy roll. As previously mentioned, wove and laid papers receive their characteristic texture here. Uncoated papers receive their smoothness in the calender stack. Coated papers are more likely to be calendered or super-calendered off the machine. Distinctive finishes such as ripple and stucco are created by embossing the paper.

For book papers, the roughest finish is called **antique**. This is an uncoated paper with high bulk. A smoother, pressed version is **eggshell**. **Machine finish** (**MF**) paper has been calendered and is smoother and less bulky than eggshell. **Machine glazed** (**MG**) paper has been dried against a highly polished cylinder and has one glossy side with the other remaining relatively rough. It is an example of **duplex stock**— paper with a different finish or color on either side.

Coating covers the paper fibers with clay. Super-calendering coated paper gives it a highly glossy appearance. Coating produces a paper with excellent ink holdout, which is ideal for color reproduction. Thus coated papers are often called art papers.

HOT TIPS & COOL TRICKS

Top dots on uncoated stock

High-quality jobs can be successfully printed on uncoated paper stock—if you compensate for dot gain and choose the correct screen ruling. Ink dries partially by absorption, so the dots will spread. As they expand and merge, detail is lost in the shadow areas and the whole image flattens. Dot gain is especially critical in the case of textured papers and on darker or warmer-toned papers, and dot-gain compensation might range from two to three percent in the highlights, to seven to 10 percent in shadows to "open up" the dots on film. Waterless plates require less dot-gain compensation because the ink dot sits on the surface rather than being absorbed. The type of stock also dictates the screen ruling. Well-formed, ultrasmooth stock can take screens from 200 to 300 lpi; smooth vellum or wove 150–175 lpi; lightly textured stock, such as laid and antique, 120–135 lpi; while for heavily textured, open-fibered, and embossed stock, stick to 110–135 lpi.

The coating can be applied by rollers on the machine (film coating, or machine coating), or by rollers or blades off the machine (conversion coating). Conversion-coated papers generally have a thicker coating and are of a higher quality. Blade coating produces a **matte** (dull) surface. Gloss is produced by calendering and super-calendering papers after they have been coated. The highest possible gloss is called **cast coated**: the wet coated web is dried in contact with a highly polished chromium-plated drum. **Chromo paper** is polished on one side only.

Other important characteristics include strength and wet strength, dimensional stability (the ability to stay the same size), rigidity, and **picking** resistance (a binder is used in coatings to prevent fibers from lifting on the press).

And bear in mind that all machine-made papers have grain. Paper folds more easily with than **against the grain**, and ideally books should be designed so that the printed sheets have the grain parallel to the binding (Fig. **6.12**).

Stock can be ordered grain long, with the grain running lengthwise, or grain short, with the grain running across the width of the sheet. Grain-long paper stretches less, so gives better color registration with web offset. Grain-short paper is better for fast print runs, because it bends easily around the press rollers and speeds up the printing process.

You can determine the direction of the grain by tearing a piece of paper—it will tear straighter along the grain than against it. Here are two other methods: run one edge of the sheet between the thumb and finger, through the fingernails. If it crinkles into a wavy pattern; that's the edge across the grain (Fig. **6.13**). Or mark a swatch and dampen it: it will curl in the direction of the grain. On paper specifications, machine direction is indicated by the symbol (m). Thus 25 × 38(m) is grain long, and 25(m) × 38 is grain short.

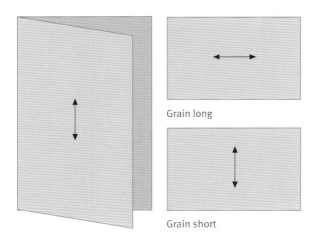

Grain long

Grain short

6.12 All machine-made paper has grain, caused by the orientation of the drying fibers. It is important to know the direction of grain, so that it can run parallel to any folds in your publication.

Choosing the right paper stock

There is a rich but bewildering range of papers available, and you should begin to collect samples, along with technical specifications on the characteristics described above. You can buy paper direct from the mill, or from a paper merchant. The first paper merchant in the US was Benjamin Franklin, who helped to start 18 papermills in Virginia and surrounding areas. Paper merchants stock a wider variety of papers, obtained from many mills, both at home and abroad. Some merchants specialize in particular kinds of paper. Most mills and merchants will supply you with a designer's pack of samples (Fig. **6.14**). Collect printed samples of paper, too, and always choose a paper in consultation with the person who is going to have to print on it.

As mentioned earlier, for some jobs the printing process itself will narrow down your choice—you would never dream of putting blotting paper through a litho press, for example. Price, too, will be a limiting factor. Handmade paper must be reserved for the most prestigious jobs. And it is possible to over-specify paper. There is little point, for example, in specifying a high-gloss stock if it is to be laminated or varnished later.

Sheet-fed offset litho machines require papers with good surface strength and dimensional stability; web offset paper must also have a low moisture content. Surface finish is

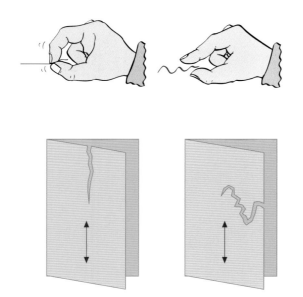

6.13 You can test for grain either by tearing a sheet of paper—it will tear more cleanly in the direction of the grain—or by running an edge between your finger and thumb: if it crinkles, then that's the edge across the grain.

6.14 Every designer should aim to collect "designer packs" of paper samples at every opportunity. Try, too, to collect printed samples.

not such an issue, as modern offset presses can make a good impression on a wide range of surfaces. Offset ink is tacky, however, and the paper should be well sized to prevent "picking"—the pulling out of surface fibers.

The prerequisites for letterpress printing are smoothness, absorbency, opacity, and compressibility. Paper has to be smooth enough to accept a uniform transfer of ink, and strong enough to take the pressure of the sharp edges of metal type without tearing.

The most important characteristic for gravure is smoothness. However, the paper must not contain any abrasive material on its surface—as matte coated stock does. It must also be absorbent enough to draw the ink out from the cells below the smooth surface of the cylinder.

And the silkscreen process demands papers that are not too absorbent.

The trick is to find the stock that matches the brief for the job—a paper just opaque enough to prevent strike-through, but not too heavy (remember the mailing bill), and with a finish appropriate to the design content. Antique may be fine for type and line illustrations, but for good halftone reproduction you will need a coated stock. Glossy is best for color reproduction, but its shine can interfere with readability in the type sections.

Glossy art paper can sometimes feel thinner than the same weight of matte-coated stock, so you may need to increase the weight when going for glossy. Increasing the weight of the stock on some jobs—on a small print run of small-scale booklets, for example—can be a relatively inexpensive way of improving the overall quality of the print.

It is also important to think hard about what other rigors your paper will have to withstand. There may be a reply coupon on your booklet. If so, is it possible to write on the stock in ballpoint or fiber-tip pen without it skipping or smudging? And will that exquisite set of corporate stationery accept additional text from a photocopier or laser printer? A print job may leave your studio looking good, but it also has to perform well in real-life conditions.

Odd-shaped booklets and posters can seem like a good idea at the time. But they can be wasteful on paper, so find out the sizes of stock that the printer can handle, and have a sheet in front of you when you are calculating the size and shape of your layout (see Appendix, pp. 246–7). Remember, however, that if the sheet is too large, this can affect the quality of color reproduction. And instead of requesting a paper by brand name, try asking printers what they have available—you may get a good deal. But beware—if you need reruns in the future, you may not be able to obtain that stock again.

Paper can represent a large proportion of the cost of any printed job, but, in the words of British typographer Ruari McLean, "can be a relatively inexpensive luxury, when luxuries—so often illegal, immoral, or fattening—are also harder and harder to obtain." Paper can give pleasure, and should always be chosen with a great deal of care.

Inks

Printing inks are completely different from the inks used for drawing and writing. They are generally thick and sticky—similar to the consistency of paint.

The various printing processes make very different demands of the characteristics of the ink: its formulation, viscosity (degree of runniness), tackiness, and rate of drying. Of course, a printer running an offset litho machine will buy ink specially formulated for offset litho (Fig. **6.15**). What a designer has to know, however, is that not all offset litho inks are the same, nor do they act in the same way. Even the standard process colors can vary subtly from manufacturer to manufacturer, and from different countries of origin. Until the discovery of phthalocyanine blue in the 1950s, process colors could be very variable indeed.

Formulation

So what are printers' inks made of? All inks are made from three basic constituents: **pigments and dyes**, a **vehicle** (or binding substance), and some additives. The pigments and dyes give an ink its color. Like the pigments in paint, they come from a wide range of natural and synthetic sources; some organic and some inorganic. Pigments are usually dry and powdery, and have to be ground finely. Dyes are liquid and have to be "coated" (attached to solid particles) before they can be mixed with the other ingredients. Black ink is made from carbon-black, manufactured by burning mineral oil in a restricted air supply.

Colored pigments come from so many different sources and have such individual characteristics that there has to be a great deal of adjustment to the vehicle and additives in order to make them behave with any kind of consistency. Different colored inks behave differently on the press, and dry at different rates. And because of the scarcity of certain pigments, there are variations in price between different colors. Metallic inks, in particular, are expensive. The choice of inks has been made simpler, however, by the adoption of the four process colors for full-color work, and by Pantone's standardization of 11 basic colors, from which over 1000 flat colors can be mixed to formula (see pp. 90–1).

The vehicle is the carrier that binds the dry, powdery pigment together. It can be an oil, a natural resin, or an alkyd (a synthetic resin). The type of vehicle is determined by the process. Litho and letterpress inks are oil-based. Screenprint, gravure, and flexographic inks are resin-based and are thinned with a highly volatile solvent, such as alcohol. Non-tainting formulations have to be specified for food packaging.

Very few printing inks are water-based, though a water-based ink would be welcomed by those caring about the environment. Litho could never use a water-based ink, because the process is based on the fact that oil and water do not mix. But water-based inks have been used, for example, for printing candy wrappers by gravure and in newspaper printing by flexography.

As well as the pigment and vehicle, printing inks contain various additives—mainly dryers, but also a selection of antioxidants (added to stop the ink from drying in the machine), fillers, and other agents that give the ink particular properties such as slip-resistance (Fig. **6.16**). Printers sometimes mix in further additives to meet the requirements of a specific job.

Different dryers are used depending on the process, the material the job is being printed on, and the intended end use. They are metallic salts or compounds of cobalt and manganese, and speed the rate of drying chemically. Paradoxically, too much dryer can slow down the rate of drying. And too much dryer on the litho press will mix with the watery fountain solution and cause pigment particles to be deposited on the non-image portions of the plate.

Most inks dry by a process called oxidation. The drying oil of the vehicle absorbs oxygen from the air, causing cross-polymerization (linking) within its molecular structure. This makes the ink gel, and then harden. Quick-drying inks and varnishes are "cured" by exposure to ultraviolet light, producing a hard and scuff-resistant film.

The quality of the paper has a marked effect on the ink's drying time. The vehicle soaks quickly into newsprint, leaving the pigment on the surface. That is why ink from most newspapers leaves your fingers (and clothes) dirty. But vegetable oils are now being used to replace the mineral oils, for improved rub resistance, as well as better **brightness** and sharper dots.

For the higher-quality coated stock used for magazines printed by web offset, the ink is dried in high-temperature

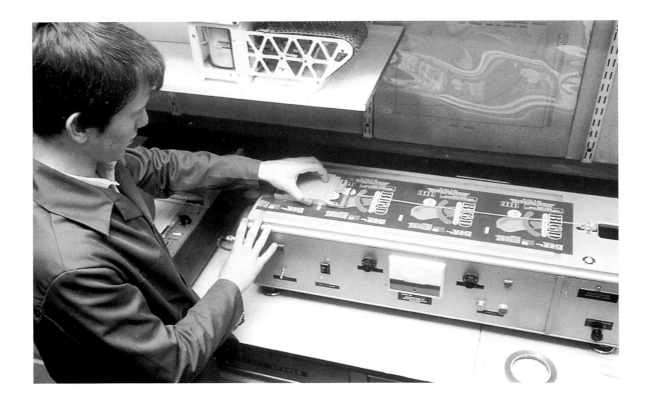

ovens and then chilled. The sheets are folded straight away, so the ink has to be dried quickly. Naturally, it has to be able to cope with this rough treatment, and a special solvent-based formulation called **heat-set ink** is used.

Other additives include extenders, which increase the coverage of the pigment and improve ink transfer from press to paper; distillates, which improve the flow characteristics of the ink; and waxes, which improve the slip and scuff resistance of inks employed in packaging. Inks with added wax cannot subsequently be varnished.

Viscosity and tackiness

The most important characteristic of an ink is its **viscosity**—how runny it is. This property is measured using an instrument called an **inkometer**, or tackoscope.

Litho inks have to be relatively viscous, with high **tack** (stickiness). They must also have a high concentration of pigment. The nature of the process demands the thinnest possible ink film of the strongest possible color. The amount of ink arriving at the paper during the offset litho process is half that of the more direct processes of letterpress and gravure. Litho inks are relatively transparent: yellow printed over blue will produce a recognizable green. They also have to perform well while being almost constantly "contaminated" with the water that coats the litho plate.

Letterpress inks are similar to litho inks, but contain a smaller proportion of pigments. They generally have a higher

6.16 The slip-resistance of many forms of printed packaging is important.

viscosity, but lower tack. Because there is no water used in the process, the chemistry of letterpress ink can be far less complex.

Inks for gravure and flexography are much more fluid than litho and letterpress inks. Gravure inks are thinned down with additional solvent before printing begins, and deposit a similar amount of pigment on to paper as letterpress. Flexographic ink is the thinnest of all, and has to be formulated so as not to attack the rubber rollers used in the process.

Silkscreen inks are semi-liquid with good flow characteristics and are mostly acrylic-based these days. They have to get through the holes of the screen, but not be so fluid as to spread into the non-image areas. These inks, too, have to be thinned before printing to arrive at the correct viscosity.

Specifying inks

Some inks react unpredictably with other finishes. Colored inks for **wet-on-wet** printing on a multicolor press, for example, must be "tack graded" to arrive at an ink film of full density. Some colors will **mottle**, or change shade, when varnished; purples and reflex blue are particularly susceptible. Colors print differently on different substrates: inks on art paper may appear stronger and brighter than on recycled paper (Fig. **6.17**), and different again on plastic.

Colors appear different under different lighting conditions. Printers view colors under standard lighting conditions, an area surrounded by neutral gray and illuminated by a light source with a color temperature of 5000 Kelvin. If you are designing packaging destined for supermarkets, for example, standard conditions will give a false reading. Supermarkets use different colored lighting to seduce people into buying more things, and to make food look more succulent. The colors in the packaging must compensate for these effects—it is essential to view your designs under the lighting conditions for which they are being designed.

Lightfast inks should be specified if the job is to be exposed to sunlight. Magenta and yellow tend to fade faster than black and cyan (look at the covers of paperbacks in the windows of secondhand bookstores). Inks prone to fading are called **fugitive** inks. Silkscreen inks are more light-fast than the others.

Fluorescent and **metallic inks** often need to be underprinted to achieve a satisfactory result, just as black is often underprinted with a percentage of cyan to increase its density. Fluorescent dyes can be added to the process colors to improve the quality of reproduction of illustrations, particularly vibrant watercolors. "Metallic integrated process printing" is a term coined by Pantone to describe a method for adding percentages of gold and silver inks to the process colors. This results in an expensive six-color process, which is printed in the sequence silver, yellow, gold, followed by the remaining process colors. Since normal photography cannot record a metallic finish, the designer or repro house has to estimate the amounts to use, based on charts supplied by Pantone. (Gold and silver can also be applied by blocking and hot-foil stamping; see pp. 210–12.)

Other specialty inks include the magnetic inks used on bank checks and business forms, microencapsulated or "scratch and sniff" inks that add a fragrance to printed work (but be aware of a potential allergic reaction by some innocent end user), invisible ink for children's books and fraud-resistant lottery tickets, and moisture-resistant inks for packaging applications.

Varnishes are a kind of colorless ink used to add gloss to halftones, particularly in prestigious publications such as annual reports. They are also used to add ultraviolet protection to color work that will be exposed to sunlight. If you intend to **spot varnish** photographs or illustrations, you may need to provide artwork or keylines on the mechanical to indicate the areas to be covered. Be sure to discuss any special requirements in the design brief with your printer, and together you will be able to find the correct ink for the application.

6.17 Recycled papers are more absorbent and can be less white than conventional stock, and printing on them can result in colors lacking in brilliance and saturation—hence the need for different ink formulations, which may themselves be helping to destroy the environment. Calculating the ecological cost of a print job is a complex process. (Cartoon by Phil Dobson.)

Selecting your supplier

You may not be able to look over the shoulder of your printer as your design is being printed. But you can make sure that you have chosen the right supplier for the job, and that the printer is in no doubt as to your requirements. There are three main considerations: quality, cost, and the schedule. If you are running to tight deadlines, you may have to pay more. Similarly, quality means more care, and that too can cost money. This is not to say that you cannot produce beautiful printing on a small budget—there are plenty of examples of imaginative design that have used cost constraints to great advantage.

You can play your part by submitting clean, uncomplicated designs and clear, unambiguous instructions, and by avoiding any superfluous processes that are going to add labor costs to your bill—unless you decide that a special shape or finish is absolutely necessary.

How do you select the supplier appropriate to the job in hand? First, clearly you should not think of asking a small jobbing printer to undertake a complicated color job for a prestigious client. Nor should you ask a fine-art printer to bid for a short-run black-and-white newsletter. There are horses for courses. Second, do not be afraid to ask around for personal recommendations from colleagues. Look for the name of the printer on the examples of printing jobs you have collected. If their credit line is not there, ask their client. Then obtain some competitive bids.

For small jobs, find printers somewhere nearby. If they consistently do good work, stick with them, and build up a friendly relationship. Ask them to bid for jobs, but don't make it too formal a process. They may be able to help you out of a jam one day.

For large-scale jobs, provide each prospective supplier with a clear specification of the job in writing, outlining the size, **print run**, and finish you want. Insist that their prices are to a format that you specify, so that you can compare like with like. Tell them that if they do not follow the rules, their bid will not even be considered. Listen to them, however, and give as much information as they need to make a sensible bid—you may end up working with them, after all. Listen to any suggestions they may have to reduce costs, and adapt your specification if you can. Ask what possible economies can be made, by adjusting the schedule, the imposition scheme, or the paper stock. Visit the print works if possible, to familiarize yourself with the company's equipment and its capabilities. Examine samples of work that have been done on stock similar to your job.

Indicate whether you or the prospective printer will supply color separations and film, and list the finishing operations you will require. Ask if the printer has these facilities in-house or will have to send out to sub-contractors. If the latter is the case, you may do better to negotiate finishing separately. Likewise, ascertain whose responsibility it will be to buy in the paper stock.

Show a detailed dummy to each company, and take no chances that they may misinterpret any aspect of the job. Decide also if you need a simple bottom-line figure for the whole job, or whether you need a breakdown into ink, paper, platemaking, proofing, prepress, printing, mailing, and shipping.

When you have all the bids, make a decision, and inform everyone who has quoted. You may wish to negotiate a better price, but do not try to act the bigshot by playing one supplier off against another—you may wish to use several of them at a later date. But you may want to promise bigger jobs in future, conditional on this crucial one.

You must now draw up a contract. If the deal is done on the nod or handshake, the terms of a job in the United States once reverted to the Printing Trade Customs, originally drawn up in 1922 by the United Typothetae of America and amended by the PIA (Printing Industries of America), and NAPL (National Association of Printing Leadership). *Graphic Communications Business Practices* replaces the former set of "trade customs" and are a set of recommendations not intended to be legally binding. This voluntary set of guidelines can be found at http://www.piasd.org/trade customs.html and covers best business practices in digital asset management, terms and conditions of sale including quotations, orders, delivery, and production schedules, and a glossary with definitions of various workflow terms used in the printing industry, based on common usage. They are not set out as "recommended" practices and their use must be an individual business decision based on customers' wishes, relationships with potential customers, and other competitive issues. In the United Kingdom it will be based on the Standard Conditions of Contract for Printers, published by the British Printing Industries Federation; there are other more specialist documents such as the Customs of the Trade for the Manufacture of Books. Other countries have similar codes of conduct. It is as well to be familiar with them—ignorance is no defense.

These "trade customs" set out the business relationship between the printer and the client. They recommend, for example, that quotations not accepted within 60 days are subject to review; that negatives, positives, flats, plates, and other items, when supplied by the printer, remain the printer's

Printing processes

exclusive property unless otherwise agreed in writing; that a "reasonable variation" in color between color proofs and the completed job shall constitute acceptable delivery; and that "overruns and underruns not to exceed 10 percent on quantities ordered, or the percentage agreed on, shall constitute acceptable delivery."

Although these "trade customs" are recommended, any contract made between you and your printer will have legal standing. If any of the terms contained in the former "trade customs" are to be adapted, they must be spelt out precisely, in writing. An underrun of 10 percent, for example, on a print run of 10,000 is a perfectly legal shortfall of 1000 copies! You may want to prohibit a shortfall and instead risk a 20 percent **overrun**.

Make a realistic schedule that includes each stage in the process—design and mark-up of copy, typesetting, paste-up, prepress, **make-ready** (setting up the press), printing, and finishing—and let everyone concerned have a copy for comment. Anticipate any delays in ordering paper, vacations (use a calendar with weekends and holidays clearly marked), and shipping. Check proofs meticulously, bearing in mind that any error you miss will be multiplied hundreds or thousands of times. Things may go wrong, but careful planning and communication should eliminate too many surprises.

HOT TIPS & COOL TRICKS

Choosing a printer

Are you printing a rough-and-ready circular, a company's stationery or a glossy lifestyle catalog? The type of job determines which of your regular printers to use. Jobbing printers have small-format machines able to print one or two colors in one pass. They will most likely use plastic plates, and close registration can be a problem. They will happily print newsletters, letterheads and disposable pamphlets, but for more demanding jobs, they will have to send out for metal plates, and the price will rise. Better to use a mid-range printer with a press that can handle bigger plates and more colors—you might actually save money. Stick to standard paper and inks, the kind they always have in stock. For jobs where color matching and premium paper stock are really important, you will need to find a printer specializing in four-color or even hi-fi color work.

The various printing technologies have been mentioned many times so far. Paper, ink, and printing process are all interdependent, and a choice of any one of them cannot be made in isolation. Once the decision to choose a particular printing process has been made, there is very little that a designer needs to or can do. If the mechanical or digital file is perfect, and the scans are good, then a good printer will produce a good result. There are things that can go wrong, however, and a little knowledge of how the printing processes work will go a long way in helping you to choose the right supplier and thus avoid any problems.

Printing processes can be categorized into five main types: relief, intaglio, planographic, stencil, and digital (Fig. **6.18**). Letterpress is a form of **relief printing** invented by the ancient Chinese. Dating back to about AD 730, it is by far the oldest of the printing technologies. Flexography is another form of relief printing, which had to await recent advances in materials technology. In relief printing, the printed **impression** is made by a raised surface coated with ink and pressed against the paper, or other substrate.

Intaglio printing uses a plate with incised lines or grooves. Ink is applied, and then wiped from the surface. An impression is made when the substrate is pressed against the surface of the plate, drawing the ink out from the recesses. Gravure is a kind of intaglio process. The **planographic printing** process, of which lithography is the only example, is perhaps the most mysterious, as everything happens on the surface of the plate. It works simply because oil and water do not mix. **Stencil printing**, or **screenprinting**, is, like relief printing, an ancient technique; early Oriental stencils were held together by meshes of human hair. What we term digital, can be any one of several different technologies (see p. 203) ranging from offset litho to inkjet and xerography.

Offset lithography is the most common form of printing nowadays, although direct digital is making inroads and one day could take over. There will be some designers who in the course of their careers use nothing else. It is rare these days for anyone to print by letterpress, but its historical *significance* is great. Unless you work in packaging design, it is unlikely that you will ever come across flexography or screenprinting. And unless you design mail-order catalogs or glossy magazines, you may never have to work with gravure. But you never can tell!

Relief

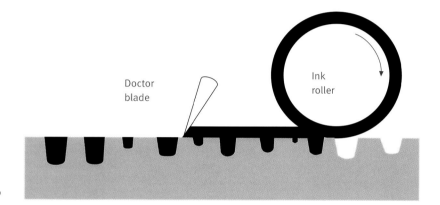

Doctor
blade

Ink
roller

Intaglio

Ink
roller

Damp
roller

Lithography

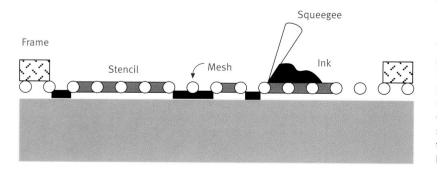

Frame

Stencil

Mesh

Squeegee

Ink

Screenprinting

6.18 Traditionally there were four main printing methods. Relief has ink sitting on the raised surface of the plate or type. Intaglio has ink in the grooves and recesses, while lithography is a planographic process with the ink on the surface, sticking only to the dry areas of the plate. And screenprinting forces the ink through a mask supported by a mesh.

Offset lithography

In Prague (now in the Czech Republic) in around 1798, Alois Senefelder was experimenting with Solnhofen limestone to find a cheaper alternative to engraving images on copper. His experiments with etching in relief were a failure, but he did notice that he could print just as well without the relief. That discovery, along with the invention of photography in the mid-19th century, changed the course of printing history. It rendered letterpress virtually obsolete, and made **offset lithography** the predominant print technology of the 20th century.

The word **lithography** means "writing on stone." Senefelder discovered that if a design is drawn on a limestone surface using a greasy crayon, and then the surface is "etched" with a solution of gum arabic, water, and a few drops of nitric acid, the area that has been drawn on will become permanently receptive to grease. The undrawn area desensitized by the gum solution will be permanently resistant to grease. If the stone is later dampened and greasy ink is applied from a roller, the ink will stick to the design but not to the rest of the surface. Impressions can then be taken that are exact replicas of the original design.

Over the years, the same properties were discovered in more manageable zinc and aluminum plates. Then the **offset process** was developed to overcome the limitations of these metal plates. It involved taking an impression not directly from the plate but from an intermediate **blanket**. The offset process has several clear advantages. Metal plates are easily damaged, and offsetting the image on to rubber protects them from damage. The resilience of the rubber blanket enables impressions to be made on even quite rough papers, and other substrates such as tin plate. Furthermore, the design on the original stone had to be drawn as a mirror image of the finished design for it to print correctly; but because the image is first offset—printed to the blanket—and then on to the paper, the design for offset litho can be positive and "right reading."

Lithography would have become much more popular a lot sooner if it had not been for the fact that typesetting was a problem. It was possible to transfer type set by letterpress on to the litho plate using paper with the ink still wet. But it wasn't until the invention of photography that type could be put on to a litho plate with any kind of quality control.

Platemaking is the process by which the design is transferred on to a printing **plate** from the artwork or mechanical, either photographically or electrostatically, by a process resembling photocopying (Fig. **6.19**). Offset litho plates have to be thin and flexible enough to wrap around a cylinder. Small plates are supplied pre-sensitized with a light-sensitive diazo compound or photopolymer, and are made from metal, plastic, or paper. Paper and plastic are used for short runs, up to 1000 copies. Because they stretch and distort on the press, they are only suitable for single-color work. They are exposed under a process camera, "developed" electrostatically, and then "fixed" by heat. Alternatively, the plates are placed in direct contact with the artwork and the image is transferred using a photographic process similar to the production of PMTs (see p. 80).

Metal plates are made from aluminum with a granular surface, which gives the plate water-carrying properties, and provides anchorage to the image. Litho plates for larger machines and some smaller conventional metal plates can be exposed from either negative or positive film. As we have seen in Chapter 5, stripping and film make-up for black-and-white work is generally done using negative film. It follows that negative-working plates will be used for single-color work. Negative-working plates are less expensive than positive-working ones and are used in print runs of up to 100,000 copies. Most multicolor work, however, makes use of flats assembled from positive film, because it is easier to keep the separations in register. In this case, positive-working plates are used.

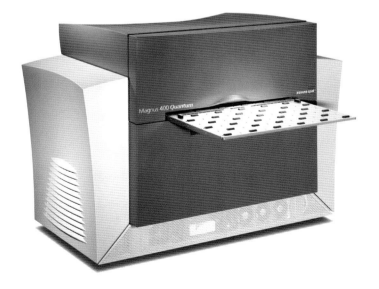

6.19 Kodak's Magnus 400 four-page CtP platesetter delivers up to 32 thermal plates per hour and features Squarespot laser imaging, which delivers a fine swath of energy at 10,000 dpi reducing Gaussian fuzziness around the edges of the dot, combined with 20-micron or optional 10-micron Staccato (stochastic) screening.

The exposure or **burn** is made by ultraviolet light in a printing-down frame which holds the plate in direct vacuum contact with the flat. On exposure, the diazo or photopolymer resin coating of a negative-working plate radiated by the ultraviolet light undergoes a chemical reaction to become ink-attracting. This then forms the image on the plate that will print. The rest of the coating, unexposed to the ultraviolet light, is washed off during subsequent processing. Finally, a gum arabic solution is applied to the surface to make the non-image areas water-attracting and ink-rejecting.

When positive-working plates are exposed in the frame, it is the sensitized photopolymer coating radiated by the ultraviolet light that is made unstable on exposure, and it is this portion that is removed during processing. The unexposed areas are the ones that will print. Again, the plate is gummed to make the non-image areas unattractive to ink. Since the image can be further destabilized by light, positive-working plates have a shorter life than negative-working ones. Some plates can be baked to "fix" and harden the image. Deletions can be made to a positive-working plate, by using a special eraser or brush-applied fluid. This can be useful for printing run-ons of a poster, for example, with dates or venues deleted.

All plates are subject to wear. After around 500,000 copies (or sometimes much lower numbers) have been printed, both the image and the surface grain start to break up. Multi-metal plates with surfaces of hard-wearing chromium are specially designed for long print runs of between 800,000 and a million.

Positive-working plates produce less dot gain than plates made from negatives and are popular for web offset magazine printing. Bimetal plates are even better at controlling dot gain. Here in detail are the main types of plate:

- Electrophotographic plates are produced like photocopies. The photoconductor is charged using a corona discharge, and on exposure to the artwork, the charge is dissipated in those areas struck by light. The charge remaining on the unexposed areas attracts a dry or liquid toner with an opposite charge. An organic photoconductor is coated on a substrate or paper, and the toned image is either fixed or transferred to another substrate. Plates used for laser imaging are coated on electrograined anodized aluminum. During processing, the coating is removed in the non-printing areas, and the plates are treated with etch and gum to make them water receptive. During the chemical removal process, the dots can become slightly ragged, so these plates are not recommended for fine screens and process color printing. It is also possible to make short-run polyester plates direct from a laser printer.

- Presensitized diazo plates are coated with organic compounds and have a shelf life of about a year; wipe-on plates that are coated at the printers have a shelf life of one to two weeks. Most are made from negatives and, once exposed, are treated with an emulsion developer consisting of a lacquer and gum-etch in acid solution. As the unexposed diazo is dissolved by the solution, the gum deposits on the non-printing areas for water-receptivity, and lacquer deposits on the exposed images, making them ink-receptive. When developed, the plate is rinsed with water and coated with gum arabic solution. These are known as additive plates and can produce runs as long as 150,000. Some diazo plates are prelacquered and are capable of runs of up to 250,000. These plates are developed using a special solvent, and are known as subtractive plates.

- Photopolymer plates are coated with inert and abrasion-resistant organic compounds and are capable of press runs up to 250,000. These too are available as negative- and positive-working plates. Some photopolymer plates can be baked after processing to produce runs of over a million. Dye-sensitized photopolymers that can be exposed by lasers are used in digital CtP (computer-to-plate) systems.

- Silver halide plates are coated with photosensitive compounds similar to slow photographic film. The emulsions are very light-sensitive to blue so must be handled in yellow-filtered light. The coatings can be exposed optically using negatives, or digitally by lasers. The processing solutions contain heavy metal pollutants (silver) which must be treated with silver-recovery chemicals before being discharged into municipal sewers.

- Bimetal plates use presensitized polymer coatings consisting of a metal base with one or more metals plated on to it: either copper plated on to stainless steel or aluminum, or chromium plated on to copper, which may be plated on to a third metal base. These are almost indestructible, have good dot control and are capable of runs in the millions—they are also the most expensive. But should anything go wrong, a single acid treatment can restore the plate to its original condition.

- **Waterless plates** consist of ink on aluminum for the image areas and a silicone rubber for the non-printing areas. Silicone rubber has very low surface tension and thus will repel ink. However, because of the pressure and heat of printing, regular litho ink will smear over the silicone and cause scumming or toning. Waterless printing must therefore use special inks and temperature control. The technique also demands good grades of paper in order to avoid debris accumulating on the blanket.

- Heat-sensitive plates are made from polymers that respond to heat rather than light, so can be handled in daylight or artificial light. They are exposed using infrared laser diodes in special imagesetters and processed in an aqueous solution. With baking, they are capable of runs of over a million.

- Hybrid plates use two separate photosensitive coatings on metal plates: a silver halide coating that can be

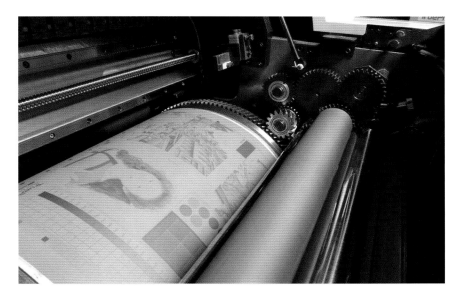

6.20 The Dainippon Screen TruePress 344 is a four-color A3+ (13⅜ × 18½ in) digital offset press featuring tf-200 thermal polyester plate technology. The image is created by thermal exposure from a multi-array laser diode to a heat-sensitive layer on the plate. This creates a hydrophobic layer on which ink is applied. The unexposed area is then removed by the fountain solution and ink during the initial press rotations.

exposed either optically to film or digitally by lasers over a bottom coating of conventional photopolymer. When the top coating is processed, the bottom coating is exposed to UV light. The top coating is then removed and the photopolymer (bottom) coating used for printing.

- **Ablation plates** are made by a laser selectively burning tiny holes into thin coatings on a polyester or metal base. These can be produced digitally, require no chemical processing, and can be printed waterless. All the plates for a job can be imaged directly on the press, simultaneously and in register.

As you can see from the above, most plate coatings can be imaged digitally by laser. High-speed dye-sensitized photopolymers, silver halide, electrophotographic, and ablation plates, coupled with PostScript-based digital systems have paved the way for CtP (computer-to-plate) systems. So say goodbye to the imagesetter and say hello to the platesetter. Your PostScript data comes in one end from the RIP, and out comes a plate ready for the press, with no need for film, stripping, or further processing. CtP on-press images the DTP layouts direct to a plate already in position on the printing press (Fig. **6.20**) or involves spraying a substance on a press cylinder and imaging it using thermal lasers. Plates can also be exposed in a vacuum frame conventionally and mounted on-press—processing takes place during make-ready. The dampening solution first disperses the coating in the non-image areas, then the ink rollers absorb this now loosened coating.

Of all the CtP technologies, thermal (infrared) laser imaging seems to be taking over from visible-light systems. The advantages are that they don't need darkrooms or light-proof cassettes; they produce sharp images with little or no dot gain when exposed above the threshold temperature and no image below it; and require little or no processing.

Other thermal technologies include: ablation (see earlier), transfer, and crosslinked. Transfer plates are produced in an adapted platesetter in which spots of ink-receptive polymer are transferred from a donor sheet to the receiving plate by laser. In a crosslinked system, the infrared dye in the plate's coating absorbs the laser's energy, causing an accelerator to be released which activates the crosslinking of resins, thus making the image area insoluble.

The litho press

Offset litho presses range from the small-scale **sheetfed** machines found in jobbing printers all over the world (Fig. **6.21**), to the huge presses used to print magazines and newspapers on to continuous webs, or rolls, of paper. The basic principles of the process are always the same (Fig. **6.22**). A litho machine comprises: a **plate cylinder** on to which the plate is securely clamped; a resilient rubber-coated cylinder, called the **blanket cylinder**; an **impression cylinder**; a system of inking rollers called the **ink pyramid**; and a **plate-damping unit**. The litho plate is dampened, and then inked. Next, the inked image is transferred (offset) to the blanket. The paper moves between the blanket and the impression cylinders, which are "packed" to ensure complete contact, and the image in ink is transferred from the blanket on to the paper stock.

A single-color sheetfed machine prints single sheets in one color at a time. A mechanism called a feeder pushes each sheet in turn between the blanket and the impression cylinder. Sheets are lifted one by one by vacuum suckers, and are then sent through the machine by blasts of air and conveyor belts. High-speed presses use a **stream feeder**, which presents sheets to the rollers overlapping slightly. Detectors cut out the printing unit if a sheet is defective or if two sheets are picked up together.

The front and side lays are adjustable stops which position the sheet before it enters the machine. The grippers—sets

6.21 The Heidelberg Speedmaster CD 74-sheet offset litho press is available as C-format, 530 × 740 mm (20.87 × 29.13 in), or F-format, 605 × 740 mm (23.82 × 29.13 in), with or without a perfecting device. It prints from four to 10 colors, with an optional coating system.

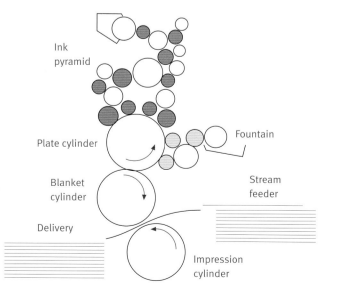

Ink pyramid

Plate cylinder

Blanket cylinder

Delivery

Fountain

Stream feeder

Impression cylinder

6.22 The layout of a small, sheet-fed offset litho machine. The plate is first dampened by the fountain, then inked by the ink pyramid. The image is transferred to the rubber blanket cylinder and on to the paper, which is pressed between the blanket and impression cylinder.

of metal fingers on the impression cylinder—grab the sheet and pull it through. A gripper allowance of ½ inch (15 mm) must be made when estimating the printed area of a sheet. After it has been printed it is released, and the delivery mechanism stacks it with the others, **jogging** them constantly to neaten the pile. To stop the wet image from **offsetting** on to the next sheet in the pile, anti-**setoff** spray is applied as the sheet falls on to the pile, separating it from its neighbors by a layer of fine particles.

Meanwhile, inside the machine, the damping system deposits a fine layer of moisture on to the plate's surface before it passes under the inking rollers. One or two cloth-covered rollers, supplied by a **fountain** roller, are used to regulate the amount of dampening. Alcohol can be used for up to 20 percent of the solution, to lower the surface tension and lessen the moisture uptake of the paper. Damp paper stretches, and anything that reduces this effect will improve the quality of the printing, especially in close-register color work. Because of the cost of alcohol and environmental considerations, fountain solutions with oxidizing chemicals have been developed that speed up the ink drying and reduce the need for anti-setoff sprays.

Ink is introduced to the roller pyramid from a reservoir via an adjustable metal blade. Ink flow can be controlled by a computer taking densitometer readings from the printed sheets. This can also record ink settings that can be re-used if the job is to be reprinted. It is possible, though very messy and unpredictable, to print two colors from a single plate on a single-color offset press by using one color at one end of the fountain, another at the other end—the colors will blend in the middle. This is called **split fountain** printing.

A perfecting press (Fig. **6.23**) is a printing press that can print both sides of the sheet in one pass. One type of perfector is a **blanket-to-blanket press**, which has the two blanket cylinders printing at the same time, so that an impression cylinder is unnecessary.

Multicolor work can be printed in many different ways. An **in-line** machine has several single units arranged to print one color after another. Stock is conveyed to the next unit by grippers on transfer cylinders. A **converter** machine (Fig. **6.24**) has a drum mechanism that can reroute the paper so that it can print either two colors together on one side of a sheet or (when converted) one color on each side of the sheet. A four-unit converter can print four colors on one side, or two each on both sides.

Web-fed machines (Fig. **6.25**) print from a continuous roll of paper stock, which is printed and then folded and cut into sheets in a single pass. All web-fed machines print both sides of the sheet, and in web-offset, blanket-to-blanket designs are common. The length of the final sheet is determined by the circumference of the cutting cylinder. This cut-off length determines the press printing size you choose for a job. A single-width press with a width of 34 inches (850 mm) and a cut-off length of 24 inches (600 mm) produces eight 8¼ × 11¹¹⁄₁₆ in (A4) pages to view, or 16 pages perfected (printed both sides) to a section.

A multiple-unit web-offset machine can have several web reels in operation. A five-unit web-offset machine with one reel in operation has the capacity to print four process colors plus one Pantone color, or one 16-page full-color section and one black-and-white 16-page section at the same time. A six-unit press, using only one or two printing units for each of two or three reels, can produce printings of flat color and black in many different permutations. On newspapers, for example, one cylinder might be reserved for printing late "stop press" items.

Web tension in the press is controlled by a dancer roller, which can apply a brake to the reel. When the reel runs out,

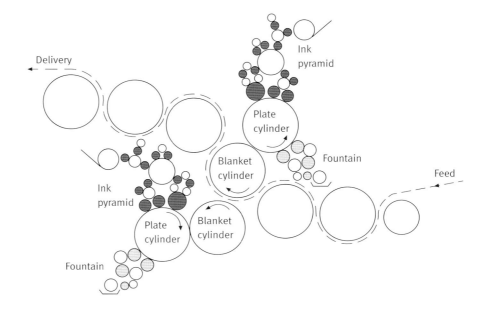

6.23 A perfecting press can print both sides of the sheet in one pass. Here there is no impression cylinder—the two blanket cylinders press against one another.

the press is stopped and a new one is connected. On larger presses, this can be done automatically by a "flying paster," which attaches the end of the old reel to the beginning of the new one, then accelerates the new reel up to press speed, all while the press is running.

After printing, the web is dried in a series of gas-fired ovens, then chilled (however, newspapers often use **cold-set ink**, which does not require this treatment). To avoid smudging, it is vital that the ink is dry before the web passes over a former, or kite, which makes the first fold in the direction of motion. This is the part of the press always shown in old films, where it looks as though the web is disappearing into a slit (Fig. **6.26**).

The paper is then cut into sections, and folded again down to the correct page size. Magazines are trimmed with a three-knife trimmer. Newspapers are usually left untrimmed. For books, the web is slit into ribbons, which are passed over polished turner bars on cushions of air, for better alignment during trimming.

Web machines are used for long print runs, typically over 20,000 copies, on jobs with tight deadlines. With web, all the colors can be printed, both sides, on one pass, with folding done in-line. However, registration is often not as accurate as it is on sheetfed presses. Trim sizes are restricted as well; non-standard sizes and finishes are better handled by sheetfed machines.

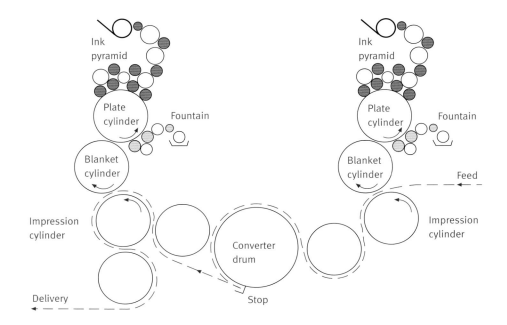

6.24 Using a converter configuration, you can either print both sides of a sheet in one pass, or one side in two colors.

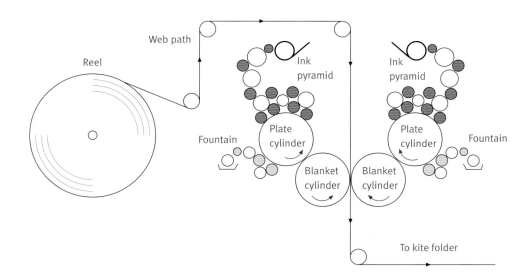

6.25 In this web offset configuration, the web is printed on both sides in one pass. A typical web press consists of several units like this, one after the other.

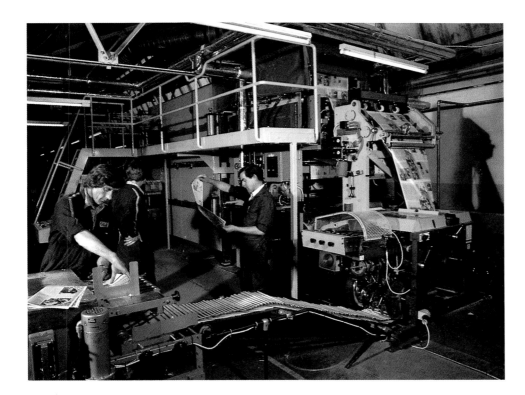

6.26 After printing and drying, the web is folded down the middle on a kite folder — as here at Headley Bros in Ashford, England.

Computer control has improved production quality considerably. The acidity (pH) and conductivity of fountain solutions can be monitored constantly and accurate temperature control of the inking system means less dot gain, smoother running of the moving parts, lower water consumption, and reduced energy consumption overall.

Temperature control is also important in waterless presses to maintain a constant viscosity in the ink so as to prevent smearing. Careful control results in faster make-ready, more saturated and consistent colors, higher ink density with improved contrast and better detail in the shadows, and the ability to use higher resolution screening, up to 500 lpi.

Many finishing processes can now be carried out in-line, with coating towers eliminating the need for off-press varnishing and coating. IR (infrared) drying or UV (ultraviolet) curing also speeds up the production process.

Gravure

The biggest rival to the huge web-offset presses is **gravure**. This is an intaglio process that is used to print everything from the highest-quality postage stamps and banknotes, through glossy magazines and mail-order catalogs, down to rough-and-ready wallpapers and gift wrapping paper.

Although related to earlier intaglio methods of printing, such as etching and copper engraving, gravure is a relatively recent process, invented in the middle of the 19th century by photographer Fox Talbot, as a means of reproducing **continuous tone copy** (see p. 18).

Present-day gravure machines are huge high-speed **rotary presses** that print from a web of paper. (Gravure is sometimes also called **rotogravure**.) The engraved cylinder is partially immersed in a bath of thin, solvent-based ink (Fig. **6.27**). Its surface is flooded with ink, and as it revolves it is wiped clean with a flexible steel blade called a doctor blade, leaving ink only in the image areas. A web of paper is pressed against the surface of the engraved cylinder by a rubber-covered impression cylinder, and the ink is transferred to the paper. The web passes to a folder and then a dryer, similar to those found on web-offset machines.

The important point about gravure is that it prints continuous tones by means of cells—containers of ink cut into the surface of the cylinder (Fig. **6.28**). Larger-diameter or deeper cells hold more ink, and thus deposit a thicker layer of ink, hence making a darker printed image. This produces continuous-tone images that are almost screenless, as the ink from neighboring cells merges during printing. A drawback is that type is also printed this way, so it is less sharp than that produced by offset litho.

In the original process, cells were of equal size but different depths. This arrangement has been superseded either by cells of both varying depth and size, or by cells of constant depth but varying size. The latter method is used mainly for textiles and packaging design.

Preparing artwork for gravure is exactly the same as for offset litho (see Chapter 5), except that the typesetting is scanned as well as the tone. The complete artwork for the job is scanned in one pass. This is converted into signals that control a diamond

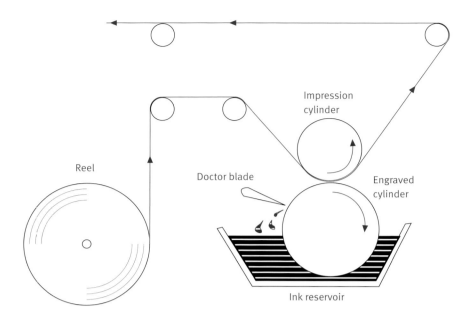

6.27 A gravure press is invariably web-fed. The engraved gravure cylinder is inked and then its surface is wiped clean by a doctor blade. The paper is printed as a result of pressure between the plate cylinder and the impression cylinder.

Impression cylinder

Reel

Doctor blade

Engraved cylinder

Ink reservoir

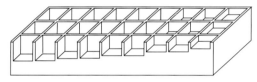

Constant area, variable depth

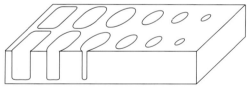

Variable area, constant depth

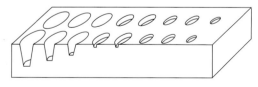

Variable area, variable depth

6.28 Conventional gravure cells have equal area but differing depth—the deeper the cell, the darker the impression (top). Other kinds of cell include those with variable area and equal depth, used mainly for packaging (center), and—for the highest-quality work—those with variable area and variable depth (bottom).

engraving stylus which cuts into the surface of a blank copper cylinder, producing the pattern of cells (Fig. **6.29**). After engraving, the cylinder can be chromium-plated for extra durability.

Because of the considerable expense involved in engraving the cylinders, gravure is reserved for jobs such as glossy magazines with very high print runs—typically 250,000 copies or more—or for jobs demanding the highest quality of halftone reproduction.

Hell Gravure Systems have produced a laser engraver powerful enough to cut gravure cells directly into a copper or chromium surface. Under laser control, depth profiles can, to a large extent, be freely selected. The write resolution of the laser can be set independently of the gravure screen, achieving a level of contour definition comparable to the screening of offset litho.

Photopolymer plate systems for gravure consist of photopolymer coatings on stainless steel plates that can be mounted on magnetic cylinders. These plates make gravure a viable process for runs below 100,000 and can make gravure competitive with lithography and flexography for packaging runs.

Gravure was the first printing process to use digital imaging. Digital information from the prepress system is fed directly to the diamond styli in the engraving heads that produce the printing cells. This process is also called **filmless gravure**.

6.29 Cylinders at the press of R. R. Donnelley in Chicago. Engraving gravure cylinders is very expensive, and thus the process is only economical for long runs.

Paula Scher

**"I've always been what you would call a 'pop' designer.
I wanted to make things that the public could relate to and understand."**

Manifesto

As the name of the partnership suggests, Pentagram was founded in London by five designers in 1972: graphic designers Alan Fletcher, Colin Forbes, and Mervyn Kurlansky, product designer Kenneth Grange and architect Theo Crosby. It currently has offices in New York (1978), San Francisco (1986), Austin, Texas (1994), Berlin (2002), and London.

Pentagram has no dominant style, but demonstrates a clean and confident visual appearance and a sense of humor, often expressed through graphic wit and visual puns. This is accompanied by exacting standards in photography, illustration, and typography. The partners are all practicing designers, each recognized in his or her particular discipline. Although each usually works independently, one partner may collaborate with another and draw upon the resources of the whole organization.

Each partner runs his or her design practice as a separate profit center, deciding which work to take on, how much to charge, and who to hire for the design team. The only requirement is that every partner should be comfortably in profit when the monthly financial report—the "blue sheet"—ranks the partners by profitability. Each partner gets exactly the same salary, however. Taking financial competition out of the equation encourages partners to share work with partners who may be less busy. This acts as a safety net and allows partners to take on larger, more exciting projects that spread beyond the boundaries of pure graphic design or pure architecture.

The firm has a certain civility in its office management, in their celebrated in-house luncheon facilities and twice-yearly partnership meetings, held in locations such as Leeds Castle or the American Academy in Rome. Pentagram style is also expressed in their publications.

Forbes believes no designer can stray very far from the craft of design. Even his analytical skills, he believes, were developed by his designing with type. The other craft that informs all his work is drawing, and he quotes approvingly a drawing teacher who told him that the reason he didn't draw correctly is that he didn't see correctly. Forbes agreed: "If I hadn't been trying to learn how to draw, I might never have been forced to learn how to see, which is far more important for a designer."

Paula Scher was born in 1948 in Washington, DC, USA. She studied illustration at the Tyler School of Art in Philadelphia, Pennsylvania, earning a Bachelor of Fine Arts, and was awarded a Doctor of Fine Arts Honoris Causa by the Corcoran College of Art and Design, Washington, DC. She'd avoided graphic design because she said she lacked the necessary "neatness skills" and didn't like arranging Helvetica on a grid. What she was good at, she discovered, was coming up with concepts and illustrating them with type. She is now best known for identity design, packaging design, publication design, and environmental graphics, with her graphic identities for Citibank and Tiffany & Co. becoming case studies for the contemporary regeneration of classic American brands.

In the 1970s she designed hundreds of album covers for CBS and Atlantic Records, before moving into art direction for magazines. She worked at Time Inc. before co founding design firm Koppel & Scher with Terry Koppel in 1984. Since 1991, she has been a principal at the New York office of the Pentagram design consultancy. In 1996 Scher's much imitated identity for The Public Theater in New York won the coveted Beacon Award for integrated corporate design strategy.

In 1998, Scher was inducted into the Art Directors Club Hall of Fame, she received the Chrysler Design Award for Innovation in Design in 2000, and a Gold Medal from the American Institute of Graphic Arts in 2001. Her work is in the permanent collection of the Museum of Modern Art and the Cooper-Hewitt, National Design Museum. Her album designs have earned her four Grammy Award nominations.

She holds an honorary doctorate from the Corcoran College of Art and Design and is a member of the Alliance Graphique Internationale (AGI). She currently serves on the board of directors of The Public Theater, and in 2006 she was named to the Art Commission of the City of New York.

Assessing her work, Scher comments that she wants to raise expectations about what the "mainstream" can be." As an artist she also is known for her large-scale paintings of maps, covered with dense hand-painted labeling and information.

Her teaching career includes over two decades at the School of Visual Arts, New York, along with positions at the Cooper Union, Yale University, and the Tyler School of Art. In 2002, Princeton Architectural Press published her career monograph *Make It Bigger*.

Resources

http://pentagram.com/en/partners/paula-scher.php

Paula Scher, *Make It Bigger*, Princeton Architectural Press, New York, 2005

Kit Hinrichs, *The Pentagram Papers: A Collection of 36 Unique Publications Designed by Pentagram*, Thames & Hudson, London, 2007

Susan Yelavich and various, *Profile: Pentagram Design*, Phaidon Press, London, 2004.
The first Pentagram book to include the design firm's "new guard": partners Fernando Gutiérrez, DJ Stout, Lisa Strausfeld, and Abbott Miller.

THE PUBLIC.

New York's first public pay toilet opened in Madison Square Park. The exterior sports a poster designed by Paula Scher, featuring the identity she developed for the park. The toilet is self-cleaning and costs a quarter to use, and is conveniently located just across the park from Pentagram's office. Paula Scher/Pentagram.

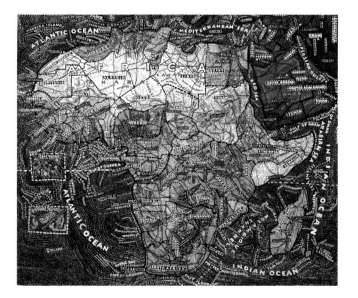

Africa, 2003, acrylic on canvas, 120 x 104.5 in (3048 x 2654 mm). Paula Scher started painting opinionated maps in the 1980s and over the years they have become bigger. Her large-scale canvasses are intricate, colorful and obsessively detailed maps of newsworthy regions of the world, often surrounded by swirling seas of typography—information overload. Africa is more sombre than most and, like the others, is not 100 percent accurate, but in its way it illustrates a world view that's always changing. Paula Scher/Pentagram.

In 1994 Paula Scher designed a poster for the New York Shakespeare Festival that introduced a new identity for the Public Theater. For the 2008 Shakespeare in the Park productions (Hamlet and Hair), Scher introduced a refreshed identity, with the Victorian wood-block letterforms redrawn using the Hoefler & Frere-Jones font Knockout. The posters utilize the strict 90° angles of a De Stijl-inspired grid organized by angled printers' rules, a throwback that also adds structure. Paula Scher/Pentagram.

Letterpress

Until the 1960s, **letterpress** was the most popular form of printing. Now it is virtually obsolete, except for small limited-edition presses producing fine editions of books and prints. Large letterpress machines have been converted to flexography (see opposite), in which the heritage of letterpress lingers on.

Letterpress is a relief process, invented by the Chinese. It was adapted to Western use by Gutenberg, and perfected in the late 19th century, with the introduction of iron steam-powered presses. The beautifully crafted Stanhope, Columbian, and Albion presses from the golden age of letterpress, with their ornamental cast-iron eagles and fanciful beasts, have long been relegated to science museums and the entrance halls of modern printers. But like steam locomotives, some have been lovingly restored by enthusiasts and put to use (Fig. **6.30**). They create that three-dimensional tactile quality of impression that litho and gravure cannot achieve.

There are three types of letterpress machine: flatbed, platen, and rotary. The flatbed is the oldest, being derived from wine and textile presses (Fig. **6.31**). The forme containing the locked-up wrong-reading type and blocks is placed horizontally on the bed of the press. Paper is placed over it, and a screw is turned or a lever pulled to apply pressure. The cylinder flatbed is a press that has the forme and paper on a bed that is inked and then moved under a heavy impression cylinder. The cylinder is lifted to allow the bed to return to its starting position.

The **platen** principle has the forme positioned vertically, with the platen—a heavy metal plate—swinging forward and upward with the paper (Fig. **6.32**). It makes an impression as it snaps shut, like a clamshell, vertical and parallel with the forme. Platen presses can still be seen in operation, printing business cards and wedding invitations.

A rotary press cannot print directly from the forme. A curved copy of the forme, called a stereotype, must first be cast. A papier-mâché mold, called a flong, is taken from the forme, and is used to make a one-piece metal, rubber, or plastic plate. It is then fixed around the cylinder. Rotary presses can be sheetfed or web-fed. During the changeover of newspapers from letterpress to offset litho, a process called photopolymer direct relief was used to make plastic or nylon plates for letterpress from photoset mechanicals. Flexography (see the next section) uses a similar process.

Letterset is a process whereby the image is first offset on to a rubber blanket, as in offset litho. It is used for printing on metal and plastic cartons and cans.

6.30 Most old iron letterpress machines, such as this Columbian, have been relegated to the foyers of large corporations as mere ornamental features. Thankfully, many are being restored and put back to work at open-access print workshops such as here, at Brighton Independent Printmakers.

6.31 On a traditional letterpress machine, paper is laid face down on to the inked forme and the whole flatbed assembly is moved beneath a screw- or lever-powered press.

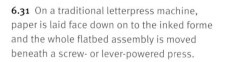

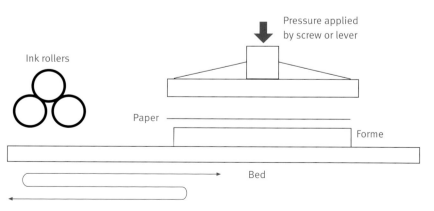

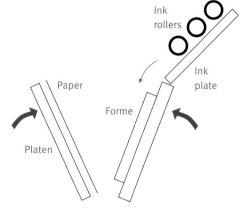

6.32 The platen press operates like a pincer—the two halves are brought forcibly together into a vertical position by lever action.

Flexography

Flexography is a relief process, a form of letterpress, which prints using flexible rubber or photopolymer plates. The process was first demonstrated in 1890 by Bibby, Baron & Sons of Liverpool, United Kingdom, as a means of printing on non-absorbent packaging materials. It was further developed in the 1920s to make use of **aniline dyes**, derived from coal tar, and had various names. The term flexography was coined in 1952 as a result of a competition sponsored by the packaging industry. It was thought that any name containing the words "coal tar" had connotations that would not be acceptable by the general public in the context of packaging for foodstuffs.

Flexography presses are rotary web-fed machines, similar in layout to gravure machines (Fig. **6.33**). Like gravure, flexo generally uses thin inks, usually solvent-based and uses a two-roll inking system. A smooth metal fountain roll transfers the ink first to an etched metal or ceramic **anilox** roll, which is covered in dimples or cells of fixed size and depth (rather like a gravure cylinder) that act as ink-carrying reservoirs, and then to the printing plate or sleeve. Water-based inks containing fluorescent dyes can also be printed using flexography. It is an economical process only for very large print runs, typically measured in millions of copies.

Artwork is prepared exactly as for offset litho. The plates or seamless sleeves are produced in the same way as the stereotypes for letterpress (Fig. **6.34**), and are flexible enough to be attached to the printing cylinder using adhesive. Corrections can be patched into existing plates. The plates do distort in use, and some image spread should be catered for in the design.

Because of the plates' squashiness, flexo is used for food-packaging applications that require flexibility—printing on plastic bags and other non-absorbent stock, such as cellophane and metal foil, and corrugated surfaces.

The process competes with gravure for printing magazines and paperback books on cheap newsprint. The plates do have a tendency to "plug up" with fibers from rougher stocks, however.

Direct laser engraving of rubber printing plates has been used since the 1980s. Lasers have also been used for producing photopolymer plates since 1995. With improved lasers producing conical dots, and with UV-cured inks, it is now possible to print at 150 lpi with three percent dots.

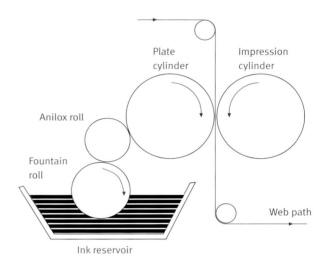

6.33 The configuration of a flexography machine is very similar to that of a gravure press. The Anilox roll even has a gravure-like cellular texture to carry the thin ink to the flexo plate.

6.34 DuPont's Cyrel FAST 1000TD processes flexographic printing plates using thermal technology, eliminating solvents and aqueous solutions from the plateroom. It can produce finished plates up to 35.4 × 47.2 in less than an hour. Photograph courtesy of DuPont.

Screenprinting

At the other end of the spectrum, the **silkscreen** process, or **screenprinting**, is used only for relatively short print runs of up to 15,000 copies. The name derives from its craft origins, when a screen of silk material was used to support the stencil bearing the image through which ink was squeezed (Fig. **6.35**). Today, the screen is made from synthetic gauzes or metal meshes.

Despite its almost exclusive associations with poster design and the prints of Andy Warhol, screenprinting is an extremely versatile process. It is a simple and direct method of delivering ink, and can thus be used to print on any kind of substrate, even on curved and uneven surfaces. It can produce thick and opaque deposits of ink, in brilliant, saturated colors, and with high chemical and abrasion resistance. Applications for screenprinting range from printed circuit-boards in electronics, through bottles and cartons, to T-shirts, point-of-display advertising, compact discs, and logos on the sides of vehicles.

The screen has two functions: to support the stencil, and to regulate the ink. The screen itself is supported in a wooden or metal frame, evenly tensioned using air-powered or mechanical devices. Most screens are made from polyester. This is a precision woven mesh for close register work, with high stability and low sensitivity to variations in temperature and humidity. Other screen materials include polyamide, which has good wear resistance and elasticity. It is used for printing three-dimensional objects. Stainless-steel screens have the highest dimensional stability, plus chemical and physical resistance. They are used for ceramic decoration and printed circuitboards.

The mesh has two main characteristics: the count and the grade. The **mesh count** is the number of threads per inch. The lower the count, the less support there will be for detail, and the heavier the deposit of ink. The **mesh grade** relates to thread thickness, which influences the weight of the ink film. There are four grades: S, M, T, and HD. S is the thinnest, giving a 50 to 70 percent open area; HD is the heaviest, giving a 20 to 35 percent open area. One chooses a count and grade depending on the application, ink, and halftone screen being used.

Stencils can be cut by hand from water- or solvent-soluble laminate film, and are either ironed on to the screen using heat or mounted using a solvent. A pen plotter equipped with a cutting knife can be used by the designer to cut out "line" stencils direct from a computer system (see Fig. 4.34). The unwanted areas are "weeded out" and discarded (don't forget enclosed areas like the counters of letters such as b).

6.35 Screenprinting is mainly associated with poster and T-shirt printing, but can also be used where a non-impact process is required, for printing directly on to the surfaces of compact discs and CD-ROMs, for example.

More complex stencils are made photomechanically. Artwork is prepared as for offset litho, and a film positive is made at the repro house. One method uses presensitized gelatin film exposed to ultraviolet light in contact with the positive. This is then hardened in hydrogen peroxide, and the sticky stencil is mounted to the underside of the frame. When it has dried, the polyester base is peeled off and discarded.

A more direct method uses a screen coated on both sides (more thickly on the underside) with a light-sensitive polymer emulsion. After exposure to ultraviolet light in contact with positive film, the image areas are washed away with water from a high-pressure jet. This leaves a stencil that completely encapsulates the screen mesh.

Presses for screenprinting range from simple bench-mounted configurations operated by hand (using a rubber squeegee to force ink through the mesh) to fully automatic rotary machines (Fig. **6.36**). On bench presses, a metal blade called a flo-coater, which is mounted behind the squeegee, returns the ink to its pre-printing position. The angle, pressure, and speed of both the squeegee and the flo-coater can be adjusted. Once set, the machine will produce consistent results throughout the print run. Fast cylinder-bed presses have the squeegee and flo-coater stationary. The stock, supported on a vacuum bed, moves in unison with the screen.

Screenprinting is a direct non-impact process producing thick, bright colors, but it is not recommended for close registration work, nor for smaller sizes of type. Halftones pose problems because of possible moiré effects caused by the gauze of the mesh interfering with the screen. Moiré can be minimized, however, by using a stencil production system with good dot formation; by angling the mesh between four and nine degrees to the axis of the frame; or by using a "grained" or textured screen rather than a pattern of dots.

6.36 Most screenprinting is very labor-intensive, using a hand-operated bench configuration—literally pulling the squeegee across the surface of the screen. The process can be automated on a rotary machine—the squeegee and flo-coater remain in the same position while the screen moves. Paper is pulled by a gripper between the screen and a vacuum cylinder.

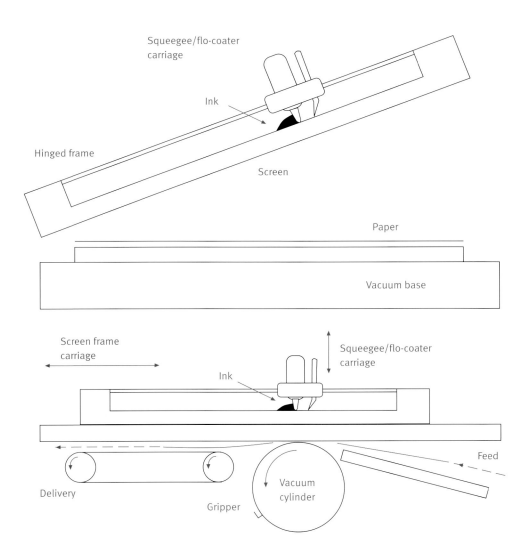

6.37 Collotype is the only process that can print a full tonal range without screening. It is relatively rare, and examples are impossible to show in a book that has been printed by offset litho (see also Fig. 1.9).

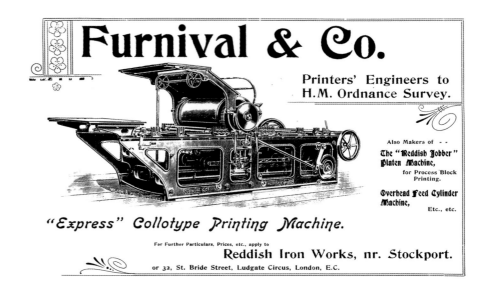

Collotype

Collotype, or photogelatin, was and still is the only process that can print continuous tone without screening (Fig. **6.37**). It is used for limited-edition art prints of exceptional quality, and is a slow process capable only of small print runs.

To produce a collotype, a right-reading unscreened negative is first made from the original. This is contact printed to an aluminum plate coated with light-sensitive gelatin. The gelatin hardens in proportion to the amount of light falling on it: highlights remain soft; darker areas are harder. The plate is prepared for printing by flooding it with a solution of water containing glycerine—the soft areas absorb more than the harder ones. Ink is then applied. It adheres to the hardened areas, and progressively less in the softer parts. An impression is made, producing a continuous tone image with a mottled grain.

Xerography

Xerography, or photocopying, may well replace small-scale offset litho in the near future. A photocopier can print direct from artwork or a mechanical, enlarging and reducing instantly. For small print runs, photocopying is cheaper than offset litho with all its set-up costs. The results are dense and black, and photocopiers can now print on a wide range of paper stock. Systems such as the Xerox DocuTech (Fig. **6.38**) are used for small-scale (less than 1000) "on-demand" runs of manuals and books. Machines such as the Canon CLC (Color Laser Copier) can produce full-color work direct from artwork, or from a computer system. The cost per sheet is relatively expensive, but falling all the time.

6.38 Xerox's DocuColor iGen3 Digital Production Press prints up to 6000 A4 ($8\frac{1}{4} \times 11\frac{11}{16}$ in) impressions an hour, both sides, at 600 dpi. In-line finishing modules for mechanical (ring) and perfect binding, imposing, folding, stapling/stitching, trimming, and UV (ultraviolet) coating can be added to produce booklets and manuals on demand. Paper stock can be up to $14\frac{1}{3} \times 22\frac{2}{5}$ in (364 × 570 mm).

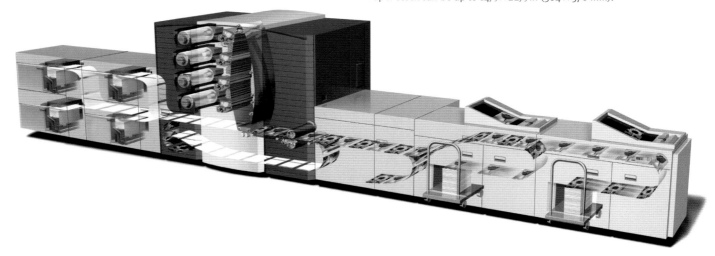

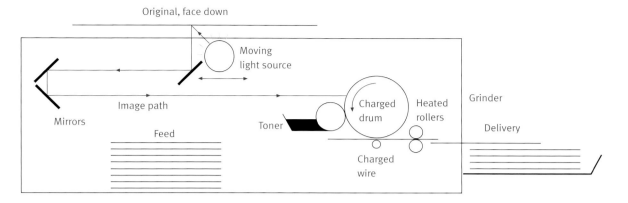

6.39 Inside a photocopier, a light source scans the artwork and this image is transferred via mirrors on to an electrostatically charged drum. Toner adheres to the image, and is transferred to the paper and fixed by heat. In a laser copier, all this is done digitally, just like a combination laser scanner and laser printer.

Xerography was invented in 1938 by Chester Carlson, and developed by the Xerox Corporation. Artwork is placed face down on a glass plate, and is illuminated by a fluorescent light which travels the length of the image. The reflected image is directed through lenses on to an electrostatically charged drum. This charge leaks away where light from the image falls on the drum. A resin-based powder, called toner, is attracted to the image areas. This pattern of toner is transferred to a sheet of paper, where it is fixed by heat (Fig. **6.39**).

Laser copiers work like combined scanners and imagesetters by scanning the image digitally, and using a laser to write the image on to the electrostatic drum.

Digital print

One day, all printing will be digital. For now we can define **digital print** as any printed output that is imaged directly on to a blanket, plate, or substrate from an electronic file, with no intermediate film stage. The first black-and-white production devices meeting this description appeared in the 1970s. The first digital presses, the Indigo E-Print 1000 and Xeikon's DCP-1, were launched in 1993 (Fig. **6.40**).

6.40 The Xeikon 6000 is an LED array-based dry toner electrophotography digital press that can print 160 A4 pages per minute in fully collated order; 9,600 full-color pages per hour. With an optional Jumbo Unwinder, it can print different jobs without having to stop.

6.41 HP's Indigo 5500 press uses ElectroInk liquid-ink technology to produce 68 ppm full color, 136 ppm in two-color, and 272 ppm monochrome, regardless of media type or thickness, 800 × 1200 dpi at eight bit, up to 2400 × 2400 dpi addressability (high definition imaging); at 144, 160, 175, 180, and 230 lpi screens. CMYK is augmented with up to three optional ink stations that simulate Pantone colors.

The HP Indigo uses liquid ink to produce a result close to that of conventional offset litho. All the colors are squirted on to the plate in one go and then transferred to an offset blanket, in a similar way to conventional offset printing. Unlike conventional printing, however, the blanket of the digital printer is left clean for the next image which could well impart a different message for each printing revolution from its PostScript server. Each individual page is RIPped to the electrostatic plate in parallel with the information being held in memory before printing the next page. The HP Indigo 5500 (Fig. **6.41**) can print 68 four-color A4 (8¼ × 11¹¹⁄₁₆ in) images per minute (two-

up) using liquid ink at 800 dpi resolution and line screens up to 230 lpi. Adaptive halftoning analyzes text as it is being printed, adding dots to fill gaps at the edges, and producing crisp, sharp text and images on paper 47–236 lb (70–350 gsm) for coated stock or 44–200 lb (65–300 gsm) for uncoated. Three additional optional inking stations augment process colors with HP IndiChrome's seven-color printing to simulate Pantone colors off-press.

The Indigo also has some finishing capabilities, with online collating and stapling of up to 100 pages in one go, which, with its variable page information, makes for a versatile machine. Web-fed presses are designed for the packaging market, printing on such materials as pressure-sensitive labels, films, foils, and other flexible packaging substrates.

The Xeikon press uses CMYK toners and heat fusion similar to a color copier, but that is where the similarity ends. Each dot can have variable amounts of toner at 600 dpi to give a quality similar to that of offset litho and much better than a conventional color copier. Also, variable dot-density screening means that there is no dot gain.

Digital print technologies

Today, there are three basic technologies being described as process color digital print:

- **Electrophotographic**, in which a dry or liquid toner is deposited on the substrate by varying its electrostatic properties and then fixed by absorption, chemical reaction, or heat. This includes xerographic photocopiers (see Fig. 6.38) and the HP Indigo and Xeikon digital print engines.

- **Digital litho**, which uses a CtP (computer-to-plate) device to image a plate on press and then prints using a normal litho process.

- **Inkjet**, in which a liquid ink is sprayed either directly on to the substrate, or on to an intermediate blanket (Fig. **6.42**).

One characteristic shared by all these devices is their ability to reduce, or almost eliminate, make-ready times. This allows short runs (roughly, up to 1000 copies) to be produced more economically than with non-digital presses. It also makes it more feasible to print "on-demand," the cut-off point being somewhere in the area of 700 to 1000 copies. One key difference is that with digital printing every copy costs the same in material costs as the previous print. In conventional print, the more copies that are produced, the cheaper each sheet becomes. Digital print, however, can vary text and images on a page-by-page basis creating opportunities for "tailored print" such as:

- Personalization, where a person's details, such as name and address, are changed between each document printed;

- Customization, where substantial amounts of the content of, for example, brochures or catalogs is altered to match the preferences and interests of readers;

- Versioning, where larger runs of a generic document are broken down into many slightly amended shorter runs (with details of a local office or staff on a sales brochure, for example).

6.42 The 5000 from InfoPrint, a joint venture between IBM and Ricoh, uses piezo-electric drop-on-demand inkjet technology to produce 916 full-color letter-size impressions/minute in two-up tandem duplex mode (862 A4 impressions) on a 20.4 in (520 mm) wide web. It only jets water-based pigment ink when it's needed on the paper.

Emerging print technologies

As discussed on page 205, there are three basic technologies being described as digital print: digital litho using CtP (computer-to-plate), electrophotography (including xerography; Fig. **6.43**), and inkjet. Although currently used for short runs, digital print is changing the workflow pattern of print production, from "print and distribute," to "distribute (digital files such as PDF) and print" (on location).

The first digital presses were either glorified color laser copiers or, like the Indigo E-print, a converted sheet-fed offset press with a reusable organic photoconductor mounted on the plate cylinder, and the inking system replaced by a corona charger and four, six, or seven toning nozzles for applying colored liquid toner to a heated blanket. Paper either rotates one revolution for each color or the image is built up on the blanket before being transferred to the paper in one pass. The "ink" is comprised of microscopic particles of toner dispersed in a thermoplastic resin and diluted in a light mineral oil. The heated blanket evaporates the ink leaving a tacky polymeric film which cools and sets on contact with the substrate.

The Xeikon is web-fed and has eight LED-exposed photoconductor plates for printing four colors on both sides of the paper in one pass. Dry toners are fused by heat after imaging.

Inkjet is a non-contact technology. Printers are of two main types: continuous jets, in which charged drops of ink are deflected to form the image or fall to a gutter to be recycled; and impulse or drop on demand, such as piezo-electric, bubblejet, and solid ink/phase change printers. Large format inkjets are used as proofers and for printing posters, displays, and fine-art prints. UV-curing ink can be used for light-fast and water resistant applications.

Electro-coagulation or **Elcography** is a novel technology developed by Canadian vendor Elcorsy. In 1971, the company's founder Adrien Castegnier was working in a rotogravure plant in Paris. He wanted to obtain photographic-quality images on plain paper without the environmental problems of silver halide. His original idea was to build a gelatin gravure cell using gas bubbles generated by an electrolytic reaction. If the cavities were then filled with ink, the image could be printed on regular paper.

The Elco 400 press uses water-based polymeric ink that is sensitive to electric fields. This pigmented liquid ink is sprayed onto a metallic cylinder and coagulates into 400 dpi gel dots in 256 different thicknesses, controlled by pulses of electricity. The lightest dot is done in 100 nanoseconds, while the darkest dot is written in four microseconds. By comparison, the time to access data on your hard disk is a thousand times slower. The imaging cycle is repeated for each revolution of the press. It can print at 1700 pages per minute and can switch print jobs without stopping, making it ideal for short-run printing. The quick-drying water-based inks are environmentally friendly, odorless, and easy to clean with high light-fastness.

Other emerging technologies include ionography, ion or electron charge deposition printing, and magnetography, in which spot opaque colors are produced from a cold-fused magnetic toner and charged drum—these are used mainly for the printing of barcodes, tickets, and labels.

6.43 Kodak's 600 dpi Nexpress S3000 electrophotography press delivers 6000 A4/US Letter sheets per hour (100 pages per minute) with offset litho quality. The five-color configuration enables in-line coating, glossing, or a fifth color to expand the printing gamut or reproduce spot colors. Maximum sheet size is 14 × 20.47 in (356 × 520 mm) for uncoated, matte and glossy papers, paper-backed transparencies, and opaque foils.

Find out more

HP Indigo: www.hp.com
Xeikon: www.xeikon.com

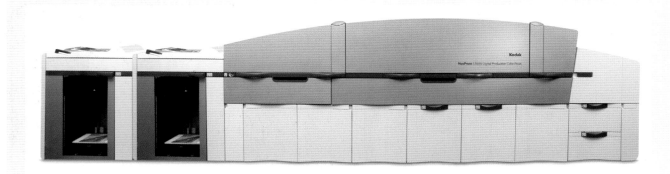

Printing processes: the pros and cons

Offset litho
Advantages Extremely flexible and cost-effective for most jobs, wide range of presses from jobbing sheet-fed machines to large web-fed presses, relatively short set-up time, positive-working or negative-working, prints effectively on wide range of stock.

Disadvantages Needs more attention than gravure for consistency over long print runs, ink translucent and prone to more problems than in the other processes. Higher set-up costs than digital print.

Gravure
Advantages High-quality, high-speed continuous-tone repro-duction and rich blacks, prints well on cheaper stock, very economical for long print runs, fast process after make-ready.

Disadvantages Type is screened, solvent-based inks, only viable for large print runs, expensive to set up, corrections require new cylinder, proofing expensive.

Flexography
Advantages Fast make-ready, prints well on non-absorbent stock, possibility of using water-based ink, prints well on cheap paper stock.

Disadvantages Image spread, poor halftones, usually have to use solvent-based ink, expensive to set up.

Screenprinting
Advantages Non-impact process, versatile, prints on any kind of substrate and on curved or uneven surfaces, can be used to produce thick and opaque deposits of ink in brilliant saturated colors and with high chemical and abrasion resistance.

Disadvantages Small print runs, not recommended for halftones because of the possibility of moiré effects, close reg-istration and four-color work difficult, cannot print smaller sizes of type.

Letterpress
Advantages Quality of impression, wide range of original typeface designs (hand-set repro proofs can be taken for printing by offset litho).

Disadvantages Inflexible for design, expensive now that big presses have largely been taken out of service.

Collotype
Advantages High-quality screenless and continuous-tone reproduction.

Disadvantages Slow, very expensive, short print runs only.

Xerography
Advantages Inexpensive for short print runs, no set-up costs, no film or plates, no ink, can print direct from computer disk.

Disadvantages Cannot print large sheets, color reproduc-tion is often poor and is almost always variable, restricted paper stock.

Digital print
Advantages Cost-effective for short runs, print can be per-sonalized, very fast turnaround, electronic collation, delivers a book or brochures that only need trimming and gluing to be ready for delivery.

Disadvantages Expensive machinery and consumables, requires a digital workflow.

6.44 Catch-up (below left).

6.45 Hickies (below right).

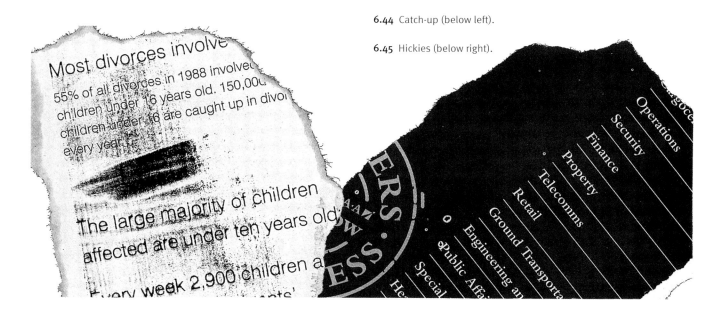

Things that can go wrong

There are all kinds of problems associated with the paper, the ink, and the press, and how they interact with each other. Some of these have been mentioned earlier, but for the sake of completeness, they will be listed here in alphabetical order.

Backing is a lightening of color that occurs if ink removed from the fountain roller is not replaced by the flow of new ink.

Catch-up occurs in offset litho when insufficient water on the plate causes non-image areas to print (Fig. **6.44**).

Chalking, or powdering, happens mainly with matte coated stock and is caused when the vehicle from the ink is absorbed, leaving only pigment on the surface. It becomes apparent when dry ink starts to rub off the image or smudge, and unfortunately is noticed only after the job is finished. In emergencies, the original plate can be used to overprint a layer of transparent size to try to bind the ink to the paper.

Color variation during a run is caused by altering ink-to-water balance, or by stopping the press.

Crawling is an imperfection in the surface of the ink, occurring when thick ink overprints wet ink.

Crocking is smudging or transfer of dry ink on to printed sheets.

Crystallization is a result of careless overprinting. If the ink of the first printing dries too hard before overprinting is done, it can repel the second color.

Damper marks are patterns over the print caused by worn damper covers or too much pressure.

Dot gain shows when halftone shadows fill in or if the print looks too dark, and is caused by bad film-to-plate contact, over-exposure of the plate, over-absorbent paper, or over-inking. However, it will always occur to some degree, so an allowance should be made at the proofing stage.

Doubling—two dots where there should be only one—is caused when wet ink is picked up by the blanket on a subsequent printing. If it is slightly off register, it prints as a ghost dot nearby.

6.46 Setoff (below left).

6.47 Misregistration (below right).

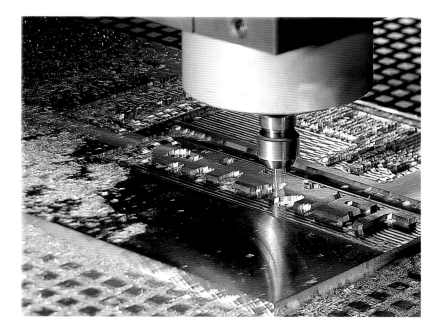

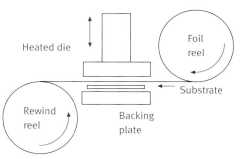

6.49 A brass die for hot-foil stamping being cut by a computer-controlled machine. These brass dies are able to surpass a million stamping cycles.

6.50 In hot-foil blocking, the foil passes from a roll and is stamped on to the substrate by the action of heat.

6.51 Cold-foil stamping is used to decorate bottle labels, cosmetics, food, and pharmaceutical packaging.

Cold-foil stamping (Fig. **6.51**) is used for decorating bottle labels, cosmetics, food, and pharmaceutical packaging. Metallic stamping foils are transferred to a substrate by means of a UV-curable adhesive applied to the substrate by either offset or flexo printing. Then the cold-stamping foil, comprising a carrier foil and stamping layer, is laminated onto the substrate. When the adhesive is cured, the carrier foil is stripped from the substrate.

The process does not require stamping tools, but instead uses printing plates, which are not only much cheaper but, because the delivery time for an engraved or etched stamping tool can be up to two weeks, can cut production times considerably. More importantly for the designer, gradients and halftone images can be introduced.

Spot varnishing of halftones to add gloss and intensity has already been mentioned in the discussion of inks (see p. 183). Overall **varnishing**, as a finishing operation, is carried out by running printed sheets through rollers. Machine varnish (lacquer) can be applied using a conventional litho machine, but the sheen it produces is barely noticeable. High-gloss or liquid lamination is a nitrocellulose coating requiring a special machine. Ultraviolet varnish, which dries on exposure to ultraviolet light, also produces high gloss and scuff-resistance. Two layers of varnish, printed wet-on-wet, give a very smooth glossy finish.

Lamination adds strength as well as gloss. Film lamination is glued to the stock as it goes through a heated roller under high pressure. It is applied from a roll on to overlapping sheets, leaving the gripper edge and the sides free for any other processing. But laminated sheets must be left for the adhesive to dry completely, before operations such as guillotining or embossing can be performed with confidence. Ultraviolet lamination cures more quickly.

Ink that is to be varnished or laminated should be quick drying, with little residual solvent, and absolutely no wax additives. Too much anti-setoff spray can have an adverse effect on either process. Metallic inks should not be varnished. They have their own sheen, after all.

How does a designer specify finishing effects?

Adding embossing, hot-foil stamping, or both to your design is similar to adding a spot color, metallic ink, or area of varnish. These print on extra plates to the four used for CMYK, either on-press or on an in-line module downstream of the press. Cold-blocking, or stamping, can also be done in-line to the press.

They can be indicated as spot colors in QuarkXPress or InDesign, or as a spot channel in Photoshop. To export a file from Photoshop to QuarkXPress or InDesign, it must be in DCS (Desktop Color Separations) or PDF format to retain the extra channels and create the extra plates.

Using varnish on your document will affect trapping. In InDesign choose "transparent" in the "ink manager" to ensure that underlying items will trap.

For metallic, pearl, or hologram hot-foil blocking you will need to have a die made, which adds time to the production cycle. So discuss any finishing operations with your printer as early as you can. You will also have to tell them how high and how many levels the emboss (or deboss) should be raised (or depressed) from the surface of the substrate, and whether the edges should be beveled, rounded, or sculpted.

Artwork should be black line or bitmap with no grayscales or halftone screens. Avoid type smaller than 8 pt, lines thinner than 2 pt, and tight intricate detail which can cause foil to plug. Areas to be embossed should be slightly larger and heavier than for a normal spot color.

Folding and binding

After these print-related finishes have been applied, the stock can be folded (Fig. **6.52**). There are three types of folding machine. **Buckle folders** (Fig. **6.53**) are the most commonplace. The sheet enters a pre-set distance and is stopped and buckled back at the fold line by two inward-revolving rollers. These nip the flat sheet, then fold it and carry it forward to the next "plate," where the process is repeated. **Knife folders** (Fig. **6.54**) are used in bookwork. Here a blunt knife is used to nip the sheet between two rollers. They are very precise, but slower than buckle folders. **Combination folders** give the best of both worlds.

Single-sheet jobs then go straight to the guillotine for trimming. Multi-page jobs first have to be united with the other pages, **gathered** on conveyor belts, bundled flat, and collated (put in order). For books, the sections are gathered one next to the other. Printed marks on the spines of sections, called backstep marks, indicate the correct sequence visually. Letters or numbers printed on the signatures serve as a double check.

Loose **inserts** are single sheets of paper or even sometimes booklets, which are added, generally by hand, to a magazine. They fall out when the magazine is shaken.

Tipping-in is adding a single page to a publication, either by pasting down the inside edge, or by wrapping a short strip around the fold. This is a labor-intensive process, and thus very expensive. Illustrations that were printed intaglio, or on art paper, used to be tipped in to books. **Tipping-on** is pasting a smaller illustration, an erratum slip, or a reply coupon on to a page.

Perforation can be done on the printing press, by means of a perforating strip attached to the impression cylinder (eventually ruining the blanket), or on a special finishing machine.

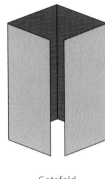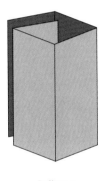

6.52 There are many different ways to fold a folder. Here are some examples—but remember to make economical use of your printed sheet before you specify an exotic fold.

Single-fold
four-page
folder

Accordion
eight-page
folder

Gatefold
eight-page
folder

Rollover
eight-page
folder

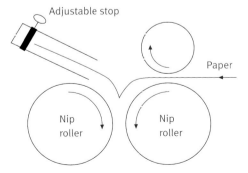

6.53 In a buckle folder, the sheet is brought to rest by an adjustable stop before being forced between a pair of nip rollers.

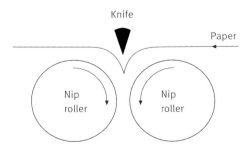

6.54 A knife folder is used for more exacting work—a knifelike device pushes the sheet between two nip rollers, producing a much sharper fold.

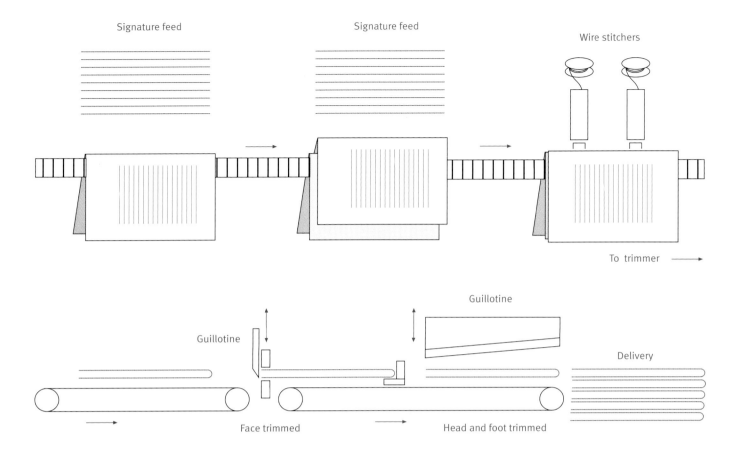

Signature feed

Signature feed

Wire stitchers

To trimmer →

Guillotine

Guillotine

Delivery

Face trimmed

Head and foot trimmed

6.55 In saddle-stitching, the folded and collated signatures move along a conveyor on saddles the shape of inverted Vs. Wire staples are then inserted along the fold of the spine.

Magazines and booklets are bound in one of two ways: by saddle-stitching or perfect binding. **Saddle-stitching** (Fig. **6.55** and **6.56**) is a fancy way of saying stapling, though the wire staples used in saddle-stitching are longer and rounder than office staples. Saddle-stitching gets its name from the inverted V saddle on to which the sections are placed. Sections are opened out and placed one inside another, inserting larger sections inside smaller ones, and with the cover on top. This is the least expensive form of **binding**, but can only be used with publications of up to around 128 pages, depending on the paper stock. On thicker publications, take note of paper creep—pages near the center will be narrower after trimming than those near the covers (see p. 145). Specify stainless steel wires so that they don't rust.

Side-stabbing (Fig. **6.57**) inserts the wires from front to back, near the spine, disguised by the creased **hinges** of the covers.

Calendars, cookbooks, and technical manuals are sometimes **spiral-bound** (Fig. **6.58**) so as to lie flat. The sheets are punched with a line of round or slotted holes near the **spine**. Wire is then coiled through the holes and crimped. **Wire**

comb, or Wire-O, bindings and **plastic comb** bindings give a more finished appearance.

Perfect binding (Fig. **6.59**), unsewn binding, or cut-back binding, can be far from perfect unless a good glue is used. For this process, the sections are gathered and collated as before, and presented to the machine spine down. The edge is notched, or milled off and roughened, and adhesive is applied. The covers are folded, scored, and wrapped around the pages. The adhesive is then cured by heat, and the pages are trimmed. Perfect-bound magazines have a flat spine, on to which a title, date, and a résumé of the contents can be printed. But the process is slower and more expensive than saddle-stitching, and double-page spreads can be a problem with copy disappearing into the gutter. Fold the magazine back and it falls apart! Mass-market paperback books are often printed two-up, head to head, and only cut apart after perfect binding.

Hardback books are sometimes perfect bound, but the sections can instead be sewn through the spine with thread—this is called **section sewing**. They are then gathered together into a book block. **Thread-sealing** combines features of perfect binding and section sewing (but no thread runs between sections).

Side-sewing is a method used for children's books, in which the thread goes front to back, as in side-stabbing. This produces a stronger binding than section sewing, with the disadvantage that the book will not lie flat when folded.

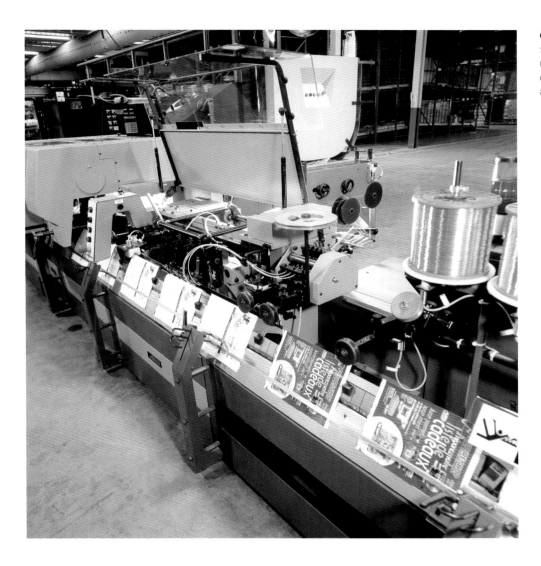

6.56 Heidelberg's Pacesetter 1100 saddle-stitcher can stitch up to 20,000 A4 (8¼ × 11¹¹/₁₆ in) copies an hour from both web- and sheetfed offset presses.

6.57 In side-stabbing, the wire staples are inserted through the front of the signature, along the back edge close to the spine.

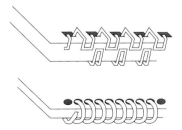

6.58 Spiral binding is used for calendars, manuals, and cookery books—wherever the publication has to fold perfectly flat. Wire-O gives a neater finish.

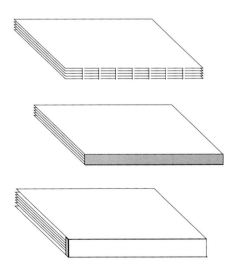

6.59 In perfect binding, the signatures are collated, then the spines are cut off, roughened, and spread with glue to attach the covers.

Score before folding

Heavy paper or card should always be scored before folding—enough to produce a raised ridge. A fold should always be made with the ridge or hinge on the inside. Booklet covers must have a score wide enough to accommodate all the pages to be inserted inside.

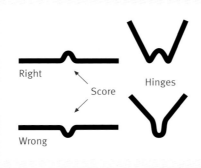

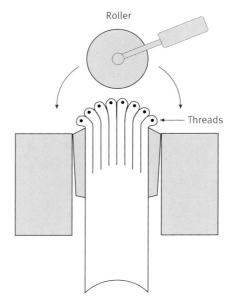

6.60 The thread used to sew the book-block makes it thicker at the spine. Rounding keeps the book in good shape; backing produces a neat shoulder.

A case-bound, or hardback, book (Fig. **6.61**) has a hard case made apart from the pages. The book-block and cover are assembled, along with tipped-on endpapers, at the final stage of binding. Endpapers are usually of heavier stock than the text pages, and are sometimes decorated. **Rounding and backing (R & B)** is a combined operation that puts a rounded shape into the spine of the book-block, and a joint below the shoulder (Fig. **6.60**). Some books are rounded; others are left with flat spines. Linings are glued to the spine; **headbands** and **tailbands**—and perhaps a bookmark—are added; and the endpapers are glued to the insides of the cases. Book jackets can then be wrapped around the cased book by hand or by machine.

Cases are made from heavy board, with the grain parallel to the spine to prevent warping. The material used to make the case of a hardback book look attractive is known as the covering. It can be of non-woven material, such as embossed paper, fiberfelts, or plastic-coated fiber, or a form of starch-filled cloth or **buckram**. A **quarter-bound** book (Fig. **6.62**) has the spine and an adjacent strip of the cover bound in an expensive material, maybe leather, with the rest of the sides in something cheaper. A **half binding** has, in addition, triangles at the corners in the expensive material. Leather, embellished with gold blocking and tooled decorations, is reserved for expensive limited-edition books. Expensive paperbacks sometimes have card covers that fold in on themselves to add thickness and a neater edge. These are called **French folds**.

After binding and counting, the job is parceled up in waterproof packaging or shrink-wrapping, is boxed, correctly labeled, put on to pallets, and shipped to its destination—and your job is done.

6.61 Case-bound books consist of a book-block, a hard cover, and endpapers that are assembled at the final stage of binding.

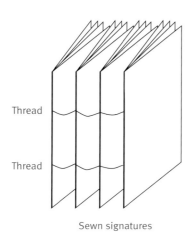

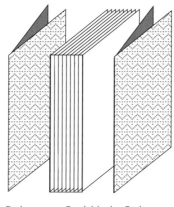

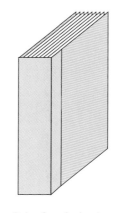

Sewn signatures   Endpapers   Book block   Endpapers   Strip of crash glued on   Headband and case added

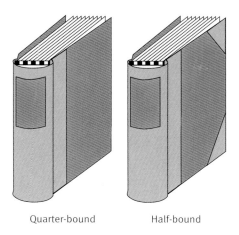

Quarter-bound   Half-bound

6.62 A quarter-bound book and a half-bound book, with its additional triangles at the corners.

Eco-friendly finishing

Many finishing operations can render a print job unrecyclable. The most environmentally friendly method of binding is wire stitching—metal staples can be removed during recycling and then recycled themselves. Cotton thread, comb, and Wire-O bindings are more difficult to separate from the paper. Any type of glue is generally bad news for recycling and can also be toxic. Foil blocking and laminating may also make your product unrecyclable. If you need to use varnish, choose water-based coatings, which can be gloss—although not as shiny as UV varnish. Vegetable-oil metallic inks are coming onto the market, so ask your printer if they are using them.

Summary

On press is that part of the production process over which the graphic designer has the least amount of hands-on control. What the designer does possess, however, is the power of *selection*. An appropriate choice of paper, ink, and printer should ensure a predictable outcome, given that the designer's input is as near perfect as can be, and bearing in mind the merits and limitations of the various printing processes.

Paper, ink, and printing process are all interlinked. The size of the print run and the budget for the job are also important considerations. Offset litho and letterpress demand thick and sticky inks; conversely, the inks for gravure and flexography need to be thin and runny. Consequently, gravure and flexo are able to print at high speed on to relatively poor stock—and flexo can print on to the most difficult surfaces, such as cellophane and waxy board. But there is a trade-off. Flexo and gravure cylinders are expensive to produce, and so the process is only viable for large print runs.

Most designers will spend most of their careers working with offset lithography, which is perhaps the most economical and versatile process of all. But there will perhaps come a time when you need to produce a design for a plastic carrier bag, for example, and have to evaluate the relative advantages and constraints of flexography and screenprinting, and modify the design appropriately. Or there may come a time when you wish to produce a high-quality invitation card on handmade paper using letterpress. With the information outlined in this chapter, you will be confident of making the right choice.

So, too, with finishing. The expected end use of a printed product and the budget are key factors in the choice of perfect binding, say, over wire stitching, or varnishing over lamination. Only experience will teach you to make the correct choices every time, but, forearmed with the knowledge contained in this chapter, you will at least be aware of all the options open to you.

Malcolm Garrett

"If you don't speak to an audience in a language it can understand,
then communication is unlikely to take place."

Manifesto
A Pragmatic Anarchist

The primary objective when designing digital media is to hide the technology, to make the design transparent, and make it do the right job for the user in an effortless manner. Garrett is a big believer in communication. His definition of good design is: does it do its job? Did message A get communicated to audience B? "If you don't speak to an audience in a language it can understand," says Garrett, "then communication is unlikely to take place. This either means that you educate an audience in the nuances of your own personal language, or you explore the languages that exist, which can be efficient yet conceptually restrictive." His work often seems to adopt a vernacular approach, but is not constrained by convention. He's a pragmatic anarchist.

Garrett has always loved technology. "If you're going to succeed and move forward, you do have to be pigeonholed. So despite calling myself Assorted images in an early idealistic vision of never being pigeonholed, I figured, well, if I'm to be pigeonholed anyway, it will be for computers, technology, something I'm good at, something I've got involved in early on, something I have a view about. I decided it was time perhaps to have people reappraise what they think I'm about. I would much rather be known as Malcolm Garrett, the guy who plays with computers, than Malcolm Garrett, the guy who designs record sleeves.

"I'm genuinely excited by the things that are happening now and things that haven't happened yet. I figure it is my job to be this kind of blinkered believer. You know: I am the new futurist, I will live in the technological world. That appeals to me and I will ignore the current technical problems because someone else will sort out the technology. That's the Japanese approach. You go to Japan and everybody is positive and optimistic and you look at what Japan's done in the last 50 years. If it can happen, it should. Is that irresponsible?"

Malcolm Garrett was born in Northwich, England, in 1956. He studied typography and psychology at Reading University from 1974 to 1975, and graphic design at Manchester Polytechnic from 1975 to 1978. His first professional work in 1977 made an immediate impact with his album sleeves for Manchester punk-rock band the Buzzcocks. In the late 1970s and early 1980s, Garrett was identified, along with colleagues Peter Saville, Jamie Reid, and Neville Brody, as one of the most influential designers working for youth-culture clients. In 1983, with partner Kasper de Graaf, he set up Assorted images (Ai).

In projects for Simple Minds, Duran Duran, and Culture Club, Garrett applied corporate identity to pop groups. Using logos, emblems, and other decorative typographical devices, and the iconography of technology, he turned bands into brands. Other work in the entertainment industry followed, including television graphics. Over the years, Garrett has designed using every possible spelling of his own name (one R, two Rs, one T, two Ts) and under various trade names, including Aesthetic Images and Assorted images. Ai could mean "love" in Japanese or stand as an acronym for artificial intelligence.

Ai was an early advocate of computer graphics—first with an Apple II-based CAD system (yes, Apple II not Mac II) called the Robocom Bitstik, used to distort and stretch logos, then more mainstream Macs. In the late 1980s, Garrett's focus shifted decisively in the direction of new technology, and in 1994 he broke with Ai and joined up with multimedia director Alasdair Scott, with whom he had collaborated since 1989. Together they set up AMXdigital in London (later AMXstudios). Garrett left AMX in 2001 when they merged with Zinc to form Arnold Interactive. He then worked at I-mmersion in Toronto, Canada, and returned to London in 2005 where he is Creative Director at AIG (Applied Information Group). He is also Creative Director of dynamo london, an online showcase for the digital and interactive media industry in London. He has developed DVD, Enhanced CD and CD-based multimedia titles and internet sites for Saatchi & Saatchi, *Dazed&Confused* magazine, and WEA records, and has pioneered "webcasts" in Europe.

Garrett taught multimedia design at the School of Visual Arts in New York, and Savannah College of Art & Design, Georgia. He is a Royal Designer for Industry, visiting professor at London's University of the Arts, and an honorary Doctor of Design at Robert Gordon University, Aberdeen. He is Fellow of the RSA and past committee member of BAFTA.

Resources

Website: www.aiglondon.com
Interview by Alan Pipes, *Design*, July 1985, pp. 44–5
Graphis Nov/Dec 1988, No. 258
Emigre 11, 1989, Ambition/Fear issue
Emigre 13, 1989, Redesigning stereotypes issue
Malcolm Garrett, "The book is dead," *Graphics World* Feb 1991, No. 90
Malcolm Garrett, "Multimedia: who needs it?" *Baseline* No. 18, 1994, pp. 30–3
Interview by Rick Poynor, *Eye* 12/94, pp. 11–16
Interview by Joe Shepter, Adobe, www.adobe.co.uk/web/gallery/amx/main.html

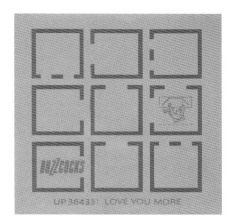

The record sleeve for the Buzzcocks' *Love You More/Noise Annoys* (1978) is among the earliest of Garrett's published works, produced toward the end of his final year studying graphic design at Manchester Polytechnic. It features matching illustrations that represent two themes: one of isolation, and the other of inescapable audio-assault, which are addressed in each of the songs. It draws references from illustrations in HMSO home architecture guidelines, and from photographic studio lighting techniques. Its candy colors are typical of the pop aesthetic with which Garrett chose to address industrial and hi-tech imagery.

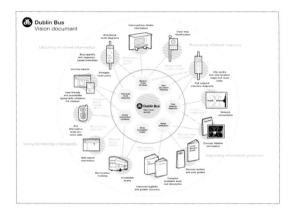

Malcolm Garrett and Matt Cooper at AIG worked with Dublin-based design company Image Now, having introduced a new visual identity in 2007, to completely overhaul the provision of information across the Dublin Bus network. The Vision Document shows the extent of the review in progress, with new street furniture also informing the design process.

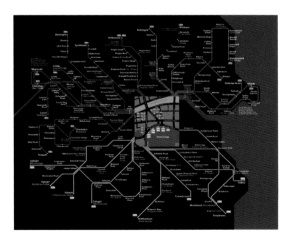

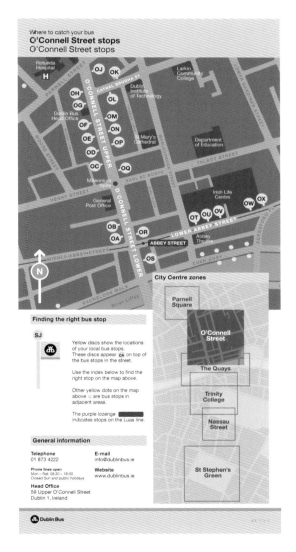

Work is ongoing to develop a comprehensive diagram of all the Dublin Bus routes, where none has previously existed. The first iteration of how this will appear can be seen in the subset of routes which form the NiteLink network of night buses.

Dublin's unique geography, which demands that most routes cross a single city-center bridge, forming a confluence of buses down the main street, AIG identified six areas, which effectively form a large city-wide "terminus." This has helped define a way of providing a more manageable and comprehensible index of routes and destinations.

start code display<html><!--This file was created on 29/2/2008 by me--><head><title>My home page</title></head><body><h1>Welcome to my world!</h1><p>This is my as yet still under construction home page.</p> <p>It was last updated on 29 February 2008.
</body></html>end code display<start code display><html><!--This file was created on 29/2/2008 by me--><head><title>My home page</title></head><body><h1>Welcome to my world!</h1><p>This is my getting there slowly home page.</p><p>My favorite artiste of all time is <a href="http://www.elvisnet.com">Elvis</a>.</p><p>You can find more musical links on my <a href= "music.html">Music</a> page.</p> <p>It was last updated on 29 February 2008.
Why not email me with your comments on<p><a href="mailto:pipes@brighton.co.uk">pipes@brighton.co.uk</a>.</p></body></html>end code display<start code display><html><!--This file was created on 29/2/2008 by me--><head><title>My home page</title></head><body><h1>Welcome to my world!</h1><p>This is my as yet still under construction home page.</p> <p>It was last updated on 29 February 2008.
</body></html>end code display<start code display><html><!--This file was created on 29/2/2008 by me--><head><title>My home page</title></head><body><h1>Welcome to my world!</h1><p>This is my getting there slowly home page.</p><p>My favorite artiste of all time is <a href="http://www.elvisnet.com">Elvis</a>.</p><p>You can find more musical links on my <a href= "music.html">Music</a> page.</p> <p>It was last updated on 29 February 2008.
Why not email me with your comments on<p><a href="mailto:pipes@brighton.co.uk">pipes@brighton.co.uk</a>.</p></body></html>end code display<start code display><html><!--This file was created on 29/2/2008 by me--><head><title>My home page</title></head><body><h1>Welcome to my world!</h1><p>This is my as yet still under construction home page.</p> <p>It was last updated on 29 February 2008.
</body></html>end code display<start code display><html><!--This file was created on 29/2/2008 by me--><head><title>My home page</title></head><body><h1>Welcome to my world!</h1><p>This is my getting there slowly home page.</p><p>My favorite artiste of all time is <a href="http://www.elvisnet.com">Elvis</a>.</p><p>You can find more musical links on my <a href= "music.html">Music</a> page.</p> <p>It was last updated on 29 February 2008.
Why not email me with your comments on<p><a href="mailto:pipes@brighton.co.uk">pipes@brighton.co.uk</a>.</p></body></html>end code display<start code display><html><!--This file was created on 29/2/2008 by me--><head><title>My home page</title></head><body><h1>Welcome to my world!</h1><p>This is my as yet still under construction home page.</p> <p>It was last updated on 29 February 2008.
</body></html>end code display<start code display><html><!--This file was created on 29/2/2008 by me--><head><title>My home page</title></head><body><h1>Welcome to my world!</h1><p>This is my getting there slowly home page.</p><p>My favorite artiste of all time is <a href="http://www.elvisnet.com">Elvis</a>.</p><p>You can find more musical links on my <a href= "music.html">Music</a> page.</p> <p>It was last updated on 29 February 2008.
Why not email me with your comments on<p><a href="mailto:pipes@brighton.co.uk">pipes@brighton.co.uk</a>.</p></body></html>end code display

Digital Design

You are reading this book and you come across a term you don't quite understand or the name of a person or place you'd like to know some more about. The words may be highlighted by being in **bold type**, so that means you can flick to the back of the book and look them up in the glossary. But think how amazing it would be if you could just "click" on the word somehow and be transported to a place with all the answers in as much detail as you need! Well, if you were online using the internet, that's exactly what would happen.

It is difficult to imagine life without the internet, but what exactly is it? It is simply a global network of computers, and a means of connecting your computer, TV, or mobile telephone to other computers. It is merely a medium. But on the internet you'll find lots of useful tools, the main three being email (electronic mail), newsgroups, and the World Wide Web.

With email, you can send messages and digital "attachments"—anything from images, scanned photographs, and artwork to audio samples—anywhere in the world.

Newsgroups are online "bulletin boards" or discussion groups that enable you to keep in touch with other designers, exchange tips and experiences, or download "shareware" fonts and programs.

The World Wide Web (WWW) is a collection of "pages," probably running into several billions by now, containing text, images, sound, movies, and, most importantly, "hot links" to other pages. You view these pages using a program called a browser, such as Apple's Safari or Microsoft's Internet Explorer. WWW pages can also have forms built in so that you can, say, order books from an online bookstore, or send fan mail (or perhaps a job offer) to an illustrator or photographer who's showing their virtual portfolio at an online gallery.

So what's in the internet for the designer? First, it is a cheap and fast way to send artwork to the client and printer. Second, it's an inexpensive and effective way to advertise yourself and your work worldwide. Third, it is a potentially huge source of new clients, interactive projects, and job opportunities.

What is the internet?

In only a decade or so, the **internet** has become an essential part of most people's lives, as indispensible as a telephone or television. But what exactly is it? And how does it work? The internet is a global network of computers or, more accurately, a network of computer networks—*the* network of networks—after all, there is only one internet. It enables you to connect your computer to every other computer on the internet, initially via a telephone line or wireless connection. It is basically a medium of communication, like the telephone network, but capable of much more.

First, as always, some history. In 1962, Dr J. C. R. "Lick" Licklider was chosen to head research into improving the military's use of computer technology. The result was ARPAnet (ARPA stands for Advanced Research Projects Agency—the funding body), which was set up to connect together just four computers at sites around the United States in order to distribute resources where they were needed. Computers were extremely expensive in those days (even though they probably only had around 12k of memory each) and had to be shared around. The first ARPAnet node was installed at the University of California at Los Angeles in September 1969. Additional nodes were soon added at Stanford Research Institute, the University of California at Santa Barbara, and the University of Utah.

This was all made possible by packet switching. The reasoning went that in a nuclear war, the communications infrastructure—the networks of wires, command centers, and antennae—would become prime targets. By decentralizing the network, communications would keep flowing even if parts of the network were destroyed. The key idea was that messages were broken down into "packets" and sent off in the general direction of their destination, where they would then be reassembled. Paul Baran of the Rand Corporation published such a scheme in 1964. The National Physical Laboratory in the United Kingdom set up the first test network based on these principles in 1968.

ARPAnet was developed from the outset to be both resilient and decentralized—designed, in other words, to survive a nuclear attack. By 1971 approximately 20 nodes had been installed. In 1972, the First International Conference on Computer Communications was held in Washington, DC to discuss communication protocols in order that different kinds of networks around the world would be able to "talk" to each other. The International Network Working Group (INWG) was created, and Vinton Cerf, who was involved with ARPAnet at UCLA, was chosen as the first chair. The first international connections to the ARPAnet were made in 1973: to University College, London, and the Royal Radar Establishment in Norway.

In September 1973, Bob Kahn and Vint Cerf presented their basic internet ideas at a meeting of the INWG at the University of Sussex in Brighton, United Kingdom. The system of protocols they came up with became known as the **TCP/IP**, after the two initial protocols developed: Transmission Control Protocol (TCP) and Internet Protocol (IP). These were first published in September 1981, became the standard internet protocols in January 1983, and are still used today.

The internet was opened up to commercial networks such as CompuServe and AOL (America OnLine) in 1991 and continues to grow and grow. The number of computers on the internet reached a million in 1992 and by the end of 1993 this number had doubled. At the time of writing, the number of computers connected to the internet was estimated at 940 million.

Who invented the internet? Who coined that word? The definitive primary source for internet history is the collection of email memos called RFCs (Requests for Comments). RFC791, for example, is the September 1981 specification for Internet Protocol (IP). The oldest reference to the word "internet" that I could find was in the title of RFC675: V. Cerf, Y. Dalal, and C. Sunshine, "Specification of Internet Transmission Control Program," dated 1 December, 1974.

So who runs the internet? No one actually owns the internet and no one body runs it. That is both its strength and its weakness. If a resilient network has been designed to find a route around physical damage, so it can always find a route around censorship. Some people see the internet as much more than a collection of cooperating computer networks. They see a new community called Cyberspace, with its own culture, language, and laws. But fascinating as that concept might be, it is really outside the scope of this book. Check out Further reading, pp. 261–2, if you'd like to know more.

In summary, the internet is:

- A network of networks based on the TCP/IP protocols

- A community of people who use and develop those networks.

- A collection of resources that can be reached from those networks.

How to get started

You may already have access to the internet at home, school, or college. If not, you can rent time at a Cybercafé or invest in your own equipment. You need a **modem**, although these are generally built into computers these days, and either a dial-up or broadband account with an **ISP** (**internet service provider**). The modem connects your (digital) computer to the (analog) telephone network and your ISP should be a local telephone call away.

ADSL (**asymmetric digital subscriber line**—or loop), or broadband, is much faster. Here the bandwidth available for downstream connection is significantly larger than for upstream and is well suited to web browsing and client–server applications as well as some emerging applications such as video on demand.

The data-rate of ADSL depends greatly on the length and quality of the line connecting the end-user to the telephone company's exchange. Typically the upstream data flow is up to 3.5 Mbit/s while the downstream data flow is up to 24 Mbit/s.

The easiest way to get online is using an ADSL modem. Just insert the CD, install the drivers, and plug the modem into the USB port. An Ethernet or wireless router is a device that connects your local area network of computers to the internet. They can act as a gateway to the internet, group disk server accessible to all computers on the network, and a **firewall** to prevent unwanted access to your files (Fig. **7.1**).

A DSL cable modem allows people to access the internet via their cable television service, and can transfer data at up to 1 Gbit/s, although most users will experience maximum speeds of 20 Mbit/s.

Email

With **email** (**electronic mail**) you can send messages and "attachments" to other people connected to the internet: you type a message on your computer, connect to the internet, and send it down the telephone line to your local ISP (Fig. **7.2**). It then finds its way to the destination computer and waits in the recipient's "mailbox" until they check their mail. If they wish to reply, they hit the "reply" button on their computer, type a message (perhaps highlighting parts of your original message), and—you have new mail.

Trivial, you may think. But it's much easier and faster than faxing, it's the cost of a quick local phone call, and you have a digital record of the correspondence. What's more, you can send "attachments," which could be scanned-in drawings or photographs, digital artwork, programs, audio samples, anything that can be digitized. It's fast, cheap, and energy-saving (green); another plus point is that precious artwork doesn't get delayed, lost, or bent in the mail.

In October 1963, computer-consulting company Bolt, Beranek, and Newman (BBN) published a paper demonstrating that users could communicate remotely with computers using ordinary telephones. BBN had already patented the modem earlier that year.

In 1971, Ray Tomlinson of BBN invented email. By the second year of ARPAnet's operation, the main traffic was news and personal messages. Researchers were using the network not only to collaborate on projects and trade notes on work, but to gossip. People had their own personal-user accounts on the ARPAnet computers, and their own personal addresses

7.1 The Linksys Wireless-G broadband router with SpeedBooster is a wireless router with a built-in four-port switch to let your network share a high-speed cable or DSL internet connection.

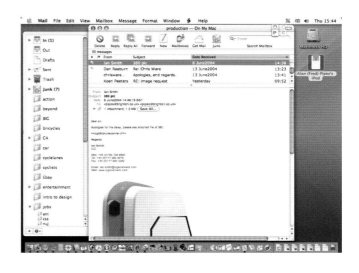

7.2 Email screenshot—the program being used was Apple's Mail.

Newsgroups

for electronic mail. It wasn't long before the mailing list was invented, with which a message could be broadcast to anyone "subscribing" to a particular list. One of the first mailing lists was for science-fiction fans.

Eudora (named after Eudora Welty, the author of "Why I live at the P.O.") was once a popular email program for Macs but Apple's own Mail now predominates; Outlook Express is an email program for PCs. Most email programs allow you to store contact lists of recipients and to add your "signature" to the end of each and every message.

Decoding internet addresses

Everyone on the internet has an email address in the form username@site.dom, in which username is your name or a nickname you have chosen, site locates your ISP or personal domain, and dom is a "domain" type, possibly including subdomains. These are generally separated by periods.

>   Domain types include:
>   .com—commercial organizations
>   .edu—educational institutions

Note that most of the sites in the .com and .edu domains are in the United States. Outside of these functional domains, sites in the States have the .us domain, and there are subdomains for the 50 states, each generally with a name identical to the state's postal abbreviation. Within the .uk domain, there is an .ac subdomain for academic sites and a .co domain for commercial ones. Note that .ca can be both California and Canada, depending on the context.

It is a good idea to register your own domain while it is still available. Not only will you have an easy-to-remember email and website address, but if you should change your ISP, you won't have to inform all and sundry about your change of address. The domain acts like a mailbox number—your mail is redirected to your actual address. Domain names are administered by companies such as Network Solutions, Inc. in the United States and Nominet in the United Kingdom, but as you must have two servers for the domain to "live on," it is usual to buy a domain through a third party. Prices have come down, but beware of companies that charge you exorbitant amounts if you choose to move your domain at any time in the future.

Usenet (**Unix user network**) was established in 1979 between Duke University and the University of North Carolina to exchange news and views. The original programs were written by graduate student Steve Bellovin. These were rewritten and extended by Steve Daniel and Tom Truscott.

Usenet is an example of a **client–server architecture**. A user (the client) connects to a machine (the server) where the Usenet postings for the past few days, weeks, or hours are stored. You can look at the headings of postings in the newsgroups of interest, and then request the full text of a particular posting (message or article) to be forwarded to your machine (Fig. **7.3**). You may then read or store the article, reply directly to the poster via email, or post a follow-up article (starting or joining a "thread"). You can also initiate a new subject heading with a new posting. The newsgroup program on your computer keeps track of which articles you have already read.

Newsgroups are supposed to be limited to a single topic, and the name of the group should give you some idea of the content to be expected. In 1986 to 1987, seven main hierarchies were created: **comp**, **misc**, **news**, **rec**, **sci**, **soc**, and **talk**. The **alt** hierarchy was proposed at a barbecue in Mountain View, California, on 7 May, 1987, and implemented by subterfuge.

At the time of writing, there were over 100,000 different newsgroups—not all of them active—covering everything from keeping fish to font design. Not all ISPs carry all newsgroups, however. Some refuse to carry some sexually explicit groups, especially those used for posting "binaries" (image or audio files), which also take up a lot of "bandwidth" (here meaning throughput of traffic). The function of newsgroups has largely been taken over by forums on the WWW.

Thoth is a popular newsgroup program for Macs; Agent is a newsgroup program for PCs.

Netiquette

Network etiquette, or **netiquette**, is something that a **newbie** (new user) will come across sooner or later. In the absence of any governing body, certain netizens take it upon themselves to police the newsgroups and will **flame** any transgressors (post a harshly critical message in public on Usenet or send very long messages to you via email). Newbies are encouraged to lurk for a while (a lurker is someone who reads but never posts) and consult the newsgroup's **FAQ** (**frequently asked questions**) list before posting for the first time.

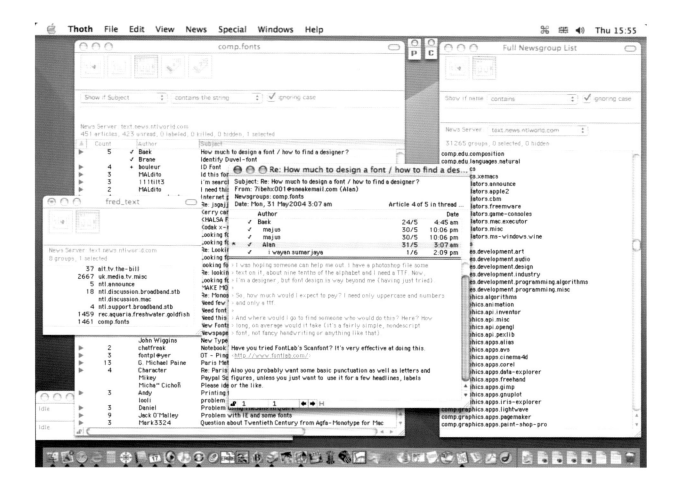

7.3 Newsgroup screenshot taken from a comp.fonts discussion thread. The program is Thoth.

Postings that are "off topic" often elicit a flaming. **Crossposting** (posting the same message to several groups) is particularly frowned upon, but real venom is reserved for **spamming** (from the Monty Python song "Spam"), which is crossposting a carelessly inappropriate message or advertisement to many different groups or individuals. Messages set all in capitals (interpreted as "shouting") or with overlong signatures (especially ones containing so-called ASCII art) are discouraged, but it is considered very bad form to criticize a poster's poor grammar or spelling. The latest versions of newsreading programs have useful "kill files" which enable you to filter out unwanted messages from particular people or on particular topics.

Acronyms and smileys

Because of the need to conserve bandwidth, and for speed of typing, many acronyms are in common use. Here are a few you may encounter:

AFAIK	as far as I know
BTW	by the way
FYI	for your information
IMHO	in my humble opinion
LOL	laughs out loud
ROFL	rolls on the floor laughing
RT*M	read the * manual (clean version!)
YMMV	your mileage may vary

And because gestures or inflections of speech are impossible on the net, symbols made from ASCII characters, called **smileys** or "emoticons," have evolved. These are particularly useful to avoid causing offense—your harmless joke may be taken literally, but a smiley makes everything OK! Here are a few (turn your head 90 degrees to the left):

:-) or :)	basic smiley
;-) or ;)	winking smiley (for irony)
:-(or :(	sad smiley

You may also see these non-smileys: <g> grins; <s> sighs.

FTP: uploading and downloading

FTP (**file transfer protocol**) lets users transfer files between computers. There are many sites around the internet where users can **download** programs, documents, and images (Fig. **7.4**). **Mirror sites** keep copies of the files from the main sites, but may be geographically closer to you. If you have a website (see next section), you will use FTP to **upload** your files to the server. Transmit is a popular FTP program for Macs; WS_FTP is an FTP program for PCs.

Gopher and Archie are other terms you may come across: they are ways of locating files via FTP. However, they are becoming much less important as the World Wide Web and all-in-one browsers such as Safari, Firefox, and Internet Explorer take over their original role.

7.4 You can download software or upload to your ISP's server using an FTP program such as Transmit.

Make yourself known

Search engines such as Google send out robots to rove the web, reading the first few words of websites and then trying to classify them so that someone initiating a search with a few keywords will not be inundated with thousands of likely matches to plow through. Help them out by using the <meta> tag in your HTML document so that search engines will know all about you. Place something like this in your document and you will stand a good chance of coming top of the list in a search for "Palo Alto poodle parlors":

```
<head>
<title>Acme Pet Parlor</title>
<meta name=description
content=We specialize in grooming pink poodles.>
<meta name=keywords
content=pet grooming, Palo Alto, dog>
</head>
```

World Wide Web (WWW)

While consulting for CERN (the European Laboratory for Particle Physics) between June and December 1980, Tim Berners-Lee wrote a hypertext-based program called "Enquire-Within-Upon-Everything." In October 1990, the name **World Wide Web** (**WWW**) was decided, and in November, with Robert Cailliau as co-author, the first WWW program was developed. On 30 April, 1993, CERN placed the software for the WWW in the public domain.

In September 1993 a group of graduate students from the University of Illinois at Champaign-Urbana developed Mosaic, a software package that used the WWW protocol. Mosaic was a major factor in the explosion of business interest in the internet, because it made the internet accessible to inexperienced users. Many other browsers have evolved since Mosaic's development, including its direct descendant Netscape Navigator, Apple's Safari (Fig. **7.5**) and Microsoft's Internet Explorer (Fig. **7.6**).

The World Wide Web is a huge collection of interconnected "pages," probably running into several billions. These pages are viewed by a **browser** (which, like most internet software, can be downloaded for free) and can contain text, images, sound, movies, and hypertext "hot links" to other pages, which may reside on servers anywhere around the world. These pages can be about anything: football, recipes, bands, illustration. The biggest growth area is in commercial sites, where corporations entice users to visit their online "advertisements" with the promise of free screensavers and other entertaining programs to download. Pages may also have built-in forms, so that you can, say, order books from an online bookshop or CDs from the Cyber Mall pages, or send fan mail (or a job offer) to an artist showing at an online gallery. Many sites encourage you to register

7.5 Safari screenshot.

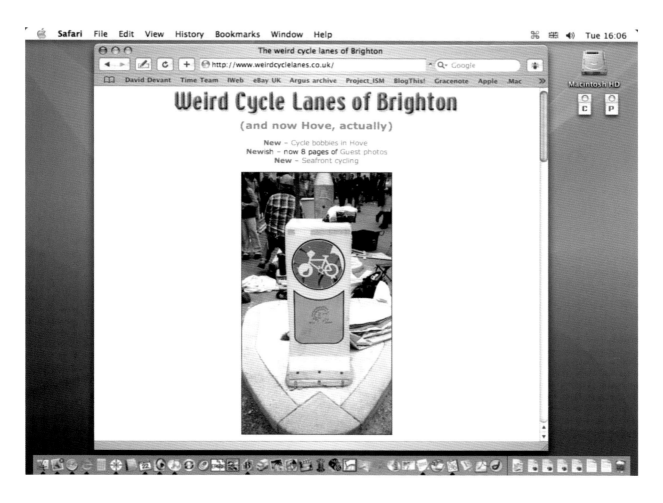

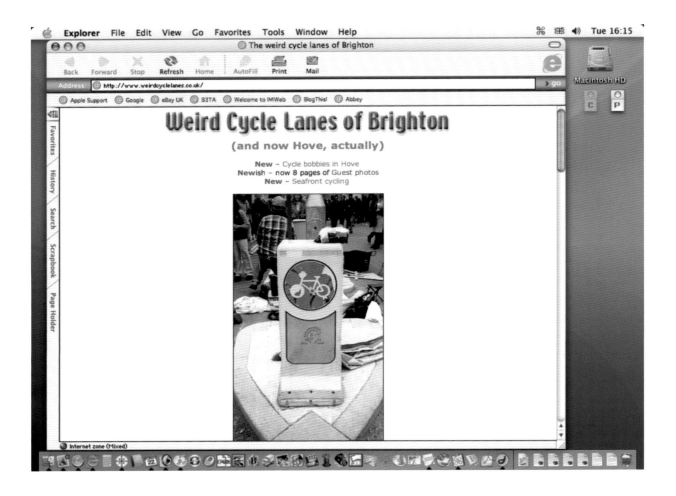

7.6 This is the same page as in Fig. 7.5 but viewed in another browser—in this case Microsoft's Internet Explorer.

(giving them valuable marketing information), and you are issued with a password for subsequent visits.

Most people on the net have a **home page**. Your ISP or college may provide you with disk space on their server, and there are many sites around the world that offer free space for home pages. These can also be used as test areas to develop your web design skills.

The WWW is based on a client–server model where the client (your browser) communicates with the servers (the sites storing the web pages you want to view) using **HTTP** (**hypertext transport protocol**). **HTML** (**hypertext markup language**) is used to create and communicate the page. The address of a page or its **URL** (**uniform resource locator**) is thus in the form: http://www.yourISP.com/username/index.html

The so-called Web 2.0, a term coined in 2004, takes the WWW to a second generation, with more user participation. Read-only websites are making way for online communities, such as the virtual world Second Life, and hosted social-networking sites, such as Facebook and MySpace, blogs (weblogs), and user-generated information-sharing sites such

as the encyclopedia Wikipedia and the photo-sharing site Flickr. Basically, the technology hasn't changed very much at all, but the way people are interacting with the web has, and this means many more opportunities for designers in, for example, producing templates for hosted services—on the whole the user customized designs on MySpace for example are a dog's dinner. Blogs, from sites such as Blogger, are a great way to quickly gain a web presence. They require very little knowledge of HTML to create and update, and uploading of images is made very simple. Although the format is a reverse-date order diary, it can be adapted into a portfolio site, or just used as a "latest news" resource within a more traditional website.

HOT TIPS & COOL TRICKS

How to find out how it's done

View the HTML source code of any web page that impresses you to see how it was done. Do this often and you'll learn all sorts of new tricks. But don't use any of their GIFs or JPEGs without the permission of the creator.

Designing for the World Wide Web

The World Wide Web is a wonderful opportunity for the graphic designer, but it does have some curious challenges. For a start, until recently you didn't have a lot of control over how your designs and layouts would be seen! You can only specify fonts that the user already has, and have little control over what size they will be viewed at or the measure used. You have very little influence over the use of white space, and there are many trade-offs to be made to keep downloading time to a minimum (if your page doesn't download quickly then it won't be seen—the user will just carry on surfing!).

You have to accept that your design is going to appear differently on different browsers and on different machines. On some browsers, for example, the user may be able to increase the viewable text size—this is great news for the partially sighted, but it can play havoc with your carefully crafted layouts. But on the upside, some designers find these constraints liberating: you don't have to worry about the resolution of images (everything is 72 dpi), CMYK concerns, color management, or anything at all to do with print production! The web is an ideal publishing medium: it is cheap (almost free), global, instantaneously updateable, and, despite what was said earlier in this paragraph, extremely versatile.

So what is there left for the designer to do? Basically what all graphic designers do all the time in any case: communicate the client's message in the most effective way; make it easy for the user to "navigate" around the site; and make the pages distinctive, attractive, eye-catching, and entertaining. You may have to use ingenious work-arounds to achieve all the results you envisaged at concept stage, but the web is also a great leveler—college graduates in their bedrooms have exactly the same tools available to them as the most prestigious design groups working for the largest multinational corporations.

Perhaps the biggest difference between designing for print and for the WWW—and this applies equally to CD-ROM design—is that the layouts for a book or magazine are designed in linear fashion: readers are expected to start at the beginning and work their way through to the end. In interactive media like the WWW, the reader is encouraged to leap from one hot link to another, so page organization is important. Designing a WWW site is more akin to making a movie, but one with multiple narratives. Remember, the reader may be entering any page in your site from an outside link, so every page must be self-contained, with all the navigational aids necessary to help them carry on surfing. A concept plan with flowcharts and maybe a storyboard is essential (Fig. **7.7**). WWW designers need directorial skills too—with sound and animation available, you may well be asked to coordinate the efforts of a whole team of other professionals.

7.7 Concept design of a website for the 1997 British General Election, designed by New Media Labs for The *Guardian* newspaper.

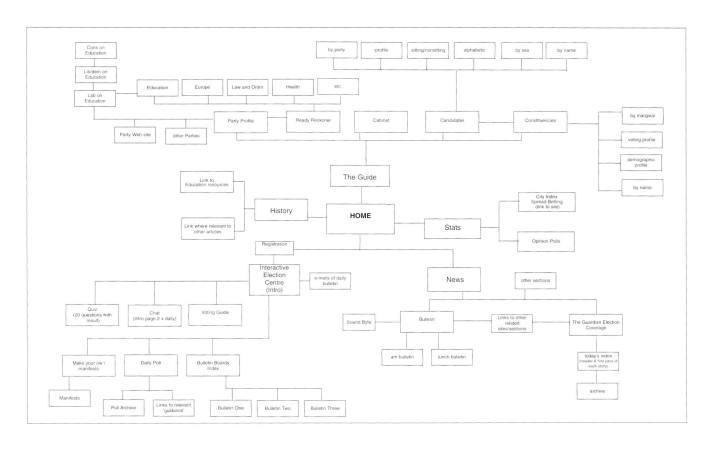

Do designers really have to learn HTML?

Well, yes and no. The internet at present is rather like the early days of automobiles, when you had to carry a toolkit around with you and know enough about the engine to make running repairs. QuarkXPress and InDesign can convert existing page layouts into HTML, but the results generally need fine-tuning later, particularly in relation to making links work.

There are several very good stand-alone **WYSIWYG** web-design programs, such as Adobe Dreamweaver (Fig. **7.8**) which claim that you can design web pages without ever having to come into contact with HTML code—after all, you don't need to be able to program in PostScript to lay out pages in QuarkXPress, do you? In practice, however, you will need a working knowledge of HTML to delve into the code if something peculiar happens to your design. They can toggle between the layout and code, which is very useful for trouble-shooting. There are excellent programs that never allow you to look at the code. Freeway, for the Mac, has a QuarkXPress feel to it, with a pasteboard, master pages and text boxes. It can import Photoshop images and convert them to GIFs or JPEGs (more later). And when you have finished, the program "compiles" and exports (and ftps) the entire website.

Most websites are now so complex that it would not be economic to write the code by hand, and programs like Dreamweaver are essential if you are working with freeform layouts using tables (more later) and frames, with mouse rollovers and other Javascript effects, or developing database-driven e-commerce sites.

7.8 Programs such as Dreamweaver enable you to create web pages quickly.

A complete description of HTML is beyond the scope of this chapter, but there are many excellent books on the subject (see Further reading, pp. 261–2), and the joy of the internet is that there are many online teaching resources available. To start with, your browser will have built-in links to "How to …" pages, and your ISP's home page is always a good place to start surfing for advice. If you do find a page that you like the look of, all you have to do is hit the "View document source" button on your browser for it to display the HTML code for the page you are viewing (so long as it is not a frames-based page!). It's then a relatively easy step to figure out how that designer achieved that effect.

Writing your own home page

A good way to get a taste of HTML is to design a simple home page. A first encounter with the internet is often quite a culture shock. It's like going back 20 years in time to the days of ASCII-only typewriter terminals. Email and newsgroups are ASCII based—thus many characters are unavailable, and you have to remember to insert carriage returns at the ends of lines. HTML is no exception; the simple reason is that the web is accessed by every possible kind of computer—the files that travel around the internet must be of the lowest common denominator, and that means ASCII text. Likewise, images have to be in a format understandable by all types of computer, and that means they are most commonly in **GIF** (**graphics interchange format**) or JPEG (joint photographic experts group) format.

A simple web page will thus comprise a text document plus GIF and/or JPEG files all in the same directory (equivalent to a Mac folder), or preferably with the images in a sub-folder.

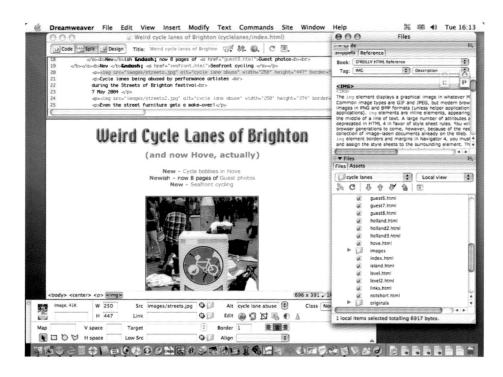

Getting yourself organized

Append notes to yourself in your HTML code by using the tag – –a note to myself– – to make future debugging easier, especially if someone else has to maintain your pages. It can be harder than you think to update complex HTML pages, even if you created them yourself. And use lots of white space between paragraphs—unless you use <p> or <br> any formatting in the code will be ignored by the browser. And remember to turn off curly quotes if you're writing HTML on a word processor: browsers only understand feet (') and inches (").

To create a home page, you will need either a simple text editor, such as TextEdit for a Mac or Notepad on a PC, a word processor that can output text files (but remember to turn "smart quotes" off), or a simple shareware web-page design program such as BBEdit or PageSpinner which will also provide menus of useful commands and options. You will also need a graphics program, such as Photoshop, that can export GIF and JPEG files. And finally, you will need FTP access to a server—you can create the pages on your computer, but for anyone else to be able to see them they must first be "published" by uploading them to a server.

7.9 BBEdit screenshot showing the HTML code of your home-page document.

HTML works its magic by the use of **tags** that the browser interprets as the web page arrives from the server to the client. Tags should have a start and an end, "containing" the item in question. The first part of the tag turns an attribute on and the second turns the attribute off. Tags themselves are surrounded by angled brackets (the < "less than" and > "greater than" symbols), and the closing tag is usually preceded by a forward slash symbol (/). An exception is the tag for line break <br> which only exists at the end of a line. To make it consistent with other start-end tags, it is best written <br />. Other exceptions include the img tag and the meta tags in the header that help search engines find your site. For example, the tag for the title of your page is written in HTML like this:

```
<title>My home page</title>
```

All HTML documents contain the following code:

```
<html>
<!--This file was created on 29/2/2008 by me-->
<head>
<title>My home page</title>
</head>
<body>
Text and images to be placed here.
</body>
</html>
```

A program such as BBEdit or PageSpinner will present this sequence whenever you open a new document—it also colors the tags to distinguish them from the text (Fig. **7.9**).

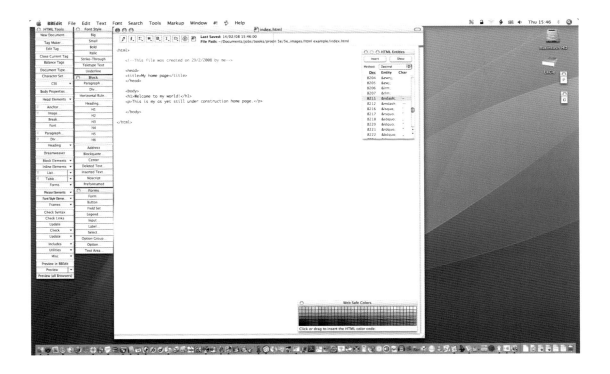

The <html> tag tells the browser that an HTML document is on the way. The name of the text document should end with the suffix ".html" (although PC users, restricted to filenames of eight characters plus a three-letter suffix, can use just ".htm" for their extension). By default, the first page of a website is always called index.html.

The text within the <title> tags will appear at the head of your browser window and as the description of a URL in the bookmark file of your browser. Everything within the <body> tags will appear in the main window of the browser.

Filenames and tags should always be lower case.

Now you can import or type in a heading and some text (Fig. **7.10**):

```
<html>

<!--This file was created on 29/2/2008 by me-->

<head>
<title>My home page</title>
</head>

<body>
<h1>Welcome to my world!</h1>
<p>This is my as yet still under construction home page.</p>

</body>

</html>
```

HOT TIPS & COOL TRICKS

Don't be a cliché

Avoid "Click here" links and try to make the hyperlink part of the description. For example, use: "Do you like Elvis?" instead of "Click here to go to the Elvis site." Don't just make lists of links, try to add content and narrative to your site.

Headings Unlike in print, in web design you cannot specify a particular font and sizes of headings; all you can say about a heading in HTML is that it will (probably) be bigger and bolder than the regular text. There are six headings in HTML: h1 through h6. The default for an h1 heading is 24 pt Times. It is best always to start with an h1 heading and not to skip levels. If you miss off the </h1> end tag, the whole document will be one big heading! h6, strangely, will be smaller than the body text, at around 9 pt.

Anchors One of the best things about the web is that you can create hypertext "hot links" to other parts of your page, to other pages on your site, or to other unrelated pages on any other computer anywhere in the world. To do this, you insert

7.10 This is how the HTML code in the text (left) will look when interpreted by the browser (below).

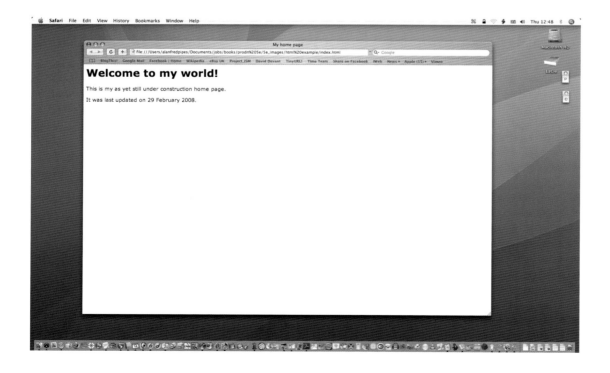

anchors: either local relative ones pointing to another text file in the same directory, or absolute ones containing the full URL of the page you want to link to. An anchor is the form

<a href=URL>the hot text</a>

where the URL is either relative, i.e. music.html—another page on your site—or absolute, i.e. http://www.elvisnet. com, the URL of the ElvisNet site. If you are experimenting with HTML in a word processor, remember to turn off the "curly quotes" option. HTML only understands the inches () symbol. An example of anchors in use follows (Fig. **7.11** and **7.12**):

Note that other type of anchor at the end: the mailto: attribute automatically opens an email program.

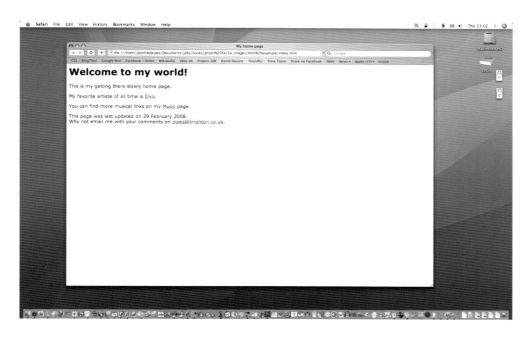

7.11 This is how the code is interpreted, or parsed, by the browser. The font, colors, and the way hot links are underlined and colored blue are all defaults of the browser, in this case Apple's Safari.

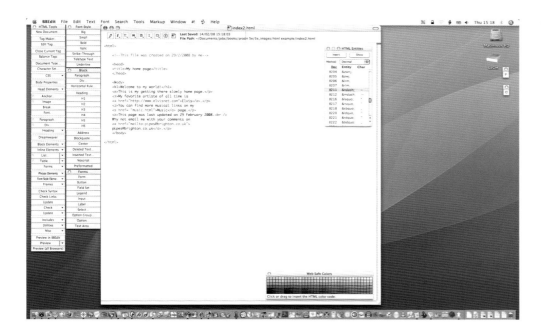

7.12 This is how the raw HTML code looks in the text editor BBEdit. Note that different colors are used to distinguish the tags from the text.

```
<html>

<!--This file was created on 29/2/2008 by me-->

<head>
<title>My home page</title>
</head>

<body>
<h1>Welcome to my world!</h1>
<p>This is my getting there slowly home page.</p>
<p>My favorite artist of all time is
<a href=http://www.elvisnet.com>Elvis</a>.</p>
<p>You can find more musical links on my
<a href= music.html>Music</a> page.</p>
<p>It was last updated on 29 February 2008.<br />
Why not email me with your comments on
<p><a href=mailto:pipes@brighton.co.uk>
pipes@brighton.co.uk</a>.
</p>
</body>

</html>
```

Be aware that if you publish your email address on a web-page, it may be "harvested" by robot spammers or mass email advertisers and you will then start to receive much unwanted email. You can obfuscate the spammers by, for example, converting each character in the address into its hexadecimal equivalent, adding spaces (which a human will understand must be removed to send an email), or making a GIF image of the address. More tips on www.u.arizona.edu/~trw/spam/.

Character formatting You can influence the choice of font to some extent, but must give the end-user a lot of leeway: if you specify <font face=Verdana, Arial, Helvetica, Swiss, Geneva, Sans-serif>, for example, then if the user has Verdana, the browser will use it, if not it will use Arial or Helvetica, or at least any old sans serif face instead of the default Times. You can at least make words **bold** or *italic*. HTML, however, has two classes of styles: logical and physical. Logical styles, such as <strong>, tag the text according to its meaning, while physical styles, such as <bold>, indicate the specific typographical appearance of the text.

Logical tags are supposed to help enforce consistency in your documents. Remember, the WWW was developed by scientists used to the conventions of academic papers, not graphic designers with their own set of needs. Most browsers render the <strong> tag in **bold** text. However, it is possible that a browser might display the word in bright red instead. If you want something to be displayed in **bold** (for example) and do not want a browser's setting to display it differently, use physical styles.

Try to be consistent about which type of style you use. If you tag with physical styles, do so within the whole document. If you use logical styles, stick with them throughout a document.

Here are some of the logical styles:

<em>	for emphasis, typically displayed in *italics*
<cite>	for titles of books, films, etc., typically displayed in *italics*
<strong>	for strong emphasis, typically displayed in **bold**.

And here are some examples of physical styles:

<b>	**bold** text
<i>	*italic* text
<tt>	typewriter text, i.e. fixed-width font, usually Courier.

Escape sequences Three ASCII characters—the left angle bracket (<), the right angle bracket (>), and the ampersand (&)—have special meanings in HTML and therefore cannot be used "as is" in text. (The angle brackets are used to indicate the beginning and end of HTML tags, and the ampersand is used to indicate the beginning of an escape sequence.) Double quote marks may be used as is, but a character entity may also be used (").

To use any of these in an HTML document, you must enter their escape sequence instead:

&lt;	is the escape sequence for <
&gt;	is the escape sequence for >
&amp;	is the escape sequence for &

Escape sequences begin with an ampersand (&), followed by the sequence (a mnemonic or a number preceded by #) and end with a semi-colon. They can be expressed in decimal or hexadecimal forms: an en-dash, for example, can be written as – or – or –.

Color By default, the background color is white and the text is black. Hot links are blue and these change to purple when that link has been visited (browsers have a cache, a portion of your hard disk, in which they store recently visited sites). These can be changed, however, by adding attributes to the <body> tag. The bad news is that the RGB colors you specify must be converted to hexadecimal! Programs such as Photoshop allow you to do this quite painlessly. For example,

<body text=#000055 bgcolor=#CCFFFFlink=#CC0000 vlink=#005522>

results in dark blue text, a light blue background, and red hypertext links which, when visited, change to green.

Website designers get to work in RGB all the time, and at a screen resolution of 72 dpi (dots per inch), so what they see on the screen will be the same as in the finished product. There are slight differences, however, in the way Macs and PCs display colors, and how browsers, such as Safari and Explorer, interpret the color information. Most people are assumed to have at least a 256-color monitor, and, taking into account the above constraints, we arrive at 216 **websafe colors**, which will be displayed without resorting to dithering (optically mixing two or more colors). Thus white is FFFFFF and black is 000000.

Web colors are described using three sets of hexadecimal numbers, one each for red, green, and blue. Some web creators prefer to specify colors by name rather than by hexadecimal value. There are 136 standard colors with names that are recognized by most browsers. Many of these colors are not among the 216 browser-safe colors, and may be dithered. These include such exotic names as Blanched Almond (FFEBCD), Chocolate (D2691E), Dodger Blue (1E90FF), Fuchsia (FF00FF), Old Lace (FDF5E6), Thistle (D8BFDB), and Tomato (FF6347). Charts of websafe colors can be found on the internet: try www.lynda.com/hex.asp and the-light.com/colclick.html.

Today, most people have computers that display thousands or millions of colors, so the need to use a browser-safe palette is less important. There may, however, be a resurgence when designing for newer online publishing devices with reduced color gamuts, such as mobile phones and PDAs (Personal Digital Assistants).

Images To add an image, use the tag <img src=picture.gif>, where picture.gif is the file name of the image, in this case a GIF file (Fig. **7.13**). img says place image here and src tells the browser that the source is an image in the same directory as the text file called picture.gif. By default, images are ranged left, but you can center them using the <center> tag. It is also useful to specify the dimensions of the image, in pixels, using width and height attributes. If you do this, the browser will leave a space for the image and display any text that follows without waiting for the image to load. Images always take longer to download than text and this gives the user something to read while waiting for the pictures. The alt attribute describes the image in text and is a courtesy to users with a browser, such as Lynx, that doesn't support graphics, and to visually disabled people who rely on their computer to speak the websites out loud.

Other attributes may define the space between the image and text, and whether the image has a border or not. You can use an image as a link, and the default is a blue rectangular border, which may look odd on an image with an irregular outline. For example,

<img src=fido.gif alt=my poodle Fido" width=200 height=50 border=0>

displays a centered image without a border. If you were using a browser such as Lynx or had your images switched off, all you would see would be the text "my poodle Fido."

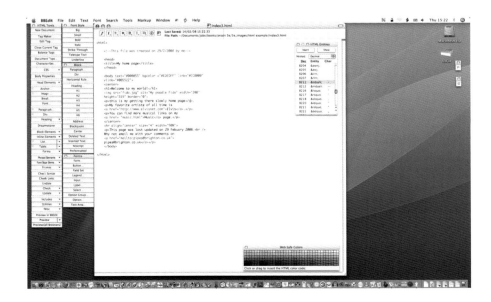

7.13 The code as seen in BBEdit.

Graphics formats: GIFs and JPEGs

One way to be in control of the look of your pages is to put all the typography into graphic images—and some web designers used to do this. On a lot of web pages, you will find that headings are often GIFs, and so are other graphic devices such as bullets and buttons. The GIF (Graphics Interchange Format) was originally developed for CompuServe (it's still called CompuServe GIF on the Photoshop menu) and it is very good at compressing 8-bit (256-color) files that have areas containing flat color, such as logos and typographic headings. A later version, called GIF89a, also supports transparency (so that images with irregular outlines can appear to blend into the background) and interlacing, so that the image first appears as a highly pixelated picture that sharpens up as it downloads (Fig. **7.14**). GIF89a also allows animated GIFs to be assembled from a series of still frames in programs such as Adobe ImageReady (bundled with Photoshop).

All browsers (except completely non-graphical ones like Lynx) support GIFs. Most also support JPEG (Joint Photographic Experts Group) files. JPEGs (files with the suffix .jpeg, or .jpg can display 24-bit color and are much better than GIFs for displaying continuous-tone photographic images. Photoshop has a "Save for web" feature that does wonders to compress JPEG and GIF images.

There are other formats in use, but these are the most common. The PNG (Portable Network Graphics—pronounced "ping") format was designed to replace the older and simpler GIF and, to some extent, the more complex TIFF format. For the Web, PNG really has three main advantages: alpha channels (variable transparency), gamma correction (cross-platform control of image brightness), and two-dimensional interlacing (progressive display). PNG also compresses better than GIF in almost every case, but the difference is generally only around 5 to 25 percent. It does *not* try to reproduce GIF's multiple-image support, especially animations; PNG was and is intended to be a single-image format only.

For image editing, either professional or otherwise, PNG provides a useful format for storing intermediate stages of editing. Since PNG's compression is fully lossless—and since it supports 48-bit color or 16-bit grayscale—saving, restoring, and re-saving an image will not degrade its quality, unlike a JPEG (even at its highest quality settings). PNG's compression is among the best that can be had without losing image information and without paying patent fees. Most applications and browsers now support the PNG format.

Whichever you use (remember GIFs are good for graphics with areas of flat color; JPEGs are best for photographs) you must keep the file sizes to a minimum. For designers dealing with print images of several megabytes, this may seem an impossible task, but remember you are only dealing with resolutions of 72 dpi and using as few colors as you can get away with.

Optional extras

You can also use GIFs to tile a background, you can create tables of data, and forms for feedback using CGI (Common Gateway Interface) scripts. You can make a graphic into an "image-map"—when users click on specified portions of the graphic they are linked to other pages. A feature called "frames" will divide the main window into lots of smaller scrollable ones—so that you can have a permanent table of contents in a sidebar, say, with the current content in the main window.

Frames were once used to solve a lot of layout problems, such as true centering of page elements within the browser window, and the use of different background colors or gifs in different areas of the window. The drawbacks include uneven browser support, difficulty in bookmarking specific pages within the website, and being listed by search engines, and problems printing out the pages. Frames also cause confusion to the speech programs that help visually impaired people.

With programs such as Macromedia Flash and Director, Real Player, and Apple's QuickTime, you can add audio, animations, movies, and virtual-reality panoramas to your website. Your end-user may have to download up-to-date plug-ins from the vendor's website. Programs such as Macromedia Fireworks help you create animated buttons and other graphic elements.

Sun's **Java** programming language (named after the amount of Mount Java coffee drunk during its development) allows you to incorporate "applets" (no relation to Apple computers) into your HTML code. These are tiny programs embedded into the HTML which, when downloaded, will run on any computer to produce animations, for example. Sun describes Java as a "simple, robust, object-oriented, platform-independent, multi-threaded, dynamic general-purpose programming environment." With Java you don't need to download plug-ins—the ability to run Java is built into browsers and operating systems.

Javascript allows you to have features such as mouse rollovers on your website, where the graphic changes as your mouse moves over it. Web-design programs such as Dreamweaver and Freeway help you create these without having to learn Javascript.

7.14 An interlaced GIF looks rough at first, but sharpens up as the image downloads.

Remember the automobile simile earlier? Web design is also like the early days of "desktop publishing" when anyone purchasing a copy of PageMaker or QuarkXPress and a handful of fonts was led to believe that they too could be a graphic designer. And the result? A lot of publications looking like Victorian handbills. Just because you can do something, you don't have to incorporate every feature into every document. Everything can be used appropriately somewhere, but in general try to exercise some restraint!

There are sound reasons for this: the more features you add to your pages, the longer they will take to download and the more chance there is that the user will get bored and move on. It may be convenient for you to write the page in Flash, say, but it can be a bore to have to download the latest version of a plug-in first, and then to have to wait ages for the "movie" to download before you can even decide whether to surf on to another page. Some of the better pages, in my opinion, have few frills, just plain white backgrounds, the minimum amount of graphics, a logical structure, and legible text.

Cascading style sheets

CSS (**cascading style sheets**) is an extension to HTML to allow styles—color, font, font sizes, and now layout—to be specified for certain elements of a hypertext document. Style information can be included within the HTML file or in a separate CSS file (which can then easily be shared by multiple HTML files). Multiple levels of CSS can be used to allow selective overriding of styles.

SGML (Standard Generalized Markup Language) is a generic mark-up language for representing documents—an International Standard that describes the relationship between a document's content and its structure. Since 1998, almost all development in SGML has been focused on XML—a simple (and therefore easier to understand and implement) subset of SGML suitable for use on the World Wide Web. XHTML is a reformulation of HTML 4.01 in XML. (For more information, check out www.w3.org/XML.)

Until recently, designers had few ways to lay out web pages. They had to use either frames or tables with spacers (transparent single-pixel GIF images resized to a specified width and height) to attempt any form of controllable layout. Both methods are unsatisfactory for various reasons. The only way to publish an exact layout on the web is to link to a PDF, a slow, cumbersome method, requiring the user to download plug-ins. CSS has been used for many years to style fonts and colors. Before CSS, if you wanted to assign certain typographic characteristics to, say, all <h1> headings, designers had to use the <font> tag to mark up every occurrence of that heading type, making document code more complex and difficult to maintain. Fewer HTML tags in a document reduces page download times and bandwidth. The only drawback to CSS at present is in uneven browser support, so hacks or workarounds sometimes have to be introduced to cater for older

versions of browsers such as Internet Explorer. In 2006, the W3C (World Wide Web Consortium) considered CSS to be superior to previous methods and has therefore deprecated their use for presentational HTML markup. The <font> tag is now obsolete.

In CSS, presentation is separated from structure, such that a single stand-alone CSS document can define color, font, text alignment, size, and many other attributes. Change the CSS document and every page attached to it are automatically updated. But it can do much more, and designers are now using CSS for layout, with <div> tags to position the "containers" of design elements.

CSS separates design and content. The content is in HTML (or, strictly speaking, XHTML) documents; the design is in the CSS file. Tableless web design also improves accessibility—screen readers and braille devices have fewer problems with CSS designs because they follow a more logical structure. It is also possible to provide multiple layouts for different devices, such as handheld computers and mobile phones.

Why cascading? Styles can be specified inside a single HTML element, inside the <head> element of an HTML page, or in an external CSS file. Multiple external style sheets can be referenced inside a single HTML document. And a single CSS document can be shared by many HTML pages. All the styles will "cascade" into a new "virtual" style sheet, in order of priority:

1 An inline style inside an HTML element
2 Internal style sheet contained within the <head> tag
3 An external style sheet
4 The browser default.

Thus an inline style, such as

<p style=color: #009900; margin-left: 20px>
This is a green indented paragraph
</p>

for a paragraph with a different color and left margin to the rest, will override a style declared inside the <head> tag or in an external style sheet. If the CSS should fail completely, your website will degrade gracefully—you will still have a legible document, displayed using the browser's default styles (usually Times on a white background, with blue underlined links).

An external style sheet is merely a text file with the suffix .css, for example style.css. The instructions in a style sheet are called statements, or rules, which have two parts: a selector (an HTML tag) and a declaration (enclosed by curly brackets {}). The selector tells a browser which elements in a page will be affected by the rule; the declaration tells the browser which set of properties to apply.

selector {property: value}

A statement with a selector for the <h1> heading, for example might look like this:

```
h1 {
font-family: Verdana, Helvetica, Arial, sans-serif;
font-size: 36px;
text-align: center;
color: #00248F;
font-weight: bold;
}
```

Size can be measured in px (pixels), as here, or in points, ems (equal to the current font size), exs (the x-height of a font), picas, inches, or mm. Colors are defined in hexadecimal RGB. Doubled-up numbers such as 00FF55 can be abbreviated to three numbers, 0F5. W3C also has 16 color names that will validate: aqua, black, blue, fuchsia, gray, green, lime, maroon, navy, olive, purple, red, silver, teal, white, and yellow.

Similarly, all other HTML tags can be styled. The syntax is very precise, but there are programs available, such as Style Master, with every possible permutation of properties accessed by pull-down menus to take care of it. To style the body text, for example, the body tag <body> and the paragraph tag <p> will be given certain typographic properties. To create a minor variation of a tag, such as a caption to an image, that you may want to look smaller than the body text, a class attribute is used. In the style sheet it will look like this:

```
p.caption {
font-size: 10px;
}
```

In an HTML document, the <p> tag for the caption will be modified thus:

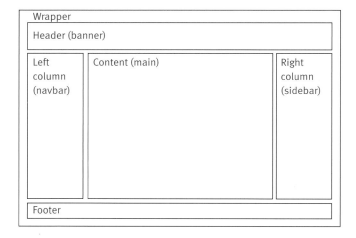

7.15 A schematic diagram of a typical web page, which will generally have a header containing a banner, sidebars for navigational menus and other standard matter, a central area for content (which may include nested <div>s), and perhaps a footer for copyright and contact information.

<p class=caption>This the caption</p>

For layout, <div> elements, each with an id so that we can identify them and give them positioning properties in the style sheet, are the main building blocks used in CSS page layouts. A web page layout will typically comprise a header or banner, the main content, a navigation bar or menu, either horizontally under the banner or vertically in the left column, a sidebar in the right-hand column, and perhaps a footer (Fig **7.15**). For a simple website with just a header and area for content, the HTML would look like this:

```
<!DOCTYPE html PUBLIC -//W3C//DTD XHTML
1.0 Strict//EN http://www.w3.org/TR/xhtml1/DTD/
xhtml1-strict.dtd>
<html xmlns=http://www.w3.org/1999/xhtml xml:
lang=en lang=en>

<head>
<!--This file was created on 29/2/2008 by me-->
<title>Simple layout</title>
<link rel=stylesheet type=text/css href=style.css />
</head>

<body>
<div id=wrapper>

<div id=header>
This is the Header
</div>
<div id=content>
<p>This is the main content area</p>
</div>

</div>
</body>

</html>
```

Note the complicated-looking "DOCTYPE" declaration at the beginning, which states that this is a valid strict XHTML 1.0 web page, and will thus validate at http://validator.w3.org/ and receive a seal of approval. A website does not necessarily have to validate for it to work, but being standards-compliant can avoid problems later. Note also the link to the external CSS document. The wrapper contains the whole page and constrains its width and enables the website to be centred in the browser window, for example.

The part of the CSS code that defines the layout will look like:

```
#wrapper {
margin: 0 auto;
width: 922px;
```

```
}
#header {
width: 900px;
padding: 20px;
border: 0px;
height: 100px;
margin: 10px 0px 0px 0px;
background: #809FFF;
}
#content {
width: 900px;
border: 0px;
background: #BFCFFF;
margin: 0px 0px 10px 0px;
padding: 10px;
}
```

Note that the borders of the boxes here are measured in pixels, as are the margins (the space around the box) and padding (the space inside the border) (Fig **7.16**). The order in which the margins are defined is: top, right, bottom, left. Adding our content to the code results in:

```
<!DOCTYPE html PUBLIC -//W3C//DTD XHTML
1.0 Strict//EN http://www.w3.org/TR/xhtml1/DTD/
xhtml1-strict.dtd>
<html xmlns=http://www.w3.org/1999/xhtml xml:
lang=en lang=en>

<head>
<!--This file was created on 29/2/2008 by me-->
<meta http-equiv=Content-Type content=text/html;
charset=UTF-8 />
```

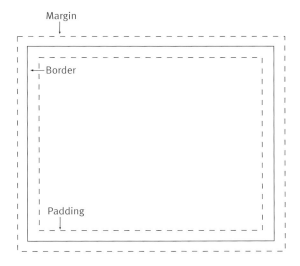

7.16 A CSS ‹div› box can have a border (solid, dotted, or invisible), margins outside the box to keep it at a distance from other elements, and padding within the box to keep content away from the border. It can also have a fill color or contain a background graphic.

```
<title>My home page</title>
<link rel=stylesheet type=text/css href=style.css />
</head>

<body>
<div id=wrapper>

<div id=header>
<h1>Welcome to my world!</h1>
</div>

<div id=content>
<img src=fido.jpg alt=My poodle Fido width=200
height=319 />

<p class=caption>My poodle Fido</p>

<p>This is my getting there slowly home page.</p>

<p>My favorite artist of all time is
<a href=http://www.elvisnet.com>Elvis</a>.</p>

<p>You can find more musical links on my
<a href=music.html>Music</a> page.</p>

<p>This page was last updated on 29 February
2008.<br />
Why not email me with your comments on
<a href=mailto:pipes@brighton.co.uk
pipes@brighton.co.uk</a></p>
</div>

</div>

</body>
</html>
```

The CSS will look like this:

```
body, p {
font-family: Verdana, Arial, Helvetica, sans-serif;
font-size: 12px;
text-align: center;
line-height: 150%;
}
p.caption {
font-size: 10px;
}
h1 {
font-size: 36px;
text-align: center;
color: #00248F;
font-weight: bold;
}
#wrapper {
```

```
margin: 0 auto;
width: 922px;
}
#header {
width: 900px;
padding: 10px;
border: 0px;
height: 70px;
margin: 10px 0px 0px 0px;
background: #809FFF;
}
#content {
width: 900px;
padding: 10px;
border: 0px;
margin: 0px 0px 10px 0px;
background: #BFCFFF;
}
```

To save having to repeat definitions, the selectors body and p have been grouped, using a comma. The finished page now looks a lot more interesting (Fig. **7.17**) and merely changing the CSS will change the whole appearance of the website, with the content staying the same. For links, this design still uses the browser defaults. We can go on to define link properties of the form:

```
a:link {
}
a:visited {
}
a:hover {
}
a:active {
}
```

Where hover, for example, changes the color of the link or its background when the mouse rolls over it. Obviously a complete outline of CSS would take up another book, so this

7.17 This is how the code looks as a web page in Safari.

simple introduction aims only to demonstrate that CSS need not be daunting. Its versatility and flexibility make learning to use CSS for layouts well worthwhile, and it is the only field in which the graphic designer can have complete control over the design and production process. CSS is the future!

Testing your pages

Web pages are cheap and fast to produce, and the temptation is to "publish" as soon as you possibly can. After all, if there are mistakes, then they can soon be rectified and the original files at the server overwritten. True, but it is still good practice to test, test, and then test again.

You can view your emerging pages on a browser such as Safari without going online, and this should be the first step. Then try viewing your pages on another browser, such as Firefox (they can all be downloaded free, or can be installed from CD-ROMs that come with computer magazines). Try uploading your pages to a home-page site and go online to check that they still look OK and that everything works.

If you designed the pages on a Mac, find a friend with a PC and see how they look on that platform. PCs have different color tables, and your subtle background color could turn into a dithered mess, or even render the text illegible. A PC might have a 96 dpi monitor, so your text will appear larger and your 72 dpi graphic will appear smaller! The default font on most browsers is Times, and the Times New Roman on PCs is different from the version of Times on Macs!

You may not need or want to start writing Java applets or CGI scripts, so make friends with your local HTML geek: the local newsgroups are a good place to start. And talk to the people at your ISP about what you can and can't do at the server end. You will at least now know what is possible.

Publicizing your pages

How do you tell the world that you have a website? You can send out postcards, by snailmail. Add your URL to your letterheads and to the signature on your email and newsgroup postings. And you can make it easy for people searching for your site to find it!

Some people still seem to think that the internet is one huge encyclopedia—you type in a word somehow and it comes up with an answer. Well, not yet. But there are search engines that can help. The best known is Google. You can speed up the process by sending them details of your site. Most search engines send out "robots" to search out pages and then try to classify them. Users can search for words and phrases using logical operators; for example, to find a bedtime story, type "fairy tale" + frog – dragon (Fig. **7.18**). Sometimes you have to use quite a lot of lateral thinking to find a site you know is there—and that's where the surfing comes in. It's like detective work: one page leads to another, nearer and nearer, until you find what you're looking for. Some search engines just look at the first few words of a page, and you can have some influence by using the <meta> tag within the head of your page:

<meta name=description content=We specialize in grooming pink poodles.>

<meta name=keywords content=pet grooming, Brighton, dog>

will result in a "hit" if you type in either poodle or dog.

Human factors in website design

Surfing the web and trying to take in information is hard on the eyes. It is estimated that reading speed and comprehension of websites is a quarter of that of print. People don't want to read a lot of text from computer screens, so avoid long pages and use plenty of subheads; to avoid the reader having to scroll, break long pages into screen-size pages. Use radio skills to boost readability: one idea per sentence; one breath per idea. Try to use italics sparingly as they are hard to read online. Instead use bold or colored text for emphasis. Text on navigation bars and buttons should be concise but not cryptic—reading a heading should tell the user quickly what the page or section is all about.

Impatient users tend not to read streams of text fully. Instead, they scan text and pick out keywords, sentences, and paragraphs of interest while skipping over those parts of the text they care less about. Jakob Nielson (www.useit.com) is a web-usability guru. In his research, he found that 79 percent of test users always scanned any new page; but only 16 percent read word-by-word. As a result, he recommends that web pages employ scannable text.

Because the reader can determine the order of access and choose which ideas to pursue, make each page a self-contained entity, with navigation back to the home page and perhaps your email address. Online readers arrive through many portals and can go anywhere they like—they will not necessarily read the pages in sequential order.

Links can be useful to take readers to extra information, but they can also disrupt flow—be careful when peppering a site with external links. Place them in a "Find out more" section. Grouping links to other sites at the website's end means readers are retained and rewarded. You also have space to describe the link before the users choose to go there.

What can you do online for your target audience that you can't do on paper? Would the site content be brought alive by including multimedia and interactive elements? Pop-up windows that bring a page up in a smaller window over the top of the page you were looking at can be used to display bigger versions of maps, photos, and illustrations. You can also use them for glossaries or box stories. But be aware that users can block pop-ups to prevent spam. Consider how repeat visitors will know what has been changed or added. "Sticky content" is the stuff that keeps users coming back day after day, week after week for their fix. Unlike print, websites can be updated fairly easily, but they can also easily be neglected. So think hard about what "sticky content" will bring lasting enjoyment to your audience.

Designing for the small screen

Until recently, graphic design for print, and graphic design for screen-based applications such as television and multimedia were seen as two distinct disciplines, employing very different kinds of designer. Print designers have long been used to working with high-resolution but static visual information; screen designers have to think more like movie makers. The popularity of the internet has been responsible for breaking down some of these divides and many designers are now expected to "repurpose" their layouts for use in many diverse and different kinds of media.

As we have seen earlier in this chapter, designing a website is more than just feeding a QuarkXPress document into an HTML plug-in and uploading the result to an ISP. A job destined to be published both in print and on the internet will ideally have to be planned very carefully to take advantage of the strengths of both media while avoiding their relative weaknesses. And even if you can turn your hand to designing wonderful web pages, creating designs for television and multimedia means taking on an entirely new set of challenges. For television and film work, designers used to produce lettering on boards, which were then placed in front of the camera. Nowadays, everything is created on a computer system (Fig. **7.19**) and output direct to video, or, in the case of sports and current-affairs programs, broadcast live.

Programs like Flash have introduced designers to animation and the possibilities of sound. You can add the time dimension to graphic design—the words and letters can move!

7.18 Google is a popular search engine that presents you with possible sites based on keywords. Sometimes a good deal of lateral thinking is needed to find a particular site.

Cheaper digital video cameras and programs like Apple's iMovie may have tempted you into film making. Designing for television is not an unreachable aspiration (Figs **7.20–7.21**). Everyone is now familiar with the clichés of flying chrome-plated logos and drop shadows, but you don't need to use sophisticated solid modeling with photorealistic rendering techniques such as ray tracing to achieve a memorable effect, as the award-winning idents for British TV's BBC Four by Martin Lambie-Nairn prove.

Other areas opening up to graphic designers include games and interaction design—designing the icons and interfaces of software applications—and interactive database design, for use in art galleries and museums, or for distribution on CD-ROM or DVD. These may also take the form of freestanding "kiosks" with touch-screen interaction.

Collectively known as hypermedia, and created using computer programs such as Adobe Director, these "stacks" mimic conventional books. The difference is that the "reader" can flip around at will, usually by pointing to a highlighted word in the text, or by choosing a new topic from a menu. The problem for the designer—apart from organizing the stack so as not to frustrate the reader with too many dead ends—is one of legibility. The amount of text on any one page must be kept to a minimum (although it is possible to scroll a large amount of text within a window) because low-resolution text on a screen is tiring to read. The graphics must also be carefully laid out to avoid unwanted effects such as "pixel beards," where a letter or graphic interacts unfavorably with a background tint.

7.19 The Building the Biggest title sequence for UK TV station Channel 4 was designed by Emmy-winning designer Bernard Heyes using Quantel's Hal video editing system with added effects by Discreet Logic's Flame. It incorporates computer-aided design images provided by architects Norman Foster and Partners, which were rendered using Alias Wavefront's 3D-animation package Maya.

HOT TIPS & COOL TRICKS

TV design dangers

Computer monitors have non-interlaced screens; television sets are interlaced—so avoid very thin horizontal lines (one pixel thick or a small, odd number of pixels) and tight patterns (like herringbone), or they will flicker. The same applies to fonts with fine serifs, like Bodoni—use sturdy, bold faces like Verdana and Century Schoolbook instead. Avoid excessive kerning and type below 14 pt. TV screens aren't as sharp as computer monitors and have a narrower color gamut, and bright, saturated colors, particularly yellows and reds, can cause problems of "blooming," so use the NTSC/**PAL** filter in Photoshop to make sure your colors are broadcast-legal. And keep important elements away from the edge of the screen—they may be cropped!

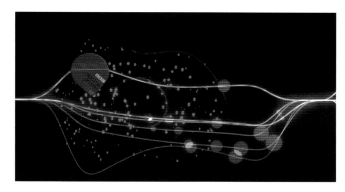

7.20 London-based Minivegas created a series of 20-second idents for S4C/, the Welsh version of Channel 4. Animated elements in the images come to life in synch with the announcer's voiceover. The brief was picture-postcard views of Welsh life. In the lighthouse sequence, the electric wires in the scene warp and wave as the channel announcer speaks. Client: S4C/; agency: proud; director/animator: Minivegas.

7.21 For the 2007 Electric Proms, the BBC encouraged participants to try something different. Minivegas took the challenge and put animated graphics to music in this abstract trailer. Client: BBC; agency: Red Bee; director/animator: Minivegas.

Summary

What's in the internet for the designer? Many things. First, it is a cheap and fast way to transport artwork to the client. Second, it's a cheap and effective way to advertise yourself and your work worldwide, using online galleries of work. You don't have to wait for a source book or CD-ROM to come out, and you can change round your portfolio daily, if need be. OK, putting lots of graphics on to WWW pages can make them slow down, but technology is improving all the time.

Third, it is a source of new work and clients. The fastest-growing area of graphic design is in making the WWW pages themselves, as many of our Trailblazers can testify. Everyone has to have one. As with CD-ROM design and production, huge opportunities exist for designers who understand and appreciate the possibilities (and limitations) of the medium.

You may not wish to learn all the ins and outs of HTML, but with the working knowledge you have gained here you will be able to assemble sample WWW pages quickly and clearly using a WYSIWYG page designer, and then be able to fine-tune the source code. You will at least be able to produce a working prototype of the look and feel for a site, which can then be completed by a team of other professionals. You may even be inspired to do it all yourself. At long last, in WWW design, the entire concept-to-production cycle is back in the hands of the designer. Gutenberg must be smiling.

Airside

"Airside combine graphics, animation, and music in flat vibrant colors, with jolly characters and large amounts of digital playfulness."

Manifesto
Going green

From the Airside website:

"Last year [2007], we invited auditing company The Green Mark to help us improve our environmental performance. Airside achieved an 'Outstanding' score for the Level 1 award."

"In order to achieve this, we addressed the following areas:

Resource use and waste management

We now monitor waste and set targets, we print double sided where possible, reuse envelopes and use electronic formats when possible. We show how all waste (including hazardous waste) is dealt with through legal, responsible, and proper measures.

Energy use and efficiency

We have implemented a switch-off policy for electrics, we use energy saving lightbulbs, we have replaced the water cooler with a filter tap.

Transport

Only one Airsider owns a car, and most of us cycle. We use public transport or a green-accredited taxi company to get to meetings, and use bike couriers when practical.

Purchasing and procurement

We consider everything we buy, and where we buy it from. We buy recycled paper, envelopes, and toilet paper, refilled inks, and environmentally friendly cleaning products.

Products and services

We aim to work with responsible companies. Where possible we are using ethically sourced T-shirts and vegetable inks on products.

Awareness and communication

Everyone at Airside is on board with being an environmentally aware organization, and we align all our thinking and products to our environmental policy."

www.green-mark.co.uk

London-based Airside was founded in 1998 by Alex Maclean, Nat Hunter, and Fred Deakin, and is currently a 12-strong team—plus regular freelancers. Co-founder Fred Deakin is one half of ambient/electronica music duo Lemon Jelly (named after the smell of Fred's kitchen) with Nick Franglen. All promotional material for Lemon Jelly to date, including posters, album covers, and videos, has been produced by Airside.

The name came from a dictionary of new words, meaning the place between an airplane and where you enter a country at customs control. Airside began when the three freelancers shared a studio space in Islington, London. They decided to set their desks up as though they were a company and immediately their clients started treating them differently—with more respect. After a year they hired their first employees—Mark Swift and Henki Leung—and have gone from there. Nat, Alex, and Fred do all the new business, then after that the hierarchy is flat; everyone has an equal share of the profits and a say in how things are run.

Alex Maclean originally studied interior design at the Royal College of Art but whilst there experimented with animation, film, and three-dimensional modeling, ending up as a Research Fellow working for a charity promoting democracy via the web. There he met fellow RCA student Nat Hunter, who had studied human-computer interface psychology at Edinburgh University and then, after a spell with Bridges & Woods designing for bands, joined the RCA's interaction design course. She co-designed the interface for the Jupiter II spaceship in the movie *Lost in Space* as well as performance installation work for Blast Theory before starting Airside. Nat also makes things from clay and wool in her spare time.

Fred Deakin did an MA in communication design at Central St Martins. He'd also been in Edinburgh—studying for a degree in English Literature—where he met and eventually married Nat. Self-taught in graphic design, he developed his strong illustrative style by designing flyers and posters for club nights, mostly using Letraset and photocopies. Between Edinburgh and St Martins he ran a design agency called Funny Man and did the MA so he could feel like a real designer. While Alex and Nat were freelancing at Pinewood Studios, Fred was working for Swifty Typographix and teaching at St Martins. Frustrated by lack of control and wanting to be able to speak directly to the client, they set up Airside.

One of their first big jobs was a digital radio project for BBC Radio 3, with ambient animation accompanying music by Evan Parker. This was followed by a website for Jay Joplin's White Cube Gallery. Clients include Apple, Coca-Cola, Fiat, MTV, Panasonic, Sony, and Suzuki. They recently worked on the opening and closing title sequences for Anthony Minghella's film set in Africa, *The No 1 Ladies' Detective Agency*. They also sell T-shirts and other fun items through their online shop.

In 2007 Airside became officially green, being accredited to Level 1 Green Mark certification. They're also nearly carbon neutral, minimizing general office waste by recycling and re-using, they turn off all machines at night, have sourced non-toxic printers for their T-shirts and calendars, are looking into green energy suppliers, and many of them cycle to work. They're adding up their air miles to offset at the end of the year with tree-planting. Nat has joined forces with Sophie

Panasonic asked Airside to decorate four limited-edition mobile phones they were launching in Japan. They wanted covers and an animated ringtone to bring the phone to life and to make it a collectible item. Airside came up with storyboards for spunky ghosts, a pooing monkey, an angry giant Cyclops, and a happy hand. By combining each of the animated sequences with music composed specially for the project by Fred, they came up with the final animated ringtone to please the most twisted Japanese phone fiend.

Orange wanted a series of commercials to bumper a music video program they were sponsoring. So obviously singing farmyard animals were the solution. The inspiration behind these commercials came from a kid's T-shirt Airside made (Bear in Tree). The Orange characters were brought to life using Flash.

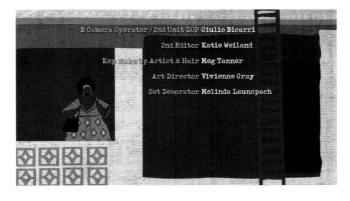

Airside has worked on all of Lemon Jelly's music packaging to date. This is the band's 2004 *Lost Horizons* album. There are two versions of the same landscape: by day the city is dull and gray while the countryside entices you to its delights, but by night the countryside disappears into darkness while the city lights up. These images were created using Maya and rendered to look as if they had been drawn in 2D.

Thomas (co-director of design studio thomas.matthews) and Caroline Clark (of ecologically-aware design site, lovelyasatree.com) to set up social enterprise, Three Trees Don't Make A Forest, which aims to provide a one-stop shop for creatives seeking information on sustainability issues and how their working life affects the environment.

The opening and closing title sequences for Anthony Minghella's film set in Botswana, *The No 1 Ladies' Detective Agency* use painterly graphics in vibrant African colors.

Resources

www.airside.co.uk
www.apple.com/pro/profiles/airside/
www.threetreesdontmakeaforest.org

Appendix: Standard sizes for paper, books, and envelopes

US standard paper sizes

Grade classification	Basis size* in	Basis size* mm	Weights, lb/ream	Design applications
Bond	17 × 22	432 × 559	13, 16, 20, 24, 28, 32, 36, 40	Letterheads, newsletters
Book	25 × 38	635 × 965	30, 40, 45, 50, 55, 60, 65, 70, 75, 80, 90, 100, 120	Books, catalogs, calendars, annual reports, brochures, magazines
Text	25 × 38	635 × 965	90, 100, 120, 140, 160, 180	Posters, self-mailers, announcements
Cover	20 × 26	508 × 660	25, 35, 40, 50, 55, 60, 65, 80, 90, 100	Business cards, annual report covers, greeting cards

*Basis size: the standard size in a particular grade that determines basis weight

US book sizes

Grade classification	in	mm	Grade classification	in	mm
Medium 32mo	3 × 4¾	76 × 121	Medium 12mo	5⅛ × 7⅔	130 × 195
Medium 24mo	3⅝ × 5½	92 × 140	Demy 8vo	5½ × 8	140 × 203
Medium 18mo	4 × 6⅔	102 × 169	Small 4to	7 × 8½	178 × 216
Cap 8vo	7 × 7¼	178 × 184	Broad 4to (up to 13 × 10) (330 × 254)	7 × 8½	178 × 216
12mo	4½ × 7½	114 × 191	Medium 8vo	6 × 9½	165 × 254
Medium 16mo	4½ × 6¾	114 × 171	Royal 8vo	6½ × 10	165 × 267
Crown 8vo	5 × 7½	127 × 191	Super Royal 8vo	7 × 10½	178 × 267
Pos 8vo	5½ × 7½	140 × 191	Imperial 8vo	8¼ × 11½	210 × 292

Note that American and European usage is to express the width dimension of the book first. In the UK and Far East, depth is shown first. Sizes quoted are not absolute and may vary slightly.

Trimmed page sizes from standard US sheets

Trimmed page size in (mm)	Number of pages	Number from sheet	Standard paper size in	Standard paper size mm
3½ × 6¼ (89 × 159)	4	24	28 × 44	711 × 1118
	8	12	28 × 44	711 × 1118
	12	8	28 × 44	711 × 1118
	16	6	28 × 44	711 × 1118
	24	4	28 × 44	711 × 1118
4 × 9 (102 × 229)	4	12	25 × 38	635 × 965
	8	12	38 × 50	965 × 1270
	12	4	25 × 38	635 × 965
	16	6	38 × 50	965 × 1270
	24	2	25 × 38	635 × 695
4½ × 6 (114 × 152)	4	16	25 × 38	635 × 965
	8	8	25 × 38	635 × 965
	16	4	25 × 38	635 × 965
	32	2	25 × 38	635 × 965
5¼ × 7⅝ (133 × 194)	4	16	32 × 44	813 × 1118
	8	8	32 × 44	813 × 1118
	16	4	32 × 44	813 × 1118
	32	2	32 × 44	813 × 1118
6 × 9 (152 × 229)	4	8	25 × 38	635 × 965
	8	4	25 × 38	635 × 965
	16	2	25 × 38	635 × 965
	32	2	38 × 50	965 × 1270
Oblong 7 × 5½ (178 × 140)	4	8	23 × 29	584 × 737
	8	4	23 × 29	584 × 737
	16	2	23 × 29	584 × 737
8½ × 11 (216 × 279)	4	4	23 × 35	584 × 889
	8	2	23 × 35	584 × 889
	16	2	35 × 45	889 × 1143
9 × 12 (229 × 305)	4	4	23 × 38	665 × 965
	8	2	23 × 38	665 × 965
	16	2	38 × 50	965 × 1270

US standard envelope sizes

Commercial/official Window Number	Size, in	Booklet Number	Size, in
6	3⅜ × 6	2½	4½ × 5⅞
6¼	3½ × 6	3	4¾ × 6½
6¾	3⅝ × 6½	4¼	5 × 7½
7	3¾ × 6¾	4½	5½ × 7½
7¾	3⅝× 7½	5	5½ × 8½
Data Card	3½ × 7⅝	6	5¾ × 8⅞
8⅝	3⅝ × 8⅝	6½	6 × 9
9	3⅞ × 8⅞	6¾	6½ × 9½
10	4⅛ × 9½	7	6¼ × 9⅝
10½	4½ × 9½	7¼	7 × 10
11	4½ × 10⅜	7½	7½ × 10½
12	4¾ × 11	8	8 × 11½
14	5 × 11½	9	8¾ × 11½
		9½	9 × 12
		10	9½ × 12⅝
		13	10 × 13

Catalog Number	Size, in	Announcement Number	Size, in
1	6 × 9	A-2	4⅜ × 5⅝
1¾	6½ × 9½	A-6	4¾ × 6½
2	6½ × 10	A-7	5¼ × 7¼
3	7 × 10	A-8	5½ × 8⅛
6	7½ × 10½	A-10	6¼ × 9⅝
7	8 × 11	Slim	3⅜ × 8⅞
8	8¼ × 11¼		
9½	8½ × 10½		
9¾	8¾ × 11¼		
10½	9 × 12		
12½	9½ × 12½		
13½	10 × 13		
14½	11½ × 14¼		
14½	11½ × 14½		

International A sizes of paper

Size	mm	approx. in
4A0	1682 × 2378	66¼ × 93⅜
2A0	1189 × 1682	46¾ × 66¼
A0*	841 × 1189	33⅛ × 46¾
A1	594 × 841	23⅜ × 33⅛
A2	420 × 594	16½ × 23⅜
A3	297 × 420	11¹¹⁄₁₆ × 16½
A4	210 × 297	8¼ × 11¹¹⁄₁₆
A5	148 × 210	5⅞ × 8¼
A6	105 × 148	4⅛ × 5⅞
A7	74 × 105	2⅞ × 4⅛
A8	52 × 74	2 × 2⅞
A9	37 × 52	1½ × 2
A10	26 × 37	1 × 1½

*Nominal size: in the A series, this equals one square meter

All A series sizes mentioned here are trimmed. A sizes can be cut from two stock sizes—R, for trims, and SR, for extra trims or bleeds. A listing of R and SR metric sizes and inch equivalents is below.

Size	mm	approx. in
RA0	860 × 1220	33⅞ × 48⅛
RA1	610 × 860	24⅛ × 33⅞
RA2	430 × 610	17 × 24⅛
SRA0	900 × 1280	35½ × 50⅜
SRA1	640 × 900	25¼ × 35½
SRA2	450 × 640	17⅞ × 25¼

ISO envelope standards

Sheets from the A series can be inserted in the C series envelope, flat or folded. For example, a C5 envelope will accommodate an A5 sheet flat, or an A4 folded once. ISO envelope sizes are all taken from B or C size sheets.

Envelope	mm	approx. in
C3	324 × 458	12¾ × 18
B4	250 × 353	9⅞ × 12⅞
C4	229 × 324	9 × 12¾
B5	176 × 250	7 × 9⅞
C5	162 × 229	6⅜ × 9
B6/C4	125 × 324	5 × 12¾
B6	125 × 176	5 × 7
C6	114 × 162	4½ × 6⅜
DL	110 × 220	4¼ × 8¾
C7/6	81 × 162	3¼ × 6⅜
C7	81 × 114	3¼ × 4½

ISO B and C Sizes of Paper

Size	mm	approx. in
4B0	2000 × 2828	78¾ × 111⁵⁄₁₆
2B0	1414 × 2000	55¹¹⁄₁₆ × 78¾
B0	1000 × 1414	39⅜ × 55⅝
B1	707 × 1000	27⅞ × 39⅜
B2	500 × 707	19⅝ × 27⅞
B3	353 × 500	12⅞ × 19⅝
B4	250 × 353	9⅞ × 12⅞
B5	176 × 250	7 × 9⅞
B6	125 × 176	5 × 7
B7	88 × 125	3½ × 5
B8	62 × 88	2½ × 3½
B9	44 × 62	1¾ × 2½
B10	31 × 44	1¼ × 1¾
C0	917 × 1297	36⅛ × 51
C1	648 × 917	25½ × 36⅛
C2	458 × 648	18 × 25½
C3	324 × 458	12¾ × 18
C4	229 × 324	9 × 12¾
C5	162 × 229	6⅜ × 9
C6	114 × 162	4½ × 6⅜
C7	81 × 114	3¼ × 4½
C8	57 × 81	2¼ × 3¼

Japanese B Sizes

Japan has developed its own standards for paper sizes. While the JIS (Japan Industrial Standard) A series of sizes is identical to the ISO/DIN A series of sizes, the JIS B series is different to the ISO B series; and Japan has no series of envelope sizes comparable to the ISO/DIN C series. JIS B sizes are just over six percent larger than ISO/DIN B sizes. While ISO/DIN B sizes can be cut from JIS B stock, JIS B sizes cannot be cut economically from ISO/DIN B stock.

Size	mm	approx. in
B0	1030 × 1456	40⁹⁄₁₆ × 57⁵⁄₁₆
B1	728 × 1030	28¹¹⁄₁₆ × 40⁹⁄₁₆
B2	515 × 728	20¼ × 28¹¹⁄₁₆
B3	364 × 515	14⁵⁄₁₆ × 20¼
B4	257 × 364	10⅛ × 14⁵⁄₁₆
B5	182 × 257	7³⁄₁₆ × 10⅛
B6	128 × 182	5¹⁄₁₆ × 7³⁄₁₆
B7	91 × 128	3⁹⁄₁₆ × 5¹⁄₁₆
B8	64 × 91	2½ × 3⁹⁄₁₆
B9	45 × 64	1¾ × 2½
B10	32 × 45	1¼ × 1¾

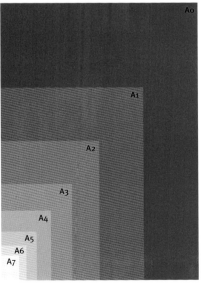
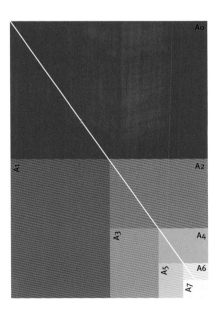
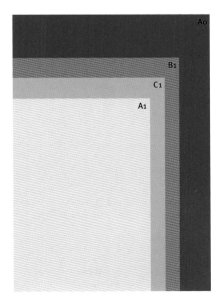

Paper sizes

Glossary

ablation plates in OFFSET LITHO printing, a laser is used to burn tiny holes into thin coatings on a polyester or metal base. These can be produced digitally, require no chemical processing, and can be printed waterless. All the PLATES for a job can be imaged directly on the press, simultaneously and in register

accordion fold or **concertina fold** a folding method in which two or more parallel folds are made in opposite directions

acetate a clear film used as an overlay on a MECHANICAL, for the production of SEPARATIONS for FLAT COLOR, for example, or KEYLINES

achromatic stabilization see GRAY COMPONENT REPLACEMENT

additive colors the primaries of TRANSMITTED LIGHT: red, green, and blue-violet

addressability a measure of how close the centers of the dots that make up type or images can be placed next to each other on an output device such as a LASER PRINTER; see also RESOLUTION

ADSL (asymmetric digital subscriber line— or Loop) telephone line for connecting to the INTERNET in which the bandwidth available for downstream connection is significantly broader than for upstream

against the grain folding or feeding paper stock at right angles to the orientation of the fibers

Agfaproof a proprietary PREPRESS color-proofing system

alignment placing type or images so that they line up either horizontally or vertically

alkaline papermaking a process in which calcium carbonate replaces clay as filler, and titanium dioxide as whitener. Synthetic sizes replace rosin and alum. The result is an inexpensive paper with a longer life and improved bulk and opacity

alphanumeric character set a complete set of letters, numbers, and associated punctuation marks; see also FONT

AM screening (amplitude modulated) conventional screening which uses an array of dfferently sized dots; see also FM SCREENING

anchor in HTML code, a means of pointing your BROWSER to another web page.

The TAG is of the form <a href= "url"> the text to be linked </a> where the url is either relative, i.e. music.html—another page on your site—or absolute, i.e. http://www.elvisnet.com, a site elsewhere on the INTERNET

aniline dye synthetic dye used in flexographic ink

anilox a metal or ceramic roll, used in FLEXOGRAPHY, covered in cells of fixed size and depth that act as ink-carrying reservoirs, rather like a GRAVURE cylinder

anti-aliasing an optical trick to make hard, jagged edges on low-RESOLUTION computer screens and color output look smoother

antique paper a book paper with a rough finish

application computer software that does a particular task, such as page layout

APR (automatic picture replacement) this uses a low-RESOLUTION HALFTONE in a digital page layout, which will be replaced later at the repro house by a high-resolution scanned image

ascender the part of a lower-case letter such as k or d that extends above the body of the type

ASCII (american standard code for information interchange) a text-only format of 256 codes used to represent ALPHANUMERIC CHARACTERS with no additional information about size, font, or spacing

assembler a low-level computer-programming language which uses mnemonics, such as MPY for multiply

assembly collecting and arranging design elements on film to create the FLAT used for platemaking

author's corrections corrections that are made to a GALLEY PROOF by the author or editor, which may contain new material or changes of mind that will have to be paid for

auto-reversing film film that can be used to copy negative-working film to negative-working film without the need for an intermediate positive

avatar on the INTERNET, in IRC, your visual human-like representative in a virtual scene speaking your words. In mythology, an avatar is an incarnation of a Hindu deity

back edge the MARGIN closest to the SPINE

backing a problem of lightening of color in printing which occurs when ink removed from the FOUNTAIN roller is not being replaced by the flow of fresh ink

backstep mark black mark printed on a SIGNATURE which shows where the final fold will be. After collation, the marks should fall in a stepped sequence

back up printing on the other side of the sheet; in computer terminology, to copy important work onto removable hard drives, or other storage media

bad break in JUSTIFIED setting, hyphenation of a word which looks wrong

baryta smooth paper used for LETTERPRESS repro proofs

baseline the imaginary—or, where a computerized layout GRID is used, the actual—horizontal line on which letters sit

basis weight the weight in pounds of 500 sheets (a REAM) of paper. Also called poundage or substance

bastard size any non-standard size, especially of paper

binding fixing together folded SIGNATURES into multipage publications, using glue, thread, or metal wires. Also the cover and backing of a book

bit the primary unit in computing—a binary digit (a 1 or a 0)

bitmap an image or letter made from a pattern of dots or PIXELS on a RASTER device such as a computer screen or LASER PRINTER

blanket the intermediate rubber roller on an OFFSET LITHO press which transfers the image from the PLATE to the paper

blanket cylinder the cylinder on an OFFSET LITHO press to which the BLANKET is attached

blanket-to-blanket press an OFFSET LITHO press that can print both sides of a sheet in one pass—the sheet passes between two BLANKET CYLINDERS and there is no need for an IMPRESSION CYLINDER

bleed part of the image that extends beyond the TRIM MARKS of a page

blind a method of DIE-STAMPING or EMBOSSING in three-dimensional low relief without foil or ink

blocking producing the lettering on the SPINE of a hardback book, usually in gold or silver leaf, by means of a die; see also STICKING

blue and red keys a method for ensuring the close REGISTRATION of COLOR SEPARATIONS using a key image in blue or red as a guide

blueprint or **blue** a DYELINE PROOF for checking the position of design elements and STRIPPED-IN HALFTONES before the PLATE is made, also called OZALID

bluetooth a wireless protocol used to communicate between devices such as mobile phones and computers over a short range

body type type below 14 POINT, used for the main body of text, as opposed to DISPLAY type

boilerplate a set piece of text, such as a disclaimer or copyright statement; in the days of hot metal, a boilerplate was cast or stamped in metal, ready for the printing press and distributed to newspapers

bond a durable grade of paper, used mostly for stationery

brightness the brilliance or light reflectivity of paper

bromide smooth, high-contrast photographic paper used for PMTS and as output from IMAGESETTERS

brownline or **brownprint** a PROOF made from a LITHOGRAPHIC negative similar to a BLUEPRINT but producing a brown image

browser a computer program that allows you to view and interact with WWW pages on the internet. An example is Firefox

bubblejet printer a form of INKJET PRINTER in which a heating element causes bubbles to eject the ink

buckle folder a folding machine that uses an adjustable stop to buckle the sheet, which is then forced between two nip rollers

buckram a heavy, coarse-thread BINDING cloth

bug a mistake in a computer program which makes unexpected things happen

bulk see CALIPER

burn exposure of a LITHO PLATE

burnishing rubbing down pressure-sensitive lettering such as Letraset

byte eight bits, corresponding to one ASCII character

C++ a structured computer-programming language, the basis of JAVA

calendering smoothing and compressing paper as it travels through the paper machine

caliper the thickness of paper, also called BULK

camera-ready copy (CRC) or **mechanical** a complete and finished layout of type and images ready to be scanned or photographed by a PROCESS CAMERA

cast coated paper with a high-gloss finish

casting off calculating how much space the text in a MANUSCRIPT will occupy when set into type

catch-up printing on non-image areas, caused by insufficient water

CD-ROM (compact disk-read-only memory) a plastic disk, like an audio CD, onto which tiny holes are "written" by a laser beam to store up to 650 Mbytes of digital data or programs; see also DVD-ROM

CEPS (color electronic publishing system) low-RESOLUTION images are used as for-position-only visuals. High-resolution scans, straight from the original TRANSPARENCIES, are reunited with the layouts in the IMAGESETTER at the repro house

chalking PIGMENTS smudging or rubbing off, caused by improper CURING of paper which results in too rapid an absorption of the binding vehicle in ink

character the smallest component of written language that has semantic value; refers to the abstract meaning and/or shape, rather than a specific shape (see also GLYPH)

chase in LETTERPRESS, the rectangular metal frame holding type and blocks; when locked up, it is called a FORME

chromo paper a type of paper polished on one side only

client–server architecture a user or a user's program is the client and connects to a remote machine (the server) where, for example, USENET postings or WWW pages are stored

clip art royalty-free illustrations

clock speed the length of the processing cycle in a computer, measured in Mhz

CMM (color-matching module) converts images from one COLOR SPACE to another and simultaneously applies the information in the profile to correctly render the image

CMS (color-management system) a library of scanner, monitor, and output device profiles to ensure consistency of color reproduction by mapping color from the GAMUT of one device, such as a display, into a device-independent model, and then to the gamut of another device, such as a color printer; see also COLORSYNC

CMYK cyan, magenta, yellow, and key (black). This is the system used to describe and separate colors for printing. Other color systems include RGB (red, green, blue) for transmitted color, such as for computer screens, and HLS (hue, luminance, saturation), a more theoretical description. The PANTONE MATCHING SYSTEM matches colors by mixing 11 basic colors

coating adding a layer of china clay to paper to increase its smoothness

cold-metal setting or **strike-on** typesetting produced directly onto paper using a typewriter or rub-down lettering

cold-set ink solid ink that is melted and used with a hot press, solidifying when it contacts the paper

collating or **gathering** bringing pages and SIGNATURES together for BINDING

collotype printing process using plate coated with gelatin, the only process to reproduce CONTINUOUS-TONE images without screening

color bar a printer's check appearing on color PROOFS to show up any faults in color REGISTRATION, print density, DOT GAIN, and SLURRING

color blindness the inability to distinguish one or more of the three colors red, green, and blue. Blindness to red is called protanopia; to green, deuteranopia; and to blue, tritanopia

color calibrate to adjust the output values of a computer screen to correspond more faithfully to printed colors

color cast an unfaithful color on a color image, often found on a subject photographed against a strongly colored background

color-display system the color computer display screen or monitor itself, and the graphics card that drives it

Color-Key a proprietary dry-proofing system using plastic laminates

color-management system see CMS

color separations a set of films for the cyan, magenta, yellow, and black components of a full-color image

color space see GAMUT

ColorSync Apple's proprietary COLOR-MANAGEMENT SYSTEM

combination folder a folding machine that uses both the KNIFE and BUCKLE methods in combination

CompactFlash memory cards for Canon and Kodak digital cameras; see also SMARTMEDIA

composing stick a device used in handsetting for assembling a line of type

compositor the person who sets type

computer-to-plate (CtP) or **direct-to-plate** making OFFSET LITHO PLATES in a PLATESETTER direct from a POSTSCRIPT file without the need for film

concertina fold a type of fold in which two or more parallel folds are made in opposite directions, also called an ACCORDION FOLD

continuous-tone copy artwork or photography containing shades of gray, as opposed to LINE copy, also called contone

contract proof the final PROOF before going to press, which the printer promises to reproduce

converter an OFFSET LITHO press that can be converted to print either two colors on one side of a sheet or one color on both sides in one pass

copy the raw material of the graphic designer: the text, type, artwork, and mechanicals

copy fitting marking up type so that it fits a given space in a layout

copy preparation adding the instructions to text that define how it is to be set; MARK UP is the manual method of copy preparation

copyright the right in law to prevent copying of your work

CPU (central processing unit) the "brain" of a computer, a microprocessor, chip, or chipset

crawling an imperfection in the surface of the ink, occurring when thick ink overprints wet ink

crocking smudging or transfer of dry ink on to printed sheets

Cromacheck proprietary off-press proofing system from DuPont which uses plastic laminates

Cromalin proprietary off-press PROOFING system from DuPont which uses dry toners and light-sensitive sheets

crop marks lines to indicate which portions of a photograph or illustration are surplus to requirements

cropping choosing not to use portions of a photograph and marking an OVERLAY on the original to indicate which portions of the image are to be printed

cross-headings DISPLAY TYPE used to interest the reader and break up gray areas of body type

crossover when an image, text, or tint extends from one page of a publication to a facing page, which may or may not be from the same printed sheet

crossposting posting the same message to several newsgroups on the INTERNET—not a good idea, especially if it is off-topic

crystallization when the ink of the first printing dries too hard before OVERPRINTING, it can repel the second ink and produce poor TRAPPING

CSS (cascading style sheets) an extension to HTML to allow styles—color, FONT, font sizes, and other attributes—to be specified for certain elements of a hypertext document

cure procedure of acclimatizing paper to the temperature and humidity of the pressroom

customization in digital print, where substantial amounts of the content of, for example, brochures or catalogs is altered to match the preferences and interests of particular groups of readers

cut-out photograph in which certain portions are removed to make a subject stand out

cyan PROCESS blue—really more a turquoise

damper marks patterns over the print caused by worn damper covers, or too much pressure

deckle the natural wavy edge to paper; also the frame used to make handmade paper

densitometer an instrument used to measure the density of printed color

descender the part of a lower-case letter such as p or g that extends below the BASELINE

DHTML (dynamic HTML) a term used by some suppliers to describe the combination of HTML, style sheets, and scripts that allows documents to be animated

diazo PROOF made by direct contact with film positives; see also BLUEPRINT and BROWNLINE

didot point a unit of measurement used in continental Europe equivalent to 0.0148 in (0.376 mm), seven percent larger than the American POINT

die-cutting using sharp steel rules in a wooden die or laser to cut shapes from paper

die-stamping producing a three-dimensional low relief effect on paper or cover board using a metal die and counter-die

diffusion transfer a semi-automatic process for making enlargements or reductions of LINE or HALFTONE copy. A negative is produced in the PROCESS CAMERA and transferred to a receiver sheet to create the BROMIDE positive; see also PMT and VELOX

digital camera instead of capturing an image on light-sensitive film that has to be sent away to be developed and printed, a digital camera uses an array of CCD (chargecoupled device) sensors to convert the image into a form that can be stored in the camera's RAM and then downloaded into your computer

digital litho a press which uses a CTP (COMPUTER-TO-PLATE) device to image a PLATE on press and then prints using a normal litho process

digital printing any printed output that is imaged directly on to a BLANKET, PLATE, or SUBSTRATE from an electronic file, with no intermediate film stage

dingbat a symbol or ornament such as ☛ or ❤ treated as characters in a FONT

direct digital printing POSTSCRIPT files are sent directly to special OFFSET PLATES (direct to press) on the press or to ELECTROPHOTOGRAPHIC cylinders in XEROGRAPHY machines, without the need for artwork or film

direct thermal printer an output device that burns an image into special paper

direct-to-plate see COMPUTER-TO-PLATE (CTP)

display type type above 14 POINT set for headlines or other display purposes; some fancy display faces are available in capitals only

dithering a crude computer method of screening. THERMAL-TRANSFER and INKJET printers produce their colors by interspersing PIXELS of CYAN, MAGENTA, and yellow (and sometimes black) in regular patterns, grouped together in either two-by-two or four-by-four MATRICES

document in computer language, any job you are working on is called a document, whether it is a drawing, a piece of text, or a page layout

dot-for-dot a method of screening already screened HALFTONE to prevent MOIRÉ patterns

dot gain or **dot spread** as individual dots begin to join in darker areas of a HALFTONE there can be an apparent jump in what should be a continuous tone

dot-matrix printer an output device that uses pins striking a ribbon to transfer ink on to the paper

doubling two dots where there should only be one. It is caused when wet ink is picked up by the BLANKET on a subsequent printing. If it is off REGISTER, it prints as a ghost dot nearby

download use FTP to transfer files from a remote server to your computer

dpi dots per inch, a measure of the RESOLUTION or ADDRESSABILITY of a RASTER device such as a LASER PRINTER

DPS (double-page spread), two facing pages treated as one design layout, also called a spread or double truck

drawdown a smear of ink from a smooth blade used to check the quality of an ink on a particular paper stock

draw program or **object-oriented program** a computer program that stores and manipulates images in terms of the lines and curves used to create them, usually in POSTSCRIPT; see also PAINT PROGRAM

drop cap a large initial letter dropping into the lines below and signaling the beginning of the text

drop-out complete removal of the dots in highlight areas of a HALFTONE

dry proof a color PROOF made without ink, such as a CROMALIN

DTP desktop publishing—digital page make-up

dummy a "concept model" of a publication, usually a miniature folded version, showing the position of pages; also a book without printing made up to the correct number of pages in a particular paper stock for the purpose of weighing, designing the dust jacket, and generally seeing how the finished product will look

duotone a high-quality HALFTONE with a full tonal range made from two printings, either black and one other color, or black twice

duplex stock paper that has different finishes or colors either side

dusting accumulation of paper particles on the BLANKET of a LITHO press, also spraying powder on to sheets coming off the press to stop wet ink touching the other sheets above and below

DVD-ROM (digital versatile disk–read-only memory) a storage medium similar to a CD-ROM but which can hold more than 5 Gbytes of information

dyeline see DIAZO

dye sublimation prints color PROOFS of near photographic quality produced by mixing vaporized dyes on the surface of the paper

earmarks distinguishing features of a TYPEFACE used for identification, named after the ear of a lower-case g

e-book a book in digital form. It can be a document scanned into PDF (Portable Document Format), retaining all the formatting, typography, and illustrations of the original paper document it can be output into PDF directly from a layout program such as QuarkXPress or InDesign or it can just be pure text

ECF (elemental chlorine-free) in papermaking, chlorine-free bleaches, such as chlorine dioxide; see also TCF

eggshell paper a smooth, pressed type of book paper

electro-coagulation (Elcography) DIGITAL PRINT using water-based polymeric ink sprayed on to a metallic cylinder which coagulates into 400 dpi gel dots in 256 different thicknesses, controlled by pulses of electricity

electrophotographic printers DIGITAL PRINT technology in which a dry or liquid TONER is deposited on the SUBSTRATE by varying its electrostatic properties and then fixed by absorption, chemical reaction, or heat. This includes XEROGRAPHIC photocopiers and the Indigo and Xeikon digital-print engines

em the width of a letter M, or a square em-QUAD space, which will be different for each typeface, unlike a PICA EM, which is ⅙ inch

email (electronic mail) a means of sending messages and "attachments" to other people, mainly connected to the INTERNET, but also within organizations on a local-area network or INTRANET. You type a message on your computer, connect to the internet using a MODEM, and send it down the telephone line to your local ISP

embossing a FINISHING process producing an image in low relief

emulsification what happens when water gets into the litho ink. Most litho inks are designed to accept some emulsification, but too much results in a wishy-washy appearance

emulsion side the duller side of film, which can be scratched

en the width of a letter N; half an EM

EPS (encapulated PostScript) a format for transferring drawings created in Illustrator and FreeHand, for example, into digital layout programs

escape sequences the left angle bracket (<), the right angle bracket (>), and the ampersand (&) have special meanings in HTML and cannot be used "as is"; you must enter their escape sequence instead—&amp, for example, is the escape sequence for &

Ethernet a local-area network developed by Xerox, Intel, and DEC for connecting PCs, Macs, and printers together so they can share data

ezine a magazine that exists only on the INTERNET or on CD-ROM

face see TYPEFACE

family a set of FONTS related to a basic ROMAN TYPEFACE, which may include italic and bold plus a whole spectrum of different "weights"

FAQ (frequently asked questions) a list of questions and answers, usually relating to a particular NEWSGROUP. NEWBIES are encouraged to consult the FAQ before posting, so as not to annoy the old hands

feathering ink spreading from the edges of type, caused by poor-quality ink or paper

fillers additives in papermaking that improve the properties of the stock, for example increasing BULK and preventing FEATHERING

filling in when HALFTONE dots or the bowls of letters such as a or b fill solid with ink

film high-contrast photographic film used to transfer the image to the PLATE; can be positive (when the image is the same as the MECHANICAL) or negative (the white areas show black and vice versa)

filmless gravure in GRAVURE printing, digital information from the prepress system is fed directly to the diamond styli in the engraving heads that produce the printing cells

film recorder output device for making TRANSPARENCIES from an image created in the computer

final film containing all the pages and design elements assembled ready to make the plate

finish artist person who makes a neat camera-ready MECHANICAL from a designer's rough layout

finishing all the processes that convert printed sheets into folded and bound publications

firewall a security system consisting of HARDWARE and SOFTWARE that limits the exposure of a computer or computer network to attack from undesirable people on the INTERNET

FireWire (IEEE 1394 or I-link) a serial bus interface standard found mainly in digital video cameras but offering high-speed communications between computers, SCANNERS, and HARD-DISK drives; see also SCSI and USB

flame to post a harshly critical message in public on USENET or send very long abusive messages via EMAIL

flapping an overlay of tissue or ACETATE protecting artwork and mechanicals

flash memory a type of memory that can be electrically erased and reprogrammed, but needs no power to maintain the information stored in the chip

flat all the film assembled by the STRIPPER to make a 16- or 32-page plate

flat color, match color or **spot color** a single printing of a PANTONE color, printed solid or as TINTS, in REGISTER with the black

flatplan a diagram showing the position of pages in a publication along with a brief description of their content, used mainly to identify full-color and FLAT-COLOR sections

flat-tint halftone a black HALFTONE printed over a TINT of color, faking a DUOTONE

flexography (flexo) a form of relief printing, using fast-drying inks and rubber or plastic PLATES on a rotary LETTERPRESS

flocculation an ink defect that produces a surface like orange peel, caused by the PIGMENT not being properly dispersed in the VEHICLE

flong see MAT

flopped laterally inverted—normally applied to HALFTONES that have been STRIPPED into film wrongly

FM screening (frequency modulated) or **stochastic screening** using dots arranged randomly to reproduce CONTINUOUS-TONE artwork; see also AM (amplitude modulated) or conventional screening, which uses an array of differently sized dots

fold lines marks usually in the TRIM areas showing where sheets are to be folded

folio page number, or a single sheet of a manuscript

font a complete set *in one size* of all the letters of the alphabet, complete with associated LIGATURES (joined letters), numerals, punctuation marks, and any other signs and symbols

font masters a set of type designs in one or more sizes that are scaled (enlarged or reduced) to create all the intermediate sizes

font metrics the information about horizontal spacing built into a TYPEFACE by its designer

foot the bottom MARGIN of a page

fore edge the MARGIN of a page furthest from the SPINE

forme a locked-up CHASE in LETTERPRESS; also another name for a FLAT

fountain the ink reservoir in LETTERPRESS, or the container for the solution that dampens the rollers of an OFFSET LITHO press

four-color process full-color printing in which colors are approximated by various percentages of the PROCESS COLORS CYAN, MAGENTA, yellow, and black. A full-color image is separated by filters into four different films—one for each of the four process colors—and four PLATES are used for the printing

frame buffer computer memory that holds the current image on the screen; see also VRAM

frame grabber an input device that uses a television camera to capture a picture or three-dimensional object, or a video frame; it converts it into digital form readable by a computer program

French folds the double-thickness card covers that fold in on themselves to add thickness and a neater edge to expensive paperbacks

FTP (file transfer protocol) a protocol to let users transfer files between computers

fugitive inks that fade when exposed to light

furnish the liquid pulp that is converted into paper

galley proof a typesetting PROOF for checking the setting before the type is made up into pages; they are generally long and thin

gamut or **color space** the range of colors that can be reproduced on a color display, output device, or by a particular color-printing method—some colors available on a computer screen may not be printable using the CMYK process

ganging up grouping together several TRANSPARENCIES to be scanned together; also printing a group of different jobs on the same sheet of paper using a single PLATE

gathering see COLLATING

ghosting printing fault of a repeated image appearing next to the correct image, caused by faulty IMPOSITION; also a dull image on the other side of the sheet—this happens when the printed image affects the drying and TRAPPING of wet ink on the reverse

giclée (from the French for "spraying" or "spreading") medium-to-large format INKJET devices printing onto SUBSTRATES such as watercolor paper using archival ink

GIF (graphics interchange format) a common format for graphics containing flat areas of color; see also JPEG

glyph the specific form that a UNICODE CHARACTER can take: a lower case "a" and an alternate swash lower case "a" are the same character, but they are separate glyphs

Goldenrod orange or yellow opaque masking paper used to assemble negatives for exposure to PLATES

golden section an aesthetically pleasing proportion with many examples in nature; the ratio is 34:21 or 8.1:5

grain the orientation of fibers in paper, which lie in the direction of flow in a papermaking machine. "Grain long" means the grain is in the direction of the sheet's length. "Grain short" means the grain is in the direction of the sheet's width

gravure or **photogravure** an INTAGLIO PRINTING process in which the image is etched below the surface of a cylinder. The deeper the ink, the darker the tone.

gray component replacement or **achromatic stabilization** removing percentages of CYAN, MAGENTA, and yellow that cancel each other out to produce neutral grays, and replacing them with a tint of black

grayscale artwork or photograph in continuous tones of gray, between the extremes of black and white

greeking gray lines that indicate the presence of type on a computer screen; also the nonsense setting (usually Latin!) used by designers to show the position of type on a rough layout or DUMMY

grid the underlying structure for a page layout as prescribed by the designer, usually preprinted onto layout sheets or boards, or programmed into master pages in a digital page-layout program

gripper edge the edge of a sheet held by metal fingers in the press—a term used in IMPOSITION. The gripper margin is the allowance that avoids any damage caused by the grippers to the printed image

GUI (graphical user interface) what you see on the screen when you want to communicate with the program, the most famous being the WIMP (windows, icons, mouse, pull-down menus) interface of the Apple Macintosh, derived mostly from the smalltalk project at Xerox's PARC. Other "standards" include Windows for the PC and X-Windows for workstations.

gutter the combined MARGIN of a book or folder on each side of the SPINE; the margin on one side of the spine is called the BACK EDGE. The term gutter is also used for any vertical space, such as that between two columns

Gyricon "digital paper" having many of the properties of paper, but electronically writeable and erasable

hairline rule a rule thinner than 0.5 POINT

halation or **halo effect** when ink builds up around letters or dots, leaving the center lighter

half binding the SPINE, adjacent strips of the cover, and triangles at the corners are bound in one material, maybe leather, and the rest of the book in a less expensive material

halftone a CONTINUOUS-TONE image converted to line by turning it into a pattern of dots, either digitally, by laser, or by photographing it through a screen

hardcopy output from a computer system that you can hold in your hand—usually a paper PROOF

hard disk permanent magnetic memory, usually within the computer

hard dot a clean, regular, and sharp HALFTONE dot

hardware the parts of a computer system that you can see and touch

head the MARGIN at the top of a page

headband a decorative feature added to a case-bound book at the top of the SPINE

heat-set ink web ink that is dried quickly by heat and then chilled

Hexachrome a proprietary six-color system from PANTONE using brighter (fluorescent) versions of CMYK plus vivid orange and green; also referred to as HiFi color. See also FOUR-COLOR PROCESS

hickies imperfections in LITHO printing caused by any dry, hard particles on the cylinder or BLANKET, also called fisheyes, bull's eyes, donuts, and Newton's rings

high-fidelity printing or **HiFi printing** uses additional process inks to increase the GAMUT. PANTONE's hexachrome, for example, adds green and orange inks to the regular CMYK

hinge the crease in a book cover near the SPINE

hinting in computer FONTS, a method for changing the shapes of characters—especially those of small sizes— so that they look better on low-RESOLUTION printers

HLS (hue, luminance, saturation) a method for specifying colour; see CMYK and RGB

holdout the property of paper that makes it resist the absorption of ink

hologram a three-dimensional image created by laser photography, reproduced by hot-foil stamping or embossing on to reflective-backed mylar

home page your own WWW site, in which you can indulge your hobbies, try out your INTERNET skills, or publish an EZINE

hot-foil stamping transferring a foil coating from a carrier roll of polyester to paper or cover board by means of a heated die

hot-metal setting casting molten metal into molds to produce type for LETTERPRESS printing

house style standards of consistency concerning spelling and use of English (or any other language) as laid down by a particular publisher, or to be used within a particular publication

HTML (hypertext markup language) text-based language used to create and communicate **WWW** pages

HTTP (hypertext transport protocol) the protocol of the World Wide Web

hue the rainbow parameter of a color that distinguishes, for example, red from blue

hyphenation the division of words, usually between syllables, pairs of consonants, or pairs of vowels

icon a small picture on a computer screen representing an application, tool, or document

imagesetter a high-RESOLUTION output device that produces film or BROMIDE prints from a POSTSCRIPT file, so called because it can output LINE art and HALFTONE images as well as type; see also PLATESETTER

imposetter IMAGESETTER which, with imposition software, produces film negatives with pages in position ready for platemaking

imposing table in LETTERPRESS, the place where galleys are assembled

imposition the layout of pages such that after printing, folding, collating, and trimming they will all end up in the correct order and the right way up

impression the process of transferring ink from PLATE to paper during printing

impression cylinder in an OFFSET LITHO press, the cylinder that presses the paper against the BLANKET CYLINDER

InDesign a page-layout program from Adobe, and successor to PAGEMAKER

inkjet printer an output device that creates an image by spraying tiny drops of ink on to paper; see also BUBBLEJET PRINTER

inkometer or **tackoscope** an instrument for measuring the tackiness of ink

ink pyramid in an OFFSET LITHO press, the system of rollers that conveys ink to the PLATE

in-line an in-line press has several single units arranged to print one color after another; also a process, such as folding or gluing, that happens straight after the printing, in the same pass

insert any printed material that is included during BINDING. Material wrapped around a SIGNATURE is called a wrap. A loose insert is not attached to the "parent" publication and will fall out when it is shaken

intaglio printing a method in which the ink is contained in grooves below the surface of the PLATE and transferred to dampened paper by pressure

internet a network of networks based on the TCP/IP protocols, a community of people who use and develop those networks, and a collection of resources that can be reached from those networks

intranet a local network, such as within a corporation, using the same tools as the INTERNET, EMAIL, and WWW pages, for example

IRC (internet relay chat) a means of communicating in text in real time with other INTERNET users employing a program such as Homer

ISDN (integrated services digital network) a dedicated digital telephone line—you don't need a MODEM

ISP (internet service provider) the company you dial up to get on to the INTERNET

Java a C++ based programming language from Sun that is object-oriented and platform-independent—tiny programs called applets are downloaded and embedded in the HTML code

JDF (job definition format) an open standard for a digital job ticket, reducing the need for information to be re-keyed

jogging vibrating paper stock before trimming to bring all the edges into alignment

JPEG (joint photographic experts group) a common format for graphics containing CONTINUOUS TONES of color, such as photographs; see also GIF

justified type set with edges that are aligned both left and right. Justified setting requires hyphenation and variable spacing between words

k–p distance the distance from the top of a letter k to the bottom of a letter p

kenaf a plant from Asia and parts of Africa, and now grown in the USA, that has many environmental advantages over trees in papermaking

kerning adjusting the spacing between pairs of letters, such as T and A, to improve the aesthetic appearance; see also TRACKING

key black in four-color printing; see CMYK

keyline the marks on a MECHANICAL's OVERLAY that indicate the position of TINTS, HALFTONES, and BLEEDS. A keyline artist is a person who assembles the finished mechanical

knife folder a folding machine that uses a knife to force the sheet between two nip rollers

L*a*b a device-independent color model proposed by the Commission Internationale de l'Eclairage: L is for luminance; a and b are chromatic components—a for green to red, and b for blue to yellow

lacquer see VARNISHING

laid a paper texture created on the Fourdrinier wire; it has a characteristic lined appearance

lamination coating paper or cover board with a clear film to add strength and gloss

landscape the orientation of a page when the width is greater than the height

laser printer an output device in which TONER is attracted to an image on a drum that has had electrostatic charge removed by the action of a laser; the image is transferred to paper and fixed by heat

late binding the term used to mean last-minute changes within POSTSCRIPT files while they are in the RIP, such as adding TRAPPING and IMPOSITION information, particularly for digital presses

laydown sequence the sequence in which colors are printed—usually yellow, MAGENTA, CYAN, and finally black

lay edge the left side of the sheet as it passes through the press; the lay edge will change to the right side if the sheet is to be printed on the reverse

LCD (liquid crystal display) thin, flicker-free computer-display technology

leading or **interline spacing** the space between lines of type; in LETTERPRESS these were strips of lead

leave edge the edge of a sheet opposite the GRIPPER EDGE

letterpress a RELIEF PRINTING process, in which ink is transferred from the raised surface of metal or wooden type directly on to paper

letterset an indirect LETTERPRESS printing process, in which the image is first transferred to a BLANKET, and then on to the paper

ligature two or more letters, such as fi and ffl, joined together into one character

line artwork in black (or any other single color) and white only, with no intermediate tones of gray, which will print without first being screened

linen tester see LOUPE

Linotype a typesetting machine for LETTERPRESS in which a whole line of type (line o' type), or SLUG, is cast in one operation

linters in papermaking, the fibers left on the cotton seed once the longer fibers have been removed for yarn-making

linting a printing problem caused by paper fibers that get on to the BLANKET, PLATE, or rollers of a press

literals in proofreading, the spelling mistakes and transposition of letters caused by typing errors

lithography a PLANOGRAPHIC PRINTING process in which greasy ink is transferred from the surface of a dampened plate or stone directly on to paper. OFFSET LITHOGRAPHY, usually shortened to offset litho, prints first on to a rubber or plastic BLANKET, and then on to the paper

loupe designer's magnifying glass, also called a linen tester or eyeglass; used for checking color TRANSPARENCIES and HALFTONE dots

low spot loss of image caused by an indentation in the BLANKET of an OFFSET press

luminance see VALUE

machine code the lowest level of computer language—lists of hexadecimal numbers

machine finish (MF) paper that has been CALENDERED and is smoother and less bulky than EGGSHELL PAPER

machine glazed (MG) paper that has been dried against a highly polished cylinder and has one glossy side while the other remains relatively rough

machine proof see PRESS PROOF

magenta the PROCESS COLOR red, really more a purple

mailing list an EMAIL discussion group, in which a message sent to the list server is broadcast to anyone "subscribing" to that particular list

make-ready setting up the press ready to print

make-up to assemble, position, and paste type and graphic elements to produce a MECHANICAL or FLAT

manuscript the original COPY for typesetting, shortened to Ms

margins the areas of white between the text and the edges of the page

mark up to write instructions on text to define how it is to be set in type

mask shape cut out of opaque material such as RUBYLITH or GOLDENROD to shield film from exposure to light; also used in image manipulation programs such as Photoshop

master proof a clean and neat PROOF on to which the corrections and comments of all interested parties are collated

mat or **flong** in LETTERPRESS, a papier-mâché mold taken from the FORME and used to make a STEREOTYPE; an abbreviation for MATRIX

match color see FLAT COLOR

Matchprint a proprietary prepress proofing system from Imation

matrix a metal mold used to cast metal type; also any array or pattern of PIXELS, as in DITHERING; see also MAT

matte dull finish, the opposite of glossy

measure the width of a line of type—usually the column width, specified in PICA EMS

mechanical camera-ready artwork on boards, or all the LINE artwork for a page layout with the HALFTONES marked "for position only", also called camera-ready copy. Mechanical SEPARATIONS are sets of OVERLAYS in REGISTER containing the artwork for FLAT COLOR

mechanical tints patterns of dots simulating shades of gray or FLAT COLOR added by the process blockmaker (Ben Day tints) or printer according to the designer's instructions

menu in computing, a list of options or commands from which you are invited to choose

mesh count a measure of the fineness of the mesh in the screens used in SCREENPRINTING—the number of threads per inch

mesh grade thread thickness in the screens used in SCREENPRINTING

metallic inks inks that contain metal dust, producing a sheen when printed

micrometer an instrument for measuring very small distances, such as the thickness of paper; also one millionth of a meter

mil one thousandth of an inch

mirror site stores copies of files from main internet sites, but may be geographically closer to you

modem (MOdulator DEModulator) a device to convert digital data from your computer into analog data that can travel down the telephone line

moiré patterns unwanted "basketweave" effects caused by superimposed regular patterns, such as HALFTONE dots. Screens must be set at angles that minimize the moiré effect

mold-made paper paper made by a semi-automatic process to resemble handmade paper

mono, monochrome black and white, or the various tones of one color

Monotype a LETTERPRESS typesetting machine that casts individual metal letters in a two-stage process

mottle an uneven impression caused by too much dampening water or the wrong choice of paper and ink

mouse in computing, a small pointing device used to control a cursor on the screen

M weight the weight of paper as measured per thousand sheets

negative-working plate OFFSET LITHO PLATE prepared by exposure to negative film

netiquette a code of conduct or good manners for the INTERNET

networking linking computers together so that they can communicate with each other and share output devices such as LASER PRINTERS and file servers

newbie a new user to the INTERNET, particularly to NEWSGROUPS

newsgroup a "bulletin board" of articles on a specific topic, arranged in threads; see also USENET (UNIX USER NETWORK)

newsprint inexpensive, rough, absorbent paper used for printing newspapers and some magazines

NTSC (national television systems committee) the US standard of the FCC (Federal Communications Commission) for broadcast television

offset abbreviation for offset lithography; also the same as setoff—when ink transfers from one printed sheet to the back of another

offset lithography or **offset litho** a PLANOGRAPHIC PRINTING process in which greasy ink is transferred from the surface of a dampened PLATE first on to a rubber or plastic BLANKET, and then on to the paper

offset process see OFFSET LITHOGRAPHY

one-up printing a single job on one PLATE. Quality is better controlled, but it is usually more economical to print two-up, i.e. two different jobs, or the same job in tandem, on one plate

opacimeter an instrument for measuring the OPACITY of paper

opacity the property of a paper affecting the SHOW-THROUGH of printing from the other side of the sheet

operating system behind-the-scenes computer software that takes care of the internal workings of the computer

OpenType a FONT format developed jointly by Adobe and Microsoft compatible with Macs and PCs, also supporting expanded CHARACTER SETS

OPI (open prepress interface) a protocol, originally proposed by Aldus, which enables files from different digital prepress programs to be used together

optical brighteners additives to paper that increase its brightness by glowing under the influence of ultraviolet light

opticals OPENTYPE FONTS optimized for use at specific POINT sizes: caption (6–8 pt), regular (9–13 pt), subhead (12–24 pt), and display (25–72 pt)

oriented polypropylene (opp) lamination the standard book jacket lamination film

orphan(s) a single word or a few words, usually less than a third the MEASURE of the setting, forming a line of its own at the end of a paragraph; see also WIDOW

orthochromatic film sensitive to the blue end of the spectrum used for LINE work—red records as black, and marks in light-blue pencil are invisible; see also PANCHROMATIC

out of register the blurred effect that occurs when film SEPARATIONS or PLATES are misaligned

overlay a sheet of ACETATE or tissue over a photograph or in REGISTRATION with a MECHANICAL, containing artwork for FLAT COLOR, KEYLINES, or instructions to the printer

overmatter setting or images that are excess to requirements, to be used in the next issue of a magazine, for example

overprint color, usually black, printed over FLAT COLOR

overruns or **run-ons** sheets printed beyond the quantity specified, to compensate for spoilage or for the client's own use

ozalid see BLUEPRINT and BROWNLINE

PageMaker a page-layout program from Adobe, originally developed by Aldus, and superseded by InDesign

page proof a PROOF showing type arranged on a page, along with FOLIOS, RUNNING HEADS, captions, and sometimes the position of illustrations

pagination the sequence of pages in a book or folder

paint program or **paint system** a computer program that stores the image on the screen as a bitmap; see also DRAW PROGRAM

PAL (phase alternation line) the standard in the UK and most of Europe for broadcast television

panchromatic film that records all colors equally, as opposed to ORTHOCHROMATIC which does not "see" the blue end of the spectrum

Pantone Matching System (PMS) a widely used proprietary system for specifying FLAT COLOR in percentages of eleven standard colors; papers and markers corresponding to Pantone colors can also be purchased

paper-creep allowance allowing for the thickness of paper at the SPINE of a thick, SADDLE-STITCHED publication by shifting the MARGINS on the MECHANICAL so that the margins remain consistent after the sheets are trimmed

paper curl wavy edges caused by the stack of paper having a lower moisture level than the surroundings, or tight edges caused by the stack having a higher moisture level

paste up to cut and assemble typesetting, LINE art, and HALFTONES on to board using gum or wax, so as to produce a MECHANICAL

PCF (processed chlorine-free) in papermaking means that the recycled fiber in the sheet is unbleached or bleached with non-chlorine compounds

PDF (portable document format) a DOCUMENT format that uses a reader such as Adobe Acrobat to recreate the appearance of FONTS and spacing in your page layout

pen plotter a point-to-point output device used mainly for engineering drawings; if equipped with a knife in place of the pen it can be used to cut stencils for SCREENPRINTING or vinyl letters for signs

perfect binding trimmed single sheets of paper bound with glue to produce a book or magazine with a flat SPINE

perfecting press a press that prints both sides of the sheet at the same time

perforation producing the tear-along lines on coupons or stamps, for example, by piercing with sharp metal strips

personal computer a stand-alone desktop computer; a PC is an IBM Personal Computer or a software-compatible system from a supplier such as Compaq

personalization in digital print where a person's details, such as name and address, are changed between each DOCUMENT printed

photogravure see GRAVURE

phototypesetting or **photosetting** a process in which type is set on to BROMIDE paper or film by exposure of light through a MATRIX containing tiny negatives of the letters, or directly by the action of a laser beam

pica or **pica em** a unit for measuring type equal to ⅙ inch, or 12 POINTS; on a typewriter, the normal PITCH of 10 characters per inch

pi characters Greek and mathematical signs, used with but not typically part of a FONT

picking removal of some of the surface of paper during printing

PictBridge an open standard for connecting a digital camera directly to a DYE-SUBLIMATION or INKJET PRINTER

pigments and dyes components of printing inks that give it color

piling sticking or caking of ink PIGMENT on the BLANKET or PLATE

pin register accurate positioning system for COLOR SEPARATIONS—both films and plates—with punched holes and corresponding pins

pitch on typewriters, the number of characters per inch

pixel pixel is short for picture element and is the dot on a computer display. The RESOLUTION (sharpness) of a RASTER display is measured by the number of pixels horizontally by the number of scan lines vertically, e.g. 1280 × 1024

planographic printing any process using a PLATE on which both the printing and non-printing areas are on the same surface, e.g. LITHOGRAPHY

plastic comb a type of ring BINDING found on reports and manuals

plate a metal or plastic sheet with photosensitive face on to which an image is chemically etched, either changing the characteristics of the surface as in LITHOGRAPHY, or cutting below the surface as in RELIEF or INTAGLIO PRINTING

plate cylinder in an OFFSET LITHO press, the cylinder to which the PLATE is attached

plate-damping unit in OFFSET LITHO, the system of rollers that dampens the plate before inking; see also FOUNTAIN

platen a small LETTERPRESS that acts like a clamshell, bringing a flat PLATE and the paper together in an opening and closing motion, as opposed to a ROTARY PRESS

platesetter a device that processes PLATES direct from a POSTSCRIPT file; see also IMAGESETTER

PMT (photomechanical transfer) a DIFFUSION TRANSFER process for enlarging or reducing LINE art; also called a BROMIDE

PNG (portable network graphics) a lossless, portable format coming into use that provides a patent-free replacement for GIF and can also replace many common uses of TIFF

point a unit for measuring type equal to approximately ½2 inch (exactly ½2 inch in computer systems), abbreviated pt; also a measure of paper BULK equivalent to one thousandth of an inch (a MIL)

portrait the orientation of a page when the height is greater than the width

positive-working plate an OFFSET LITHO PLATE prepared by exposure to positive film

PostScript an outline description language for type developed by Adobe and licensed to suppliers such as Linotype, Monotype, Agfa, and AM Varityper. Type 1 PostScript FONTS contain HINTING and encryption; see also EPS and TRUETYPE

PPP (point-to-point protocol) the gateway from your client SOFTWARE, e.g. Mail for EMAIL, to the INTERNET, see also SLIP

preflighting checking output from page-layout programs such as InDesign and QuarkXPress to see if all images and FONTS are present and that there will be no problems with files at the printers

prepress proof a PROOF taken directly from the film SEPARATIONS, to check that the color will print correctly

press proof a PROOF taken from the PLATES that will be used to print the finished job, and on the specified paper stock, usually on a special proofing press, also called MACHINE PROOF or WET PROOF

printing-down frame in OFFSET LITHO, a device for holding the film and PLATE in contact during exposure to ultraviolet light

print run the number of copies to be produced in one printing, also called the press run

process camera a camera designed to enlarge or reduce artwork and MECHANICALS, and produce film positives and negatives

process colors the four colors—CYAN (process blue), MAGENTA (process red), yellow, and key (black)—used to approximate full-color artwork

progressives a set of PROOFS showing the four color SEPARATIONS printed in various combinations; also called hollywoods or progs

proof hardcopy that allows you to check the accuracy of setting, the position of design elements on a page, or the fidelity of color after separation

proofing press a small press used to produce PROOFS

proportional scale see REPRODUCTION CALCULATOR

quad a square space in typesetting used as a unit of measurement, such as an EM quad or EN quad

QuarkXPress a digital page-layout program

quarter binding the SPINE and adjacent strips of the cover are bound in one material, maybe leather, and the rest of the sides in a less expensive material

RAM (random access memory) quick-access temporary memory in a computer, containing the job in hand, in the form of chips

ranged left/right ranged left is a method of setting type in which the type is aligned on the left-hand side and ragged on the right. Ranged right is ragged on the left and aligned on the right

raster a horizontal scan line on a computer screen or output device

RAW (no acronym) a "digital negative" format for digital cameras that is not directly usable as an image, yet comprises the information needed to create an uncompressed image within image-processing software, such as Photoshop

ream 500 sheets of paper

recto the front of a sheet of paper, or the right-hand page of a publication; opposite of VERSO

reflected light colors from an object or flat artwork, as opposed to TRANSMITTED LIGHT from a light source or TRANSPARENCY

reflection copy any original art viewed by light reflecting from its surface, as opposed to TRANSMISSION COPY such as a 35 mm slide

register or **registration** correct positioning of one COLOR SEPARATION in relation to the others during printing. A register mark is a symbol used on COPY and film to ensure accurate registration

relief printing a printing process, such as LETTERPRESS and FLEXOGRAPHY, in which ink lies on the raised surface of the PLATE but not in the grooves and is transferred to the paper by pressure

reproduction calculator or **proportional scale** a slide-rule type instrument for estimating the size of an illustration after reduction or enlargement

reproduction proof or **repro proof** a crisp PROOF on art paper of LETTERPRESS setting to be used on a MECHANICAL

repurposing adapting an existing page layout to become a different format or medium, such as a WWW page

resist a substance used on PLATES for preventing the non-printing areas from etching

resolution a measure of the fineness and quality of an output device, usually measured in dots per inch (DPI)—the number of dots that can be placed end to end in a line an inch long; see also ADDRESSABILITY

retouching modifying or correcting photographic images either manually with dye and airbrush, or electronically to a scanned image using a program such as Photoshop or Quantel Paintbox

reversed out when type is set in white against a black or flat-color background

RGB (red, green, blue) a system for specifying color on a computer screen; see also CMYK

rich black a black object or area that prints even darker with the use of undercolors, usually CYAN

right-reading emulsion down (RRED) film used for OFFSET LITHO platemaking in which the image appears the correct way round when the film is viewed from the shiny (non-EMULSION) side, also called WRONG-READING EMULSION UP (WREU)

right-reading emulsion up (RREU) film used for direct forms of platemaking, such as LETTERPRESS and FLEXOGRAPHY, in which the image appears the correct way round when the film is viewed from the dull EMULSION SIDE, also called WRONG-READING EMULSION DOWN (WRED)

RIP (RASTER image processor) a device that converts a POSTSCRIPT file into a BITMAP that can be output from an IMAGESETTER or PLATESETTER

rivers unwanted space running vertically and diagonally in chunks of (mainly JUSTIFIED) type—to be avoided

rolling ball a pointing device that controls the position of a cursor on the computer screen

ROM (read-only memory) permanent unalterable computer memory in the form of chips; also abbreviation for ROMAN

roman normal type, as opposed to italic or bold; also a kind of type with SERIFS such as Times New Roman

rotary press a press that uses a cylinder as its printing surface, as opposed to a flatbed or PLATEN press

rotogravure see GRAVURE

rounding and backing (R&B) putting a rounded shape into the SPINE of a book-block, and a joint below the shoulder

Rubylith a red, transparent MASKING material

runaround type set around a photograph or other design element, deviating away from the normal MEASURE

running heads headlines that appear in the same (or a symmetrical) position on every page of a publication, except where chapter titles occur or if illustrations outside the GRID area displace them

saddle stitching a BINDING method using wire staples along the fold of the publication

sans serif a typeface without SERIFS

saturation or **intensity** a measure of the color's position in the range from neutral gray to fully saturated, or bright, color

scaling enlarging or reducing—usually applied to an image—and calculating the percentage of enlargement or reduction so as to anticipate the space it will occupy in a layout

scanner an electronic device used to convert artwork or TRANSPARENCIES into digital form

scatter proofs PROOFS with several illustrations printed randomly together on one sheet, not in their correct positions on the page

score creasing a sheet of paper or board so that it will fold easily

screen a piece of glass or plastic used to convert CONTINUOUS-TONE COPY into a HALFTONE; also the frequency of dots, expressed in lines per inch or lpi

screenprinting a printing process using a stencil supported on a mesh or screen; ink is forced through the open mesh but is prevented from reaching the non-image areas of the paper by the stencil

SCSI (small computer system interface) a parallel interface used to connect computers with SCANNERS and other peripherals; see also USB and FIREWIRE

scuffing a problem in packaging design, where print is more likely to receive rough handling; scuffproof ink, LAMINATION, or a coat of varnish is the solution

scumming a printing problem caused when the plate accepts ink where it shouldn't

section sewing a BINDING method in which SIGNATURES are sewn through the SPINE with thread before being casebound

self cover a cover printed on the same paper stock as the rest of the publication, using the same PLATE as pages from the inside

separation film in REGISTER relating to one of the four PROCESS COLORS; also artwork or film in register relating to FLAT COLOR

series a complete range of sizes in the same TYPEFACE

serif the mark that terminates the ends of the letters in some TYPEFACES

service bureau a place where you can rent expensive equipment by the hour, or have laser prints, BROMIDES, and film output from an IMAGESETTER from your disk at a price per sheet

set the width of a letter

setoff or **offset** this occurs when the wet image on a sheet of paper prints on to the paper above or below it in the pile. Anti-setoff spray should separate each sheet with a fine layer of particles

set solid type set without LEADING, for example 10/10 pt

set-up time the time it takes to MAKE-READY and set up the press to run your job

SGML (standard generalized markup language) a generic MARKUP language for representing DOCUMENTS—an international standard that describes the relationship between a document's content and its structure

sheetfed a press taking single sheets of paper

sheetwise a form of IMPOSITION using one PLATE to print the front of a sheet, and another to print the back

shingling see PAPER-CREEP ALLOWANCE

show-through or **strike-through** being able to see through a sheet of paper to the printed IMPRESSION on the other side

side bearings the space allocated on either side of a letter by its designer to stop adjacent letters from touching and to achieve an aesthetically pleasing appearance when words are set

side sewing a form of BINDING used mainly for children's books in which the thread is sewn near the SPINE, front to back, as in SIDE STABBING

side-stabbing a form of BINDING in which wire staples are inserted near the SPINE from front to back

signature several pages for a book, printed from the same PLATE and arranged so that they can be folded and trimmed to make a section, usually of 16 pages. A BACKSTEP MARK on the SPINE shows how several signatures are to be arranged so they bind in the correct sequence

silkscreen see SCREENPRINTING

size in papermaking, substances added to the FURNISH to make the paper less absorbent, which can also be coated or sprayed on to the WEB at a later stage of the process at the size press; sizing can also be used to mean SCALING

skewing a printing problem that occurs when paper, BLANKET, and cylinder are not in proper contact

SLIP (serial line internet protocol) the gateway from your client SOFTWARE, e.g. Mail for EMAIL, to the INTERNET; see also PPP

slug a line of LETTERPRESS type from a LINOTYPE machine, or a piece of metal used for word spacing

slurring distortion of the image, with dots appearing elongated or smeared, caused by too much ink or slippage of stock

slurry in papermaking, fibers with lots of water

SmartMedia memory storage cards for Olympus and Fujifilm DIGITAL CAMERAS; see also COMPACTFLASH

smiley symbol made from ASCII characters meant to convey emotions, e.g. :-)

snowflaking in OFFSET LITHO, a problem of water droplets in the litho ink that spoil solid areas; in GRAVURE the effect is caused by inadequate pressure which prevents the paper from taking the ink from one or more cells

soft dot HALFTONE dot slightly out of focus

soft proofing a way of simulating the look of a paper proof on a computer screen

software the list of instructions that turn a general-purpose computer into a machine for a particular purpose, such as digital-page layout or image manipulation

sorts in LETTERPRESS, individual pieces of metal type

spamming (from the Monty Python song "Spam") CROSSPOSTING a carelessly inappropriate message or advertisement to many different groups or individuals

spine the bound edge of a book or magazine, where the fold is

spiral-bound a method of BINDING used for calendars, cookery books, and manuals, using a wire spiral inserted through holes in the pages

split fountain printing two colors on an OFFSET press by using one color at one end of the FOUNTAIN and another at the other end—the colors blend in the middle

spoilage wasted printed sheets that are discarded

spot color see FLAT COLOR

spot varnish applying patches of varnish, often to make HALFTONES glossy

spreading an enlarging of the image caused by too much ink, or too much pressure between BLANKET and PLATE

standard lighting conditions a light source with a color temperature of 5000° Kelvin

standard viewing conditions an area to view color PROOFS, surrounded by neutral gray and illuminated by STANDARD LIGHTING CONDITIONS

starvation ghosting an unwelcome effect that results in uneven printing and is due to some extent to the placement of dense black elements in certain positions on the PLATE

stencil printing a printing process, such as SCREENPRINTING, using a stencil supported on a mesh or screen; ink is forced through the open mesh but is prevented from reaching the non-image areas of the paper by the stencil

step-and-repeat a method for copying film, so that two or more parts of the same job can be printed from one PLATE

stereotype or **stereo** a LETTERPRESS PLATE made by casting lead in a papier-mâché mold (a MAT or flong) taken from the FORME. It can be flat for flatbed presses or curved for ROTARY machines

stet a proofreading mark meaning reinstate, or "let it stand," i.e. print what was there originally

sticking or **blocking** so much SETOFF that the sheets stick together

stochastic screening or **FM screening** using dots arranged randomly to reproduce CONTINUOUS-TONE artwork; see also AM (amplitude modulated) or conventional screening which uses a regular array of differently sized dots

stream feeder a mechanism on high-speed sheetfed presses that presents sheets to the rollers overlapping slightly

strike-on setting see COLD-METAL SETTING

strike-through see SHOW-THROUGH

stripping in inserting HALFTONES on film into the film made from a MECHANICAL. A stripper is a person who assembles film into the final

style sheet a paper document or feature of a page-layout program that sets out the specifications for a publication or series of publications, listing such things as the TYPEFACE, size, LEADING of body text headlines, and captions

substrate any sheet material to be printed— paper, board, plastic, or another substance. Also the carrier material in film, for example, on to which a layer of emulsion is deposited

super-calendering smoothing paper by pressing it between highly polished cylinders, done off the machine

surprint superimposing type on to a TINT of the same color—they share the same film and are printed together

swatch book a book of tear-off color samples; the most commonly used come from PANTONE

SWOP (specifications for web offset publications) standard ink colors and DOT-GAIN tolerances established by the magazine publishers' association

system a catch-all term meaning all the computer equipment you need to make things work (as in "the system's down"); also the operating system (as in System 7); or a set of SOFTWARE tools (as in a digital prepress system)

tack the adhesive property of an ink

tag HTML code that the BROWSER interprets "on the fly" as the web page arrives from the server to the client. Tags usually have a start and an end, "containing" the item in question. The first part of the tag turns an attribute on and the second turns the attribute off. Tags are surrounded by angled brackets (the "less than" and "greater than" symbols) and the closing tag is preceded by a slash symbol (/)

tailband a decorative feature added to a casebound book at the bottom of the SPINE

tail-end hook when solid areas near the back edge of a sheet make it curl down, caused by paper that adheres to the BLANKET too tightly as it is pulled off by the delivery grippers because the ink is too tacky

TCF (totally chlorine-free) in papermaking, chlorine-free bleaches, such as hydrogen peroxide

TCP/IP (transmission control protocol/ internet protocol) the standards that enable computers to pass information between each other on the INTERNET

telnet a program that lets you log on to another computer, anywhere on the INTERNET, as if you were using a terminal attached to that computer

thermal-transfer printer an output device that prints by "ironing" colored wax on to paper by the action of heat

thermal-transfer prints color PROOFS produced by melting colored waxes on to paper

thermography creating a raised IMPRESSION by using a heat-treated resinous powder

thermojet printer a form of INKJET printer which sprays melted plastic onto the paper, also known as a phase-change inkjet

thread-sealing a combination of some of the features of PERFECT BINDING and SECTION SEWING, but no thread runs between sections

TIFF (tagged image file format) a protocol for dealing with scanned photographs in digital prepress programs

tint shades of a FLAT COLOR created by patterns of dots similar to HALFTONES, specified as a percentage of the solid color

tinting a printing problem of PIGMENT finding its way into the FOUNTAIN, discoloring the background

tip in a page-size INSERT glued to the edge of a signature

tip on a small insert glued to the surface of a page, such as a coupon

toner digital "ink," used in photocopiers and digital presses

tool a facility in a computer program that makes something happen—a circle tool, for example, allows you to draw circles in different ways; tools are usually represented by ICONS

tracking adjusting the spacing between all letters, as opposed to KERNING, which only adjusts the space between pairs of letters; also, when several colored images are printed in a row and inking becomes uneven as a result

transmission copy COPY, such as TRANSPARENCIES and film positives, viewed by TRANSMITTED LIGHT

transmitted light colors from a light source or a TRANSPARENCY, as opposed to REFLECTED LIGHT from a print or flat artwork

transparency a color slide, usually either 35 mm, 5 in by 4 in, or 10 in by 8 in, so-called TRANSMISSION COPY

trap a small nick in the design of letters to allow for ink spread, especially around junctions

trapping creating an overlap between areas of FLAT COLOR to compensate for any misregistration—usually the lighter color overlaps the darker; also any area of color overlapping another. A **spread** traps a light foreground object to a dark background; a **choke** traps a light background to a dark foreground object. Rich blacks require keepaway: the undercolor is made smaller than the black, so that should the inks misregister the undercolor is covered by the black

trim and center marks indications of where paper sheets are to be trimmed and folded; they mark out the finished page area

TrueType an outline description format from Apple and Microsoft which rivals POSTSCRIPT

turnkey system a packaged and integrated assembly of HARDWARE, SOFTWARE, and support. Turnkey suppliers buy in equipment from third parties and repackage or "badge engineer" the components, perhaps adding some proprietary go-faster boards as well as their own software, before passing on the "value-added" system to the end user

TWAIN standard for connecting SCANNERS and PERSONAL COMPUTERS, from Kipling's "The Ballad of East and West"— ". . . And never the twain shall meet . . ." aka "Technology Without An Interesting Name"

two-up see ONE-UP

typeface the design of a FONT

type specification a list of all the TYPEFACES, sizes, and LEADING to be used for body type, headlines, captions, and so on, in a publication or series of publications; see also STYLE SHEET

undercolor addition (UCA) adding a TINT of PROCESS COLOR to add density to a black; see also RICH BLACK

undercolor removal (UCR) reducing the amount of color in areas of shadows, to save ink and improve TRAPPING

Unicode an international standard for CHARACTER encoding, for most languages

units letters of different widths in a TYPEFACE are allocated different numbers of units in accordance with a scheme that is devised by the typographer and the type foundry and dependent on the output process being used

upload using FTP to send a file from your computer, such as your WWW home page, to a remote server

URL (uniform resource locator) the unique address of a WWW page, of the form: http://www.your_isp.com/user_name/index.html

USB (universal serial bus) a hot-swappable interface used to connect computers with SCANNERS and other peripherals; see also SCSI and FIREWIRE

Usenet (unix user network) a collection of NEWSGROUPS, each containing articles on a specific topic, arranged in threads

value or **luminance** the parameter of color describing lightness or darkness, changed by adding black or white to a particular HUE

varnishing coating areas of a page with a colorless varnish or lacquer to improve gloss on HALFTONES, for example

vector uses geometrical formulas for lines, curves, and shapes to represent images. Compare with BITMAP

vehicle the component of a printing ink that carries and binds the PIGMENT

velox a HALFTONE on BROMIDE paper that can be pasted on to a MECHANICAL and used for undemanding printing

versioning in digital print where larger runs of a generic DOCUMENT are broken down into many slightly amended shorter runs (with details of a local office or staff on a sales brochure, for example)

verso the back of a sheet of paper, or the left-hand page of a publication, opposite of RECTO

VGA (video graphics array) developed by IBM for the PS/2 computer. Its standard resolution is 640 x 480 PIXELS, extendable to 1024 x 768, and it can display 256 colors from a palette of 256k

vignette a HALFTONE that fades to nothing around the edges

virus a pernicious and self-replicating piece of mischief that can cause havoc in a computer or via the INTERNET

viscosity the amount of flow and tack in an ink

VRAM (video random-access memory); also known as FRAME BUFFER

VRML (virtual reality modeling language) a platform-independent language for describing 3D virtual-reality scenes

waterless plates in OFFSET LITHO printing, waterless plates consist of ink on aluminum for the image areas and a silicone rubber for the non-printing areas. Silicone rubber has very low surface tension and thus will repel ink.

watermark a symbol or mark manufactured into paper which can be seen when the sheet is held to the light

web a continuous roll of paper used on web-fed presses, cut into sheets after printing; also short for World Wide Web

web proofing a PDF stored centrally so everyone always has access to an up-to-date proof, with a full history of changes. Also called Web-to-print or Web2Print

websafe colors 216 colors that will be displayed by a BROWSER without resorting to DITHERING (optically mixing two or more colors)

wet-on-wet one color is still wet as another is printed

wet proof see PRESS PROOF

widow a single word or part of a word from the end of a paragraph left at the top of a new column or page; see also ORPHANS

WIMP windows, icons, mouse, and pull-down menus (or windows, icons, menus, and pointing device), the original Mac GUI with which the user tells the computer what to do by pointing and clicking at ICONS (little pictures) and MENU items (lists of available options) on the screen using a MOUSE or other pointing device

window a transparent hole in a negative awaiting a HALFTONE to be STRIPPED IN; also an active and independent area of a computer screen

Windows a WIMP operating system for PCs developed by Microsoft

wire comb a form of spiral BINDING used for reports, cookery books, and manuals

woodfree chemical woodpulp for papermaking

woodpulp wood that has been debarked and separated into fibers for papermaking, either by grinding (mechanical WOODPULP) or by cooking in chemicals (chemical or woodfree woodpulp)

work-and-tumble an IMPOSITION scheme in which both sides of a job can be printed, in two passes, by a single PLATE: one side is printed, then the sheet is turned head-over-heels so that the GRIPPER EDGE changes ends

work-and-turn an IMPOSITION scheme in which both sides of a job can be printed, in two passes, by a single PLATE: one side is printed, then the sheet is turned sideways so that the lay edge changes sides but the GRIPPER EDGE remains the same

workstation a type of networkable computer, more powerful than a personal computer, made by companies such as Sun and Silicon Graphics

wove a paper texture introduced on the Fourdrinier wire; it has a characteristic woven appearance (or sometimes no detectable texture); see also LAID

wrong-reading emulsion down (WRED) see RIGHT-READING EMULSION UP (RREU)

wrong-reading emulsion up (WREU) see RIGHT-READING EMULSION DOWN (RRED)

WWW (World Wide Web) interconnected INTERNET "pages" viewed by a BROWSER, such as Firefox, containing text, images, sound, movies, and hypertext "hot links" to other pages

WYSIWYG (what you see is what you get) in computer SOFTWARE, a screen-based representation of a printed or WWW page that approximates what you will see in the finished product, as opposed to a list of computer code

xerography a copying process using black TONER attracted to an image on an electrostatically charged drum; the toner is transferred to paper and fixed by heat

x-height the height of a letter x in a particular TYPEFACE—a typographic measurement which ignores the height of the ASCENDERS and DESCENDERS

XHTML a reformulation of HTML 4.01 in XML

XML (extensible markup language) a simple subset of SGML suitable for use on the World Wide Web

Abbreviations and acronyms

AFAIK as far as I know
AM amplitude modulated
APR automatic picture replacement
ASCII American Standard Code for Information Interchange
ADSL Asymmetric Digital Subscriber Line—or loop
A/UX a workstation operating system, a version of Unix
A/W artwork
BTW by the way
C++ a high-level computer language
CCD charge-coupled device
CD-ROM Compact Disk-Read-Only Memory
CEPS Color Electronic Publishing System
CIE Commission Internationale de l'Eclairage
CIP3 Cooperation for the Integration of Processes in Prepress, Press, and Postpress
CMM color-matching module
CMS color-management system
cm³/g cubic centimeters per gram
CMYK cyan, magenta, yellow, key (black)
CPU central processing unit
CRC camera-ready copy
CRT cathode ray tube
CSS cascading style sheets
CtF computer-to-film
CtP computer-to-plate
DCS Desktop Color Separations
DHTML Dynamic HTML
DMA direct memory access
dpi dots per inch
DPS double-page spread
DTP desktop publishing
DVD Digital Versatile Disk
ECF elemental chlorine-free
EPS Encapsulated PostScript
FAQ Frequently Asked Questions
FM frequency modulated
FSC Forest Stewardship Council
FTP File Transfer Protocol
FYI for your information
Gbyte gigabyte
GIF Graphics Interchange Format
g/m² grams per meter squared
gsm grams per square meter
GUI graphical user interface
HD grade of mesh for screenprinting with 20–35 percent open area
HLS hue, luminance, saturation
HP hot-pressed, a handmade-paper finish
HP-GL Hewlett Packard graphics language
HTML Hypertext Markup Language
HTTP Hypertext Transport Protocol
Hz Hertz, or cycles per second
IBC inside back cover
ICC International Color Consortium
ICE Image Correction and Enhancement

IFC inside front cover
IMHO in my humble opinion
IRC Internet Relay Chat
ISDN Integrated Services Digital Network
ISP Internet Service Provider
JDF Job Definition Format
JIS Japan Industrial Standard
JMF Job Messaging Format
JPEG Joint Photographic Experts Group
k kilobyte, 1024 bytes (kbyte is more accurate usage)
kbyte kilobyte, 1024 bytes
L*a*b L is for luminance; a and b are chromatic components—a for green to red and b for blue to yellow
LAN local-area network
l.c. lower case
LCD Liquid-Crystal Display
lpi lines per inch
M grade of mesh for screenprinting
(m) machine direction in paper
Mbyte megabyte
MF machine-finish paper
MG machine-glazed paper
MHz megahertz, or millions of cycles per second
MICR Magnetic Ink Character Recognition
MIPS millions of instructions per second
Ms manuscript
NOT not hot-pressed, a handmade-paper finish
NTSC National Television Systems Committee
OBC outside back cover
OFC outside front cover
OPI Open Prepress Interface
OPL oriented polypropylene lamination
OS operating system
OSHA Occupational Safety and Health Administration of the US Department of Labor
PAL Phase Alternation Line—broadcast television standard in the UK
PC personal computer
PCB printed circuitboard
PCF processed chlorine-free
PDA Personal Digital Assistant
PDF Portable Document Format
PEFC Programme for the Endorsement of Forest Certification schemes
PJTF Portable Job Ticket Format
PMS Pantone Matching System
PMT photomechanical transfer
PNG Portable Network Graphics
PPF Print Production Format
ppi pages per inch
PPP Point-to-Point Protocol
pt point, a measurement of type size
RAM Random Access Memory—short-term computer memory

RAW an uncompressed data format for digital cameras
R&B rounding and backing
RC resin-coated
RGB red, green, blue
RIP raster image processor
RISC reduced-instruction-set computer
ROFL rolls on the floor laughing
ROM Read-Only Memory—permanent computer memory
RRED right-reading emulsion down
RREU right-reading emulsion up
RSI repetitive-strain injury
RT*M read the * manual (clean version!)
S grade of mesh for screenprinting with 50–70 percent open area
SFNT spline font
SGML Standard Generalized Markup Language
SIMM single in-line memory module
SLR single lens reflex
SPARC scaleable-processor architecture
S/S same size
stet reinstate deleted material
SWOP Specifications for Web Offset Publications
T grade of mesh for screenprinting
TCF totally chlorine-free
TCP/IP Transmission Control Protocol/Internet Protocol
TIFF Tagged Image File Format
TPD two-page display
TWAIN Technology Without An Interesting Name
u.c. upper case
UCA undercolor addition
UCR undercolor removal
URL Uniform Resource Locator
USB Universal Serial Bus
UV ultraviolet
VRML Virtual Reality Modeling Language
W3C World Wide Web Consortium
WIMP windows, icons, mouse, and pull-down menus
WOB white-on-black
WRED wrong-reading emulsion down
WREU wrong-reading emulsion up
WRULD work-related upper-limb disorders
WWW World Wide Web
WYSIWYG What You See Is What You Get
XHTML Extensible HyperText Markup Language
XML Extensible Markup Language
YMMV your mileage may vary

Further reading

Tricia Austin and Richard Doust, *New Media Design*, Laurence King Publishing, London, 2007. Explains how graphic designers use computers to combine word, image, motion, sound, and user interaction in designing for the internet, TV, games, animation, CDs, and exhibitions.

Jeremy Aynsley, *Pioneers of Modern Graphic Design: A Complete History*, Mitchell Beazley, London, 2005. Profiles over 60 of the most influential designers worldwide, from Peter Behrens to Saul Bass, plus exponents of today's digital technology such as Jonathan Barnbrook.

Phil Baines and Andrew Haslam, *Type & Typography*, Laurence King Publishing, London, and Watson-Guptill Publications, New York, 2005. A definitive guide to help you navigate among the typefaces available, as well as scores of no-fail techniques for using type as a meaningful element of design.

David Bann, *The All New Print Production Handbook*, RotoVision, Hove, 2006. Well-illustrated guide to print production in PVC cover.

Fernand Baudin, *How Typography Works (and Why It is Important)*, Lund Humphries, London, 1989 An idiosyncratic handwritten text based on a series of blackboard lectures by the Belgian graphic designer.

Michael Bierut, William Drenttel, and Steven Heller, *Looking Closer: Critical Writings on Graphic Design: Five*, Allworth Press, New York, 2007. A fifth collection of essays on contemporary graphic design from 2001 to 2005.

Lewis Blackwell, *The End of Print* (revised edn), Chronicle, San Francisco, and Laurence King Publishing, London, 2000. A book about and designed by innovative graphic designer David Carson.

Lewis Blackwell, *David Carson: 2nd Sight: Grafik Design After the End of Print*, St Martin's Press, New York, and Laurence King Publishing, London, 1997. The sequel to *The End of Print* examines David Carson's intuitive approach to graphic design.

Lewis Blackwell, *Twentieth-Century Type*, Laurence King Publishing, London, and Yale University Press, New Haven, CT, 2004. A decade-by-decade look at typography and graphic design.

Lewis Blackwell and Neville Brody, *G1*. Rizzoli, New York, and Laurence King Publishing, London, 1997. A collection of work by contemporary graphic designers, including Zuzana Licko and P. Scott Makela, along with the found images that have inspired them.

Michael H. Bruno (ed.), *Pocket Pal: A Graphic Arts Production Handbook* (20th edn), International Paper, Memphis, TN, 2007. A handy concise pocket-sized guide to graphic-arts production.

Rob Carter, Philip B. Meggs, and Ben Day, *Typographic Design: Form and Communication* (3rd edn), John Wiley & Sons, New York, 2002. An overview of the fundamentals of typographic design, incorporating desktop publishing, digital type, and bitmapped design.

Sebastian Carter, *Twentieth-Century Type Designers* (3rd edn), W.W. Norton & Company, New York, and Lund Humphries, London, 2002. A standard reference work on the lives of 24 designers worldwide, from Frederic W. Goudy to Carol Twombly.

James Craig, William Bevington, and Irene Korol Scala, *Designing with Type: The Essential Guide to Typography* (5th edition), Watson-Guptill, New York, 2006. Part textbook and part reference work, this is the fifth edition of this classic, first published in 1971.

Hillman Curtis, *MTIV: Process, Inspiration and Practice for the New Media Designer*, Markt + Technik Verlag, Munich, 2005. Making the invisible visible, outlines and explains the design process used by the author's graphics design company to produce digital media projects.

Andy Ellison, *The Complete Guide to Digital Type*, Laurence King Publishing, London, 2006. A comprehensive guide to creating and using digital type, both in print and for the web.

Stephen Eskilson, *Graphic Design: A New History*, Laurence King Publishing, London, 2007. A scholarly and accessible account of the field from Gutenberg to today, discussed in the light of prevailing political, social, military, and economic conditions, nationalism, and gender.

James Felici, *The Complete Manual of Typography*, Adobe Press, Berkeley, CA, 2002. A beautifully designed and richly illustrated reference for anyone who works with type.

Nathan Gale, *Type 1: Digital Typeface Design*, Laurence King Publishing, London, 2002. Collects together the best digital typefaces from around the world.

Mark Gatter, *Getting it Right in Print: Digital Prepress for Graphic Designers*, Laurence King Publishing, 2005. Gives designers the confidence to do everything necessary to ensure trouble-free, high-quality printing.

Mark Gatter, *Software Essentials for Graphic Designers: Photoshop, Illustrator, InDesign, QuarkXPress, Dreamweaver, Flash and Acrobat*, Laurence King Publishing, London, 2006. The essential knowledge to run seven major graphics and web-design programs in one book.

Bob and Maggie Gordon, *The Complete Guide to Digital Graphic Design*, Thames & Hudson, London, and Watson-Guptill, New York, 2002. The basic design principles used by graphic artists designing for print, advertising, packaging, signage, exhibition, the internet, and multimedia.

April Greiman, *Something from Nothing*, Rotovision, Hove, 2002. Explores digital design as pioneered by April Greiman—bold, kinetic explorations of typography and imagery as objects in time and space.

Andrew Haslam, *Book Design*, Laurence King Publishing, London, 2006. From the components that make up a book, to understanding how books are commissioned and created, to the intricacies of grid construction and choosing a typeface.

Steven Heller, *Design Literacy: Understanding Graphic Design* (2nd edn), Allworth Press, New York, 2004. An analysis of the key works of graphic design, exploring classic and contemporary works, explaining why they are aesthetically significant and how they function as good design.

Seven Heller (ed.), *The Education of a Graphic Designer* (2nd edn), Allworth Press, New York, 2006. Designers and educators, including Milton Glaser and David Carson, examine how graphic design is taught, learned, and practiced.

Steven Heller, *Education of a Typographer*, Allworth Press, New York, 2004. Features more than 40 essays from top experts and educators in typography introducing the themes of type and typography.

Steven Heller and Gail Anderson, *New Vintage Type: Classic Fonts for the Digital Age*, Thames & Hudson, London, 2007. A lighthearted survey looking at the role of old and classic fonts in contemporary graphic design.

Steven Heller and Teresa Fernandes, *Becoming a Graphic Designer: A Guide to Careers in Design* (3rd edn), John Wiley & Sons, New York, 2005. A clear and comprehensive overview of the many types of careers available to today's graphic designer: advertising, corporate work, editorial, and other key design disciplines, with case studies from Pentagram, Margo Chase Design, and Landor Associates.

Steven Heller and Mirko Ilic, *The Anatomy of Design: Uncovering the Influences and Inspirations in Modern Graphic Design*, Rockport Publishers, Beverly MA, 2007. Fifty examples of graphic design dissected to reveal their influences and inspirations.

Richard Hendel, *On Book Design*, Yale University Press, New Haven, CT, and London, 1998. Hendel and eight other book designers from both sides of the Atlantic discuss the challenges of the "invisible" craft of book designing.

Kenneth J. Hiebert and Armin Hofmann, *Graphic Design Sources*, Yale University Press, Yale, CT, 1998. Practical advice for those seeking to understand the principles and process of good design.

Jost Hochuli, *Detail In Typography*, Hyphen Press, London, 2008. Hochuli begins with a consideration of how human beings read, moving on to considerations of letter, word, and line as well as word-space and line-space.

Jost Hochuli and Robin Kinross, *Designing Books: Practice and Theory*. Princeton Architectural Press, New York, 2004. The basic principles of "macrotypography" by the Swiss designer with a detailed commentary of 27 of his designs by a design historian.

Richard Hollis, *Swiss Graphic Design*, Laurence King Publishing, London, 2007. By the 1950s Switzerland had developed a clear graphic language examined in this fascinating account of a key period in graphic design history.

Dard Hunter, *Papermaking: The History and Technique of an Ancient Craft*, Dover, New York, 1978. An authoritative history of papermaking.

Kaj Johansson, Peter Lundberg, and Robert Ryberg, *A Guide to Graphic Print Production* (2nd edn), Wiley, New York and Chichester, 2007. An introductory textbook covering all aspects of print production and manufacturing.

John Kane, *A Type Primer*, Laurence King Publishing, London, 2002. A practical guide for the beginner, presenting the basic principles and applications of typography.

Robin Kinross, *Modern Typography* (2nd edn), Princeton Architectural Press, New York, 2004. A completely updated and revised edition of Robin Kinross's classic survey of European and North American typography since 1700.

Robert Klanten et al, *The Little Know-it-all: Common Sense for Designers,* Die Gestalten Verlag, Berlin, 2007. Pocket-sized handbook full of facts and diagrams for designers of print and websites.

Dean Kuipers (ed.) and Marvin Scott Jarrett (introduction), *Ray Gun: Out of Control*, Simon & Schuster, London, 1997. Since 1992, *Ray Gun* has set the parameters of the cutting edge in publishing. David Carson served his apprenticeship as Art Director at *Ray Gun*.

Brian P Lawler, *Official Adobe Print Publishing Guide: The Essential Resource for Design, Production, and Prepress* (2nd edition), Adobe Press, Berkeley CA, 2005. Easy to read guide to the print production workflow.

Jeremy Leslie, *Magculture: New Magazine Design*, Laurence King Publishing, London, 2003. Following *Issues,* this book explores the latest trends and creative design styles in magazines from around the world.

Ellen Lupton, *DIY: Design It Yourself*, Princeton Architectural Press, New York, 2005. All the tools you'll need to create your own projects, from conception through production.

Ellen Lupton, *Thinking With Type: A Critical Guide for Designers, Writers, Editors, & Students*, Princeton Architectural Press, New York, 2004. A primer providing clear and concise guidance for anyone learning or brushing up on their typographic skills.

Patrick J. Lynch and Sarah Horton, *Web Style Guide: Basic Design Principles for Creating Web Sites*, Yale University Press, Yale, CT, 1999. The essence of the Yale University Center for Advanced Instructional Media's wonderful online website-design guide translated in traditional print format.

Ruari McLean, *How Typography Happens*, Oak Knoll Books, CA, and the British Library, London, 2000. Based on the Sandars lectures at Cambridge University in 1983.

Ruari McLean (ed.), *Typographers on Type: An Illustrated Anthology from William Morris to the Present Day*, W.W. Norton, New York, and Lund Humphries, London, 1995. An illustrated anthology of essays from type designers as diverse as William Morris and Matthew Carter.

Daniel Mason, *Materials, Process, Print*, Laurence King Publishing, London, 2007. An analysis of materials and print and manufacturing processes is combined with case studies showing innovative practice from major international design studios.

Philip B Meggs and Alston W Purvis, *Meggs' History of Graphic Design* (4th edn), John Wiley & Sons, New York, 2006. The 4th edition adds 450 new images and new educational tools to this comprehensive reference tool.

Jennifer Niederst, *Learning Web Design: A Beginner's Guide to HTML Graphics and Beyond* (3rd edn), O'Reilly & Associates, Sebastopol, CA, 2003. A guide for beginners to web design, updated to include CSS.

Jennifer Niederst, *Web Design in a Nutshell: A Desktop Quick Reference* (3rd edn), O'Reilly & Associates, Sebastopol, CA, 2006. Slim but full of understandable, readable segments.

Jakob Nielsen, *Designing Web Usability: The Practice of Simplicity*, New Riders Publishing, Indianapolis, IN, 1999. Web usability guru sets out many of the design precepts all web developers should follow.

Rick Poynor, *No More Rules: Graphic Design and Postmodernism*, Laurence King Publishing, London, and Yale University Press, New Haven, CT, 2003. A comprehensive overview of modernism as applied to American graphics and a look at the explosion of creativity ushered in via digital design.

Adrian Shaughnessy, *How to be a Graphic Designer Without Losing Your Soul,* Laurence King Publishing, London, 2005. Straight-talking advice addressing the concerns of young designers who want to earn a living by doing expressive and meaningful work but want to avoid becoming hired drones working on soulless projects.

Herbert Spencer and Rick Poynor, *Pioneers of Modern Typography* (revised edn), MIT Press, Cambridge, MA, and London, 2004. Since its first publication in 1969, *Pioneers of Modern Typography* has been the standard guide to the avant-garde origins of modern graphic design and typography.

Erik Spiekermann, *Rhyme & Reason: A Typographic Novel*, H. Berthold AG, Berlin, 1987. A beautifully made treatise on typography, in the style of *Tristram Shandy*.

Erik Spiekermann and E.M. Ginger, *Stop Stealing Sheep & Find Out How Type Works* (2nd edn), Adobe Press, Mountain View, CA, 2002. The title refers to a quotation by Frederic Goudy: "Anyone who would letterspace lower case would steal sheep."

Victoria Squire, *Getting it Right with Type*, Laurence King Publishing, London, 2006. An introduction to the basics of typography, from choosing which typeface to use to how you can combine different typefaces in one document.

Fay Sweet, *Metadesign: Design from the Word Up*, Watson-Guptill, New York, and Thames & Hudson, New York, 1999. Erik Spiekermann's multidisciplinary design firm is one of the world's largest consultancies applying its fresh ideas to everything from websites to corporate identities.

Tomato *Bareback: A Tomato Project* Gingko Press, Corte Madera, CA, and Laurence King Publishing, London, 1999. Stunning collection of personal work by the members of Tomato, from poetry to photography.

Tomato, *Process: A Tomato Project*, Gingko Press, Corte Madera, CA, and Thames & Hudson, London 1996. Tomato's output in its first five years—an eclectic mix of artistic concepts and working ideas which offers a glimpse into the creative processes at work.

Lynne Truss, *Eats, Shoots & Leaves: The Zero Tolerance Approach to Punctuation*, Profile, London, 2003. Entertaining and informative bestseller on the correct use of punctuation.

Jan Tschichold (Ruari McLean, translator), *The New Typography: A Handbook for Modern Designers*, University of California Press, Berkeley, CA, 1998. Since its initial publication in Berlin in 1928, this has been recognized as a definitive treatise on book and graphic design.

Rudy Vanderlans, Mary E. Gray and Zuzana Licko, *Emigre: Graphic Design into the Digital Realm*, John Wiley & Sons, New York, 1997. Brimming with ground-breaking Mac-generated typography, illustration, and graphic design, and oversized to do justice to its pictorial content.

Jon Wozencraft, *The Graphic Language of Neville Brody 2*, Universe Publishing, New York, and Thames & Hudson, London, 1996. The fruits of five years' experimentation, alongside Brody's new typefaces: Blur, Pop, and FF Gothic.

Yolanda Zappaterra, *Editorial Design*, Laurence King Publishing, London, 2007. Explains the fundamentals of editorial design and layout for magazines and newspapers, including case studies, practical tips, examples of best practice, and profiles of individual designers.

Website resources

The internet is full of wonderful resources for web-design tips and tutorials. It is not possible here to list every vendor's website, but here follows a by-no-means exhaustive selection. To find a particular vendor's website, try a search engine such as Google.

101 things designers can do to save the earth
http://onehundredthings.wordpress.com/

Adobe—home of Acrobat, Illustrator, InDesign, Photoshop, and Dreamweaver
www.adobe.com

AIGA (American Institute of Graphic Arts) Center for Sustainable Design
http://sustainability.aiga.org/

Core77—resources for designers:
www.core77.com

Creativepro—topical articles of interest to graphic designers
www.creativepro.com

CSS tutorial
www.w3schools.com/css/

CSS Zen Garden—showcases what is possible with CSS-based design
www.csszengarden.com

Design can change—sustainability resources for graphic designers
http://designcanchange.org

Design Observer
www.designobserver.com

FontFont Finder Typographic Resource
www.fontfont.com

Graphic Designers' Paradise—links to graphic design sites
www.desktoppublishing.com/design.html

Jakob Nielsen's useability website
www.useit.com

Lovely as a tree—choosing eco-friendly paper and printers
www.lovelyasatree.com

Microsoft's typography website:
www.microsoft.com/typography/default.mspx

paper.print.environment—how to reduce the environmental impact of printed materials
www.ppe.uk.net

QuarkXPress
www.quark.com

Renourish—sustainability toolkit
www.re-nourish.com

Vincent Flanders' "Web pages that suck"—learn good design by looking at bad web design:
www.webpagesthatsuck.com

Webmaster Reference Library
www.webreference.com

Web-safe color charts
www.lynda.com/hex.html
the-light.com/colclick.html

Wikipedia—online encyclopedia
http://en.wikipedia.org/wiki/Printing

Yale web style guide
www.webstyleguide.com

Magazines and journals

USA

American Printer
33 N. Wabash
Suite 2300
Chicago, IL 60611
www.americanprinter.com

Communication Arts
110 Constitution Drive
Menlo Park, CA 94025
www.commarts.com

DT&G Magazine
15 Southgate
Harrisonburg, VA 22801
www.graphic-design.com

Graphic Arts Monthly
2000 Clearwater Drive
Oak Brook, IL 60523
www.graphicartsonline.com

Graphic Design USA
89 Fifth Avenue
Suite 901
New York, New York 10003
www.gdusa.com

Graphis
307 Fifth Avenue
10th Floor
New York, NY 10016
www.graphis.com

HOW
F&W Publications, Inc.
4700 E. Galbraith Road
Cincinnati, OH 45236
www.howdesign.com

i-D magazine
38 East 29th Street, Floor 3
New York, NY 10016
www.id-mag.com

MacWorld
MacPublishing
301 Howard Street
15th Floor
San Francisco, CA 94105
www.macworld.com

Print
38 East 29th Street, 3rd Floor
New York, NY 10016
www.printmag.com

Publishers Weekly
360 Park Avenue South
New York, NY 10010
www.publishersweekly.com

STEP inside design
6000 N. Forest Park Drive
Peoria, IL 61614
www.stepinsidedesign.com

u&lc (now online only)
International Typeface
Corporation (ITC)
200 Ballardvale Street
Wilmington, MA 01887–1069
www.itcfonts.com/ulc

x-height (now online only)
DsgnHaus, Inc.
2232 South Main Street
Suite 388
Ann Arbor, MI 48103-6938
www.fonthaus.com/xheight/

UK

Baseline
Bradbourne Publishing Ltd
East Malling
Kent ME19 6DZ
www.baselinemagazine.com

Computer Arts
30 Monmouth Street
Bath BA1 2BW
www.computerarts.co.uk

Creative Review
50 Poland Street
London W1V 7AX
www.creativereview.com

Design Week
50 Poland Street
London W1F 7AX
www.designweek.co.uk

Digital Arts
99 Gray's Inn Road
London WC1X 8TY
www.digitalartsonline.co.uk

Eye
Haymarket Publishing
174 Hammersmith Road
London W6 7JP
www.eyemagazine.com

Grafik
24a Unit Workshops
1–13 Alder Street
London E1 1EG
www.grafikmagazine.co.uk

MacWorld (UK edition)
IDG Communications
99 Gray's Inn Road
London WC1X 8UT
www.macworld.co.uk

Printing World
Haymarket Specialist,
174 Hammersmith Road,
London W6 7JP
www.printweek.com

PrintWeek
Haymarket Specialist,
174 Hammersmith Road,
London W6 7JP
www.printweek.com

Print & Paper Monthly
Whitmar Publications Ltd
30 London Road
Southborough
Tunbridge Wells
Kent TN4 0RE
www.paperandprint.com

Screen Process & Digital Imaging
Datateam Publishing Ltd
15a London Road
Maidstone
Kent ME16 8LY
www.datateam.co.uk

Organizations

USA

AIGA
American Institute of Graphic Arts
164 Fifth Avenue
New York, NY 10010
www.aiga.org

American Forest and Paper
Association
1111 19th Street, NW, Suite 800
Washington, DC 20036
info@afandpa.org
www.afandpa.org

American Institute of Graphic Arts
164 Fifth Avenue
New York, NY 10010
www.aiga.org

American Printing History
Association
PO Box 4519
Grand Central Station
New York, NY 10153–4519
sgcrook@printinghistory.org
www.printinghistory.org

Flexographic Technical Association
900 Marconi Avenue
Ronkonkoma, NY 11779–7212
memberinfo@flexography.org
www.flexography.org

Graphic Arts Technical Foundation
200 Deer Run Road
Sewickley, PA 15143–2600
www.gain.net

The Gravure Association of
America, Inc.
1200–A Scottsville Road
Rochester, NY 14624
www.gaa.org

IAPHC The International
Association of Printing House
Craftsmen
7042 Brooklyn Boulevard
Minneapolis, MN 55429
www.iaphc.org

Institute of Paper Science and
Technology
500 10th Street, NW
Atlanta, GA 30332–0620
www.ipst.gatech.edu

National Association of Printing Ink
Manufacturers, Inc.
581 Main Street
Woodbridge, NJ 07095–1104
napim@napim.org
www.napim.org

National Association for Printing
Leadership (formerly National
Association of Printers and
Lithographers)
75 West Century Road
Paramus, NJ 07652
www.napl.org

NPES The Association for Suppliers
of Printing, Publishing, and
Converting Technologies
1899 Preston White Drive
Reston, VA 20191–4367
npes@npes.org
www.npes.org

Printers' National Environmental
Assistance Center
www.pneac.org

Printing Industries of America Inc.
200 Deer Run Road,
Sewickley, PA 15143
www.gain.net

Specialty Graphic Imaging
Association (formerly
Screenprinting & Graphic Imaging
Association International and
the Digital Printing & Imaging
Association)
10015 Main Street
Fairfax, VA 22031–3489
sgia@sgia.org
www.sgia.org

TAPPI Technical Association of the
Pulp and Paper Industry
15 Technology Parkway South
Norcross, GA 30092
www.tappi.org

U.S. Screen Print & Inkjet
Technology
1901 E. 5th Street
Tempe, AZ 85281
www.screenprinters.net

Waterless Printing Association
P.O. Box 1252
Woodstock, IL 600
www.waterless.org

UK

British Printing Industries
Federation
Farringdon Point
29–35 Farringdon Road
London EC1M 3JF
www.britishprint.com

Confederation of Paper Industries
Papermakers House
1 Rivenhall Road
Swindon
Wilts SN5 7BD
www.paper.org.uk

Digital & Screen Printing
Association
Association House
7a West Street
Reigate
Surrey RH2 9BL
www.spauk.co.uk

Green Mark
The London Environment Centre
London Metropolitan University
133 Whitechapel High Street
London E1 7QA
www.green-mark.co.uk

Periodical Publishers Association
Queens House
28 Kingsway
London WC2B 6JR
www.ppa.co.uk

Pira International
Cleve Road
Leatherhead
Surrey KT22 7RU
www.pira.co.uk

Printing Historical Society
St Bride Printing Library
Bride Lane, Fleet Street
London EC4Y 8EE
www.printinghistoricalsociety.
org.uk

The Publishers Association
29B Montague Street
London WC1B 5BW
www.publishers.org.uk

St Bride Printing Library
Bride Lane, Fleet Street
London EC4Y 8EE
www.stbride.org

International

CIP4
Cooperation for the Integration of
Processes in Prepress, Press and Postpress
c/o VISCHER, Schützengasse 1,
8001 Zurich, Switzerland
www.cip4.org

FSC
Forest Stewardship Council
Charles-de-Gaulle 5
53113 Bonn
Germany
www.fsc.org

ICC
International Color Consortium
1899 Preston White Drive
Reston, VA 20191
USA
www.color.org

Icograda
455 Saint Antoine Ouest, Suite SS 10
Montréal, Québec
Canada H2Z 1J1
secretariat@icograda.org
www.icograda.org

ISTD
International Society of Typographic
Designers
PO Box 725
Taunton
Somerset TA2 8WE
UK
www.istd.org.uk

Organization of Black Designers
www.obd.org

PEFC
Programme for the Endorsement
of Forest Certification
2éme Etage
17 Rue des Girondins
Merl-Hollerich
L—1626 Luxembourg
www.pefc.org

W3C
World Wide Web Consortium
c/o ERCIM (Europe)
2004, route des Lucioles
Sophia-Antipolis
06410 Biot France
c/o MIT (Americas)
32 Vassar Street
Room 32-G515
Cambridge, MA 02139 USA
www.w3.org

Index

Numbers in **bold** refer to figures

Picture credits

The author and publishers would like to thank all individuals, agencies, museums, and companies that supplied pictures for use in this book. Special thanks to those designers—Airside, Jonathan Barnbrook, Neville Brody, Christine Fent of Composite Projects, Malcolm Garrett, Zuzana Licko, Bruce Mau, Stefan Sagmeister, Paula Scher, Erik Spiekermann, Chris Ware—who provided material for the Design Trailblazers spreads.

CHAPTER 1
1.1 The Art Archive/British Library; 1.2 Mansell Collection, London; 1.4–6 Ann Ronan Picture Library, Taunton, Somerset; 1.7 *The Hyena* by Thomas Bewick, Cherryburn (The National Trust) NTPL (John Hammond); 1.8 Nick Day, Whitstable; 1.9–10 Ann Ronan Picture Library, Taunton, Somerset; 1.12 Mary Evans Picture Library, London, photoshop manipulation by Dave Kemp; 1.13 David Foenander, Milton Keynes; 1.14–15 Alan Pipes; p24 The Kobal Collection; p25 top, British Heart Foundation, London (Neil Gower); bottom left, The Kobal Collection; bottom center, reproduced with the permission of BellSouth Intellectual Property Marketing Corporation; bottom right, reproduced with the kind permission of the AT&T Trademark and Copyright Counsel.

CHAPTER 2
2.3 Mansell Collection, London; 2.5 Crazy Diamond Design, Manchester; 2.6 Ann Ronan Picture Library, Taunton, Somerset; 2.8 Alan Pipes; 2.9 Mary Evans Picture Library; 2.15 Alan Pipes; 2.20 Alan Pipes; 2.24 Alan Pipes; 2.31 Alan Pipes; 2.40 Carol Kemp; 2.41 Fontworks UK, London; 2.42 Zefa Picture Library, London (J. Pfaff); 2.44 Art Director's and Trip Photo Library, London; 2.46–48 Zefa Picture Library, London (J. Pfaff); 2.50–52 Alan Pipes; 2.54 Fontworks UK, London; 2.55 Banks and Miles, London; 2.56–57 Type Solutions, Inc, Plaistow, NH, USA.

CHAPTER 3
3.1 Mansell Collection, London; 3.3 Art Director's and Trip Photo Library, London; 3.4–5 Rex Features, London (Ron Sachs); 3.8 Roger-Viollet, Paris; 3.9–10 LD Publicity; 3.11 Getty Images; 3.12 Pantone Europe GmbH, Stuttgart, Germany; 3.19 Paul Brierly, Harlow, Essex; 3.22 Alan Pipes; 3.23 Lefevre Gallery, London; 3.26 Zefa Picture Library, London (J. Pfaff); 3.28 Quantel Ltd (UK), Newbury; 3.29 Gary Thompson, Brighton; 3.31 Peter Greenwood, Brighton; 3.34 DC Comics Inc., New York; p108 Cris Cassady.

CHAPTER 4
4.1 Dell Inc, Round Rock, Texas, USA; 4.2–3 Apple Inc, Cupertino, California, USA; 4.4 Kingston Technology Company, Inc, Fountain Valley, CA, USA; 4.5 LaCie, Hillsboro, Oregon, USA; 4.6–7 Wacom Col, Ltd., Saitama, Japan; 4.8–10 Logitech Europe SA, Romanel-sur-Morges, Switzerland; 4.11–12 Canon (UK) Ltd, Reigate, UK; 4.13 Epson (UK) Ltd., Hemel Hempstead, UK; p123 top left, reproduced with the permission of IBM Corporate Identity and Design; top right, designed by Paul Rand, 1961 and FutureBrand, 2003, reproduced with the

permission of UPS Brand Management. UPS, the UPS brandmark and the colour brown are trademarks used with permission of its owner, United Parcel Service of America, Inc. All rights reserved; center left, abc; bottom left, book cover of H. L. Mencken's *Prejudices* reproduced with the permission of Marion Rand, Rand Archive, Yale University, USA; bottom right, Eye Bee M poster by Paul Rand, reproduced with the permission of Marion Rand, Rand Archive; 4.14 Kodak's Graphic Communications Group, Rochester, NY, USA; 4.15 ICG Ltd, Bristol, UK; 4.16 Nikon Inc., Melville, NY, USA; 4.17 Xerox Corporation, Norwalk, Connecticut, USA; 4.18 Agfa-Gevaert NV, Mortsel, Belgium; 4.20 Alan Pipes; 4.21 Heidelberger Druckmaschinen AG, Heidelberg, Germany; 4.22 Canon (UK) Ltd, Reigate, UK; 4.23 Alan Pipes; 4.24 Xerox Corporation, Norwalk, Connecticut, USA; 4.25 Epson (UK) Ltd., Hemel Hempstead, UK; 4.26–28 Alan Pipes; 4.29 Sony United Kingdom Limited, Weybridge, UK; 4.30 Alan Pipes; 4.31 Roland DG (UK) Ltd, Clevedon, UK; 4.32–33 Alan Pipes; p134 Jeff Knowles; p135 top left, courtesy Research Studios.

CHAPTER 5
5.1–4 Alan Pipes; 5.7 © Guardian New and Media Limited; 5.8 Courtesy Time Inc.; 5.9–16 Alan Pipes; 5.20 Amazon.com, Inc., Seattle, Washington, USA; 5.21 Square Enough, London and Brighton; 5.22 Alan Pipes; 5.23 Art Director's and Trip Photo Library; 5.24–26 Alan Pipes; 5.27 Hewlett-Packard Company, Palo Alto, California, USA.

CHAPTER 6
6.1 Sonia Halliday, Weston Turville, Bucks; 6.2 Science Photo Library, London; 6.3–4 Alan Pipes; 6.5–6 Art Director's and Trip Photo Library, London; 6.7 Alan Pipes; 6.8–9 James River Fine Papers, St Andrews, Scotland; 6.10–13 Alan Pipes; 6.14 Zefa Picture Library, London; 6.17 Phil Dobson, Brighton; 6.18 Alan Pipes; 6.19 Kodak's Graphic Communications Group, Rochester, NY, USA; 6.20 Dainippon Screen, Kyoto, Japan; 6.21 Heidelberger Druckmaschinen AG, Heidelberg, Germany; 6.22–25 Alan Pipes; 6.26 Art Director's and Trip Photo Library, London; 6.27–28 Alan Pipes; 6.29 Art Director's and Trip Photo Library, London (Archie Miles); p196 Paula Scher/Pentagram, photograph by Branson Veal (2007); p197 Paula Scher/Pentagram; 6.30–33 Alan Pipes; 6.34 DuPont Corporate Information Center, Wilmington, DE, USA; 6.36 Alan Pipes; 6.38 Xerox Corporation, Norwalk, Connecticut, USA; 6.39 Alan Pipes; 6.40 Punch Graphix International nv, Lier, Belgium; 6.41 Hewlett-Packard Company, Palo Alto, California, USA; 6.42 InfoPrint, Boulder, Colorado, USA; 6.43 Kodak's Graphic Communications Group, Rochester, NY, USA; 6.48 left to right, Hodder Headline, Pan Books; 6.50 Alan Pipes; 6.52–55 Alan Pipes; 6.56 Heidelberger Druckmaschinen AG, Heidelberg, Germany; 6.57–62 Alan Pipes.

CHAPTER 7
7.1 Linksys, a division of Cisco Systems, Inc., Irvine, California, USA; 7.7 Simon Waldman, New Media Labs, Guardian Newspapers, London; 7.15–16 Alan Pipes; 7.19 Bernard Heyes Design, London; 7.20–21 Minivegas, London.